Penguin Business

Working in Organisations

Andrew Kakabadse, Ron Ludlow and Susan Vinnicombe are all on the staff of the Cranfield School of Management in Bedford.

Andrew Kakabadse worked in the health and social services field and from there undertook various consultancy assignments concerned with local government re-organisation and large capital projects in developing countries. He is Professor of Management Development at the Cranfield School of Management and is consultant to numerous organisations, including banks, high-tech companies, public-sector organisations and multinational corporations. He has consulted and lectured all over the world and has recently completed a major world study of chief executives. Andrew Kakabadse has published over fifty articles and eleven books, including the bestselling book *Politics of Management*. He holds positions on the boards of a number of companies and is an external examiner for several universities. He is co-editor of the *Journal of Managerial Psychology* and associate editor of the *Leadership and Organisation Development Journal*.

Ron Ludlow is Lecturer in Organisational Behaviour. After a successful career in the Royal Navy, he worked for seventeen years in industry, including seven as managing director of a manufacturing company and five years as a group director in the construction industry. He has considerable experience in consultancy in management, recruitment and selection, performance appraisal and career development, both in the private and the public sector, and he is Director of Placements and Career Counselling for the MBA programme. Currently researching into British and Japanese companies in the UK and the evaluation of the effectiveness of management development programmes, he is particularly interested in the future role of management education and of simulation and gaming, to which ends he is at present designing human-resources distance-learning programmes for use both in the UK and internationally. He is co-author of *How To Accelerate Your Career* (1986) and co-editor of *Cases in Human Resource Management* (1987).

Susan Vinnicombe is Senior Lecturer in Organisational Behaviour. As well as working in industry, she has taught, researched and consulted widely in the areas of motivation, communication, group dynamics and the role of women in organisations. She is Director of the National Organisation of Women in Management Education and has written one previous book and numerous articles.

WORKING IN ORGANISATIONS

Andrew Kakabadse, Ron Ludlow
and Susan Vinnicombe

PENGUIN BOOKS

PENGUIN BOOKS

Published by the Penguin Group
Penguin Books Ltd, 27 Wrights Lane, London W8 5TZ, England
Penguin Books USA Inc., 375 Hudson Street, New York, New York 10014, USA
Penguin Books Australia Ltd, Ringwood, Victoria, Australia
Penguin Books Canada Ltd, 10 Alcorn Avenue, Toronto, Ontario, Canada M4V 3B2
Penguin Books (NZ) Ltd, 182–190 Wairau Road, Auckland 10, New Zealand

Penguin Books Ltd, Registered Offices: Harmondsworth, Middlesex, England

First published by Gower 1987
Published in Penguin Books 1988
10 9 8 7 6 5

Printed in England by Clays Ltd, St Ives plc

Contents

Preface   vii

Acknowledgements   xi

PART I: PEOPLE, JOBS AND RELATIONSHIPS   1

Introduction   3

1   The manager's job   6

2   The manager's career   31

3   The individual at work   61

4   Person to person   92

5   Motivation to work   117

6   Groups   152

7   Leadership in organisations   184

8   Power: a base for action   211

9   Increasing personal influence   249

PART II: WORKING THE ORGANISATION   277

Introduction   279

10   Mission, strategy and organisation   281

11   Organisation structure   312

12   Managing people, managing pressures   351

PART III: GUIDE TO FURTHER READING   383

Index   449

Preface

Our experience of having managed, administered and taught on graduate business degree programmes and management short courses, and having acted as researchers and consultants, has convinced us that certain common but important issues face managers. We have witnessed some managers who are able to address these issues successfully; others who struggle with them; and a third category who have asked us to provide assistance as tutors or in a consultant role. These issues form the subject of this book.

TWELVE QUESTIONS FOR MANAGERS

Commonly, participants on the various programmes at Cranfield School of Management, and clients in research and consultancy assignments, present these issues to us as questions. So we sat down to think through the content of these questions. We identified a large number of issues, which crystallised into twelve key questions. As soon as we felt confident that these questions summarised the critical issues that we needed to raise with managers, or managers with us, we began to be able to answer them. It dawned on us that these questions could form the basis for a text outlining what it means to work in organisations. Consequently, each of the twelve questions set out below is the foundation of each chapter in this book.

1 'What's a manager's job all about?' In Chapter 1 we examine the history of and thinking on managerial work, and explain recent research findings in this area.

2 'In a new job, what do I need to know to do well?' In Chapter 2 we identify the problems of entry into a new job and/or

organisation and of becoming socialised into the new organisation, and show the need for a planned approach to career development in any organisation.

3 'As a manager, what am I like?' In Chapter 3 the question is pursued through an analysis of personality and perception.

4 How can I improve my relationships at work?' In Chapter 4 we examine how effective and ineffective communication influences work relationships, how 'people needs' affect relationships, and what skills are required to improve relationships.

5 'How can I get the best out of people?' In Chapter 5 we look at motivation from two points of view. First, what does motivation mean in terms of stimulating individuals to improve performance, irrespective of job or organisation? Second, how can jobs be designed to be more motivating for their incumbents?

6 'What do I need to know to manage groups of people?' In Chapter 6 we recognise that groups have various functions and that group dynamics are a powerful force in determining the effectiveness of a performing group.

7 'What does it mean to be a good leader?' In Chapter 7 we review historical developments in leadership thinking and outline current concepts and practice.

8 'How do things happen in an organisation?' In Chapter 8 we address the theme of power in organisations, what exactly is meant by the term and why it is important for a manager to be conscious of the concept of power.

9 'How can I make an impact in my organisation?' Chapter 9 examines organisational politics as a means of increasing one's personal influence in the organisation.

10 'Where is my organisation going?' In Chapter 10 we explore the concept of organisation strategy and how strategy is formulated in order that units, departments, divisions and even the whole organisation can pursue particular goals, bearing in mind the internal issues facing the organisation.

11 'What sort of organisation am I in?' In Chapter 11 we examine the nature of organisation structure and how structure in

combination with other factors can substantially influence attitudes, values and beliefs in the organisation.

12 'How can I make my organisation work better?' In Chapter 12 we identify the various mechanisms for integrating individuals, groups, departments, sections and even divisions into a more cohesive whole, termed the organisation.

The text is divided into three parts. Part I, 'People, Jobs, and Relationships', concentrates on individual and group behaviour. Part II, 'Working the Organisation', deals with three broader organisational issues, namely organisational strategy, structure and design, and mechanisms for organisational integration. Part III provides references and a subject area guide for each chapter.

Each chapter contains two elements, the academic content and a fictional case study. The academic content is written in such a way that key concepts and implications for practice are highlighted. References to relevant books and articles are kept to a minimum in order to emphasise the important learning points. The aim of inserting a case study in each chapter is to illustrate the advantages, opportunities, problems and difficulties in implementing organisation behaviour theory. We attempt to introduce a little life and colour to concepts relating to organisations and thereby help the reader to identify with the content of each chapter. Each case study in each chapter is split into sections so that relevant aspects of organisation theory are examined and discussed from the point of view of application, whilst the underlying theme of the chapter knits together each of these sections (within each chapter) so as to form an integrated case. Further, we have been selective in the concepts and approaches we discuss in the chapters. We have tried to achieve a balance between contrasting theories and practices so as to provide an overview of the field of organisation behaviour. However, we have focused on those theories and techniques that actively address the issues, challenges and problems faced by managers. On a point of style, we have used 'he/him' to mean 'she/her' also.

Finally, we wish to thank the various people who have helped us develop the ideas for this book. Yes, some have been academics, such as ourselves. However, the people who have really provided the inspiration for this text have been the numerous middle, senior and top managers whom we have met at Cranfield School of Management or have worked with in their organisations. It is their experiences, ideas, beliefs, feelings, joys and pain that we have used to write this book. We have taken what is theirs, and moulded that into our frameworks. To all of you who have provided the true spirit behind this book, we offer our grateful thanks.

Andrew P Kakabadse
Ron Ludlow
Susan Vinnicombe

Acknowledgements

Our special thanks to Mairi Bryce and Sarah Bishton for their patience, perseverance, extraordinary sense of humour and high quality of application in typing draft after draft to produce this document: a task that would have taxed most people, but not you, the most level-headed. Thanks also to Susan Dean, Dorothy Rogers and Sarah Willett for the additional typing you undertook. A special mention for Tamazin Steele who already at an early age shows considerable potential in the field of management academia; thank you for finding the necessary references.

Our gratitude also to Malcolm Stern, surely one of the most professional editors we have experienced.

Finally, our spouses and families made no small contribution to this text in terms of their ideas, counsel and support.

APK
RL
SV

Part I
PEOPLE, JOBS AND RELATIONSHIPS

INTRODUCTION TO PART I

Part I of this book deals with the manager and those key aspects of his personality, values, attitudes, behaviours and interactions and desires that will influence his performance in the organisation. Its nine chapters cover: the nature of the manager's job, the entry and socialisation process of working in a new organisation, personality and perception, personal needs and interpersonal skills, motivation, groups and group dynamics, styles of leadership, power and its relevance to working in organisations, and the politics of managerial life.

The opening chapter explores the features of the manager's job, how work is structured ánd the relationship between work, the individual and the organisation. These features are placed in context, historically speaking, as various interpretations of managerial work, past and present, are analysed. It is assumed that understanding the manager's job is a prerequisite to managerial competence.

Bearing in mind this latter point, the problems and challenges facing the newly appointed manager are discussed. The processes of entry and socialisation into a new job and/or organisation are analysed. The inherent weaknesses of interviews are identified. We outline the transitional problems, once in the job, of recognising its true nature and changing attitude and style where necessary. One reason for transitional problems is that individuals strongly identify with a particular career pattern and become 'anchored' into pursuing one line of activity. Hence, jobs that require different skills or attitudes of their incumbent may give him a prolonged transition experience. The manager needs also to recognise that the challenges, joys and pressures of work will have repercussions on his home life.

No matter how much a manager knows his job and its problems, a key consideration in terms of effective managerial performance is the manager himself. Important elements are the personality of the manager and the way he perceives his organisational world. In addition to appreciating the inherent forces that drive each individual, personal needs and communication skills also affect managerial performance. Once the personal characteristics, drives, needs, values, attitudes and each person's approaches to communication are recognised, the interpersonal skills of listening and assertiveness can be applied to enhance interpersonal understanding and good working relationships.

Managers have not only personal needs, but work needs. Here we are referring to motivation, a central concept in organisation behaviour. Motivation is examined from two aspects: those stimuli internal to the individual, that motivate the person to undertake work for reasons of personal satisfaction; those stimuli external to the individual and built into the job that induce the individual to work well.

The groups with whom the individual interacts also influence his performance at work. Groups satisfy various functions, ranging from formal groups whose purpose is to achieve particular tasks or goals, to informal groups who can fulfil both professional and social needs. Group dynamics can influence an individual's attitudes, beliefs and even performance. Obviously, the relationship between the individual and the group needs to be positive if the individual is to stay with the group. However, effective workgroups are not simply those where the relationship amongst group members is positive. Individuals in groups need to serve particular functions or roles and the combination of roles will determine whether that group is likely to perform well or poorly.

The role of group leader is important to the development of the group. The manager has to get work done through other people, primarily subordinates and colleagues. He must be aware of the array of leadership styles he could adopt to suit various circumstances. The manager who can generate a style to suit particular circumstances is likely to be more effective.

The ability to influence others is increasingly becoming recognised as a vital managerial skill. For this reason, the topics of power and politics are essential for the development of managers. Not that power and politics are seen, in this book, as different to concepts of leadership and managerial style, though in the literature a quite separate body of knowledge and tradition has emerged that has made it impossible to combine these subjects under one umbrella heading. Power is likened to 'potential'; the potential to act and influence individuals and groups. The behaviour patterns to increase one's power need to alter according to the predominant culture and values in that part of the organisation. In this way, power can be seen as synonymous with changing people's behaviour, but equally with influencing the ideas, values and beliefs of others.

Where power is the potential to influence others, politics, the subject of the final chapter in Part I, refers to interpersonal influence and the skills of persuasion. The hypothesis offered is that the most effective means of increasing one's personal influence is to work on people's comfort zones, i.e. respond to and interact with people in a way that does not offend their views, values, beliefs and interpersonal styles, so that they will feel sufficiently attracted to you at least to pay attention to your conversation. It is appropriate that the chapter on politics should be the last in Part I, since it encompasses the learning from the previous eight chapters. By appreciating the pressures and supports in a manager's job; by understanding the manager as a person and his way of leading and managing; by recognising the issues he is or is not confronting with his subordinates, groups, colleagues and boss, and by linking all three separate areas, it is possible to influence him by interacting with him in a way he finds acceptable. That is probably the true intention of Part I; the recognition that an effective manager can achieve goals and objectives through other people.

1 The Manager's Job

Case 1.1 Electrical Enterprises

Jim Roberts checked out of his Sheffield hotel at five to seven, feeling blurred and slightly hung over. After speaking at the Institute of Marketing's Conference last night he'd had a few drinks and talked to delegates from all over the country. He'd picked up some leads, too, which he intended to follow up when he got back to work.

Jim, who was sales manager for the industrial products division of the Electrical Enterprises Group, based in Newbury, had a two-hour drive in front of him; in his present state he wasn't looking forward to it.

'Damn!' he said to himself, 'I forgot to ring Janice last night to see if young Tony's fever is any better. Even though I didn't get to bed until three, she would be expecting my call. That's the trouble - work, especially away from home, makes me forget sometimes I have a home at all.'

Jim got to the works at half past nine. The car park was full, as usual. He had to leave his car with the gatekeeper as he was already late for an interview he'd set up with two new sales representatives he'd hired last week. As he walked into his office, Elaine, his secretary, greeted him.

'Ah, there you are, Mr Roberts. Did you have a good conference? Wallace Lane, the distributors, have been on the line about delivery of those fittings which were promised yesterday. And the group marketing director wants you to call him urgently. The two new reps are waiting in the reception area for you, too, and can you go over to see Bill Ward in production about some delay he's run into?'

'Thanks, Elaine, another quiet day, I see,' replied Jim, grinning. Elaine was a good secretary, the best there was. She protected him from unnecessary interruptions when he was here, but when he was away she panicked at times.

'I'd better see those two reps first, and then I'll deal with the other things.'

Jim wanted to talk to the two newcomers to the company to see what training they needed before putting them on the road. One was an experienced salesman, but had little knowledge of the company's products, and the other was a newly qualified MBA who wanted to change functions from production to marketing and had appreciated he needed selling experience first. Jim realised he had to get to know these two quickly, and to ensure they were fully trained and briefed as soon as possible. After discussing their needs with them for half an hour he was able to sort it all out, and after they left he called the training manager to arrange the training modules they required. The headache which had started on the car journey seemed to be getting worse.

'Elaine, what about a cup of coffee, please?' he called. 'Let me have the mail while you're making one.'

Jim Roberts (Case 1.1) is a middle manager in a medium-sized company. He is accountable for his departmental staff, and has contacts outside the organisation and also with other departments within it.

He is responsible for hiring and firing, long-term activities and dealing with breakdowns such as the Wallace Lane delivery situation.

He has to plan, organise, co-ordinate, motivate and control the tasks and people in his department to achieve his and the department's goals. Jim has to act as a figurehead and in a liaison role – at the Conference in Sheffield – as a collector of information, and as a leader with his two new representatives, as a decision-maker in selecting their training programmes, and he is going to have to act as a disturbance handler and negotiator with respect to Wallace Lane and the production problem.

Jim has also to find some balance between the demands of his work and his own personal life, which, on the brief evidence so far, he does not seem to be doing very well.

Jim, in fact, is a typical manager, having to carry out a variety of activities and perform in several roles, each requiring a high level of technical competence, self-understanding and flexibility of style in social interaction in order to produce high quality performance.

Working in organisations involves all these elements. Being an effective manager means being able to diagnose people and situations, understanding basic behavioural concepts – why he and other people behave as they do – and translating these principles and techniques into the practical skills of managing his job and the people with whom he works in order to achieve his managerial goals.

This chapter will discuss various approaches, emerging from research, on managers and managerial work. A historical perspective is adopted, ranging from the classical studies in the early part of the century which identified the principles and functions of management through the studies of the manager as a handler of information for decision-making, to the recognition of the manager and the worker as human and individual, and the effects of that on managerial work and roles. Some thoughts on how to become an effective manager are offered at the end of the chapter.

MANAGERIAL WORK

Any study of management and managers must start by asking two questions:

What is a manager for?

What does a manager do?

Managers work in organisations. Those organisations may be complex structures of several thousand men, with multi-layered hierarchies, carrying out a diversity of operations all over the world. They may also be small, perhaps only two or three people doing a single set of tasks. In all cases those organisations have objectives to be met, goals to be achieved, and the smooth running of the organisation's operation is necessary to make this occur.

But who sets those objectives? The owners, or the shareholders, or the professional managers controlling the output of the organisation? And who controls the running of the operation? The managers hired by the organisation for this very purpose.

The operations of an organisation entail varying degrees of interdependence. To achieve efficiency and economy of operation, people specialise in particular tasks, and do not carry out the whole process. They specialise in sales, in production, in finance, in co-ordinating the separate functional activities.

Managers, by the very nature of their work, specialise. Some may specialise in particular technical functions and throughout their careers may stay in those functions and develop great depth of technical expertise and know-how in a specialised field. Some may find that their strengths lie more in co-ordination and integration, and prefer to work in general management. Whichever they do, they all have to work within an operational and social structure called an organisation.

All managers need to be able to co-ordinate and integrate, both within their own specialised function and also across the different functions within the organisation. They have to assimilate large quantities of data, to set priorities, to control, to communicate, to make decisions, to solve problems. They need to understand the activities and techniques which are critical to their own and their organisation's success. They have to develop the skills necessary to implement those techniques, and skills of analysis, of dealing with people, of coping with the environment, of managing their often limited resources.

Is Jim Roberts of Electrical Enterprises an effective manager? On this day most of his time has been spent reacting to events, firefighting, with only a minor part of the day being involved in long-term activities. He appears to be a good communicator and to have good relationships with other managers in the company. But it is difficult to get any real feel for his job based on the activities of his day so far. So let us take a closer look at that second question we asked at the start: 'What does a manager do?'

The rational manager

At the turn of the twentieth century, managerial work was examined from a sociological perspective. Organisations were analysed in an attempt to establish the general principles and activities of management. Certain elements were considered crucial to the survival and functioning of the organisations, for example, hierarchy, role authority and office. Further, it was assumed that the binding force behind these elements was rationality and logic. If organisations were structured as rational logical entities, it was in turn assumed that people working in organisations would behave in equally rational ways. Hence, the use of legitimate authority by management would not alienate the worker, but instead would conform with his expectations.

The renowned sociologist, Max Weber, defined such a framework of authority, a bureaucracy – an organisational framework based on (legitimate) authority and the acceptance of that authority by the people in the organisation. Bureaucracy is epitomised by standardisation – of work practices, of parameters of power within a hierarchy of command – and formality – of rules, regulations, procedures and communication (mostly in writing). From this framework it became possible to compare organisations and the managers and workers within them, the work they do, and the activities they perform.

The functions of management

The French engineer, Henri Fayol, took a functional approach to the study of managerial work. In his book *General and Industrial Administration* he concluded that the process of management in any organisation, large or small, public or private, manufacturing or services, consists of eight basic functions (Figure 1.1):

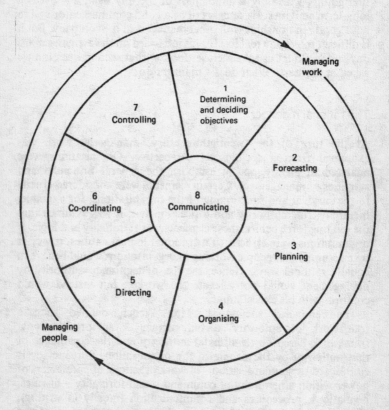

Fig. 1.1   Fayol's wheel of managerial activities

1   *Determining and deciding objectives*. Determining the priorities of organisations and departmental goals.

2 *Forecasting*. Looking ahead to predict likely conditions which will affect determination of objectives.

3 *Planning*. Turning the broad objectives of the previous activity into specific goals, and drawing up a plan of action to show how they can be achieved.

4 *Organising*. Deciding what resources are required for each task, ie both material and people; allocating resources to tasks.

5 *Directing*. Getting the work done; making decisions, giving instructions, solving problems, training staff.

6 *Co-ordinating*. Keeping everyone moving towards achievement of the objective; keeping a balance between the use and availability of resources.

7 *Controlling*. Measuring actual performance against goals set in the planning stage, and taking corrective action where necessary.

8 *Communicating*. Keeping necessary information flowing between people concerned with achievement of the objectives. Communication is the hub of Fayol's wheel; all other activities depend on the smooth flow of information.

Naturally, the weighting of these activities varies from manager to manager. The higher his position in the hierarchy, the more the manager is concerned with strategic concerns; the lower his position, the more he is concerned with day-to-day operations.

The weighting of the activities may also vary across functions, eg some jobs may be mainly forecasting, some may be mainly controlling, but the eight basic activities are common and similar for all levels and functions of management.

Fayol recognised that managerial work was different from that of the other functions which made up the activities of the organisation. The technical, financial, commercial, accounting and security functions which were the five other main activities of the organisation were primarily technique-based – managerial work, that of planning, organising, controlling, communicating etc., required the application of alternative skills.

To be a successful manager it was necessary not only to be technically competent, but to recognise that the process of working through people, and the development of the skills required for this, was the main contribution a manager could make to the maintenance of the organisation. (See Figure 1.2.)

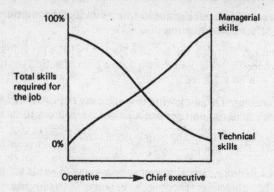

Fig. 1.2   Skills required at different hierarchical levels
Adapted from C.J. Margerison, *Career Paths. How to Assess Your Managerial Style,* MCB University Press, 1979, p. 25. Reproduced with permission from M.C.B.

Scientific management

Frederick Taylor has been hailed as the father of scientific management. The result of his studies conducted at the Bethlehem Steel Company, USA, was a scientific basis for designing and measuring jobs. His objective was to break down the elements of each task into a number of separate components and then to find the most efficient way of working on those tasks. In this way, increased productivity would generate greater economic rewards to be shared between the company and its workers. Scientific management was concerned with the measurement of work within an organisation – not of the organisation itself.

The focus was on economic reward – a fair day's work for a fair day's pay. He assumed that workers come to work solely to earn money: that money was to enable them to live their lives, and to support their families. The social responsibility of companies towards their workers was not a high consideration at this time. After all, the workers were paid fairly, productivity was being increased and fatigue was lower because of improved task design. People as individuals were not a prime concern; Taylor assumed management and workers had the same aims – economic rewards.

Management was seen to have a primary function in this system. Taylor insisted that it was management's responsibility to organise, control and design work, tasks and activities, so that workers could perform the most efficiently.

Taylor's work was carried on by Frank Gilbreth and Henry Gantt, two American pioneers, who developed time and motion study, now work study and ergonomics, to levels of sophistication which are still used extensively today.

These early studies did advance understanding of the manager's job. They told us that there were two classes of people – managers and workers. The manager's job was to organise specific tasks and activities within an organisational structure: the worker's job was to do the tasks organised by managers. This involved, for the manager, both the management of work and the management of people. It was also demonstrated that efficiency could be improved by using scientific methods of job design, and by employing the legitimate authority held by the manager within the organisational hierarchy.

The data-processing manager

Running through all the studies of the manager as a rational operator is the theme of communication – and particularly communication of information. Without this element the rational manager cannot effectively perform his other functions.

Later studies of managers and managerial work looked at the manager as an information processor within an organisational system – collecting information, filtering and monitoring it, and using it to organise and control the people and activities for which he was accountable in order to improve productive performance.

A simple model of the organisation as a system is shown in Figure 1.3.

The organisation interacts with a particular environment, such as a market place or community, in a number of ways. Such interactions will affect what happens inside the organisation. Within the system, the feedback loop is all-important. It is needed to produce the information required to monitor the standards established for the successful output of both products and services, and that people's performance, rewards and satisfaction are being achieved. Managers use this information to modify the transformation process, or to modify the people and/or material inputs to maintain achievement of the established output criteria – whether quantity or quality.

The skills of information handling thus become paramount in a manager. Quantifiable information is a basis for making decisions in this system.

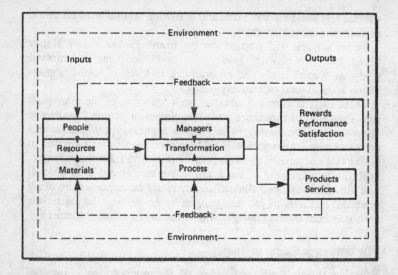

Fig. 1.3   The organisation as an open system

The collection and analysis of quantifiable information as an aid for managing to make better decisions more quickly is the task of Operations Research or Management Science, which had its beginnings in World War II, and was later incorporated successfully in industry. With increasing use of computers, management information systems (MIS) are enabling managers to make more balanced and considered decisions. Yet, as the nature of information has increasingly become more complex, additional responsibilities are placed on MIS departments to satisfy the needs of the end user (the manager). Ironically, although involved in data processing, MIS specialists need to take into account the idiosyncratic nature of different managers' situations (see the section, The Human Manager) in order to appreciate the data requirements of the end user.

Case 1.2   What's happened to Wallace Lane?

Jim Roberts' mail was the usual hotchpotch of discardable circulars, customer complaints, letters from head office, sales enquiries, and reports from his salespeople. When he had run through it he looked at his watch. 'Good God, eleven o'clock already. Elaine, let me have the file on General Products. I see I'm taking their managing director to lunch to discuss their new order requirements.'

General Products was an important new customer, an expanding company with growing requirements, and Jim wanted to establish a good working relationship with their managing director.

'And get me the group marketing director on the phone. No, let me speak to dispatch first. I'd better see what's happened to those fittings for Wallace Lane.'

Bert Jackson in dispatch was no help. 'Bill Ward just rang me yesterday and said he'd run into a snag and the fittings wouldn't be ready in time. He said he'd tried to get hold of you but you'd gone to Birmingham for the day.' Bert's disapproval of managers who could apparently 'take days off' to go to airy-fairy things like conferences dripped out of the phone.

'Thanks, Bert,' said Jim, 'I'd better get on to Bill right away, as Wallace Lane's now on my back.'

'Bill, Jim Roberts here,' he said when he got through to the production manager 'What's happening about the Wallace Lane job?'

'Oh, Jim, you're back now,' replied Bill Ward. 'Slight problem in the packaging department. The shrink wrapper has gone off line, and it looks serious - about three days before it'll be back in operation. I need to know if you'll accept box packaging without the shrink wrapping. These fittings are piling up to the ceiling now and I couldn't make a decision without consulting you.'

'I'll come back to you as soon as I've talked to Wallace Lane. They've already been on the phone about it, Bill. OK?'

'Don't be too long, Jim,' snorted Bill. 'These fittings will soon be coming out of my ears and I've nowhere else to store them.'

When we look at Jim Roberts of Electrical Enterprises (Case 1.2), do the Weber, Taylor, Fayol approaches really tell us very much about what he actually does or about the characteristics of his work? Certainly he has had to plan, organise and control, and especially communicate, in his day's work so far.

We can, however, start to make some tentative identification of the dimensions of his work from the case. A great quantity of work is conducted at an unrelenting pace. There is great variety in his work – mostly fragmented by a series of interruptions. Each episode, or critical incident, does not last very long – perhaps only minutes in some cases. Many of the episodes are superficial, where the manager is sucked into situations which he did not initiate. Contacts with other managers, employees and environmental interfaces are mostly verbal. In fact, certain studies show that managers' contacts are 80 per cent verbal, either because of pressure of time or because of their own individual approaches to managing work. They have extensive networks of contacts which they use to generate information, and these networks are not necessarily part of the formal system – managers glean 70 per cent of the information they need to carry out their jobs through informal channels.

Perhaps the main characteristic of Jim Roberts' day is the realisation that he works in a stimulus–response environment – he reacts to events, instead of controlling them; he works mostly in the short term, his work seems to consist of firefighting and crisis management rather than planning, organising and controlling. Communication may actually have become an end in itself as opposed to the hub of Fayol's wheel, facilitating all the other prescribed activities.

In Cases 1.1 and 1.2, Jim Roberts appears to be carrying out most of the functions described by Fayol. He has determined the objectives of the training of the two new reps, forecast their requirements, planned the training with the training manager. He has been involved in motivating, co-ordinating and controlling, particularly with Bill Ward, over the Wallace Lane situation. Communicating has certainly been the hub of Jim Roberts' wheel of activities: the bulk of his time so far has been devoted to communicating with others, in a spontaneous way.

However, managers are not the reflective, orderly thinkers which Fayol described, able to identify clearly their tasks, and to differentiate between them. They seem to have to switch roles quickly, and frequently, to wear different hats from minute to minute, to manage even to keep up with the pace of their short-term work, let alone consider long-term planning.

THE HUMAN MANAGER

So far in this chapter we have examined the manager as a rational, logical person who carries out tasks and activities, and uses quantitative information to make decisions and control and organise rational, logical workers.

Professor Elton Mayo and a team of associates from the Harvard University, investigating variations in worker performance at the Western Electric Company in 1924, found that people themselves affected their own performance. Mayo considered that increased performance occurred when the workers felt that they were being treated as people, when management showed that the workers were important to the business, and that the inputs and changes the workers proposed were at least considered by management on their merits.

The whole Behavioural School took off from that point. Research into the norms and dynamics of group behaviour led to hypotheses that managers should primarily act as facilitators, maintaining group morale which would lead to effective performance. Attitudes, morale, individual behaviour, management styles were researched. Conflicting arguments abounded concerning person-oriented leadership styles versus task-oriented leadership styles in order to attain maximum performance and morale. The focus of research moved from the rational, quantitative manager to the behaviourally aware, understanding and caring manager. Experience has now shown that managers need to be able to change their styles in either direction, depending on situational variables. This discussion will be taken further in Chapter 7, which concentrates on how to manage people and groups.

Out of the behavioural research some clear specification of managerial work has emerged. Managers do have to carry out all the activities already described. They have to be aware of the motives for their own behaviour, and the effects of that behaviour on other people. They have to understand their objectives and be able to devise strategies to achieve them. They need to be able to analyse situations and people and to develop the behavioural skills most effective in those situations. Managers have to perform different roles at different times.

Case 1.3   Another heavy blow

'Elaine, get me Wallace Lane, please,' Jim called out.

'The group managing director is on the phone for you. He's held on for two minutes now, so I think it must be important. Do you want to speak to him or shall I get Wallace Lane?'

'Better put him through now, Elaine,' said Jim, wondering. 'Hello, Charles, sorry to keep you waiting, I was on the other line.'

'Jim,' said Charles Howard, 'We've got problems with Richards Appliances.'

Jim's heart sank. He'd been supplying Richards Appliances for years and had a big order going through now. Only last week he'd delivered, ahead of schedule because of pressure from Richards, fittings worth £30,000.

'Their bank appointed a receiver and manager yesterday, our finance director tells me', Charles went on, 'and it looks as if there won't be very much in the kitty for anyone once it's cleared up. I'm telling you now because I know you have an order in the pipeline and it'll have to be stopped now. It's a pity about last week's delivery, but it can't be helped

> now. What you have to do now is to revise sales targets and you'll have to find some new sales from somewhere to bring us back to schedule now Richards Appliances is finished.'
>
> 'I'll look into it straight away, Charles. It's a heavy blow, for over 25 per cent of our sales were to them, but I have a few ideas that I want to look at. I'll come back with some preliminary thoughts and figures tomorrow, if that's OK?'
>
> 'That's fine, Jim. I'm really annoyed with finance. They should have had some inkling about the situation and advised us sooner.'
>
> Jim hung up the phone. This needed some immediate action. He could start the revisions now, but he felt he would have to talk to his salesmen and brainstorm this through with them before he put up any · considered plan to the marketing director.
>
> 'Elaine, do you know the reps' movements today? I'd like to get a message to those within striking distance as soon as possible.'
>
> Elaine, as a good secretary, did know. Jim explained the situation to her, and told Elaine to brief the salesmen about it and ask those available to meet him at his office at six this evening. 'Now you'd better get me Bill Ward at production too. Oh - Wallace Lane first, please.'

Jim Roberts is performing in several roles in Case 1.3. He is acting as a leader with Elaine, as a gatherer, monitor and giver of information to Charles Howard, as a disturbance handler, and as a resource allocator for his representatives for the six o'clock conference. He's not performing them consciously – it's all part of his job, and he's using different skills in each role.

The managers' roles

Professor Henry Mintzberg's study involved observing managers actually doing their work. He found an entirely different picture from the orderly, functional one described by Fayol. From this he was able to construct a model which looked at the roles which managers performed in their work because of the activities they need to carry out. This model enables the manager to identify more clearly the types of skill necessary to develop greater effectiveness in his formal job position.

Mintzberg described the manager's job in terms of various roles, or discrete sets of behaviour (see Figure 1.4), which the manager performs. He identified ten roles within the formal authority and status provided by his position in the organisation.

From the manager's formal authority derive the three interpersonal roles, which enable him to play the three

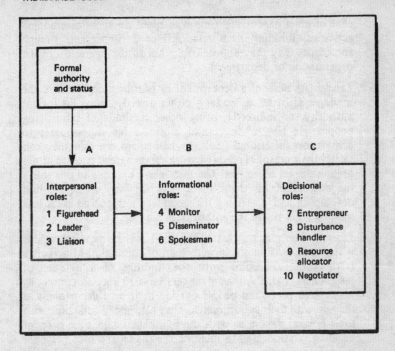

Fig. 1.4 The manager's roles
Slight adaptation of Figure 8 (p. 59) from *The Nature of Managerial Work* by Henry Mintzberg. Copyright ©1973 by Henry Mintzberg. Reprinted by permission of Harper & Row, Publishers Inc.

informational roles. These two sets of roles together enable him to perform the four decisional roles.

Interpersonal roles

By the very nature of the activities described by Fayol, the manager has to perform three interpersonal roles.

1 *Figurehead.* As head of an organisational or operational unit, the manager has to behave as a figurehead when carrying out his function. The chairman has to present a long service award; the finance director attends a board meeting in his capacity as head of the finance function. Mintzberg found that twelve per

cent of chief executives' time was spent on such 'ceremonial' activities. Building such relationships is important, though sometimes they may appear irrelevant to the operation of the organisation or department.

2 *Leader*. As head of a department or part of a department, the manager must act as leader – either directly, using his formal authority, or indirectly, using other methods of influencing people. He has to direct and motivate his subordinates to achieve organisational goals, to help them see that they can satisfy their personal needs by working on agreed tasks to attain organisational objectives. The manager is exposed in this role – the success of his department depends very much on him developing and practising the necessary influencing skills and making good use of the authority in his role.

3 *Liaison*. The manager establishes and maintains relationships with others outside his normal chain of command. Mintzberg's results are in keeping with the findings of a number of researchers, namely, that managers have to keep in contact as much with peers and people outside their own department as they do with their subordinates. They also spend little time with their bosses! Again, as with the figurehead role, time is spent building relationships to increase the manager's own personal information network, to enable him to acquire informally the information he needs for his job.

Informational roles

Managers typically spend about forty per cent of their time handling and processing information. This may be verbal, written, formal or informal. Information may be power – certainly the manager, with his development of information networks, is in a position of power in his organisational unit – but it is only useful in his job where it can be used as a basis for sensible decision-making. The manager has three informational roles:

4 *Monitor*. As monitor, he collects information from his information networks. This may not always be factual, but may because of the informal way in which much of it is gathered consist of inferences and assumptions which he has to sift and filter into some coherent and relevant form.

5 *Disseminator*. As disseminator, the manager passes on any necessary information to his subordinates.

6 *Spokesman*. As spokesman, the manager passes some information to people outside his organisation or department or unit, eg he keeps other departments and influential people in the organisation informed of his performance and the performance of his unit.

Decisional roles

An important factor in the performance of a manager is the quality of his decision-making. The time-span of his decision-making may vary from department to department, and be different at various levels of the organisational hierarchy. Generally, the higher in the hierarchy, the greater the time-span of decision-making – directors make strategic decisions, functional managers make operational ones. But no matter what that time-span may be, eventually the effectiveness of that decision can be and is measured.

Managers perform in four decisional roles:

7 *Entrepreneur*. In this role, the manager looks for changes or potential changes in the environment and tries to modify and adapt his unit to cope with these, to make it more effective. This may involve modifying objectives, task, technology or structures. It may also involve changes in people, and the manager may use his subordinates on development projects to look at new products, processes, reorganisations etc., not only to improve the department's productivity, but also to assist in the subordinate's personal growth and development.

8 *Disturbance handler*. Here is the stimulus–reactive manager, responding to pressures and unexpected events in his unit. Short-term decisions have to be made to deal with breakdowns, strikes or, shortages of materials. Because of the pressure on them for short-term results, the culture of the organisation, and their own preferred work style; many managers become excellent disturbance handlers and problem-solvers, to the detriment of planning and thinking long term.

9 *Resource allocator*. The manager decides how resources, both material and people, are to be shared on the tasks the unit has to perform. He decides who gets what and when, and how much of his own time he is going to spend on each task and decision. Perhaps his most valuable resource is his own time – and good time management is one criterion of the successful manager.

10 *Negotiator.* The manager has to spend considerable time on
negotiations, both vertically with his boss and subordinates, and
also laterally with his peers. Negotiating and influencing skills,
then, are essential for the effective manager.

Case 1.4   Managing problems

Wallace Lane's purchasing manager was fuming. 'Thanks for ringing me
back at last, Jim. What the hell's happening about our order? We should
have had it yesterday and our production's held up because of your
non-delivery. That isn't the first time, and I tell you I shall have to look
around for a more reliable supplier if you can't meet our schedule.'

Jim managed to placate him, and explained the packaging problem.

'Christ, Jim, I don't care if they come in toilet paper, but get them here
by tomorrow!' He slammed the phone down.

Jim looked at the phone, dialled Bill Ward and told him the shrink
wrapping didn't matter and to get the delivery off to Wallace Lane today
if possible.

'And, Bill, Richards Appliances. What's the state of their order which is
going through now?'

'It's in the second stage assembly,' replied Bill, 'It should be ready by
the weekend.'

Jim explained the situation.

'It's a pity these are all special fittings, Jim. We will just have to take
them into stock until you can find another customer, if you ever can!'

Jim lit a cigarette and looked at his watch. Ten past twelve already.
Elaine popped into the office.

'I've managed to get hold of three of the salesmen, and I've left
messages at the places I know they're going to today for them to phone
here as soon as they get there. I think I'd better stay in the office over
lunch in case they ring then. I'm only going to have a sandwich anyway.'

'Thanks, Elaine,' Jim said, 'I've got to meet the MD of General
Products for lunch, so I'd better go through his file first. Any other
calamities at the moment?'

'Well,' Elaine said, 'Jack Benson called in sick this morning, and will be
off for three weeks, so you'll have to reallocate calls in his area. Next
year's sales budget has to be completed by Friday, but you can't do
much about that until you've had the meeting today, can you? By the
way, do you want me to be there to take minutes?'

'No, that's all right, Elaine, thanks for the offer, but I'll make some
notes myself and give them to you tomorrow,' said Jim.

'Personnel is chasing you for the report on that accident in the office
when Jane pulled the filing cabinet on top of her and broke her finger
last week,' Elaine concluded, 'and Roger Case wants to talk to you
about unionising office staff.'

'Elaine, first things first – get me my wife, on the phone please. I want
to see how Tony's fever is.'

Jim Roberts (Case 1.4) is not having a very good day. Short bursts of various problems are forcing him into actions and giving him little time for reflection. He is having to make decisions based on limited information, and to rely on his judgement, intuition and experience to devise successful strategies. Time pressure is forcing him to deal with each situation on a superficial level. In his situation, achieving short-term goals and maintaining the status quo reduce the time available for the long-term planning he must do.

His obvious high-level skills in his interpersonal roles are enabling him to obtain and interpret a modicum of information on which to make decisions. He is, in fact, performing all three sets of roles in his job. Some of the roles overlap, but the three sets of roles form, according to Mintzberg, a complete picture of his whole job.

Clearly, in order to make sensible decisions, the manager needs adequate and relevant information. To generate this information, he needs to develop skills in his interpersonal roles. He also needs to understand his own work, and the relative weighting of the ten roles in that work, for then he will know the types of skill he needs to become effective. Such skills are developing interpersonal relationships, motivating, leading, collecting and analysing information, negotiating, problem-solving and decision-making.

The only problem is that managers are not normally measured on the quality of their performance in their interpersonal roles, but mostly on their decisional roles.

Perhaps this is the wrong way round.

Demands, constraints and choices

Like Mintzberg, Dr Rosemary Stewart of the Oxford Management Centre studied the interpersonal activities of managers. She examined particularly the interpersonal contacts they have – with bosses, subordinates, peers and external contacts. These networks of contacts are extensive.

She further observed and studied what managers specifically do in their jobs, and developed a framework for analysing the way in which managers themselves shape the nature and design of their jobs, tasks and activities as a result of the demands, constraints and choices they experience whilst doing their work.

Demands

Demands refer to those activities that need to be done by anyone holding a particular management position, the accountabilities that *must* be achieved, the performance standards and criteria that *must* be met. Basically, we are talking about meeting others' minimum expectations about what should be done, although there may be choices at the discretion of the job holder in how he meets these expectations. The level of demands may also be a function of the relative power of the job holder and his boss – the greater the boss's power, the more he can make demands and impose sanctions if these demands are not met.

Constraints

Stewart defines constraints as 'The factors, internal and external to the organisation, that limit what the job holder can do.' These may be resource, legal, technological, organisational and attitudinal. Procedures may be laid down in the organisation clearly limiting and defining how certain tasks are to be performed. Organisational policies may define the limits of sales in a particular market and the products to be sold in them. Trade union rules may clearly limit the parameters of work which may be carried out by union members.

Choices

The manager has opportunities to decide what he wants to do, and

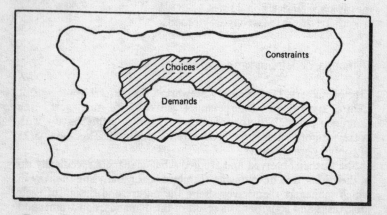

Fig. 1.5   Job A: Demands, constraints and choices
From Stewart, R., *Choices for the Manager: A Guide To Managerial Work*, McGraw-Hill, 1982, p. 7. Reproduced with permission from McGraw-Hill.

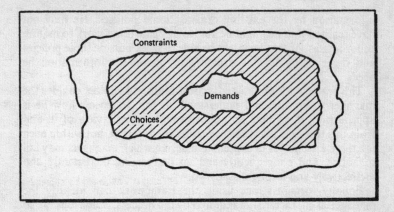

Fig. 1.6   Job B: Demands, constraints and choices
From Stewart, R., *Choices for the Manager: A Guide To Managerial Work*, McGraw-Hill, 1982, p. 7. Reproduced with permission from McGraw-Hill.

also how he does it, taking into account the existing demands and constraints of the job. Some selection is possible within most managerial jobs. Certainly, job descriptions may limit the parameters within which the job holder may work. However, within those parameters, the activities, accountabilities and tasks will vary with the preferences of individual managers. Some jobs may be tightly defined in both content and procedures, and give very few choices to the manager to change the type of work he does or the way in which he does it. Others may have a small area of demands and few constraints, giving much more choice and opportunity to the manager to define and design his own work.

In Job A (Figure 1.5), being effective means bearing in mind the many demands and constraints, and few choices, meeting the demands successfully within the constraints imposed. In Job B (Figure 1.6), success involves using one's discretion to make the most appropriate choice about what to do and how to do it under those particular circumstances. In all cases, however, demands may be only perceived demands and constraints only perceived constraints.

In turn, choices may generate further demands and impose further constraints. A manager choosing to take on an extra project may have additional demands on his time if he has to work to a strict deadline, and may be constrained in his collection of necessary information by the existing organisational policies. He may not have realised that he might be able to delegate other work to mature subordinates, or that he might be able to work outside these policies and the existing formal structure to obtain the information he needs.

This framework of demands, constraints and choices enables the manager to analyse and understand his job, to review how he is approaching it, to take an objective and strategic view of it, and from this to assess his efficiency. Jobs are different, but within each job there are choices in content and design which managers may fail to notice, and consequently end up performing inefficiently and ineffectively and feeling dissatisfied.

Equally, organisations using the framework can identify the managerial characteristics required by job holders. Some jobs are so structured that they impose many demands and constraints but few choices; what to do and how to do it are clearly defined in rules and procedures. These jobs require little initiative and creativity. Other jobs may only impose a few important demands accompanied by a wide band of constraints, where managers can be creative and innovative in their choice. In both cases, this framework aids selection and the recognition of training needs for potential job holders, and also helps develop criteria for assessing the manager.

Case 1.5   What have I achieved?

Jim's lunch went well. He and Alan Tudsbury, the MD of General Products, hit it off from the start. General Products seemed to be a well run, efficient and go-ahead company, and this was epitomised by Alan Tudsbury. Jim even managed to interest him in the Richards Appliances fittings now being made for stock; General Products were considering moving into that market and the offer of the fittings at a substantial discount was attractive to Alan.

Jim got back to his office at 3.30pm feeling rather pleased with himself. Elaine had managed to arrange the meeting with the salesmen – only two were unable to come at six.

'Any chance of organising some beer and sandwiches for us then, Elaine?' asked Jim.

In the next two hours, he took a long hard look at the sales performance figures and his original projections for next year's budget. It was obvious that some substantial reorganising needed to be done in order to meet targets with the company's existing products. New markets or new products needed to be developed quickly, and the sales force organisation would have to be changed.

'This isn't just about next year when we're going to have problems,' thought Jim. 'We're really talking about an examination of the whole business we're in. Once I've clarified some ideas with my salesmen tonight, I'll have to write a report and discuss this with Charles Howard before next year's budget is submitted. Richards Appliances have hit us harder than I thought at first.

Elaine came into the office.

'I'm leaving now, Mr Roberts. The beer and sandwiches are on my desk. I've managed to keep everyone off your phone this afternoon, but Roger Case keeps asking if he can see you before he goes about white-collar unionisation.'

'Fix an appointment and put it in my diary, Elaine. I've got more important things to do at the moment.'

Elaine left.

Jim suddenly felt very tired. He had been a bit short about Roger. 'What have I achieved today?' he wondered. Some troubleshooting, a possible way out of the temporary problem of the fittings being produced now, a good lunch with Alan Tudsbury with the prospect of continuing orders, and a brief stab at some long-term planning. To be followed by a meeting with his salesmen which he hoped would be creative and help him to revise targets realistically.

Not much of a day's work, really. Things were different when he was just a sales rep three years ago. He sometimes wondered if he was really cut out to cope with all the administrative hassle of being a sales manager.

And he'd be late home – Oh hell! He'd forgotten to tell Janice that at lunchtime. He'd better ring her straight away. He picked up the phone....

In Case 1.5, the demands of Jim Roberts' job are clear. He must achieve sales targets. This is the performance criterion which he must meet for the group marketing director.

He has constraints within which he must work: namely budgets (financial constraints), personnel (the quality and reliability of his sales force), external (the future of Richards Appliances), organisational (reliance on the production department to meet his targets), personal (his desire to maintain a balance between his work and family lives).

Between the demands and constraints of his job he has considerable opportunity for choice in what he wants to do, and also in how he does it. He likes to go to conferences – he can structure his job to enable him to attend. He likes to get personally involved with customers. He has been able to design his job and workload so that he now has time available in the afternoon for the long-term planning which was immediately and unexpectedly necessary.

Managers typically have more choices in their jobs than they may realise, but also typically (and often unconsciously) shape their jobs so that they can do the tasks and perform the roles they prefer.

SOME THOUGHTS ON MANAGEMENT EFFECTIVENESS

Management effectiveness can be considered as a function of understanding and skills: Understanding primarily the job which is held, within the context of the organisation's situation – its objectives and its needs, and the wider environment – the industry, technological developments, the social environment, all of which influence the organisation. Understanding also that managers get their work done through people and that competence at people skills are essential for achieving goals as well as the technical skills relevant to the particular function. Understanding, therefore, why the manager behaves as he does, why other people behave as they do, and what are the likely consequences of his own behaviour. Understanding the basic notions, the concepts that are paramount to good management – the concepts and techniques of leadership, motivation, delegation, communication, influencing, negotiation, problem-solving and decision-making.

Managerial effectiveness also involves skills: skills in analysing and skills of managing oneself, other people and tasks. Skills of recognising problems, what information is needed, how to get it, and how to assess its validity, skills of flexible thinking, of creative thinking, of developing insight into situations; skills of learning quickly from experience and being able to take an intuitive leap forward. Skills with people – being able to assess them, to develop open trusting relationships with bosses, colleagues and subordinates, to listen and collaborate, to create climates within which people are self-motivated; skills of communicating, skills of analysing and managing interpersonal, group and intergroup problems and conflict, skills of influencing without formal authority.

The manager's job is complex, requiring a high level of short-term problem-solving skills and techniques from its incumbent, particularly the efficient management of his own time. Free time is made, not found, and in some of that time freed from other obligations the manager needs to stand back occasionally and test out his understanding of the job – is he emphasising the role that best suits the situation, and is his perception of the demands and constraints correct? Does he, in fact, have more latitude and choice about his job content and design than he realises? Insight into his job makes for an excellent manager.

SUMMARY

The manager's job has been examined from six angles.

1   *The rational manager* is a concept based on the Weberian model
    of bureaucratic organisation. The existence of the organisation
    is based on a universal acceptance of the legitimacy of authority
    and standardisation and familiarity of work processes. The task
    of the manager is to work within the existing system, which
    makes his job predictable and also easy to compare with those
    of other managers in different parts of the organisation.

2   *The functions of management* are eight, namely determining
    objectives, forecasting, planning, organising, directing, co-
    ordinating, controlling and communicating. The relative
    importance of each of these functions to each other varies
    according to levels of hierarchy and functional specialisation.

3   *Scientific management.* Jobs are broken down into separate
    components in order to attain the most efficient way of
    working, which would lead to greater rewards for both
    operatives and management. It was assumed that operatives
    come to work for economic reasons, solely to earn money.
    Humanistic concerns did not figure highly in this formula.
    Scientific management has had a powerful impact in the field of
    management, for out of it arose techniques such as time and
    motion, work study and ergonomics.

4   *The data processing manager.* Due to the complexities of
    organisational operations, the communication of information is
    an essential component of a manager's job. The manager is an
    information processor, collecting, collating and maintaining
    information, and using it to organise and control other people
    and their activities for which he is accountable. Sensible
    decision-making depends on reliable quantifiable information.

5   *The manager's roles.* Managers have to perform different roles
    in their job at different times. Mintzberg identified three types
    of managerial roles – interpersonal, informational and
    decisional – which managers perform within the defined
    parameters of their formal authority and status in the
    organisation. Managers are mostly measured on their
    performance in the decisional roles of entrepreneur, disturbance
    handler, resource allocator and negotiator, but need to play
    their informational roles well in order to have adequate data on

which to base their decisions. However, to play his informational role well he must firstly develop skills in his interpersonal roles, to enable him to establish a network of contacts both within and outside the organisation where required, which he can tap for information not available through formal communication channels.

6 *Demands, choices, constraints.* Demands are the accountabilities of the job holder, the performance standards and criteria which must be met. Constraints are the factors, both internal and external to the organisation, that limit what the job holder can do. What is left in between are the choices, the opportunities which a manager has to decide what he wants to do, and also how he does it – the way, in fact, he can shape his job to his own preferred activities, roles and styles of working. Jobs vary in the range of choices available, but this is a useful framework for a manager in analysing and understanding his job, particularly if he can establish which demands are only perceived constraints. The framework can also be used in the recruitment and selection process, and when making career development and promotion choices.

IN CONCLUSION

Managers have to perform diverse activities and adopt different roles within the context of their everyday jobs. Managers have to achieve objectives, often not set by them, and have to achieve those objectives through the management of work and the management of people. Although historically emphasis has been placed on the controlling, planning and co-ordinating skills, it is actually people skills that decide between a good and a poor manager. Remember: 'managers get things done through others'.

2 The Manager's Career

Case 2.1   Sarah Young

'Right, Sarah. Anything else you want to cover about yourself or want to know about the job?' James Wood looked across the interview room at her.

'We seem to have gone over a lot of ground. I can't think of any more at the moment, thanks.' Sarah Young felt it had been a good interview. James Wood had been sympathetic, though searching, in his questions. She knew she'd done well to get to this last stage of the selection process, and she certainly would like to work in James' consultancy firm: it seemed just what she'd been looking for.

Sarah was in her last term at business school. She was thirty-one years old and single, with five years' experience in administration – first with a publishing company and latterly with an international cosmetics corporation. She had a first degree in business studies from a polytechnic, and had decided she wanted to move into consultancy on the personnel/human resource side. She liked people.

She'd put her name down on the list of interested students when James Wood came to the business school looking for recruits to his consultancy company, based in London, and at present employing twenty people. It seemed just the right size for her to go into and gain valuable experience, and the assignments he'd described seemed interesting. Sarah was delighted to be asked to go to London for a second interview.

'Well, I'll be making a decision this week, and I'll let you know as soon as I do so. It's been nice talking to you, Sarah.' James Wood escorted her out, walked back to his desk, sat down and relaxed.

'That's the last candidate,' he thought. 'It's been a long day, but I think Sarah is the one who'll both fit into the organisation and also be capable of high and fast performance.' He reflected on the problems of selecting good consultants for the company. 'No, not just selecting them, but training them, and making sure they get to know the ropes – that's what it's all about,' he thought.

> Sarah got her letter of acceptance a week later, and started work at
> James Wood's consultancy on 4 January.

The whole process of joining a new organisation can be viewed
from two contrasting points, that of the new employee and that of
the organisation.

From the individual's point of view, it is a process of highlighting
one's skills and attributes, of working out how to get on in the
organisation, of learning to perform well, and more generally, of
squaring the commitment involved in all of this with the
commitment to one's home/family life. The same process from the
organisation's point of view is one of selection and recruitment,
induction and training, performance appraisal and career counselling. The two processes are two sides of a complicated negotiation
which will lead to an understanding whereby the contribution of
each party aims to address the other's expectations. This
understanding may be renegotiated many times by either party, as
expectations change over time.

Any such understanding between two parties has both
quantitative and qualitative elements. The quantitative elements
refer to tasks, output and hours to be worked. The qualitative
elements are such factors as commitment, energy, drive, trust and
identity. Does the individual identify with his employing
organisation? Is he committed to what he is doing? Does he trust his
bosses, colleagues and subordinates both as people and as
creditworthy professionals? Is the individual willing to commit the
drive and energy required to make himself successful? Equally, is
the individual's boss, or are other key managers, willing to offer him
jobs or tasks of substantial responsibility? Do they trust him from
what they have seen of his performance? Because of the qualitative
nature of such an understanding, the parties may not be clear as to
its exact elements, but at least they feel that some form of agreement
has emerged.

The manner in which such tacit agreements develop is highlighted
by examining the following four areas:

1 Recruitment and selection

2 Induction and socialisation

3 Career development

4 The interaction between work and the family

Early experiences in an organisation can have one of two outcomes. Either the individual feels content and well matched with the organisation (in which case we say he is well socialised), or that he feels disappointed and out of place. Which it is rests very much on the extent to which the individual feels the organisation reinforces his personal feelings about how people should be treated at work. In periods of economic growth, where job mobility is easy, if the individual feels uncomfortable in the organisation he can leave. In periods of economic recession, where job mobility is difficult, there is increasing pressure on the individual to conform to the organisation. This in itself sets up all kinds of personal dilemmas. The many training programmes and seminars on stress today may well be one crude measure of this phenomenon. Sufficient attention to the processes of entry and socialisation can turn potentially negative experiences into an exciting and stimulating learning phase.

RECRUITMENT AND SELECTION

Both the employer and the prospective employee are trying to find out if there is a match: the employer is seeking a candidate who can be integrated into the job and the organisation; the candidate is looking for a job and organisation which will satisfy his needs and expectations.

These needs and expectations are entirely subjective; they exist in the perception of the individual. The individual who perceives the congruence of the offered rewards and the satisfaction of his needs, expects to perform the job successfully, believes that he will fit into the culture of the organisation and will like working with the people there – and so will be attracted to the job and the organisation and want to take up a job offer.

In Case 2.1, James Wood and Sarah Young were seeking a match. James's company was expanding. He needed high-performing personnel and a candidate who could quickly fit into his organisation. Sarah wanted to work with people and to move away from administration. Both had high expectations and both felt these would be met by the other.

But interviews alone are notoriously unreliable as predictors of future job performance. Some people are good performers and can project a favourable and professional image in an interview. Some selection interviewers are not well prepared or briefed, and have not developed the skills of gathering the information about candidates that enable them to make good decisions. It is easy to see how poor decisions at the selection stage can be made. Below are listed problems to which attention should be paid in order that the entry process be effectively managed.

Problems in the management of entry

The recruitment/selection and job hunting processes are problematic both for the individual and the employing organisation. Professor Ed Schein of the Massachusetts Institute of Technology (MIT) describes four problem areas:

1   *Obtaining inaccurate information in a situation of mutual selling.* Since the organisation is trying to pull in the best candidate and the individual is trying to get the best job, there are strong incentives on both sides to give an unbalanced picture. Both want to play up their strong points and play down their weak points. Careful questioning at the interview stage can help to alleviate this problem.

2   *Both the organisation and the individual unconsciously colluding in setting up unrealistic expectations about the early career.* There may be a tendency in the interview to concentrate on the long-term prospects available in the organisation, rather than spending sufficient time thinking through the nature of the immediate job. The outcome may then be that the individual joins the organisation on the basis of what it offers him/her in one or two years' time, rather than the reality of the first job. A few years ago, one of the MBA students at Cranfield School of Management took an accounts manager job in a well-established advertising agency, primarily because of the attractive likelihood of becoming an accounts director in twelve months' time. What was not discussed was that the directorship was contingent on his performance on one major account. This account had been fraught with all sorts of problems and the client was renowned throughout the agency as being difficult. Within six months the MBA despaired of the account and soon after that the account moved agencies. The MBA was made redundant.

3   *The recruitment process building an incorrect image of the organisation.* If the organisation emphasises to the individual how much it values his abilities, and subsequently he is not used

well in the first job, disillusionment may set in. Professor Van Maanen, again of MIT, has shown that there is a relationship between the toughness of the recruitment and selection process and the positive self-image and commitment of the individual. The harder it is to get into an organisation, the more highly the individual values membership of it.

4 *Deciding on a job or a person without clear reliable information about the future.* Choosing to offer a job to an individual or deciding to take up a job offer is an expensive decision and may involve a long-term commitment. It is especially important in times of low job mobility, where it is less easy for individuals to obtain alternative employment. What measures can be taken to minimise this problem? From the individual's point of view, it is essential he is clear about his abilities, needs and values. Second, individuals must learn how to communicate such information accurately to others. Third, individuals must learn how to ask the right questions at interviews and thereby diagnose potential jobs well. From the organisation's point of view, the same principles apply. Management must know the organisation's needs; they must be able to communicate clearly the nature of the job and organisation now, and the prospects for the future, and they must be able to diagnose the potential of the applicant. Last, it is necessary to streamline recruitment and selection activities with job placement and supervision. The latter might well be accomplished by bringing the new employee's boss into the process of selection and recruitment.

INDUCTION AND SOCIALISATION

Case 2.2   Where to start?

Sarah joined the consultancy company in January. She was given an office to share with Derek Malcolm, a young consultant who had been with the company two years. Derek was not in on Sarah's first day. In fact, not many consultants seemed to be in.

'I suppose if consultants are good at their jobs, they are out with clients most of the time,' she said to herself.

Still, it did leave the immediate problem as to how she would learn to do her job. At that moment, a secretary walked in.

'I'm awfully sorry, there's no one here to welcome you. Everyone is tied up today. Let me show you round and introduce you to everyone who is in. Afterwards, I'll give you some of the recent big client reports we've written. That will give you a good idea of the kind of work on at the moment.'

The client reports she was given seemed a hotch-potch. Recruitment and selection, job evaluation, advice on industrial relations, some management development programmes and some supervisory training.

'Gosh,' she thought, 'I don't know an awful lot about these areas. I hope I'll be able to cope. And how does one go about behaving as a consultant, anyway? All I know is some theoretical approaches. But I suppose they won't let me loose by myself to start with, at least on any major consultancies.'

Derek Malcolm arrived back at the office two days later. 'Hello, it's good to have you with us, Sarah. Have you managed to settle in yet?'

'Well, I'm not really sure, Derek,' she replied. 'No one seems to know what to do with me. I haven't been assigned to any specific work. All I'm doing is to try to understand the work the company does at the moment.'

'Ah, Sarah.' James Wood appeared in the office, looking harassed. 'We're doing this job for Burskeins, the construction people, trying to sort out a salary system for them. They don't know what they ought to be paying their chartered surveyors, or where their job grades should fit on their salary scales. I want you to do some desk research on the area, and look at comparative figures in other industries too. It shouldn't take you long. Let me have your results early next week so that I can include them in my report to old man Burskein then.'

He smiled. 'We'll try to get you out of the office as soon as possible, meeting some clients. But at the moment, we're really pulled out, and someone has to do this backup work.'

Derek and James vanished to have a meeting.

Sarah wondered where to start.

Sarah in Case 2.2 rightly shows concern when starting her new job. Her boss and colleagues were not available to meet her in the first days of entry into the organisation. Simply starting a new job in a new organisation is an anxiety-provoking process. However, with no introduction to new colleagues or workload, an individual is likely to be extremely anxious. On eventually meeting her new colleagues, Sarah was quite inadequately briefed as to her workload in general or her assignment in particular. It is hardly surprising that she did not know where to start.

'Socialisation shapes the person.' Socialisation is the process whereby individuals come to terms with the new job. Ed Schein points to five key elements in this process:

1   Accepting the reality of the organisation (ie the constraints governing individual behaviour).

2   Dealing with resistance to change (ie the problems involved in

getting personal views and ideas accepted by others).

3   Learning how to work realistically in the new job, in terms of
    coping with too much or too little organisation and too much or
    too little job definition (ie the amount of autonomy and
    feedback available).

4   Dealing with the boss and understanding the reward system (ie
    the amount of independence given and what organisation
    defines as high performance).

5   Locating one's place in the organisation and developing an
    identity (ie understanding how an individual fits into the
    organisation).

All five elements come together to give an individual a certain
orientation towards the organisation.

The knowledge, values and skills that individuals learn from
being socialised differ for two reasons. First, individuals are
different, holding different values and attitudes and having acquired
and developed varying levels of skills. The values, attitudes and
skills level of the person will strongly influence the way they view
the new organisation, their new job and new colleagues. Second, the
actual experience of induction and socialisation into the organisation will vary according to the prevailing circumstances.

Three assumptions underlie this discussion of socialisation. First,
individuals in a state of transition experience anxiety. They want to
learn about their new role as quickly as possible to reduce this
anxiety. Second, when an individual moves into a new job the
surrounding colleagues, subordinates, superiors and clients play
active roles in the socialisation process by giving him information
about what really happens in the organisation. Third, the
productivity of any organisation depends upon how individuals
learn to perform in their new positions.

In order to appreciate the impact of socialisation on individuals,
we shall first examine the typical problems which emerge during a
person's induction into the organisation. Then we shall review the
practices organisations use to socialise newcomers and, lastly, we
shall look at how individuals cope with the emotional stages
involved in such a transition.

Problems of induction

Just as there are problems in the recruitment/selection/job hunting process, so there are in the early induction and socialisation period. The main questions typically facing any individual are:

- Will the job test me?
- Will my contribution be valued?
- Will I be able to maintain my individuality and integrity?
- Will I be able to balance my job with my family and outside interests?
- Will I have the opportunity to develop in the job?
- Will I feel proud to belong to this organisation?

The main issues facing organisations are:

- Will this individual fit our organisation?
- Will this individual make a real contribution?
- Will the individual be able to develop within the organisation?

Organisations spend considerable time and money on the induction of employees. Usually the direct costs of induction programmes are substantial. There are indirect costs as well, since new employees generally work below capacity whilst they are learning their jobs. The possibility of reducing costs provides an important incentive for management to learn how to improve socialisation.

Mechanisms for effective induction

The three American researchers Meryl Louis, Barry Posner and Gary Powell conducted a study to compare socialisation practices and to investigate how they might affect employee attitudes. They were interested in the availability and helpfulness of various socialisation practices and about their impact on newcomers' job satisfaction, commitment and intention to stay with the organisation.

The most representative practices and influences which emerged were: formal on-site induction, off-site residential training, other new recruits, relationships with more senior colleagues, mentor and/or sponsor relationship, supervisor/boss, secretary or other support staff, daily interactions with peers while working, social/recreational activities with people from work, and business trips with others from work.

As Figure 2.1 shows, the three most important socialisation practices were interaction with peers, supervisor and senior colleagues. Interaction with peers on the job was reported to be the most widely available aid, and was viewed as most important in helping newcomers become useful employees. The two least available aids to socialisation were off-site training and business trips.

Taken as a 'set' of socialisation practices, the availability of socialisation opportunities significantly affected subsequent job satisfaction commitment and intention to stay with the organisation. Obviously the impact of these socialisation practices may vary from one setting to another, depending upon a number of factors such as how well they are performed. This study does suggest, however, that the most formal and planned aids, such as training, may be seen as only modestly helpful. It is the day-to-day interactions with peers, senior colleagues and organisations that are considered most helpful. Probably not many organisations capitalise by utilising these people. The three American professors David Nadler, Richard Hackman and Ed Lawler say that the three critical elements during an individual's early employment period are a challenging job, good boss and a supportive workgroup.

	Ranking Helpfulness	Ranking Availability
Peers	1st	1st
Senior colleagues	2nd	3rd
Supervisor/boss	3rd	2nd
Mentor/sponsor	4th	8th
New recruits	5th	6th
Formal on-site induction	6th	5th
Off-site residential training	7th	10th
Social/recreational activities	8th	4th
Business trips	9th	9th
Secretarial/support staff	10th	6th

Fig. 2.1   Availability and helpfulness of socialisation practices
Adapted from Louis, M. R., Posner, B. Z. and Powell, G. N., 'The Availability and Helpfulness of Socialisation Practices', *Personnel Psychology*, Vol. 36, 1983, p. 861.

In case 2.2, Derek, Sarah's peer, was not available at first and was not much help in socialising her into the organisation. Her role had not been clearly defined and her expectations of 'working with people' were dashed by her first job, after being left alone for two days with no support or interaction with others in the organisation. The job she was given was a mixture of administration and consultancy, and she had not expected to have to work in that way. She wanted to do consultancy, not research and administration, as this appeared to her.

Her expectations were not being met at this early stage. She could not identify with her role, and she was not sure how to go about her first job. Support was not readily available. The climate and culture of the organisation was not what she had perceived it to be at her interview. Even allowing for pressure of work, she felt it was an inadequate induction process.

The stages of transition

Sarah's (Case 2.2) experiences are not so unusual. In fact, two researchers at Cranfield School of Management, Chris Parker and Ralph Lewis, consider that all managers go through phases in the process of entry and socialisation into the organisation. Whether the manager has accepted a new job in a new organisation, been promoted within an organisation, or had a sideways move, Parker and Lewis indicate that he will undergo a transition. In essence, the person has to learn what it really means to perform effectively in the new job and/or organisation, and that process takes time. During the period of transition the person will experience problems, failures and frustrations. How well he survives these problems depends significantly on the degree of perceived change required on his part, his capacity to adapt, and the support and guidance provided for him during the process. The person's capacity to adapt to his new environment and the support provided are critical. Many organisations operate a 'sink or swim' philosophy. Casualties occur because individuals take too long to reach the required level of competence. The time taken to move through the transition phase varies depending upon the degree of perceived change. The research indicated that on average managers spend between 18 and 30 months in a phase of transition. Below are the phases of the 'Transition Curve', shown in Figure 2.2.

Phase 1: Getting used to the place

A person has just changed his job. He may or may not have changed organisations, but the job content is different. The individual was probably competent in his last job and that is why he was appointed to this next one. In other words, his effectiveness rating is on the high side.

On entering the new organisation and/or job, work effectiveness drops slightly. Everything can be so new, unintelligible and overwhelming. The way things are done in the new place is so unfamilar that the individual is likely to feel that he cannot make a contribution or even function adequately.

However, within a matter of a few weeks, the person becomes used to the new place. He has found people to talk to and to ask when he requires assistance. If he is skilled at handling people, then the old hands at the new place are more likely to give him a chance. They may make strenuous efforts to ensure that the tasks are handed to the new boy are not too complex. People may go out of their way to offer advice and guidance on particular jobs or even how to handle particular people, especially troublesome superiors.

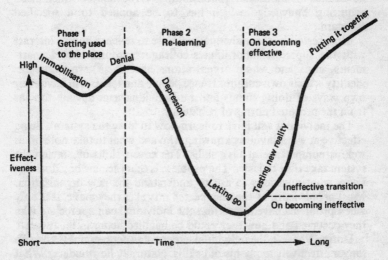

Fig. 2.2   Changes of work effectiveness during transition
From Andrew Kakabadse, *The Politics of Management*, Gower, 1983, p. 150.

Within a short time the initial shock and immobilisation have gone. The individual may by now be working quite well. Other people have given him a chance, so he is now showing what he can do. The person is, in fact, utilising the various skills he used in his last job. After all, they worked there; why should they not work here? The person has entered the stage of denial in that no great changes on his part are required. His attitude is: 'OK, so I've got a new job. But I don't have to become a different person!'

Phase 2: Re-learning

The initial immobilisation and denial stages of Phase 1 give way to Phase 2 when others begin to make real demands on the person involved.

Denial provided time for a temporary retreat. It allowed the individual to gather strength by using the skills that worked well in the past. However, within a fairly short time after entering the new job, denial can no longer work, for people cease to treat the individual as a new boy. They want him to become part of the team.

For the individual, the realities of the change and the resulting stresses become obvious. He has to learn new job skills. He may have taken on additional responsibilities in the new job which mean acquiring knowledge which has to be applied to a specified standard.

Most certainly, the individual will have to re-learn how to interact with the superiors/subordinates/colleagues around him. Departments, units and whole organisations have their own particular identity – their own culture. Hence people and teams will have their own ways of doing things and no individual can deviate too far from the accepted norms of behaviour.

The individual will have to learn how to 'play the system'. Being effective at work involves knowing who and what to take note of, as well as competence at task skills. The covert skills of playing the system take time to learn. The problem is that the new boy does not know what questions to ask to understand the new organisation. Most people learn by the unexpected mistakes they make. It is only when problems have arisen that the individual can appreciate why they occurred and how they could be handled better in the future.

During Phase 2, the individual experiences depression. He can no longer effectively apply his old skills. Naturally he wonders, 'What is wrong with me?'

The depression is the first real step to re-learning. The person is facing the fact that he has to change. He realises his performance is deteriorating dramatically and only he can do anything about it. Although frustrated and depressed, the individual can see that he has to let go of the past and face the future.

Phase 3: What does one become?

What does one become – effective or ineffective? In other words, how well has the individual negotiated his transition?

After letting go of the past, the person accepts his new reality, his new challenge. He is likely to become more pro-active. He may try out new behaviours, new workstyles and new approaches, and apply newly-learned skills. The testing stage is as frustrating as the depression stage. The individual is bound to make mistakes, become angry with himself and irritable with others. These negative feelings have to be coped with.

From the high energy of the testing phase the individual attempts to put his new world together. He seeks for new meaning as to how and why things are now different.

The final part of the process is one of internalisation, whereby new behaviours and attitudes are incorporated into what is left of the old attitudes and behaviours. The individual has consolidated his position and is operating better than the day when he was first appointed.

The initial results of research indicate that this process can take, on average, eighteen months for middle managers and up to four years for top management. However, some people do experience ineffective transitions. They end up operating at their level of incompetence. Some people are appointed to jobs beyond their capacity. Perhaps their depression during Phase 2 became intolerable; they could not pull out. Perhaps they also had to tolerate unforgiving superiors and colleagues who could not ignore the mistakes they made.

Case 2.3   I'm dissatisfied here!

Six months into the job Sarah felt she was not still fully integrated into the job. She had had a few projects of her own, but seemed to have to act as an extra resource when and where it was required. There was no continuity to her work. She felt she wasn't making sense of things. Either she wasn't cut out for consultancy, or she couldn't come to terms with what it involved.

Derek Malcolm was aware of Sarah's depression, and one Friday after work he suggested they have a drink in the local bar before going home.

'You haven't been looking very happy these last few weeks, Sarah.

What's the problem? Is there anything you'd like to share with me?' He passed her a margueritta and sipped his whisky. 'I'm not sure I can put my finger on it, Derek', Sarah said ruefully. 'I came here with such high hopes and really thought I'd make a go of it. But consultancy and I don't seem to be going together all that well.'

'Anything in particular?'

Sarah thought for a moment. 'During the last few weeks I've been reflecting on my past work experience and comparing it with what I'm doing now. Both my previous jobs were with large companies. I'd always found them very restricting – I seemed to be hamstrung by routines and systems. There was no room for innovation, or creativity. I often felt that so much time was spent managing internal administration that it stifled me.

'In addition, I like to set my own pace to the work. It was difficult to do before, but it was what I was most looking forward to in joining a small, growing consultancy. I'd visualised having a lot more freedom to do the things I wanted to do, and in my own way, but that's not what's happening here. I just seem to do the bits and pieces that have to be picked up by someone. And there's so much to learn.'

'So any job that gave you the chance to be creative and innovative would have satisfied you?' Derek asked. 'Why did you choose consultancy in particular? Some aspects of it are very boring and routine, and we also have to work to procedures and systems. And there's not much opportunity to be creative or risk-taking when we've got clients to satisfy.'

'I don't know, Derek! I do know that I've thought about this a lot lately, and the one thing I seem to want out of work most, the one thing I wouldn't want to give up, is autonomy. I didn't have a lot of it before, and I know I've got even less now. That's why I'm dissatisfied here, as well as realising that I haven't yet developed the skills I need in the job.'

Sarah (Case 2.3) is showing strong signs of transition. Her disappointment with her new job, especially when contrasted with her previous job, her inability to recognise the positive aspects of her new job, and her admission that she has not yet developed the skills required for her new position, are all signs of a person in the middle of the transition curve. As part of the process, Sarah is also examining what she really values at work, which for her is autonomy. At present, Sarah says that her present job may have even less autonomy than her previous one. From the way Sarah is feeling, it is difficult to tell whether she will stay or leave the consultancy company. Her negative attitude is fairly typical of someone in transition.

CAREER DEVELOPMENT

Many organisations have developed fairly elaborate systems of career planning and development, for two sound reasons. First, individuals in the organisation should have an opportunity to experience training or some other form of development in order to equip them for their present or future job(s). Second, the organisation gains the full benefit of the actual and latent skills of its employees by providing training and sufficient experience of the total activities of the business, in order to prepare those persons promoted to positions of responsibility adequately. It makes sense to identify, prepare and nurture on the job people who will make significant contributions to the development of the organisation.

Equally, career planning and development may tip the balance between good and bad management. Two behavioural scientists, McCall and Lombardo, conducted an interesting study at the Centre for Creative Leadership in North Carolina, USA, examining the differences between those managers considered to have succeeded and those who failed. Essentially, the differences between the two groups were small. Those considered to have failed tended to be people who were insensitive to others, were somewhat aloof, overtly played politics, were unable to delegate, could not think strategically, were poor at selecting staff and could not easily adapt to new bosses. Those managers in the study considered to be consistently effective experienced the same problems, but were able to admit they were wrong, learn from their mistakes and still maintain good working relationships with all types of people. Hence, adequate and sensitive training, as part of an integrated career planning system, can help executives to minimise their failings, capitalise on their strong points and thereby create a pool of competent executives.

Career development programmes

What, then, are the important elements of any career development programme? A recent study conducted by Professors Charles Margerison and Andrew Kakabadse of top chief executive officers (CEOs) in the USA revealed the following elements.

Identifying executive potential

In the study, the 'need to achieve results' was highly rated by the majority of CEOs. Although a personal view, it indicates the importance successful people place on results. However, few organisations try to measure an individual's need to achieve results, perhaps on the assumption that such an attribute is difficult to measure. Tests are available that can highlight this characteristic. These tests can be used in selecting people who are joining an organisation straight from college or who are moving into the organisation in mid-career.

An equally powerful measure is track record. Actual performance is a good indicator of an individual's drive and hence his future performance. Is the individual meeting his budget and target? Is he pro-active or reactive in the way he conducts his work? Actual results and the opinions of key managers on appraisal documentation provide valuable data to assess the executive potential of each manager.

Accountability for profit and loss

The job of managing, like so many other things, is learned primarily by doing. It is therefore vital that people moving toward senior positions have the opportunity to acquire the necessary experience at the right time. Rather than such experience being left to chance, opportunities can be built into the organisation's manpower planning system. The first of these is to carve out positions that enable people to have challenging jobs and overall accountability for running part of the business. This means that the organisation must not be too centrally constructed. If the organisation can divide up its work into profit and loss units, executives can gain the experience of running an operation which, while interdependent with the rest of the organisation, stands on its own as a measurable business centre.

Some businesses lend themselves more to this form of organisation than others. Consider, for example, that in the retail industry managers often have an opportunity to take over management of a retail outlet while relatively young. It may be far more difficult to find similar profit centre units in other, more technologically sophisticated, industries. Wherever possible, however, profit centres should be established so that young managers can have the experience of leading a team – whether it be five, a hundred, or five hundred people. They learn that 'the buck stops' with them for overall performance.

Early personal leadership

It is vital for prospective leaders to develop personal leadership abilities through practical experience. Unless an executive can learn how to allocate work, resolve differences of opinion, chair meetings, motivate people, resolve conflicts, and a host of other practical leadership tasks, he will not be able to move to high office. It has been argued in Chapter 1 that management is 'getting things done through persuading other people'. The way to learn this is to hold a leadership post early in one's career.

In the Margerison and Kakabadse study, most of the managers felt that this experience must come before the age of 30 and preferably before the age of 25. Two-thirds of the people responding had received their first leadership command prior to the age of 30, with all but 10 per cent being in such a position before reaching 35. Perhaps the most interesting finding, however, is that 41 per cent of all respondents had in fact gained their first leadership command before the age of 25.

It is perhaps more difficult now than in the past to gain leadership experience early in one's career. Business now requires more professional specialists, and people spend longer in the formal educational process. Again, however, the organisational structure can be designed to facilitate the creation of leadership positions. Actual leadership of people with budget and staff management accountability must take place early in an executive's career.

Breadth of business experience

Prospective leaders also need a broad view of their business. This can be gained only by experience in more than one of the business functions at a relatively early age. Too many people are held in the area of their original technical training. For example, engineers who spend all their time in the production function cannot know much about the total business. And too many accountants spend virtually all of their time in the finance and accounting function without learning much about marketing, sales, personnel and production.

If, however, senior managers are to learn how to run an integrated business, it is vitally important that they have experience in two or three functions of the business before the age of 35. They cannot be expected to be experts in each of these areas. Therefore, it is more likely that they will gain this experience by receiving assignments in which they apply their technical skills – but in an area other than their own speciality. For example, a marketing person may advise the production function on the various issues related to design, distribution, and development. Likewise, a production person could learn a great deal by working for a period in the marketing area. These moves should be part of the planned career structure rather than *ad hoc*.

In addition, people with high potential should be allocated to project groups, working committees and task forces which enable them to get a wider view of the business by working on specific tasks. This is already being done with great success in a number of organisations.

Jobs with challenge and support

Again the Margerison and Kakabadse study showed that executives respond to and learn from challenges. Therefore, managerial jobs for people in their twenties and thirties must include tasks where they can be stretched. The jobs should be designed in such a way that the manager can have identifiable goals which are sufficiently difficult to make them challenging, but not so unreasonable as to be demotivating. Organising jobs on this basis is not easy. It is also vitally important that executives receive regular feedback on their performance and report on a regular basis. The reporting relationship allows for guidance and constructive criticism on how to improve. There needs to be some tension in the design of the job and the reporting system. At the same time, the jobs must allow the individual manager sufficient discretion to make decisions and get on with the job in his own way, while having the counsel and support of senior managers.

Career anchors

A systematic approach is important to career development so that relevant learning opportunities are provided on the job. As the individual acquires further and further job experience, he learns about himself: his strengths and weaknesses, his needs and desires and, most of all, whether he holds a particular orientation or inclination in terms of the work he undertakes. Ed Schein terms this orientation a career anchor; in effect, the individual is anchored into pursuing a particular type of career for himself and thereby develops a particular occupational self-concept. This self-concept has three components which together make up an individual career anchor.

- self-perceived talents and abilities
- self-perceived motives and needs
- self-perceived attitudes and values.

The anchors act as internal driving and constraining forces on career decisions so that, if an individual moves into a work environment which fails to comply with his talents, needs or values, he will be 'pulled back' into something more congruent: hence the metaphor 'anchor'. The concept emphasises the interaction between abilities, needs and values. In essence, the individual tends to want and value things that he is good at and improves his abilities on those aspects of work he wants and values.

Because of this dominant interaction of abilities, needs and values, an individual's career anchors can be discovered only after a number of years of experience. A person's self-concept will be influenced by the career options available to him. The concept is designed to explain that part of our lives which grows more stable as we develop more self-insight from increased life experience.

Ed Schein defined six separate career anchors:

1   *Technical/functional.* The self-image of individuals in this group is tied up with their feelings of competence in their particular technical or functional area. It is the intrinsic work which interests them. Such individuals tend to disdain and fear general management.

2   *Managerial.* Individuals in this group have as their ultimate goal management *per se.* They see their competence as lying in a combination of three general areas: analytical competence, interpersonal competence and emotional competence. The latter means being able to deal with risks, uncertainty and crises.

3   *Security/stability.* Individuals in this group tend to behave as their employers wish in order to maintain job security, a reasonable salary and a stable future. They rely heavily on the organisation to look after them.

4   *Creativity.* Individuals here have an overwhelming need to buiid or create something of their own. Such individuals continually initiate new projects. They are very visible people. They may also have a variety of motives and values that overlap with other anchors, eg they want to be autonomous, managerially competent, able to exercise their own talents.

5   *Autonomy/independence*. Individuals in this group wish to be maximally free of organisational constraints to pursue their professional/technical competence. Their primary need is to be on their own, setting their own pace, life styles and habits.

6   *Social/moral*. Individuals in this group are primarily motivated to do something which is valued by society. They would be distinctly uncomfortable if asked to compromise their sense of morals or ethics. Other people's recognition of their work is central to their satisfaction.

Case 2.4   You are getting better at the job

Three months later Sarah was still unhappy. A number of her problems stemmed from being the only woman in the company. Her colleagues seemed to see her more as a woman than as a colleague. They frequently commented on her clothes, which made her self-conscious about what she wore to the office. In addition, they seemed to her to be patronising, which made her feel 'put down', particularly when this was done in front of clients. Perhaps she could have discussed some of these issues formally with her 'closest' colleagues, but unfortunately they rarely socialised. Derek hadn't asked her out again. She felt he thought she was too wrapped up in herself and her own problems, that she wasn't very good company. Perhaps he'd passed that impression on to the others, for they seemed to shun her also. She was becoming steadily more tense and frustrated at work, and couldn't turn off at home. Her social life was non-existent.

Two more weeks passed. Sarah decided that something needed to be done. The next day she burst into James Wood's office. James looked up, startled.

'James, I can't go on like this. I'm being treated like a dogsbody. You don't give me any really worthwhile projects to do. There's no degree of self-development in my work, and I feel I'm stagnating. And I don't seem to be able to talk to anyone about it – no one wants to know. Thanks for letting me work here, but I know my expectations, and probably yours too, haven't been met. I'll leave at the end of the month, if that's all right with you.'

As Sarah was talking, a look of astonishment spread over James's face.

'But, Sarah, I've just been looking at your work record. It's coming up to annual performance appraisal time, and I was just reviewing what a range of work you've done, and how you appeared to be settling in to what must be to you a completely new and difficult work environment. Some of the ideas you've put forward on management development for our clients could be very well used here. I was thinking particularly that, as we're only twenty here, we might run a career development workshop to discuss ways in which we might meet the needs and aspirations of the staff and also to ask for the staff's views on the ways in which the

> company itself might be moving in the future.'
> 'I didn't know you felt this way,' he continued. 'I know I haven't been around much, but I assumed things were OK. I had considered I could trust you to work on your own. You are learning, you are getting better at the job, and I think you will develop into a good consultant. What do you think about my idea for a career development workshop?' he asked, ignoring Sarah's preferred resignation....

Sarah (Case 2.4) has become increasingly dissatisfied with her work in the consultancy company. Her on-the-job development has been left to her. She had to learn what to do, and how, in her own way. In fact, although Sarah declared in Case 2.3 that she valued autonomy, it seems that it is the consultancy company that values autonomy. Probably with the best of intentions, the company has developed a sink or swim philosophy. In reality, Sarah seems to hold different expectations. She seems to need planned development. She needs a closer working relationship with colleagues; she wants to talk and share ideas with others. However, Sarah's work, as far as James Wood is concerned, is satisfactory. In fact, it seems that Sarah values the professional and security career anchors. James Wood, in response, seems to appreciate Sarah's professionalism and has ignored her need for security, which he could find irritating, bearing in mind the seemingly individualistic nature of consultancy practice in the organisation. In effect, Sarah is still in transition and is beginning to recognise what she really values in her working life.

The importance of the career anchor as a concept is in helping the individual discover and consolidate his self-image: what he is good at, what he wants and what he values at work. For individuals who feel they need to rethink their career, particularly during its early years, the career anchor is an exceptionally useful concept which allows individuals to analyse themselves and their present and future expectations. It helps them come to terms with and understand the decisions they have made in their careers to date.

WORK AND FAMILY LIFE

In 1979, Professors Bartholomé and Evans of the French business school of INSEAD asked an important question, 'How do managers experience the relationship between their professional lives and private lives?' Five hundred and thirty-two male middle managers took part in the survey. All of them were married, 93 per cent of them had children, and their ages ranged from twenty-seven to fifty-eight. Three important findings emerged from this study. First, the majority of the managers (79 per cent) attached a high value to both their careers and their families. Second, whilst a very high proportion of them saw family activities as the most important aspect of their lives, they frequently reported having their most satisfying experiences at work. Third, most of the managers spent twice as much time in work activities as in family activities. In addition, for many managers time spent at home was seen as an opportunity for relaxing and building up energy for the next day or next week at the office. Bartholomé and Evans concluded that the behavioural profile of the typical male manager potentially generates tensions, ambivalence and dissatisfaction for them and their families. However, the two professors equally indicated that such tensions need not become crippling if the managers consciously attempt to integrate home life with work life.

If the problems that exist in 'traditional' marriages are great, then the problems which face dual career families and particularly women are even more substantial. Women have to manage the conflicting demands of their multiple roles. These impose a tighter schedule on the personal lives of executive women than of men. The American researcher Rosbeth Moss Kanter proposed that if women comprise less than 15 per cent of the workforce in an organisation, they can be labelled as 'tokens', as they would be viewed as symbols of their group rather than as individuals. In addition, other studies have shown that professional and managerial women experience particular strains and pressures by virtue of being members of organisations dominated by men. These disadvantages derive from six factors.

1   *Work overload.* Many studies have found that women managers frequently suffer work overload due to the pressure to work harder and better in order to prove themselves. Because of this, women managers often take on demanding work. It has been suggested that this 'credibility testing' pressure felt by women managers, together with feelings of isolation, may lead them not to feel confident to delegate, which in itself exacerbates the problem of excessive overload.

2   *Visibility.* Women are often noticed because they are women, as well as because of their skills. Depending on the situation, women may have to put extra effort into being taken seriously. Dress becomes an important facet of this visibility. In fact, some

women, particularly at junior management level, see the quality of their clothes and dress sense as a kind of visible status differentiation between themselves and secretaries (visually the only other female employees).

3   *Being a test case for future women.* The feeling of being a token woman and always being responsible for representing the entire sex is a continual problem. This source of stress should be recognised by employees.

4   *Isolation and lack of female role models.* Women in management positions often complain of feeling isolated and missing female peer support. There are often no other women in senior positions to measure oneself against. In fact, certain women end up acting as the role model for others. Although such an experience may be stress-provoking for the individual, she does provide a role model for other women and in turn for male managers to help them adjust their attitudes and behaviours towards female colleagues.

5   *Exclusion from male groups – infiltrating the 'old boy network'.* Women managers in token positions are also subject to the restrictions imposed by males at work through the social structure. Some women feel uncomfortable buying men a round of drinks, or paying for a business lunch. Many men also have difficulty in reconciling themselves to such female behaviour. In addition, there are the exclusive male clubs where a lot of informal business discussion is conducted by male managers.

6   *Resisting female sex roles.* Sex role stereotypes related to management evolve from a view of males as more task-oriented, objective, independent and aggressive and generally more able than females to handle managerial responsibility. Females are viewed as more passive, gentle and sensitive and less suited than males for positions of high responsibility in organisations. Sex role stereotyping is an additional work pressure experienced by women managers, since they feel that they need to conform to the male managerial stereotype in order to succeed at work.

Professor Cary Cooper and Dr Marilyn Davidson of the University of Manchester Institute of Science and Technology believe there are solutions to these problems. First, a change of attitudes towards women managers by males is required. Managers should not be stereotyped males and females. Second, the concept of androgyny (the combination of both male and female qualities such as emotional expressiveness and task orientation) should be applied in the development of managers. Women managers who adopt the androgynous approach resist aligning themselves to any female sex roles.

Case 2.5   I'm here for quite a time

The career development workshop was a success. The staff of the consultancy company discussed where they felt the company should go in the future, what each individual would wish to do in the short to medium term and most of all the sorts of consultancy assignment individuals would wish to pursue. For Sarah, the workshop was more of a success than she had first imagined. First, she was given the task of managing it and was therefore identified as the driving force behind a valuable event. Second, as a participant at the workshop, Sarah's dissatisfaction became apparent. Colleagues listened to her views and her problems and were most supportive. It was suggested that she attend a training course. Also she was offered a small but varied workload which was much more to her liking. Most of all, Sarah really became acquainted with her colleagues. Her isolation finally ended.

Three months later, she invited James Wood for a drink one lunchtime. After a short while in the pub, James asked, 'How are you feeling these days, Sarah, about the company and your work, I mean?'

'Oh, I'm enjoying life again. I hadn't really realised what consultancy was all about, especially in this company which is growing fast, but is still vulnerable. For one thing, I thought I needed autonomy and that's what you gave me and it's only then I recognised that's not what I needed!'

'Oh?' enquired James.

'I just wanted more breathing space, especially the way I felt after my last company. It took me some time to realise it, but what I really enjoy doing is working with people. I like working in teams. I like to discuss things and share ideas, but I still don't like administration.

'I see,' responded James. He continued, 'You seem more content now than I've ever seen you.'

'Yes. I am feeling much better now. What's also helped is the fact that we have two more women consultants. Although my relationship with Valerie Moss is a little strained, it does help to talk things through with female colleagues,' said Sarah.

'Well, I must say, Sarah, after the career workshop, virtually everyone in the company is using you as an expert on women consultants. That's why I sent the two new girls to talk to you about the problems of being a woman consultant in a fairly aggressive, up-and-coming consultancy company. I think because of what you said at that workshop, the men in general are just more sympathetic to the problems you experienced and so they will be to these two new girls,' commented James. He finished, 'So I presume from what you've said you won't be leaving us?'

'That's right. I'm here for quite a time. Life is starting to look really good.'

Sarah (Case 2.5) seems to have successfully negotiated her transition. A great help in the process was the careers workshop, for it gave her the opportunity to share her feelings and ideas with colleagues. From the comments Sarah has made, she seems to value professionalism and to a certain extent creativity. She also seems to have recognised that the autonomy and managerial career anchors do not suit her. Further, she recognised that she was isolated as the only woman professional in a male dominated company. In her boss's opinion, the fact that she and others recognised her isolation helped, for not only did male colleagues become more sympathetic to her problems, she was used as the role model for the other female consultants who later joined the company. Finally, it is worth noting the factors that Sarah had to come to terms with in negotiating her transition. The key factors seemed to be her attitudes and expectations, but not her professional skills. Sarah overemphasised her need for autonomy and underplayed her needs for professionalism and creativity. Further, working in a young and growing consultancy was not quite what she expected, for the degree of professional interaction between colleagues was minimal and certainly not to her liking. As far as her skills as a consultant were concerned, she seems to have satisfied her boss as a competent individual from the very start.

Sarah's experience is common. It is difficult to be both sympathetic and understanding to someone in transition, as it requires considerable patience and sympathy to see their problems from their point of view.

Integrating work and family life: the life planning workshop

Concerns about work and career do not exist in isolation, but are related to issues of self-development, the stages in one's life, family circumstances and one's own feelings and attitudes at the time when particular constraints and opportunities arise. Inevitably, certain demands made on the individual may not fit with personal, professional or family needs and desires. In the short term, such tensions can be coped with. In the longer term, these strains may lead to demotivation, stress and a possible drop in work performance.

Management and organisation development specialists in business schools and business organisations in the USA observed that 'difficult to handle tensions' between work, self and home did, in fact, lead to ineffectiveness of performance at work. Hence, for

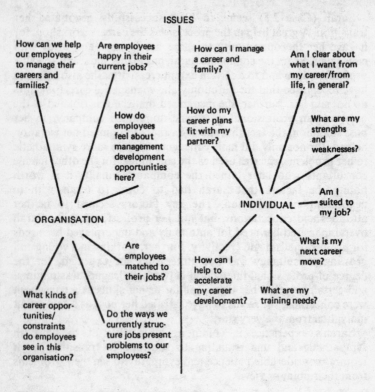

Fig. 2.3   Career/life planning issues

both business and humanistic reasons, certain behavioural scientists began to experiment with far broader concepts than just career planning, namely those of life planning. The idea spread to the point where certain organisations extended their management development portfolio to include life planning workshops.

The life planning workshop is essentially a mechanism for integrating work and family life. Such workshops, often conducted 'in-company', attempt to help individuals confront and discuss the issues that face them, and at the same time help organisations to manage their employee development. The range of issues which emerge are illustrated in Figure 2.3.

Such workshops are beneficial in two ways.

1 They provide an opportunity for participants to reflect on their careers to date in the organisation and to consider their aspirations.

2 They encourage participants to think realistically about their own abilities, needs and personal values and to consider what is a comfortable balance for them between self, work and home needs.

Although their popularity is increasing, career/life planning workshops have not been highly utilised as an integrated approach to career and personal development. The problem is one of attitude in that most individuals and the senior management of most organisations would still consider work and career as distinctly separate from home life. Such a view is likely to be severely tested in the near future, as increasingly women are pursuing careers whilst bringing up families.

SUMMARY

The processes of entry, socialisation and the integration of the individual into the organisation and the topic of career development fall into four main areas.

Recruitment and selection

Effective recruitment and selection ensure a satisfactory match between the needs of the individual and those of the organisation through the job the individual is asked to undertake. In order for the process of recruitment and selection to be effective, both the prospective candidate and the employing organisation need to:

• Seek and obtain accurate information about each other.

• Identify and clarify accurate expectations about each other.

• Project an image that is realistic and not one that can lead to disappointment at a later stage.

• Realistically appreciate one's needs, strengths and future demands.

Induction and socialisation

At induction, the employee is initiated into his job and the organisation. In certain cases this may consist of an introduction to his boss and immediate colleagues. In other organisations, it may comprise a programme of several days in which the new employee is instructed, informed and inducted into the roles and requirements of the job and the culture of the organisation. It is an occasion for clarifying mutual expectations before performance standards are agreed.

Satisfactory socialisation and the integration of the individual into the organisation take a considerable time, during which the organisation and the individual come to terms with the reality of each other. During this period, the individual has to achieve some form of congruence between himself and the way work is conducted in the organisation in order to cope with role ambiguity and limited choice in the way work can be designed or scheduled. The individual learns in this stage to interact with his peers, his supervisor and his colleagues, and to understand the performance standards required of him.

It is likely that the individual will need to learn how to perform and behave in his new organisation. This learning experience is known as the transition cycle. The stages of the cycle are:

1   Getting used to the place, ie overcoming the initial shock and immobilisation of the new organisation and job demands.

2   Re-learning, ie recognising that new skills have to be learned or how learned skills have to be re-applied.

3   Becoming effective, ie consolidating one's position in the organisation by applying new behaviours and skills or integrating newly formed attitudes with ones held from the past.

The length and depth of these phases will vary according to the degree of self-awareness of the individual and the level and complexity of the position to which he is appointed.

Career development

Career development is seen as a means of making the best use of people who exhibit potential for more senior managerial positions. Five elements make up a sensible career development system, namely:

1 Identifying executive potential by recognising the executives who exhibit a high drive to achieve results.

2 Offering managers the opportunity to be held accountable for profit and loss.

3 Providing managers with the opportunity for early leadership experience.

4 Providing managers with a breadth of experience throughout the various business units in the organisation.

5 Generating jobs which are challenging for managers.

Individuals make specific choices based on their values, ideals, motives, needs, talents and abilities. These rather subjective attributes have been termed career anchors: *Technical/Functional* where the individual strives to become highly proficient within his own function or technical profession and actively shuns moving into a general management position. *Managerial* where the individual needs to develop analytical skills and abilities, coupled with interpersonal, group and emotional skills, which can best be deployed in managing people. *Security/stability*, where the individual's prime need is for a secure and stable environment. *Creativity* where the individual requires to be innovative and creative. *Autonomy/independence* where the individual wants to 'be his own boss', to have control over his work. *Social/moral* where the individual has specific needs, talents, attitudes and values which lead him to serve the community.

Work and family life

It is increasingly being recognised that home life is an important consideration when examining the effectiveness, motivation and contentment of managers. Separate studies have shown that both male and female managers need to consider how to integrate better the demands of work and home life. An increasingly popular approach to home and work issues is the life planning workshop. Both the organisation and the individual benefit from the opportunity for individuals to reflect on their careers and think realistically about their abilities, needs and personal values, before pursuing a particular course of action.

IN CONCLUSION

The progression and development of a person in an organisation are
as much based on his attitudes and values as on the organisation's
ability to utilise his potential. Whether the individual is able,
motivated or offered the opportunity to develop latent talents
depends on his perception of the organisation, and the reaction of
key managers in the organisation to him. Such attitudes, values and
reactions begin to form as soon as the individual enters the
organisation. Although these perceptions do alter over time, the
initial impressions and reactions of the individual and organisation
to each other strongly influence the tone of the relationship for the
future. The processes of entry and socialisation and development of
the individual's career reflect the perceived compatibility,
colloquially known as 'fit', between the individual and the
organisation. More often than not, it is the question of 'fit' that
influences the individual's level of performance and personal
satisfaction, and not just the level of skills he has acquired.

3 The Individual at Work

Case 3.1   Bien Aimée fashion jewellery

Charlie Kay looked over at his brother and said, 'You know, Simon, I wish we'd never hired that guy. He's caused more trouble here in the last six months than we've had for the past six years.'

'Be fair, Charlie,' replied Simon, 'I know exactly how you feel, and I'm not very happy either, but he has come up with some very good ideas, even if he rubs us up the wrong way. We've got to decide whether to keep him, and work with him, or to give him the sack. I'd like to think about it and then discuss it further.'

Simon and Charlie Kay had founded Bien Aimée Fashion Jewellery in the early 1960s. They hadn't much money then, being both just out of Arts College, but Simon was an artistic genius, who saw a market opening in the London of the swinging sixties. He recognised that many middle-aged, middle-class women wanted to keep up with the trendy younger generation of the mini-skirt era, and designed fashion jewellery for them which was outrageous but elegant. Starting small, they raised some capital and managed to make contacts in the high street chain stores, and it caught on. Within five years they had established their name in the upper bracket of the market to the tune of a turnover of £1/3 million.

Simon had an intuitive feeling for the market, and not only followed trends, but was very sensitive to the way they were going to move, with the result that the company continued to grow in the 1970s.

Charlie looked after marketing and selling. His enthusiastic nature fitted him well for this, as did his command of figures, although he often manipulated the interpretation of those figures to fit in with his own value-laden plans. Simon was the creative artist, and in overall control - he made the decisions, although he liked to weigh up all the consequences before he committed himself. Increasingly Simon found he was being drawn into administration, which restricted his design work, and with four factories manufacturing in 1983, the Kays appointed a financial controller, James Wellard, a professional, experienced accountant, to take some of this load off Simon.

In Case 3.1, Simon and Charlie Kay, although brothers, and of similar backgrounds, are different. Charlie appears to make quick judgements, while Simon likes to take his time over making decisions. Simon looks at both sides of the coin, while Charlie seems to have his own personal view of the world. Simon is naturally intuitive, and can see possibilities in people and situations. Charlie is ebullient and extrovert. The two of them appear to have worked together well for several years, but the introduction of someone else, James Wellard, into the organisation has caused problems in their relationship. They view James Wellard differently – Charles sees him as disruptive, Simon as a person with good ideas. Charlie doesn't see James as fitting his style of working; Simon may agree with him, but sees in James qualities which the company may need.

Simon and Charles – two different people, two different natures, or personalities, and two different views of the same person. What causes their differences of view?

Although a manager may have a consistent view of the world, his organisation, and his job, he has to work in an environment consisting of other people: and this is his dilemma. One of his greatest challenges is that other people are different from him. They differ in terms of their views of the organisation, jobs and how they should be managed. They differ in other ways, such as physique, background, experience, perception, and personality. Because of these differences, the manager has to revise and modify his social interactions and approaches to other people as individuals, in order to maximise their motivation, commitment, and performance so that he can achieve his goals and objectives with and through them.

This chapter will examine two basic differences between people – personality and perception. These differences cause people to behave differently towards others in different situations. The chapter will also explore some recent work on the effects of personality on people's behaviour at work and the outcomes of that behaviour. Finally, the process of managerial mapping is outlined as a mechanism for using personality and perception information to help managers improve their performance.

PERSONALITY

Definitions of personality run into the hundreds. We all have our own idea of what the term means, but this is inextricably bound up with our own interests and values – in fact, with our own personalities! Perhaps one of the clearest definitions to emerge recently is given by the English psychologists Eysenck, Arnold and Meili in the *Encyclopedia of Psychology*, Vol. 2, 1975:

> Personality is the relatively stable organisation of a person's motivational dispositions, arising from the interactions between biological drives and the social and physical environment. The term usually refers chiefly to the affective-cognitive traits, sentiments, attitudes, complexes and unconscious mechanisms, interests and ideals, which determine man's characteristic or distinctive behaviour and thought.

This suggests that personality does not change very much (relatively stable), it is organised (there is an integration of components), it results from an interaction of internal drives and the external environment, and that each person is different (distinctive). So personality does not arise from purely inherited or environmental factors, but from a combination, an interaction, of the two, and all through our lives the two sets of factors interact with each other in complex ways, resulting in patterns of behaviour which are characteristic to us.

Inherited factors

Each individual receives a unique set of chromosomes from his parents. These forty-six chromosomes determine such physical characteristics as colour of eyes and hair, potential height and weight, etc. Research into genetic abnormalities has also suggested that genes can affect individual behaviour, although there is little evidence that they are a major influence. Nevertheless, the American, William Sheldon, attempted to link personality characteristics to physical characteristics. He categorised three basic types of physique – the *ectomorph*, thin and delicate, the *endomorph*, fat and tubby, and the *mesomorph*, strong and muscled. 'Morph's Law' suggested that ectomorphs are withdrawn, intellectual, and prone to anxiety; endomorphs are cheerful, easygoing and friendly, and tend to depend on other people; while mesomorphs are competitive, strong and dominating.

These predictions of behavioural patterns are characteristic of the extremes of each physical type. Normally everyone has elements of each of the types in them, and consequently people's behaviour is a complex of these patterns. Sheldon later discovered further evidence which corroborated this link between physique and behaviour, but the questions still remain – are behaviour patterns really only related to physique itself? Has behaviour anything at all to do with inherited genes? Because mesomorphs are strong and muscled, do they learn that being competitive and dominating is the type of behaviour most likely to achieve their goals? Are ectomorphs withdrawn because this is the natural response of thin and delicate people to the aggression of the mesomorphs?

The implication is that heredity (which to a certain extent provides us with some of our physical characteristics, and gives us the means to survive in this world) and our environment (from which we learn coping behaviours) are *both* determinants of our individual personalities.

The person/environment interaction

The first significant external source of influence on a developing personality must be the immediate family, within which a person spends most of his early years. The child is dependent on his mother and father for love, satisfaction of his biological needs, and the setting of approved standards of behaviour. These standards are influenced directly by the parents' own values and beliefs, and by what they consider acceptable in their culture and society. The parents are the main interface between the child and the environment outside the family. As the child grows, so he has more personal interaction with the outside world. At school he observes other children and their behaviour; he is exposed to and influenced by the values and beliefs of his teachers; he adjusts his behaviour to conform to the sometimes conflicting signals he receives from his school and his home environment. He is constantly receiving stimulii which increase his knowledge of his world and the people who live in it. Later he goes to work and forms associations with people in that world. He may join social or leisure groups. In fact, he finds it is almost impossible to go through life without being a member of some group, large or small, formal or informal. The group has a powerful influence on the development of his personality.

Therefore, depending on the individual's ability to interpret and utilise life's experiences in terms of his interaction with other individuals, groups and organisations, the person/environment interaction can be a fundamental influence of personality development. The range of theories in this area are summarised by examining the sorts of manager that best seem to epitomise the type of theory.

The reactive manager

Sigmund Freud suggested that man's personality make-up is a mixture of early experience and an instinctive drive for pleasure. Freud considered that humans are born with a basic drive for pleasure (the libido). The source of energy for the libido is the *id*, which provides the instinctive, unconscious impulses in individuals to pursue pleasure. Moreover, as we live in a world which involves numerous demands and imposes substantial constraints on individuals, the *ego* develops to help the person cope with the reality of the physical world and to keep the demands of the *id* under control. We also live in a social world, and in order to help individuals interact with each other the *super ego*, or conscience, develops and emphasises how to interrelate according to the social rules within particular cultures. Thus behaviour becomes the result

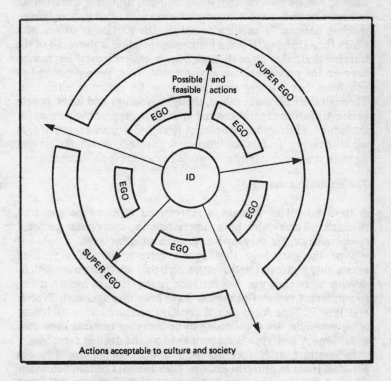

Fig. 3.1 Freud's psycho-analytical model

of complex series of interactions and perceptions which are forever being modified. In essence, the manager is constantly developing as a result of the reactions and interactions he experiences in his world, as outlined in Figure 3.1.

Freudian concepts have been popular in psychiatry, counselling and personal therapy and in management training and development. Particularly famous neo-Freudians in the management world are Karl Rogers and Karen Horney, whose original work in the area of personal therapy has been applied in the field of organisation behaviour.

The learning manager

In contrast to the reactive manager, the learning manager is capable of considerable choice and self-regulation. In effect, individuals learn to receive information, organise, plan, negotiate and transmit information and interact in complex ways with other human beings, without necessarily needing to satisfy the particular drives with which they are born. Human behaviour therefore is the result of the learning that takes place through continuous reciprocal interaction between the person and his environment. True, people respond to situations but equally they learn how to influence situations. Through their personal values, thoughts, feelings and ideas, people anticipate future experiences and attempt to prepare the present for the future. The famous sociologist Erving Goffman suggested that we all develop 'frames' of individual reference which are created through subjective interpretations of numerous social interactions.

The responsive manager?

A third school of thought is represented by the type and trait theorists. These are both interested in individual personal characteristics, but they analyse them in different ways.

Type theorists hold that people have a particular type of personality (extrovert/introvert), which they are either born with or develop at an early age. For instance, in the study of human stress, two different types of behaviour have been distinguished, Type A and Type B. Type A people put constant pressure on themselves to achieve results, always seeming to be hurrying towards their own ends. Type A and Type B are seen as two quite distinct categories.

In contrast, trait theorists believe that people use different personal traits to different extents. They feel that certain behaviour shows, not the personality of the individual, but that the individual has used particular characteristics in the situation. It follows from this that people can learn to behave in certain ways. Later trait theorists have developed a number of psychological (psychometric) tests which measure people's learned capacity to draw on particular traits. In these, extroversion and introversion, for example, are seen as two extremes of a behaviour pattern, and a person's score would fall somewhere between them.

In other words, a type theorist would proclaim somebody to be extrovert, while a trait theorist would describe the same person as more extrovert than introvert.

One particular measure that we find useful at Cranfield School of Management, based on the work of Carl Gustav Jung (originally a collaborator of Freud's), is a particularly interesting example of type and trait theories combined. The American psychologists Katherine Briggs and Isabel Briggs Myers developed a personality test which purports to reveal how a person prefers to work (ie, work preferences). This test, termed the Myers Briggs Type Indicator, identifies two inner drives which in turn are influenced or modified by two further drives showing how the person relates to the world outside him. The model, outlined below, is easy to understand and is presented in a way which we consider attractive to practising managers. (See Managerial Mapping at the end of this chapter.)

The four dimensions of behaviour that Myers and Briggs studied are:

1 Meeting, and relating to, other people.

2 Finding out, generating and gathering information.

3 Making decisions.

4 Deciding and setting priorities.

On each of these dimensions they defined a continuum of behaviour at each end of which there are two contrasting preferences. But what is meant by preferences? An individual's normal (preferred) way of doing something is discovered from experience and experimentation. Doing something in a certain way provides positive feedback, eg a person may prefer to use a certain style when running or jogging because he finds that doing it that way produces reliable results. He would therefore continue to use that style more, to the exclusion of others, in order to become more accomplished at the sport. Suddenly to use a different style may result in poor performance. Not having fully developed in the new style, the person cannot produce the results he desires. Similarly, when at work, most of us like to work in familiar ways; it helps us get results, it makes us feel more confident, so we reinforce these styles to the exclusion of others.

The Inner Drives

Two dimensions in the model highlight the preferred ways in which people tend to *generate and gather information*, and the ways in which they like to utilise that information to *make decisions*. (See Figure 3.2).

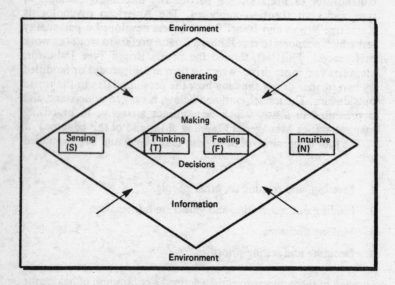

Fig. 3.2   The two inner drives of the Myers Briggs model

People collect information either by relying on their senses, by using practical, measurable data (*sensing*), or by using their imagination, intuition, insight to recognise possibilities to pursue (*intuitive*). People make decisions based on logical, rational analysis of the situation (*thinking*), or rely on their own personal values, beliefs and experiences of people and hence respond more emotively (*feeling*).

While people can use either approach on either of these dimensions, they tend to have a preference for one more than the other on each dimension.

There are therefore four basic conceptual types – intuitive thinking (NT), intuitive feeling (NF), sensing feeling (SF), sensing thinking (ST).

Case 3.2 James Wellard finds out

James Wellard was 37. A qualified management accountant, he had previously served with Ford and with a leading consultancy firm. He was looking forward to the challenge of Bien Aimée, which now had a turnover of £4 million and appeared to have two dynamic entrepreneurs at the top.

When James joined in June 1983, Simon was involved in designing his new collection. 'Get to know the system, James,' he said. 'We'll meet later to see what needs to be done. I'm going to be tied up for the next couple of months.'

James was quite happy to do this. He was more at ease with figures than with people. He started by looking at the nominal ledgers. There was no computerised or integrated information system in the company: the nominal ledgers and all other systems were entered manually by the senior clerk.

'This doesn't make sense,' James said to the clerk. 'These opening balances for 1983 don't match up with the auditor's figures, and it looks as if we're carrying forward some balances from the end of 1981 which don't tie up either.'

'Charlie said not to bother about that – just fill in the figures each month and let the auditors sort it out – that's what we pay them for.'

James shuddered, his glasses fell forward on his nose, and he sighed.

'Better let me go through them. I'll try to sort it out before this year-end, but I'll need a lot of help from you.'

As he went through the ledgers and associated books, all sorts of other discrepancies came to light. He began to feel anger towards the Kays.

'What the hell's going on?' he thought. 'I did hear that the auditors were unhappy about passing their accounts last year, and the way things stand, I'm not surprised.'

Stock control appeared to be non-existent. Several thousand pounds' worth of obsolete stock and superseded designs hadn't been written down or off. Marketing promotion expenses appeared to be inordinately high and inconsistent with sales campaigns. Cost control wasn't broken down or allocated by factory, establishment or project, and hadn't been reviewed for several years; all purchasing and selling was done centrally, and in a haphazard way.

'Who does the buying? And who does the selling? And who co-ordinates the budgets?' he asked the senior clerk.

'Charlie does it all,' he was told, 'but all the decisions are made by Simon, who gets the information from Charlie. It's a cockeyed system, but Simon insists on having every bit of data fed to him. I can't even buy any stationery without Simon's signature. He says it keeps him in touch with what's going on.'

All this offended James's systematised approach.

'We seem to have four new cars on the books - they've all been bought in the last three months. And what's this yacht and the country cottage in Berkshire - what are they used for?'

'Both Charlie's,' replied the senior clerk. 'He claims he needs them for entertaining major customers from abroad when they're over here. Says it keeps up the company image. Expensive way to do it though,' he sniffed, 'although Simon always backs him up.'

'Bloody hell, I'm surprised we haven't got a plane as well!' exclaimed James.

'Oh, we have that, too - or at least a Cessna is permanently retained for charter from Beechwood Airways any time we want - Charlie uses it about five times a year when he goes overseas on buying and selling trips.'

The senior clerk managed to say 'buying and selling' as though it was in inverted commas.

In Case 3.2 James Wellard appears to operate differently from Simon and Charlie Kay. James Wellard relies on his senses to generate information. He is a systematic thinker, making decisions based on logic and rationality – an ST type. Simon Kay sees possibilities and potential in various situations, and makes his decisions about the future market working on a feeling of what the customer will want – an NF type. Charlie also uses facts and figures to make decisions, but these decisions are often Charlie-value-laden – an SF type.

Modifying factors

Modifying factors concern the way in which people relate to others, and how they set priorities. (See Figure 3.3)

In establishing and managing relationships with others, people will prefer to behave in either an *extroverted* or *introverted* manner. Extroverts need the company and stimulus of other people. Introverts are more content with their own company. When setting priorities, people will try to establish order and resolve issues by using their judgement (*judgemental*), or will seek more information and try to understand the situation (*perceptive*).

This theory has great relevance for managers in that it relates to

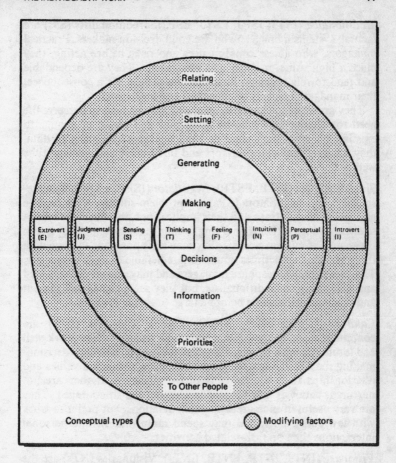

Relating

Setting

Generating

Making

| Extrovert (E) | Judgmental (J) | Sensing (S) | Thinking (T) | Feeling (F) | Intuitive (N) | Perceptual (P) | Introvert (I) |

Decisions

Information

Priorities

To Other People

Conceptual types ◯   ◯ Modifying factors

Fig. 3.3   The eight Myers Briggs types of work preference

activities which they have to pursue in their work life – they have to
relate to other people (Mintzberg – Chapter 1 – found that 80 per
cent of a manager's time was spent on this activity, mostly in
informal, verbal interactions); they have to decide on the priorities
of their work; they have to collect information, and they have to use
it in making decisions.

The Centre for Creative Leadership in North Carolina, USA,
broke down the descriptions of these combinations into five
managerial types: traditionalist, troubleshooter, negotiator, catalyst
and visionary.

Traditionalist (ISTJ, ISFJ, ESTJ, ESFJ). Traditionalists (SJs) are factual, systems managers who are good decision-makers. Practical managers, who assess consequences and risks before acting, they place a high value on order and punctuality. They are dependable and tend to rely more on facts than on people. As a consequence, their managerial style is often formal and impersonal.

They are loyal to the status quo, and may be slow to perceive the need for change and even be suspicious and afraid of change to existing systems. Very good at handling large quantities of data, they are excellent co-ordinators and integrators and manage time well.

Troubleshooter (ISTP, ESTP); *Negotiator* (ISFP, ESFP). Trouble-shooters and negotiators (SPs) are problem-solvers. Very flexible and aware of situations and their implications, they 'use' the system to effect change rather than trying to change the system. They live in the reality of current needs – they may shift positions to cope with these and thus sometimes appear unpredictable to their colleagues. They are stimulus–response managers and may appear disorganised and disorderly to traditionalists, but they are good at sniffing out and dealing with trouble before a large problem develops.

Catalyst (INFJ, INFP, ENFP, ENFJ). Catalysts (NFs) are communicators, charismatic, committed managers who work well and intuitively with people. They care for people, and their decision-making may be influenced more by their own personal values and relationships than by the facts of the situation. If they are not nurtured, catalysts can become ineffective and discouraged. They are very useful in such areas as public relations, but prefer to work with few constraints, and may spend more time in interpersonal interactions than on task-related activities.

Visionary (INTJ, INTP, ENTP, ENTJ). Visionaries (NTs) are the planners, the innovators, the creative force in organisations, the managers who are able to see the whole picture and relate it to the present situation. They look at possibilities and analyse them objectively. While they like to put new ideas into operation, they may quickly lose interest and search for new areas of challenge within their competence – and competence is one quality they expect in others. Because of this they may be insensitive to the problems of other people, and need to be reminded to expect less than perfection. They are good decision-makers, but because they expect everyone else to read situations as well as they can, they often feel it unnecessary to explain their reasons. Visionaries are ideas-men who quickly conceptualise outcomes; it is therefore not surprising that they may equally quickly leave organisations where they feel their talents are not being used.

All these types are necessary in the running of any organisation. The traditionalist keeps the system running and provides stability; the troubleshooter/negotiator senses developing problems and deals with them; the catalyst maintains communications and uses people to best effect; and the visionary looks to the future, senses needs for change, and stimulates its implementation.

Of a large sample of managers attending business school programmes, 80 per cent fall into the categories of traditionalist or visionary; troubleshooters and negotiators comprise only 10 per cent, with catalysts the remaining 10 per cent. It is quite probable, then, that many troubleshooters, negotiators and catalysts are having to perform in organisational roles which are not to their preference. Conversely, it is equally probable that organisations pay less attention to the training and development needs of those managers who do not neatly fit into line management roles.

Case 3.3 Tackling Charlie and Simon

'I'll have a word with Charlie, as Simon says, but a fat lot of good that's going to do'.

Sure enough, Charlie wasn't helpful. An extrovert character, a big man, with little formal education, he thought on his feet, and saw James's encroachment on his territory as a threat to his autonomy. He'd grown complacent over the years, confident in his own quickwittedness, and now devoted more time and energy to selecting the new cars for the staff than to scanning and forecasting the market and the environment.

James explained patiently, 'Selling and leasing back our freehold property, and leasing the cars instead of buying them, will release more revenue for the company, and we're cash-starved for growth.'

Charlie didn't understand. In fact, increasingly he'd become detached from the day-to-day running of the company, excelling at short-term promotions, but relying on Simon's judgement to direct the course of Bien Aimée. He liked his trips abroad, entertaining clients, and the dinners and weekends at the country cottage in Berkshire, for which he was renowned, which influenced many a favoured customer to buy Bien Aimee products.

James's proposal to sell obsolete and surplus stock at marginal cost met with heated and angry opposition from Charlie.

'I know we'll move it soon, I've got some feelers out,' Charlie snarled. 'To sell these models at those prices would be bloody ridiculous.'

'But it's costing us money to keep them in stock – there's no asset turnover, and things are getting worse,' replied James.

> 'You can't sell a piece of Bien Aimée jewellery for a few coppers - it would destroy our image in the market,' Charlie shouted at James. 'You've only just arrived here and you're telling us how to run the business. Bien Aimée isn't just about accounting, you know, we've got our reputation to think of, too.'
>
> Charlie stalked off.
>
> It was obvious to James that all was not well at Bien Aimée and that Charlie's role in the organisation, especially his influence over Simon, the alleged decision-maker, needed to be examined closely. Not the most tactful of men, James with his rigid background in accounting tended to trust figures rather than people, but once those figures and the problems he deduced from them were understood, he gathered courage and followed his convictions to the bitter end.
>
> He tackled Simon, but Simon was still too busy to concentrate.
>
> 'Let's get together when I've finished these designs,' Simon said.
>
> 'But do you realise that our overdraft is running at close to £1 million? If we take some action now, particularly trying to move some of that obsolete stock, we can reduce that to £400,000. If we put into practice some other ideas I have, it will certainly improve our cash management.'
>
> Simon said sharply, 'If you're thinking of moving stock, you'd better see Charlie - that's his area, and then he can let me see the figures.'
>
> Simon closed the interview with this dismissive remark, screwed his eyeglass back in, and turned his attention to a piece of jewellery on his table.
>
> 'What the hell,' thought James. 'Here's a company that isn't looking further ahead than the next few months. I know the fashion market is constantly changing, product life cycles are short and subject to the vagaries of individual preferences, but Simon can't even be bothered to look at the systems it needs to put in to survive.'

As can be seen in Case 3.3, James Wellard and Charlie Kay are having interpersonal problems not only because of their different personalities, but also because they see the situation differently. James's background in finance and accounting seems to provide him with a clear, focused interpretation of work issues. He meets resistance for his plans from Charlie who, over the years, has tended to become deaf to advice and possibly suspicious of other people's motives and defensive of his own perceived territory.

Both consider their plans and actions are for the good of the company – James wants to regularise the systems, particularly the information and control systems, while Charlie wants to maintain the image of the company. Charlie seems to place value on emotion and feelings – James on thinking and rationality. They haven't tried to 'get to know' each other, or to try to see the situation from each other's point of view. Charlie sees James as a threat, to his autonomy, and possibly to him as a person. James sees Charlie as an obstruction to his progress, to achieving his plans for rationalising Bien Aimée's operations. Their perceptions of the situation, and of each other, are different.

PERCEPTION

Perception is the process by which people select, organise and interpret external sensory stimuli and information into terms and categories which are consistent with their own frames of reference and personal views of the world. People use a selection mechanism when they are incessantly exposed to a multitude of sensory stimuli and have to filter out extraneous 'noise' to find and identify those which are relevant and important to them as individuals. Whilst listening to music on the radio, we know the baby is asleep upstairs. When she cries, we screen out the music and concentrate to hear whether the cry is a pain cry, a hunger cry, or a temper cry, to help us decide what action to take. Selection enables us to avoid distracting or unimportant sensory stimuli.

This filtered information is then organised into clusters and categories that, through remembered experience, enable people to make interpretations in relation to their internal states and frames of reference. We may say someone who accepts all information as true, without checking, is trusting. Past experiences of ourselves and of others who were trusting may have shown that the information given was not accurate – even, in some cases, was deliberately inaccurate – and that acting on the assumption of accuracy has led to unexpected and negative outcomes. We therefore link together the concepts of trust, unqualified acceptance of information, deception, and negative consequences. We say that people who are trusting are prone to deception and unexpected pitfalls. This may not be objectively real, but it is subjectively 'real' for the person described, for his experiences influence his attitude and behaviour towards people he perceives as 'trusting'.

Understanding other people

Proper understanding of other people depends very much on interacting and communicating with them, 'getting to know' them. (See Chapter 4 for further discussion on managing communication.)

In Figure 3.4, A's and B's perceptions and impressions of C are different, even though the information passed from C to A and B is

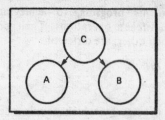

Fig. 3.4   Unshared perception and understanding

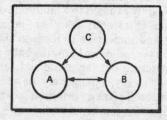

Fig. 3.5   Shared perceptions, shared understanding

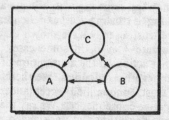

Fig. 3.6   Shared perceptions, common understanding

the same, because A and B have different values, beliefs, attitudes
and remembered experiences. When, as in Figure 3.5, A and B
communicate to each other their perceptions of C, and a process of
disclosure and feedback occurs, A and B are more likely to
understand each other's perception of C. Greater common
understanding develops when A, B and C share and feed back
perceptions of each other, as shown in Figure 3.6.

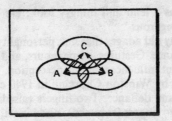

Fig. 3.7 Overlap of common perception and understanding

And even greater empathy and understanding occur when, as in Figure 3.7, A, B and C share some common values, beliefs, attitudes and remembered experiences.

Too often, however, in organisations, individuals have to make judgements of other people based on limited information. In these situations people face the conflict of needing to be as accurate as possible in their perceptions while needing also to make up their minds very quickly. Where time or information is short, individuals often tend to stereotype other people into categories which fit the aggregation of the limited information available, within the parameters of their past experiences. Prejudice occurs by simply categorising people on incomplete information, or by refusing to accept evidence about individuals which conflicts with previous experience.

However, people often have to rely on 'first impressions' in such situations as selection interviews, or in making a sale to an unknown customer. Three factors influence their judgement: the *perceived* (the person they are meeting), the *perceiver* (themselves), and the situation. We can all improve our ability to understand other people and their behaviour by being aware of these three factors throughout the relationship.

The perceived

An individual's perception and categorisation of, and his behaviour towards, other people, influence to a certain extent their apparent characteristics. Some factors which affect people's interactions are:

Physical appearance

'People with glasses are studious.' 'Red hair means a quick temper.'

'Yon Cassius has a lean and hungry look; He thinks too much: such men are dangerous.'

There are many old adages that link personality characteristics to physical appearance. Gestures, demeanours, and facial expressions are also important influences on our perception. Two fingers raised in a victory sign by Winston Churchill in 1940 evoked admiration for his courage and defiance. Two fingers raised in benediction by the Pope, and two fingers (reversed) raised in vulgar contempt by a soccer hooligan, generate entirely different feelings in us when we have to form impressions based on public behaviour. We may infer characteristics of strong self-discipline from the ramrod figure of a Sergeant-Major, while feeling that a person who is unkempt and mooches around is lazy and unmotivated. A scowl makes us unhappy, while a smile makes us want to smile back. Dress also affects our evaluation of other people – we dress smartly for an important interview in order to make a good impression, whilst perhaps feeling that people who wear individualistic clothing or hairstyles are not good team people.

Verbal and social cues

One of the most influential factors in a person's perception of other people is their verbal behaviour – how people speak, and what they say. We all have our own pictures of someone who speaks with a broad Yorkshire accent, or a Scouse accent, or a Scots, Cockney or German accent. Even UK and USA 'English' can lead to perceptual misunderstandings. In the UK, the cover on top of the engine is called the bonnet; in the USA, it is the hood. The storage space at the rear of the car is called in the UK, the boot, in the USA, the trunk. And in France, regional dialects ('patois') give different meanings to common words which the individual needs to understand in order to comprehend and be comprehended. Grammatical exactitude and the use of long words may also influence us to see people as intelligent, though this may not be the case. People's education and status are often categorised by their manner of speech. Those who attended and were pleased with public school could attribute positive characteristics to someone with a strong public school accent. People who speak loudly are often considered extrovert – or even vulgar – while people with soft voices are often thought to be shy and sensitive.

Motor behaviour

'People who won't look you in the eye are shifty and unreliable.'

'Strong handshake – strong character.'

Certain personality traits are often inferred from people's motor behaviour.

These various cues – physical appearance, verbal, social and motor behaviour – help us to form impressions of other people in a first social interaction. Some may be valid, others not. There appears to be a low correlation between most of these factors and personality traits, and how, and which, cues are selected, organised, and interpreted depends on the values, attitudes and beliefs of our particular culture and society, as well as on those of ourselves, the perceivers.

The perceiver

This is the factor over which we have most control. The more we understand and have confidence in ourselves, the more likely we are to understand others. Some of the factors specific to the perceiver which affect the perception of other people are:

- Individual values, beliefs, attitudes, prejudices and remembered experiences.

- Level of awareness and knowledge of, and confidence in, self. People with accurate perceptions of themselves are likely to be more accurate in their perceptions of others. Positive attributes are also more likely to be given to people perceived to be like the perceiver, and vice versa. If the perceiver is loyal and extremely committed to his organisation, he is likely to discount people who are not.

- Current needs, feelings and state of mind. People's perceptions, as well as their behaviour, are likely to be affected by immediate past and current events. A person seriously worried about his finances is not likely to take kindly to someone trying to sell him an expensive holiday.

- Expectations about other people. A person who is told someone is brilliant tends to see brilliance – at first. Told that someone else is a cold fish, he expects to see someone with not much consideration for people, and this influences his initial perception of, and behaviour towards, that person. People seem to see what they expect to see, and often the conflicting evidence needs to be overwhelming before it is accepted.

The situation

Situational factors can be influential when forming first impressions of people. Since individuals have few behavioural cues to help them, the context (a board meeting), the environment (the executive suite at the top of the building), and the perceived value of the other person to themselves (the managing director) affects their perception.

Attributes

As people interact more with others, they tend to infer from the behaviour of others certain characteristics about their motives, their feelings, their needs, their attitudes. Their observed behaviour is felt to be a more accurate external indication of the 'real person' than the earlier, non-behavioural cues on which first impressions were based. Attributes are inferences about people's internal states of mind and emotions based on their observed behaviour.

Reality is what we subjectively perceive to be real. Our own 'real world' – our frame of reference – shapes the way in which we behave in the external objective environment. It also tends to distort, sometimes consistently, sometimes erratically, the information which we receive from that environment, and the people who live in it. Some of the ways in which this distortion affects us are described below.

Stereotypes

Sometimes we have little information about a person apart from his demographic characteristics – his home, his education, his age, religion and nationality etc. From this very limited information a picture of the other person can be built and he can be classified in categories based on our remembered experiences and/or the frames of reference of others. We, for example, have our own pictures of the possible expected personality traits and behaviour of a red-haired person, a minister of religion, an officer in the armed services, a pop star. With no further information, we tend to deal with such people as representatives of their category in our internal picture, and not as individuals. We expect certain types of behaviour from each category, and behave accordingly ourselves. This can help to reduce our own internal conflict and ambiguity as we reject dissonant cues, and if we can be accurate in our stereo-typing it makes it easier to predict behaviour. It can, however, also lead to erroneous judgements about people.

Halo and horns effects

A manager may say: 'He's got all the technical know-how needed – he should be able to keep on top of the work and make a good supervisor.' An individual's perceptions of someone's behaviour in certain areas – whether favourable (the halo effect), or unfavourable (the horns effect) – can influence their predictions about behaviour in other areas.

The Peter Principle, that people can be promoted above their levels of competence, warns us to beware of this distortion, particularly in the area of promotions. People who are like us, or come from similar backgrounds, or have had similar experiences, are likely to be credited with more positive attributes than people who are entirely unlike us.

Expectancy

Expectancy refers to the actual occurrence of something that is expected to happen. Perhaps we expect someone to be antagonistic towards us, and display defensive behaviour, even being aggressive towards him (we retaliate first!). We reject any overtures of friendship as being inconsistent with our expectations. Eventually he really does end up by being antagonistic towards us. We then rationalise our behaviour by saying, 'See – I told you he was like that and he's certainly lived up to expectations!' The bank crash in the Depression year of 1929 was a classic example of expectancy – the self-fulfilling prophecy – in action.

Projection

Projection occurs when people attribute to other people their own feelings and perceptions. The 'them and us' attitudes between management and unions are an example of projection. Management may distrust a union and feel that under current circumstances the union also distrusts management. This, however, may not be the case. So instead of entering a negotiating situation with a win/win outcome in mind, management may ignore conflicting evidence of the union's attitudes and a win/lose situation develops.

Selective perception

We all tend to reject information which we perceive to be inconsistent with our own frame of reference and self-image. Selective perception means that we only listen to what we want to hear, see what we want to see. This is epitomised by the old adage 'Love is blind!'

Case 3.4   'This company's in a helluva state.'

James tried Simon Kay again, 'I need to set up a comprehensive set of information systems that will tell us exactly what's going on in the company to help you in your decision-making.' He had decided on a low-key approach.

'Great, James, go ahead,' said Simon, erasing a line on his sketch of an earring.

'And I can't make head or tail of some of these customer accounts,' James continued. 'What precise customer credit policy do you have here? I know that our invoices say 30 days, but two specific customers seem to be taking over four months to pay, and even then they're taking discount. I've had a word with them and they say that they have a special arrangement with you, but I can't find anything on paper. They're quite large accounts and seem out of line with everyone else.'

'Let's see who they are, James. Oh, yes. Charlie set this up when we were quite small, and we had to give that amount of credit to get the orders.... How much is this – £45.000? God's teeth! I'll have a word with Charlie about this. By the way, James, try and be a bit more diplomatic when you speak to Charlie. Some of the things you've been doing recently are putting his back up, and the staff resent you ferreting about the way you do. Heavens above, I don't think so, but they believe you suspect some of them of fiddling! Heh, heh!'

James thought long about this. Do I take this lying down as I usually do, or do I say what I think is right? He finally decided to speak out. 'Simon, this company's in a helluva state. I know it's still making profits, but the margins are coming down and soon you'll be wondering what hit you. You're getting to such a size that you now need systems to control what's going on – it's too much for you to keep making all the half-pint decisions – even down to signing requisitions for stationery – by yourself. You need to plan and organise for the future. You've got four factories, some of them duplicating production instead of getting economies of scale by specialising. Your credit policies aren't monitored. Expenses bear no relation to the amount of business going on, and there's no budgetary control to speak of. If I were your auditor I wouldn't even sign a qualified report – I'd resign. And you talk about wanting to go public. That's pie in the sky unless you get things under control here.'

James continued hurriedly, as he saw Simon glaring at him, narrow-eyed and white-lipped, 'I don't want to speak of anyone behind his back, but Charlie's out of touch with the business as it is now, and I feel he's more of a liability than an asset, although I know he's worked his guts out and done a very fine job in the past. Now I can put some systems in here. It'll take time, but it'll take a lot of the day-to-day responsibility off your back. I can make sure that you're not delayed with information and bits of paper as you are now, and you probably won't like that at first because you like to keep in touch with everything – and I do mean everything – that's going on. That's not necessary. You need time to plan and to think strategically, and especially because this company is living from day to day and it's slowly going downhill. I can do what I say with your help; it's the only way forward I can see, so it's up to you - either sack me or back me.'

Simon was furious. He wasn't accustomed to being spoken to in this way by employees and his first reaction was to take up James's first suggestion and sack him on the spot. He was too much of a realist to do anything hasty, and eventually he calmed down and said slowly and deliberately, 'I hear what you're saying. I don't necessarily agree with it, and I don't like being spoken to like that. But it's too important to sweep under the table: you've raised a lot of things I want to think about. I'll come back to you tomorrow and let you know my decision.'

When the Kays hired James Wellard (Case 3.1) they knew he had accounting and financial expertise, and were content to allow him freedom to start to put the company's finances in order. Charlie saw James's meeting with him (Case 3.3) more as a personal attack than an attempt by James to establish facts as a basis for decision-making. Simon shifted responsibility for stock control on to Charlie, removing himself from the firing line. Charlie in turn probably felt that James mistrusted him, and so he mistrusted James and his motives.

Both Simon and Charlie Kay initially rejected information which appeared inconsistent with their own terms of reference with respect to the company: they didn't want to hear information from James which would make them uncomfortable. Simon (Case 3.4) has at least acknowledged that a problem may exist. A great deal will depend on his perception of James, Charlie and the company's situation.

Improving perception

A framework called the Johari Window, developed by Joe Luft and Henry Ingham, two American psychologists, has been used in management training and counselling to help people understand the development of differences between their self-perception and others' perception of them. The Johari Window is useful in reducing perceptual biases such as stereotypes, halo and horns effects and selective perception.

In social interactions (Figure 3.10) there are facets of ourselves, our attitudes, behaviour, and personality which are known to us and also apparent to others (the *open* area). At the same time, other people may observe aspects of ourselves of which we are unaware (the *blind* area). We also keep some of our attitudes and feelings private and do not disclose them to others (the *hidden* area). There

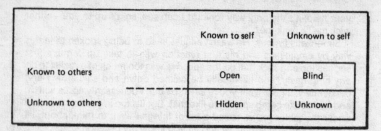

	Known to self	Unknown to self
Known to others	Open	Blind
Unknown to others	Hidden	Unknown

Fig. 3.8   The Johari Window
Adapted from Luft, J. and Ingham, H. (1955), *The Johari Window;
A Graphic Model of Interpersonal Awareness*, Proceedings of the
Western Training Laboratory in Group Development (Los Angeles:
UCLA Extension Office).

are some aspects of ourselves of which we are unaware and which
are also not apparent to others, but which do influence our
behaviour; unless we make determined efforts to increase our self-
knowledge, we are unlikely to understand some of our actions and
reactions (the *unknown* area).

Open	Blind
Hidden	Unknown

Fig. 3.9   First social interactions
Adapted from Luft, J. and Ingham, H. (1955), *The Johari Window;
A Graphic Model of Interpersonal Awareness*, Proceedings of the
Western Training Laboratory in Group Development, (Los Angeles:
UCLA Extension Office).

In first social contact situations we tend to reveal little about
ourselves; others do not get to know much about us, and their view
of us is based on non-behavioural cues. Our open area is small
(Figure 3.9).

As relationships grow we feel we can be more open with others,
and the open area expands, while the hidden area reduces. This is
achieved by *self-disclosure* (Figure 3.10).

The other mechanism by which the size of the open area can be

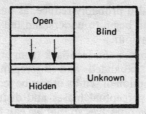

Fig. 3.10 Self-disclosure effect
Adapted from Luft, J. and Ingham, H. (1955), *The Johari Window; A Graphic Model of Interpersonal Awareness,* Proceedings of the Western Training Laboratory in Group Development (Los Angeles: UCLA Extension Office).

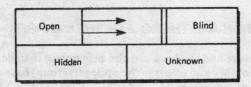

Fig. 3.11 Feedback effect
Adapted from Luft, J. and Ingham, H. (1955), *The Johari Window; A Graphic Model of Interpersonal Awareness,* Proceedings of the Western Training Laboratory in Group Development, (Los Angeles: UCLA Extension Office).

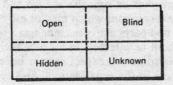

Fig. 3.12 Self-disclosure and feedback effects
Adapted from Luft, J. and Ingham, H. (1955), *The Johari Window; A Graphic Model of Interpersonal Awareness,* Proceedings of the Western Training Laboratory in Group Development, (Los Angeles: UCLA Extension Office).

increased is *feedback* from others. This reduces the size of the blind area (Figure 3.11).

Where both self-disclosure and feedback occur, the size of the unknown area will also probably reduce, as our knowledge of self increases, and we can begin to understand the underlying motives for more of our behaviour.

Only by self-disclosure and feedback from others can the size of the open area be expanded and discrepancies between self-perception and perception of self by others be reduced (Figure 3.12). In order to reduce perceptual biases and distortions we need to develop confidence in ourselves so that we can be open with others and willing to receive feedback. Feedback can sometimes damage our view of ourselves (ie self concept); we can react defensively to feedback which (in our view) places us outside our comfort zone, our 'real world' – and, particularly in counselling situations, considerable skill is needed to maintain a positive, progressive climate.

PERCEPTION AND THE ROLE OF THE MANAGER

Self-disclosure and feedback can also help people to understand the expectations they and others in their role set (group) have of them in their roles as a manager.

Role perception refers to the way in which managers understand their roles – how clearly they identify the tasks they are expected to perform, and their expected behaviour whilst doing those tasks. Frustration and anxiety, leading to role stress, can be caused both by inaccurate role perception, and by inaccurate role definition and expectations by the organisation.

When a manager joins an organisation, he and the organisation hold certain *role expectations* which may or may not be the same. The organisation, and particularly the manager's role set (the group of people with whom he interacts in his job, such as his boss, his colleagues, his subordinates), expect certain beliefs, attitudes and behaviours of others in the organisation. At a selection interview when a full exploration of expectations should take place, differences of expectations may not become apparent because of perceptual biases and simply lack of time to probe adequately.

There are several ways in which these differences may affect the manager.

Role conflict

Occurs when the job occupant has conflicting role demands in his job. He may be required by his role set to do what he doesn't want to do or doesn't think is within his role definition. His role expectations and those of the organisation or his role set are different, and role conflict occurs.

Role overload

Occurs when the manager cannot meet the organisation's requirements, although they may be consonant with the organisation's role definition and expectations, within the constraints of his job/role conditions. The number of roles expected of the manager becomes too great for him to cope with.

Role ambiguity

Occurs when a manager feels, rightly or wrongly, that inadequate information is available about his expected role. This may be due to the lack of clear objectives for the role, unclear definition of the scope, responsibility and accountabilities of the job, or too much uncertainty among the manager's role set about what precisely is his role. Role ambiguity may give managers opportunities to shape and develop their roles to match their own role expectations better. However, resistance to his changes, and perhaps his own low tolerance of ambiguity and uncertainty, may cause frustration and anxiety.

Role clarity

Occurs when the manager sees his role as straightforward and unambitious. However, clear role definition may inhibit the manager from changing and developing his role to match his own expectations. Where a manager does have a low tolerance for uncertainty, it may keep his sense of ambiguity in his role situation to an acceptable level. The problem is that he may ignore or reject activities which appear to him to be outside his clearly perceived role.

Role underload

Occurs when the organisation's role expectations fall short of the manager's own needs and abilities. In other words, he feels he should be filling bigger or a greater variety of roles. Role underload can lead to frustration, role stress, reduced performance and even, eventually, to withdrawal from the organisation.

Role stress

Occurs when the manager experiences sufficient discomfort in his job to prevent him from functioning effectively. This is a psychological or physiological response by the role holder to what he perceives to be some form of role overload/underload, role conflict, role ambiguity/clarity. Role stress can be caused by such things as:

- not being allowed to participate in decision-making.
- having poor managerial support.
- having to cope with technological changes.
- having to keep up with increasing standards of performance.
- having responsibility for people who seem unco-operative or difficult.

Let us examine what has happened so far in Bien Aimée Fashion Jewellery. Simon felt that James Wellard's role was clearly defined – he was financial controller with responsibility for administrating systems and activities which Simon had previously organised and controlled. James gradually realised that there were too many loose ends. His responsibilities and accountabilities were unclear. He interpreted his general brief to permit him to introduce improved information systems into the company.

However, he ran into problems with Charlie Kay, who, because of his withdrawal from day-to-day operations, and his own reduced performance, has role underload. Charlie's disagreement with James leads to James suffering role conflict, particularly because of the lack of managerial support he is receiving from him, and his exclusion from participating in what is to him vital decision-making.

Case 3.5   Nothing to lose

Simon was not sure what to do. He wanted to remain loyal to Charlie, but at the same time he realised that James's proposals would benefit the company in the long term. He was, however, not willing to face the short-term conflict with Charlie, and asked James to prepare a series of revised, pared-down systems which still appeared to maintain Charlie Kay's autonomy. Simon had also in the past given a fair degree of autonomy to the four factory managers who had been allowed to 'do their own thing' - which had contributed to the high stock levels causing the cash flow problem. They didn't support James Wellard's proposals, which they saw as a threat to their present levels of independence. James Wellard felt that he was going to get nowhere with his proposed improvements to the systems in the company. In a prime example of expectancy – the self-fulfilling prophecy – he became more extravagant in his demands to Simon and Charlie Kay. He felt he had nothing to lose in the situation, with the deteriorating relationships placing him in an increasingly isolated position in the company – not supported by Charlie, defended reluctantly by Simon, and resisted and resented by the factory managers.

James Wellard resigned. Bien Aimée Fashion Jewellery's cash position worsened, and nine months later it was taken over by a large conglomerate. Simon Kay was retained purely in his creative role, while Charlie Kay was removed from the company.

In Case 3.5 the different personalities and perceptions of Simon, Charlie and James caused behavioural outcomes which led to conflict and finally incompatibility.

MANAGERIAL MAPPING

One way of trying to prevent the unhappy outcome at Bien Aimée Fashion Jewellery is to apply the technique of managerial mapping. Pioneered by Professor Charles Margerison of the University of Queensland, Australia, the process helps senior executives, through the services of a third party such as a consultant or management development specialist, recognise their preferred work and leadership styles, their views of people, groups and problems in the organisation and the adjustments they would need to make. Margerison originally used this approach to help managers explore their Myers Briggs profiles. Managers were asked to consider the implications of having different types of people in key positions. Considerable emphasis was also placed on examining the balance and composition of teams. However, the approach of assisting managers to explore what it really means to be effective in a particular work situation has far wider appeal than just examining individual personality characteristics. Teams of managers are asked to share their scores and maps in order to appreciate and discuss the strengths and weaknesses in their team. With such insights discussion will then focus on finding ways to improve team and individual performance. It is, in fact, a simple but sophisticated problem-solving tool, which if well used can show further ways to

overcome individual, group and situational problems. All that is
required is an executive facing problems, a counsellor and a piece of
paper.

SUMMARY

The individual at work has been examined from the following
perspectives.

Personality

The term personality largely covers the attitudes, values, sentiments,
interests, ideals, complexes and unconscious mechanisms which
determine an individual's behaviour pattern and thought processes
– the likely results of interactions between the individual's biological
drives and the social and physical environment. Freudian theory,
social learning theory and trait and type theories all deal with this
interaction. The Myers Briggs Work Preferences Indicator, based
on Jungian theory, is a measure for managers to explore their
preferred approaches to work. It identifies four dimensions of
behaviour at work, namely meeting and relating to people,
generating and gathering information, making decisions and setting
priorities. There is a continuum of preferences for each of those
dimensions.

   Although these four dimensions of behavioural preferences are
considered independent, the combination of preferences makes up
sixteen different types whose characteristics can be used as
predictors of behaviour in the work setting.

Perception

Perception is the process whereby individuals select and filter
external stimuli and interpret them into forms consistent with their
frames of reference. To perceive other people accurately, it is
necessary to collect information from them by interacting and
communicating with them. Where the frames of reference of two
people are non-congruent, misunderstandings tend to occur. With
increased congruence, shared perception and shared understanding
are more likely to ensue.

First impressions can influence perception and understanding of people. First impressions are made up of the characteristics of the perceived, eg physical appearance, verbal and social cues, motor behaviour; those of the perceiver, eg values and beliefs, self-awareness, current needs and expectations; and those of the situation, eg the context, environment. These three elements affect the judgements we make of other people. In addition, each person's frame of reference distorts the information he receives, which affects the judgements he makes of other people, eg by forming stereotypes, the halo and horns effects, expectancy (the self-fulfilling prophecy), projection and selection perception.

Distortions in perception can be reduced by self-disclosure and feedback from other people. These processes increase the level of self-awareness. In addition managers' perception of their roles are important. The expectations of the manager and his role set can be different, leading to conflict, role overload or underload, role ambiguity, or role stress.

Managerial mapping

Managerial mapping is a process whereby executives are helped to identify their approaches to managing work, problems and people, their views of situations and how these impact on their performance in their work environment. The aim is to stimulate managers to change their behaviour pattern at work, if that is desired, in order to help them perform well.

IN CONCLUSION

Effective managers have developed the skills of matching the individual's unique personal qualities with their job within the organisation which generates maximum motivation and commit-ment in the person. The individual's personal needs are satisfied by achievement of the job's and organisation's goals, which is doubly rewarding if this perception is shared throughout the organisation.

4 Person to Person

Case 4.1   Frank and Mike

'Well, it all goes back to business school. At that time there was no real relationship between the two of us. Different groups, different accommodation; he was not one of the guys that I actually met socially. Mike was not a guy that I felt attracted to on the course.'

Why was that?

'Outward mannerisms; not that I was very well dressed, but he was pretty much a slob. He tended to go around with a group of people that I didn't feel at ease with. He had a very, very incisive mind in areas that I did not feel confident with, such as finance and accounts. Apart from on the marketing side, I never felt very happy. I admired his ability: probably more than that, I admired him for actually using the ability that he was born with. A lot of people have good brains but don't actually use them. He did. He could pick up things very fast, and he always struck me in class as a very practical man in his approach to business problems, which is close to my own heart.'

What did you do after business school?

'I tried for jobs in marketing, with large companies. International marketing, especially; got a fair number of interviews. Nothing really came up; always the same problem, overqualified for my age, lack of relevant experience, which is all that employers in the UK seem to want.

'Out of the blue comes a call from Mike, around about June time. He is thinking of buying a company; could I either go down and give him a point of view on its marketing potential or alternatively perhaps think about coming into business with him as a partner? At that time, the good thing about going into it was that I had not been able to find a job of professional stature, which I needed. To get back into the swing of things, I had to make decisions soon because the longer you are on the shelf, the more difficult it becomes. I was very keen on going ahead.'

In Case 4.1, Frank appears to have formed certain opinions about Mike at business school, based on limited information. He felt Mike was intelligent, able, and practical, but his social standards weren't the same as Frank's. These feelings were generated by observation and value-laden communication with Mike and others on his business course. Mike also had formed certain opinions about Frank. Although there appears to have been very little direct communication between them, Mike was sufficiently impressed by Frank's marketing ability to invite him to collaborate with him in a business venture.

Research has shown that a manager's job consists mostly of interpersonal transactions; senior managers spend up to 80 per cent of their time in oral communication with their superiors, colleagues, subordinates and people inside and outside their work unit, and really half of a manager's time is spent generating information. Thus the importance of developing skills in interpersonal interactions is obvious. Managing relationships forms the greater part of a manager's job.

However, a qualitative change is taking place in the nature of managerial relationships with the accelerating progress in information technology. In the future a manager may have fewer subordinates, as information processing systems take over much of the work done by people in organisations. Colleaguial relationships will become more important as information needs to be transferred and integrated across departments. Consequently, as a manager's informational roles increase, so his skill in his interpersonal roles becomes a determining factor in his effectiveness.

This chapter will examine two key functions of interpersonal communication in terms of passing information and relationship building. In addition, it considers that interpersonal communication is influenced by the personal needs of each of the individuals involved in the situation. Finally, the skills required for effective interpersonal communication are outlined.

INTERPERSONAL COMMUNICATION

Have you experienced personal satisfaction when communicating and interacting with friends, relatives and well established acquaintances; in effect, people with whom you feel comfortable? Often there is less of a need to be guarded when disclosing sensitive or even personal data, largely because of the way the relationship between the friends is managed. With good friends, one can speak openly, probably honestly, make outrageous statements and even turn a relatively serious conversation into a joke. With the best of friends, endearment can be shown by using terms of abuse. If two friends who have not seen each other for some time meet accidently, one may say to the other,

'Heh ... you old fool! I wish I had your life, being paid to go socialising and attend dinners; in fact, being paid to do nothing, which just suits you!'

Both friends laugh, inform each other of their recent experiences and probably enquire about each other's welfare. The relationship can be described as warm, comfortable, sharing, uninhibited and satisfying for each individual.

Consider another common experience. Two or more individuals are required to interact effectively in order to address business and organisational problems competently. However, the relationship between the individuals is not well developed. Frequent misunderstandings occur which may lead to arguments, or alternatively non-confrontation because the individuals feel unable to address the problems they face with each other. Under such circumstances, people may talk behind each other's back; offer minimum cooperation and generally find the work environment unsatisfactory. Ironically, in such a situation, the manner of interpersonal communication may be polite and, on the surface, people's feelings may be sensitively handled. Yet, despite such people management skills, the level of interpersonal communication is low.

The values held by each individual, their needs in terms of business and personal relationships, their perceptions of the others with whom they interact, and the importance or sensitive nature of the issues under consideration, influence the process of interpersonal communication. If the relationship between individuals can be considered satisfactory, providing information and addressing shared concerns can be more easily accomplished. People are likely to trust the data offered, both in terms of the source and content, and hence are more likely to utilise such data to help solve problems or pursue challenging strategies. If the relationships between people are not satisfactory, each person may not trust the information provided by other parties. They may consider it to be inaccurate or even falsified. They may not trust the other person's judgement, and hence consider any data and arguments provided by the other inappropriate. In extreme circumstances, the information provided may be recognised as accurate, appropriate and relevant but is considered unacceptable because of the way its proponent is perceived. People just do not like the guy!

In order to ensure that interpersonal communication is well managed, two issues must be considered: *information passing* and *relationship building*.

When the primary function of communicating is information passing, effectiveness can be measured in terms of the nature of the information received. Both the source of the data and the manner in which it has been gathered and compiled need to be scrutinised in order to assess its quality. How useful is the information? How adequate is the information? These two questions can only be satisfactorily answered if the context in which people find themselves is understood. The individuals concerned would need to appreciate the problems and challenges, supports and constraints that they need to manage in their situation. They would equally need to identify their aims and objectives, in order to recognise what is and what is not useful and adequate information. The individuals in the situation would need to consider their expectations; would need to talk to each other in order to test the assumptions each person holds, and thereby come to a realistic conclusion concerning their present and future circumstances.

Consider the following conversation.

Manager (calling to his secretary in the outer office):
'Betty, I need the up-to-date figures on the Barley Brothers account. Could you let me have them, please?' (Meaning, bring me Barley Brothers' file.)

Betty (his secretary): 'Did you say Bailey Brothers?'

Manager: 'No, Barley Brothers.'

Betty: 'Barley Brothers. All right. Coming.' (Brings Barley Brothers' file in to manager.)

Manager: 'Thanks.'

In this situation, the manager's motivation to initiate the communication process was that he had a need – he required information. He then went through a process of deciding whether to take action himself, whether to bring in someone else to help him, who that person should be, how to approach that person, what to communicate (what the message should be), how to communicate (what mode and medium to use).

Feedback from his secretary tested out the understanding of the message and the sender reinforced his original message, which was then interpreted correctly by the receiver.

In a simple situation like this, where the two people have possibly enacted similar scenes many times before, the sender and receiver share much common experience. The implicit and unstated message – bring me the file – was understood correctly by the receiver. If, however, this had been the secretary's first day at work, the manager would have had to state his message much more specifically to ensure that the receiver understood. The implicit message would have to be made explicit, until the receiver had learned through experience of the manager's style how to interpret it correctly.

Case 4.2   That should have wised me up!
What arrangements did you come to with Mike?

'At this stage, it was never actually said as such, but we both assumed that I would go in on a partnership basis. I wanted a quarter. He was willing to let me have 20 per cent of the action. That suited me, though I had no money. He had the money; he came from a rich family. He would lend me the money to buy the shares. I would have a directorship and marketing and sales were under my control.'

Was it a limited company or a partnership?

'Limited company. And he also gave a small number of the shares to another guy, with whom he was very friendly at college. I was told in the early days that he was also a director; he could always sit as an arbiter between the two of us.

'That should have prepared me for the eventual situation here. But it did not. A number of things should have wised me up to the situation, but they did not.'

In Case 4.2, Frank is making certain assumptions about his projected business relationship with Mike which are not being substantiated and reinforced by subsequent actions. First of all he assumed that he and Mike would he partners. Then this turned out to be a company in which he would have minority shareholding, and Mike, to protect his interests, would appoint another director who was a close friend. Danger signals are starting to sound for Frank but he is not aware of them. He rejects the signs because he has financial needs, and an emerging interpersonal need for his expertise, and himself as a person, to be accepted by Mike.

Case 4.2 indicates the dangers of not testing assumptions even when the relationship between the parties is positive. It is interesting to speculate the perceptions that will evolve between Frank and Mike as a consequence of not testing assumptions.

Information, once received and digested by individuals, will in turn affect their perceptions of their roles, their accountabilities, their quality of decisions and ultimately their job performance. If the information is considered satisfactory, people may be stimulated to work harder, take calculated but positive risks and be more open and honest when being held accountable for their job performance. The reverse process could occur if the information received is considered unsatisfactory. The nature of information itself can either be a positive and motivating or a negative and demotivating experience.

On certain occasions, no matter how well intended is each individual, unacceptable or undesired information needs to be offered to others who in turn are required to accept it and put it into practice. It may be bad news for an R & D project group to hear that their budget is cut and that one of the well respected group members is to be made redundant simply because there is a need to reduce head count. However, the remaining group members need to continue with their work and strive to attain group objectives. Despite the depressing nature of the information received, the group could continue to perform effectively, if the relationships between the group members, the group leader and other key managers in the organisation are positive. Hence, the other primary function of communicating is relationship building. Effectiveness can be measured in terms of an ability to relate to one another, psychological closeness, supportiveness and approachability. The nature of the relationships individuals develop at work in turn affect the ways they identify with their organisation, their degree of commitment to achieve goals and finally their overall motivation.

Individuals need to be concerned with the impact they make on others; is it positive or negative? Some may not care what others think of them. Under certain circumstances, paying little attention to the personal impact one makes on others can be considered as dogged determination or fighting against overwhelming odds. However, in most situations, paying little attention to personal impact may leave others with negative feelings such as the individual being perceived as obstructive, uncooperative and possibly creating unnecessary tensions in the work situation.

In negotiating to attain effective working relations, it is important to take account of each individual's values, drives and behaviour. Equally, body language can influence interpersonal communication. Others can misinterpret the true meanings behind the words used if body language and posture of the individual do not support the statements made.

Developing effective working relations depends on being perceived as credible and, from there on, working towards generating trusting relationships between oneself and others.

In practice, information passing and relationship building occur simultaneously. Hence, it is important to recognise the miscommunication that can take place by simply concentrating on use of language. As indicated, personal values, beliefs, assumptions and perceptions can colour, distance or enrich the effectiveness of interpersonal communication. Karl Albrecht suggested that in all social interactions, communication occurs through four separate channels; through facts, feelings, values and opinions (see also Figure 4.2).

- *Facts* are objective reality, or inferences, assumptions believed to be true on the basis of our previous experience.

- *Feelings* are our emotional responses to this situation in relation to our previous experience; our reactions to the context and content of this transaction.

- *Values* are the norms of behaviour which we feel are appropriate for us within our society and culture; reasonably permanent beliefs about what one should be or should be important for us.

- *Opinions* are attitudes which are relevant to the particular position one has taken in this transaction; short term beliefs about this situation which are subjective, not objective reality.

All four of these channels are used in any interaction.

Managing director (MD): Division A's profits are down 10 per cent this quarter (*fact*).

Finance director (FD): It's a continuing trend this year (*fact*).

MD: Why didn't they let us know they weren't going to meet their targets this time? I'm getting very angry with the general manager (*feeling*). I think he's bullshitting us again (*opinion*).

FD: The division's worth persevering with (*value*). With a new general manager I'm sure it can be turned round (*opinion*).

MD: Yes, you may be right (*opinion*). I'm over-reacting to the problem (*opinion*). Their track record has been good in the past (*fact*).

Problems of miscommunication occur when messages sent on one channel are thought to be sent on another, eg an opinion is received and interpreted as a fact. 'Connors will never beat McEnroe at Wimbledon' is an opinion expressed as a fact – perhaps a reasonable inference based on the sender's own experience – and would probably be received and viewed as a fact by most receivers.

Division A's general manager to managing director: 'We'll do much better this quarter – we're sure to meet our targets' is an opinion which was received by the managing director as a fact: hence his anger when the division's results were reported. The general manager may have thought 'He knows it's only my opinion', but the managing director saw it as a fact.

To reduce these misperceptions and avoid consequent frustration and anger, one needs to be aware that a message consists not just of content (the apparent facts) but also of the underlying feelings, values and opinions of the sender. It is important to try to separate out those elements in the 'decoding' process. One needs to *listen actively* to messages and reflect back the expressed content and feelings to be sure that the whole message is received and understood. As the brain can process data at about four times the speed of speech transmission, an individual has time after receiving a message to interpret it and consider how to respond. The process of interpretation is often neglected as time is spent in constructing a response. Certain elements of a message can trigger off programmed responses based on personal values, feelings and opinions. The sender justly complains: 'You hear, but you're not listening.'

The continuous bombardment of information to which managers are daily subjected makes matters worse. How can they evaluate the relative objective importance of the messages they receive? When should they listen and when should they not? If they decide not to listen to a particular communication, they could miss some vital piece of information affecting their performance. The similarity (or not) of the language, values, feelings and opinions of the sender and those of the receiver influence the attention given to the message. So does the apparent importance of the message to the two parties' individual needs in the situation.

If the message is threatening to the receiver or does not fit with his values or beliefs, he is likely to ignore or repress it, behave defensively, or even to forget it. Managers need to check continually that their messages are being received and decoded correctly, even though the two-way communication process takes longer. (For further discussion on information, feelings and values, see the section on the skills of interpersonal communications.)

Case 4.3   The warning

Did you and Mike go ahead and buy the company?

'The process of the negotiations was very strange. The guy who owned the company had founded it. He was superb, an absolute gem. He'd started the business from nothing, a jobbing builder – he now had a company making double glazing packs. The eventual asking price went up and up. Twice the guy tried to give us our money back. And we were taken by that and we agreed, and the price slowly crept upwards. He was exceedingly good. This was the last Christmas before the recession. That's when most of the money is made, in the three months leading up to Christmas. Of course, the economy crashed afterwards, but who was to know that? The reason we went on was that Mike had the money, and he wanted to make a go on his own, and I needed a job; I needed personal respect, I needed my ego boosting.

'Mike, I discovered later, found it very difficult to work with people. His solution was to do it all on his own, and he knew he could achieve results, although he had an inferiority complex, practically as big as mine. He had to prove that he could succeed on his own and he needed his own company to be run his own way, so the price went up and up. We kept going.

'We also met an extremely capable bank manager, Mike's bank manager, who did the deal. I'd a lot of respect for that man. I was asked quite straightforwardly by the bank manager, "Frank, how well do you know Mike? Do you realise he is not one of the easiest men in the world to get on with? I have known him a long time, and he's very capable. In the company he was working for before, the board meetings used to last all day, now they last 45 minutes."

'I did not pick that up either. I was fairly warned by his bank manager, who knew him. Mike did all the cash flow and the financial plans and analysis and did them exceedingly well, from what I can understand. I trusted him on all that, and one thing Mike never did was to betray that trust. That was one thing in his favour.'

In Case 4.3, Frank seems to want respect and recognition of his own self-image by others. He needed to be accepted by Mike, to be trusted by him as he trusted Mike himself. Mike was driven by a need to control his environment and the people in it, and didn't like others to control him. Others could perhaps predict the probable effects of these individual needs on the relationship, but Frank was so closely involved that he found it, at that time, difficult to separate himself from the situation and look at it objectively.

People's behaviour towards others is affected very much by their own interpersonal needs.

INTERPERSONAL NEEDS AND BEHAVIOUR

Some people always take charge whether they know what to do or not; others always let other people decide what they should do. Some people hang around groups at work apparently wanting to join them; others wouldn't join groups unless required to do so. Some people are friends with everyone; others are impossible to get close to. These behavioural characteristics are the result of differing levels of interpersonal needs.

Understanding what we need from other people can help us analyse why we behave the way we do in different situations. The poet John Donne said 'No man is an island.' We live in a society of people, an environment populated by people who are both similar and different to ourselves. Man is a social creature. Throughout history, he has learned to co-operate and compete with others for control over his environment, over other people, and over himself. All of us have social and interpersonal needs which we have to try to satisfy, somehow achieving a balance between their satisfaction and the minimisation of the threat to others – equally other people have interpersonal needs, and their attempts to satisfy them may pose a threat to us. The levels and intensity of these needs vary from person to person, and each person may use different methods to cope with them. These interpersonal needs were defined by Will Schutz, the American psychologist, as a need for *inclusion*, a need for *control*, and a need for *affection*. There are two dimensions of need – the behaviour we initiate towards other people, our *expressed* behaviour, and the behaviour we should like other people to initiate towards us, our *wanted* behaviour.

The need for inclusion

This is the need to have an equitable relationship with other people in respect of social transactions and 'belonging'. People's needs for inclusion vary enormously. At one end of the scale are people who want to be with others, who actually seek them out: they are group-dependent, 'people-gatherers'. Some want very little to do with other people; they are content by themselves, they want to be private, 'loners'. Some want to join every group within their environment, others shun group activity. Between these extremes, most people have ranges of behaviour, or comfort zones, within which they feel they can achieve a balance between membership of a group or society, and maintaining their own private lives. They actively work to achieve this balance in their *expressed* behaviour. On the other hand, everyone has a certain level of need for social interactions, wanting others to have him join their group activities, whilst at the same time wanting to strike a balance with being left alone. This is his *wanted* behaviour.

The need for control

Schutz defined this as the need for a certain degree of power and influence in our relationships. It is closely related to what David McClelland, the American psychologist, called the need for achievement, but again Schutz looks at it in two dimensions. Managers, in particular, need to have some control over their environment to enable them to make good decisions, and to be able to rely on the effects of those decisions through consistency and predictability. Ambiguous situations make most people uncomfortable.

From a managerial viewpoint, expressing power and influence usually manifests itself in taking charge of other people, as people are the means to getting things done, and may also be the blocks to achieving the manager's goals, by causing inconsistent and unpredictable outcomes. People's needs for control and power also vary, from those who always want to be in complete control of everyone and everything which affects them, to those who actively hold back from taking responsibility (*expressed* behaviour); and from those who reject any forms of control over them, to those who want to be told what to do in every situation (*wanted* behaviour). Between those extremes, most people find some form of balance between their need to take control and exercise power and their need to be directed and controlled.

The need for affection

This is the need for love, affection and friendship. It differs from the need for inclusion because here we are talking about relationships with others as individuals, as opposed to the need to belong to a group. Varying levels of the affection need produce different types of social transaction. Some people may actively force their friendship on others. They want close, intimate relationships with most people with whom they have contact (high *expressed* behaviour). Others may actively reject any deep personal overtures

EXPRESSED BEHAVIOUR		NEED	WANTED BEHAVIOUR	
Extreme high	Extreme low		Extreme high	Extreme low
'Come and join us'	'Go away'	*Inclusion*	'Can I join you?'	'I want to be alone'
'I'm in charge'	'You're in charge'	*Control*	'Tell me what to do'	'Keep off my back'
'Hey, let's you and me get together'	'Don't call me, I'll call you'	*Affection*	'Please, can we meet again?'	'Keep away from me'

Fig. 4.1   Interpersonal needs – the message

of friendship – they do not desire close friendships (low *wanted* behaviour).

Some of the characteristics of the extremes of these dimensions are shown in Figure 4.1.

The motives for our behaviour towards other people are the result of the relationship that develops within and between each of these needs. If, within a particular need, the expressed or wanted levels are about equal, it is likely that the way in which that person behaves will not lead to conflict; his orientation and stability with respect to that need will enable him to cope well. The greater the difference between expressed and wanted levels, the more likely are frustration, conflict and stress. A manager may have high expressed control needs which make him want to act independently and have complete autonomy in his work. His wanted control need may be very low. Such a man is likely to resent and reject any directions his boss gives him towards achievement of his targets – it's seen as an invasion of his territory: his boss, noticing this, may impose even stricter control on him.

Behavioural outcomes are also affected by the interactions between these needs: the way in which a person behaves in one area may influence outcomes in another area. A manager may have moderate expressed control needs but also high wanted inclusion needs. He may be unwilling to take positive steps to correct a situation where his group is not performing well for fear of exclusion from it.

Case 4.4   'I just do not argue.'

How did you split up responsibilities in the company?

'Mike was managing director, he also handled the purchasing and finance. I was responsible for marketing, in practice, selling. The idea was that selection of new products and pricing should be done in partnership. In other words, we should reach consensus. In a sense, this was something very difficult to reach with Mike, as a person. Consensus to me implies straightforward, logical reasoning by both parties for a common goal. It does not include hysterical screaming. This I found somewhat offputting; it was totally strange, when it first happened.

'I started off with enormous confidence, blind confidence, perhaps. This was before any talk of recession. The figures had gone up and up and up. Yes, the confidence was there. It was a good Christmas, lots of sales. These are the good things of life. After that, of course, the economy turned round, and the problems came.

'The first point at which I started seriously thinking "Can I really work with this guy on a long-term basis?" was just after Christmas. We had an old guy running the warehouse, running it quite well. Some of the people we took on, though, were quite amazingly thick. One of them had to make orders up, load the vans and make deliveries, make sure it was all down on the notes, and get the stuff out on time. This guy was trying his best but he just wasn't up to it, he couldn't actually read very well. Mike saw this and launched screaming at this guy, which is all well and good, you come across that on building sites, but not to a guy that you are employing, it just doesn't seem right. And the clipboard which had all the orders on it, Mike threw it to the other side of the warehouse. Bright red he was, pacing up and down, screaming and throwing the board.

'I thought, hold on a minute, I don't like this. Mostly because it made me feel extremely uncomfortable. Because I do not argue with people, I just do not argue. I have no knowledge or experience of heavy arguments. I avoid it, I can see an argument coming when I'm talking to someone, I can see it miles before they do, and before they realise that there is a possible conflict I have gone round it already, I have sidetracked. My wife hates me for it because now and then she would like an argument, and no way will I have it, it makes me very, very uncomfortable. When I try to have a conversation with someone like that, I always feel intimidated, which makes it very difficult to progress anywhere. So I didn't raise the situation with Mike at that time.'

In Case 4.4, Frank is now identifying the interpersonal problems he had with Mike. Mike is not meeting Frank's commitment to the relationship and his needs for inclusion and friendship. Frank, as Mike reveals more of his real personality, finds himself wanting to withdraw, but to where? Tension and conflict rise as Mike's interpersonal attitudes manifest themselves in his behaviour to the warehouseman. There is no valid communication between them over the situation as Frank feels himself unable or unwilling to face up to the conflict in their attitudes. There is no attempt by either to understand the motives behind their behaviour.

INTERPERSONAL TENSION

There may be tension between individuals when certain of these needs (inclusion, control, affection) are not being satisfied. Where person A has high expressed affection needs and person B has low wanted affection needs, person A will feel frustrated that his overtures of friendship are being rejected, while person B will become angry and overwhelmed by the continued invasion of his privacy.

Tension may occur where individuals' coping mechanisms are *unable* to cope because the individuals don't have the necessary knowledge or skills to manage interpersonal interactions. Each person's values, beliefs and attitudes may be rigidly held, and each may thus reject any view which is contrary to and appears to be a threat to his own self-image. In these situations there is likely to be a breakdown in communication ('You hear what I say, but you aren't listening'). Stereotyping and selective perception may also cause people to accept only those sensory stimuli which reinforce their preconceived ideas about a situation or other person. Perhaps person A wasn't really making strong overtures of friendship to person B, but person B, with low wanted affection needs, perceived *any* close social interaction, even at work, as a threat to his privacy.

These tensions in conflict situations arouse the emotions and can lead to anxiety and stress. People feel they're not being understood and this may manifest itself in anger, passive or active resistance (or sabotage), defensive behaviour or withdrawal from the situation.

Tension can only be reduced by really attempting to understand the other person's feelings about a situation *from his point of view*. To do this, one needs to listen actively and with empathy to the other person, to reduce any threat and to show him understanding and acceptance. He then feels it less essential to hold unwaveringly to his own beliefs and attitudes. This means that facts have to be understood by both parties as facts, feelings as feelings, values as values, and opinions as opinions – and, importantly, stated or implicit needs as real needs. After acceptance and understanding the situation can be explored in a less threatening way. The motives for each person's behaviour can become clearer when shared, which can lead to changes in both perceptions and attitudes to the situations and to each other, and steps, mutually agreed, can be worked out for a successful outcome.

THE SKILLS OF INTERPERSONAL COMMUNICATION

Tensions between managers can be reduced if the individuals develop styles of interpersonal communication appropriate to the situation. It is imperative therefore to understand the range of skills available. The American consultant, Dr Robert Bolton, suggests four key skills which he considers critical to effective interpersonal relations:

- listening skills
- assertion skills
- conflict-resolution skills
- problem-solving skills.

Active listening

Listening is not a passive process, it is an active, time and energy consuming activity. Active listening involves paying attention to the other person on three separate levels. Figure 4.2 illustrates this. Most people tend to think of listening in terms of concentrating on what the other person is saying. In fact, actual words convey only a small proportion of each message. (One psychologist reckoned this proportion was as low as 20 per cent.) Listening actively to the words of a message can be achieved by asking the appropriate questions and by giving encouragement. The general rule is to use open questions (ie, those that do not invite a 'yes' or 'no' reply, but encourage the other person to share his/her thoughts, opinions, observations, experience, etc) at first, to allow the person to explain the nature of the problem. Use probe questions to acquire additional information and then use closed questions to clarify details. Encouragement may be given verbally by such words as 'yes ...', 'Mmm ...', 'Uhuh ...'. They may seem inconsequential but they are conspicuous when absent.

When people communicate, they use their minds, emotion and body language. Words reflect the intellectual side of the message

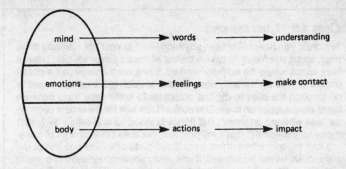

Fig. 4.2   The three levels of active listening

and provide understanding to the other person. Feelings reflect the
emotions underlying the message and they are very important
because they make contact with the other person. Compare a
message delivered totally apathetically with a message delivered
with strong emotion. It is easy to ignore the former, whilst the latter
automatically triggers a response! Lastly, people communicate with
their body. What kinds of body signals do people transmit during
conversations? Posture, gestures, facial expressions, hands and feet
movements and voice characteristics are probably the most
common of these signals. Positive body language that helps
communication include maintaining eye contact, smiling, leaning
towards the speaker, speaking at a moderate rate and in an assuring
tone. Body language that may encourage a negative response
includes averting one's eyes from the speaker, yawning, speaking
too quickly or too slowly and in an offhand way. From there on, it
is important to maintain the momentum of the conversation by
allowing the other speaker to verbalise his thoughts and feelings
with the minimum of disruption. Further, in order to provide
sufficient encouragement for the speaker to continue with his story,
certain words or phrases such as 'mm-hmm' or 'really ... I see ...
what? ... then? ... go on ... good', can provide the stimulus the
speaker needs. In addition, asking appropriate questions, paying
attention to the response and being able to reflect back to the
speaker the key elements of his conversation, all help to attain
effective communication between the two parties.

Case 4.5   I just listened

'His desk, you have never seen anything like it in your life. He had a large desk, and it was full up to twelve inches all the way over. He didn't have a bare space where he actually worked, there were always half a dozen papers or files underneath when he was scribbling things out. I used to go through the piles to dig out orders that I knew were there because there were queries on them. You couldn't ask him for the orders because he "was working on them". But if they phoned up and asked "Why isn't the order delivered?" that's *my* problem, because I'm in charge of sales.

'I had my own office, there were these glass offices at one end of the warehouse, where we worked, it was really abysmal. He used to come in with things like "What are you doing about getting the sales up?" and in the next breath, "What the hell are you getting so defensive about?" Those are the words, so you can see the problem.

'Well, we shortly had another one of our little crises. He got rid of old Bill and brought in a machine. Old Bill was the accountant, a book keeper, and he was elbowed out fairly fast. After shouting and screaming at him once or twice because things were going wrong, and the air was turning blue, old Bill left. Mike then got an accounting machine. The problem was he didn't really know how to use it. So nothing really got better.'

How did Mike handle that?

'Well ... not too well. He just blew up. Even I heard him screaming. Shortly after, he came into my office angry and upset. I asked him what was the matter. And he told me.... He told me everything. Just went on and on.'

What did you do?

'I just listened. I really listened. I murmured a couple of things, but I can't really remember what I said. All I remember was just listening and helping the guy get his problems off his chest.'

What happened then?

'He just kept talking and calmed down and for the first time we talked to each other like human beings. He just kept on talking and then, after a while, the conversation just slowed down. He got up and thanked me for listening. He said he felt a lot better. He then left my office. D'you know something? I felt good. I really felt as if I had made a breakthrough with that guy. I really felt as if I had made a contribution.'

Frank (Case 4.5) played the classic role of an active listener. The results of such behaviour are obvious to both Frank and Mike.

Both felt positive after the conversation. Little, in terms of outcomes, seems to have been achieved by the discussion. However, in terms of feelings, the relationship seems to have improved, especially from Frank's point of view. Mike also seems to have benefited in terms of calming down and presumably going back to work. Note that tangible outcomes do not necessarily have to result from active listening. Managing people's emotions can be just as valuable.

Assertiveness

How does one make an impact on another person without necessarily upsetting them? How is a person forceful and yet sufficiently sensitive to the other person's feelings?

The answer is by being assertive! Every individual has his personal space; his territory which he values and does not want others to invade. Such personal space is made up of views, values, ideas and emotions. People have a right to those values and certainly would not thank others for encroaching on their personal territory. Assertiveness is a means of making an impact on other individuals without wandering into their personal arena. It is a means of being influential with others without damaging the personal relationship. Assertiveness is the mid-point between submissive and aggressive behaviours (see Figure 4.3).

Submissive behaviours	Assertive behaviours	Aggressive behaviours

Fig. 4.3   The submission-assertion-aggression continuum
From Bolton, R., *People Skills*, Englewood Cliffs, N. J.: Prentice-Hall, Inc., 1979, p. 123. Reproduced with permission from Prentice-Hall.

Submissive behaviour involves an unwillingness or inability to express honest feelings, needs, values and personal concerns. People who adopt submissive behaviour allow others to violate their space and deny their rights. Naturally, they harbour negative feelings towards others who adopt such behaviours but they do not express them; they bottle them up. In a sense, they are dishonest with others, for they appear positive but inwardly dislike or despise others.

Aggressive people on the other hand tend to overpower others. They impose their point of view or values on other people and may express their feelings at the expense of others. Aggressive people are liable to generate resistance in others by actively blocking their demands or views or are simply unable to stimulate commitment from others.

Assertive behaviour, however, enables one person to say what he/she wants without overwhelming or abusing other people. Assertive people are clear about their own position and communicate this to others, but are also able to accept the position that others have taken, and thus may negotiate their own position accordingly. Giving an opinion at a meeting, asking for a rise in pay, stopping a conversation that is time wasting, dealing with persistent salesmen and terminating someone's employment are all good examples of situations where we need to act assertively.

Case 4.6   I told him

So the relationship improved, did it, after Mike had poured out his heart to you?

'Well, I thought it had, but a couple of days later, same old Mike. Only this time things were a little different. That guy from whom we bought the company, we still had his wife working in the company as a secretary. She was quite good as a secretary. Well, one day, Mike lost his cool with her. They had a row and she ended up crying. That surprised me because she seemed such a strong-willed woman. Well, that was it! I asked Mike to come into my office and without even thinking about what I was doing, I told him that his behaviour was unpleasant and nasty, but, most important, unproductive as far as the business was concerned. I can still remember Mike looking totally surprised.'

What did Mike do?

'Well, nothing really. He tried to say something but I stopped him. Looking back, it's so funny. I stopped him saying anything and then calmly and coolly listed my areas of concern about the business, about Mike's style and the reasons why he needed to improve his attitude. The only problem was the longer I went on, the more I thought about what I was doing, the more I began to lose confidence. I was becoming the old Frank again. Well, I just finished fairly abruptly, and waited for the onslaught from Mike.'

Did he lay into you?

'No! That more than anything else gave me confidence which I haven't lost to this day. Mike said "OK. I've heard you. I hadn't quite realised the way you felt. We need to talk. Let's get together some time in the middle of this week, and let's meet in the evening so that we can discuss things quietly." I agreed and Mike left.'

How did you feel?

'I felt great! I really felt as if I had scored a great victory. But looking back, you know, I was not aggressive. I just told Mike straight what I thought the problems were in the company and with himself. With some of the more important problems, I just stated them again and again. You know, if I had stopped to think before I said to Mike what I thought, I'm sure I wouldn't have done it.'

Frank (Case 4.6) practised assertiveness. He calmly offered opinions and information to Mike about the company and Mike himself. Frank did not attempt to hurt Mike's feelings, but rather to point out areas which required attention. Mike in turn seems to have responded positively by suggesting that the two partners meet to discuss the issues further. Mike's response is typical when confronted with assertive behaviour.

Conflict resolution

Conflicts, tensions, difficulties with individuals or groups in organisations are inevitable. People have their own views on issues their own approaches to solving problems. Conflict between individuals and groups can arise as much because of disagreement on particular issues as because of the manner in which discussions took place. Two people can agree on a particular approach to a problem, but may still end up disliking each other. The reason for that could be that the process of negotiation was unsatisfactory, although the outcome is acceptable. The question to raise, therefore, is whether the two parties will do what they have agreed – are they committed? An inability or unwillingness to apply what they have agreed can eventually lead to further conflict.

In order to achieve greater collaboration and commitment amongst people, the following approaches should be considered:

1 *Reflective listening* both improves understanding of common

problems and generates sufficient trust between individuals for them to talk to each other.

2   *Assertion skills* make a powerful impact on people and also maintain their commitment to working in the organisation.

3   *Fewer communication blocks* between individuals can be achieved by reducing dominating, threatening and aggressive behaviour, and making fewer false judgements.

4   *Issues*, rather than just interpersonal tensions should be emphasised. This means gathering facts, breaking larger issues into smaller workable units and then confronting each problem separately.

5   *Careful appraisal of the actions decided* and an assessment of the consequences of those actions is a valuable discipline to undertake, for it may deter both individuals and groups from needless disputes in the future.

Problem-solving

Problem-solving is concerned with trying to find some form of mutual agreement about decisions and actions which have to be taken. Here the manager may have one or more of three reasons for using this style. First, he may not have all the information he requires to make a decision himself, and only by sharing the problem, the facts and feelings in the situation with the other person is it possible to reach a quality decision. Second, it may be necessary for the other person to be totally committed to the required action or decision, and the only way in which that can be achieved is for both to work on the action or decision together. Third, it is a means of developing other people, particularly subordinates, by involving them in the decision-making process.

The problem-solving process is two-way. The manager and the other person share facts, feelings, values and opinions about a situation, explore it from both points of view, and resolve a solution which is appropriate to that situation rather than to either person in particular. The sharing process, the involvement of the other person (where genuine), means that he has some opportunity to influence the decisions and is likely to be more committed to it. The process can, however, be time-consuming, and the manager must balance the time and cost involved in this two-way communication process against the quality of the decision required and the commitment and motivation which it generates.

It is important to recognise and understand one's own preferred style, its appropriateness to the situation, and its possible consequences. Flexibility of style can be effective – but only when the manager has the skill to change his style according to the circumstances and the people involved.

Case 4.7   We've all got a bit of Frank and Mike in us

'I suppose what really happened is that Mike saw me in a different light. I reckon he must have respected me more.'

What makes you say that?

'Some time after I had told Mike what I thought of him, he followed up his own suggestion and said we needed to talk. "OK", I said. "When?" Well, we arranged to go for a drink and dinner to really talk things through. We did, and I must say that meeting was one of the best I ever had with Mike. We thrashed out the company, its past, present and future. Mike's style, my style, and, most of all, our working relationship. As we talked, Mike grew to respect me more and more. He must have seen it coming, but I'm not sure he wanted it to happen, when I suggested that we should consider my leaving the company. Mike asked why; the relationship now seemed to be on a better footing.'

What did you say?

'Well … I agreed, but really I had gained more confidence during that time and I recognised it was time for me to do something else. We talked about my role and contribution to the company, but really I had made up my mind. We amicably agreed that I should go when it was mutually convenient. No hassle, no fights. Just a clean break.'

Hmm. Interesting. What did you learn from that experience?

'What did I learn …? Well, in a funny way Mike brought me fairly sharply face to face with my own problems. Not that I did not know I had them in the first place. I did, but I recognised how vulnerable I was. That was also really the first time I felt what it was like to be a manager. What was also good about the Mike experience was that I learned to handle difficult situations far better. It was more by accident than design, but I did gain confidence in myself. I learned to handle difficult situations. I learned to accept responsibility.

'You know, in a funny way we've all got a bit of Frank and Mike in us. The problem is doing something about it.'

Frank and Mike (Case 4.7) developed a collaborative problem-solving style in order to confront and discuss their and the company's problems. Through calm realistic discussion Frank recognised he needed to leave the company. Despite the fact that Mike was reluctant for his partner to do so, the mature discussion between the two men led to a clean break. Looking back on the experience, Frank felt he learned a great deal about being a manager from working with Mike. Probably the most important lesson for Frank was appreciating self-responsibility. Whether Mike was an easy or difficult person to handle, it was Frank's responsibility to manage the relationship to the best of his ability. Frank learned that one reason why the relationship was not as good as it could have been was that he (Frank) was not as effective as was required in the early days of establishing the company. A salutary lesson for us all.

SUMMARY

Managing interpersonal relationships in organisations involves all the following:

Interpersonal communication

Interpersonal communication is considered as being composed of two functions: information passing and relationship building. For effective information passing to occur, the quality and quantity of data and its relevance to the situation need to be considered. In order to ensure satisfactory understanding of the data being transmitted, each party in the situation needs to test assumptions and offer feedback. Relationship building involves individuals taking into account the values, needs and desires of others in order to be more supportive and approachable towards others. Appreciating the personal impact one makes on individuals and groups, is a necessary concern in relationship building.

Messages between persons occur through four separate channels: facts, feelings, values and opinions. Problems of miscommunication occur when messages sent on one channel are perceived to be sent on another. To reduce these problems it is necessary to try to identify and separate out those elements in the process of interpretation. Active listening is important, as well as the ability to evaluate and filter the enormous amount of information to which people are subjected every day. The relevance of messages to both the receiver and sender will also affect their attitudes to 'learning' them.

Interpersonal needs and behaviour

It is essential to understand the effects of interpersonal needs, particularly those of inclusion, control and affection, and the way in which people behave in interpersonal situations and social interactions. There are two dimensions of need – expressed behaviour (which is initiated towards others), and wanted behaviour (which we want others to initiate towards us). The three sets of needs are independent, but interact to produce behavioural outcomes which may have significant effects on the manager's effectiveness in his job.

Interpersonal tension

Tension may exist between individuals when certain of the aforesaid needs are not satisfied. This can be reduced by developing the knowledge and skills to manage interpersonal transactions, to avoid breakdowns in communication. Sympathy and active listening can assist in reducing conflict and threat, and the acceptance of facts as facts, feelings as feelings, values as values, opinions as opinions, and needs as needs.

Styles of interpersonal communication

One can define four styles of interpersonal communication, active listening, assertiveness, conflict resolution skills and problem-solving skills. Active listening involves offering attention, following the conversation and reflecting back. Assertiveness is the mid-point between submissive and aggressive behaviours and is about being clear and firm while being responsive to the other person. Conflict resolution entails reflective listening and assertiveness skills, the introduction of fewer communication blocks into the conversation and assessing the consequences of one's actions. Effective problem-solving is achieved through sharing information, obtaining commitment from the others in the situation and involving others in the decision-making process. Each style is appropriate in different situations and managers need to learn to modify their communication styles accordingly. The fundamental aim in using any of these styles is to turn one-way communication into a two-way process in order to reach some form of agreement about decisions and actions.

IN CONCLUSION

To manage interpersonal relationships, to work well with other people and to be able to lead a group successfully means being able to develop the skills of diagnosis and analysis of interpersonal situations, and also the skills of effective communication. The skills of diagnosis and analysis should not be seen as just thinking skills. They need to be recognised as natural, thinking and feeling, everyday skills. Looking at the situation and the impact of communication from the other person's point of view at least ensures sufficient sensitivity to allow a meaningful discourse between two people. You do not have to 'take on board' the other person's point of view, but just appreciate that your impact on them affects their communication with you.

5 Motivation to Work

Case 5.1   The finance department of Airways International

Airways International is a large, world-renowned international airline, operating most of the major air routes of the world. In order to provide such a comprehensive service, Airways International employs over 35,000 personnel. Perhaps not a glamorous department in which to work, but one which provides a vital service, is the accounting department.

In the accounting department approximately 1,500 staff are employed to arrange all the financial transactions involved in running an airline. One of their key activities is ticketing. Ticketing is a complicated issue in the airline business, as tickets purchased for a flight with a particular airline may be changed for a different flight with the same airline, or a different flight with a different airline, or a different flight to a different location with the same or a different airline, or may be surrendered for reimbursement. The accounting procedures are naturally complex and sophisticated. In addition, the current price structure allows for six different price tickets on any flight. As a result there exists a comprehensive manual to guide staff in their processing of tickets.

For some time now the manager of the accounting department, Eamon Devera, had been concerned about the motivation of his staff. One morning, after a particularly frustrating meeting with the chief executive, Devera walked through his department, more to cool off than anything else. That walk seemed to worsen rather than improve his ill temper. 'Hell, this place just looks like a factory!' thought Devera (nicknamed Dev). Hundreds of people work on each floor of the five-storey block. Each floor is open-plan so everyone sits next to each other at separate desks, each with their own keyboard and monitor terminals and at least two telephones.

'I've done the best I can here, but these floors are so large and impersonal. In fact, it's ridiculous that placards have had to be placed on each floor labelling the north, south, east and west faces of the building', reflected Devera.

In Devera's opinion, the hierarchical structure of the department had generated its own problems. There were ten grades between the lowest clerical assistant and the departmental manager. The differences between many of those grades, however, were primarily related to pay. Most of the problems occurred amongst the lowest grades, C1 to C5. Although the whole department was roughly divided into half men, half women, women predominated in these lower grades. Staff in all of these five grades talked of being bored in their work. Both absenteeism and staff turnover were high compared with turnover in the airline as a whole. An anticipated change of location for the staff prompted Devera to ring the human resources manager, Abraham Farringdon.

'Look, Abe, with this forthcoming change of offices, I want to be heavily involved in what is happening. I'm not having the same problems taken from one building to another. I just don't want my staff de-motivated again. I think we should meet', said Dev.

The subject of motivation simply covers the fundamental question, 'What stimulates people at work'? What drives people to do the things they do in their job? Further, how can such energy be harnessed to assist individuals to improve their performance at work? In fact, the term motivation is virtually a household word, as so often problems at work are attributed to poor motivation, or vice versa, as poorly motivated individuals generate a substantial number of work problems.

In Case 5.1 Eamon Devera recognised that a motivational problem existed in his department. Symptoms of demotivation such as high staff absenteeism caused him sufficient concern to call for help to improve the situation. Interestingly enough, Devera's view as to the causes of these symptoms ranged from the structure of the building in which his subordinates worked to the organisational and pay structure of his department. Whether Devera's views of the problems in his department are accurate or inaccurate, he has at least recognised that individual motivation and work performance are integrally linked. In fact, motivation as a concept is central to an appreciation of work performance.

If motivation is a topic of such importance, to what does it then refer? Motivation derives from the latin verb 'movere', meaning 'to move'. Movement implies *action* and, in order to act, *energy* and *effort* are required from the individual. The level of individual motivation is determined by the amount of energy and effort people put into their work. In order for a person to generate such energy and effort, they need to be stimulated by the work they do and the job they hold. In general, people are highly motivated when they are well matched to their jobs. It is the fit between people and their jobs which determines an individual's level of motivation.

An examination of these two crucial factors, the individual and the job, provides the basis for this chapter. We shall focus on individuals and explore the question of what determines individual motivation. We shall also examine jobs and analyse those properties of jobs that are considered motivational. Communication is important in that an individual's ability to negotiate for what he desires, and the ability of key managers in the organisation to respond appropriately, influence levels of motivation. Finally, we suggest what needs to be done in order to improve the levels of motivation of people in organisations.

WHAT DETERMINES AN INDIVIDUAL'S MOTIVATION?

An individual's motivation is the result of the interaction of needs, incentives and perception. Figure 5.1 indicates the motivational process for an employee in an organisation. Quite simply, individual motivation is determined by the extent to which the needs he brings to the job are matched by the incentives (such as rewards) provided by the organisation. This is a subjective process, for what one individual perceives as a satisfying incentive (eg a good salary) may not be satisfying for another. This subjective element in motivation is critical,

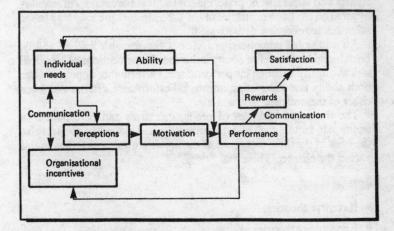

Fig. 5.1   What determines an individual's motivation?

for individuals react to their jobs in terms of how they see them. For this reason, managing workgroups is a difficult process. Not only does the manager of the group have to consider the objectives to be achieved and the means and resources available to achieve them, but he also has to raise the level of motivation of each individual in the group. A group that is poorly motivated is unlikely to make best use of the resources available or even attempt to acquire new resources. Under these circumstances, the whole group will require the manager's attention. Poorly motivated individuals in a group are likely to function below their level of effective performance and could also influence the other, more positively stimulated members and demotivate them. In this case, the manager will need to attend to the poorly motivated members, not only to improve their performance but also to minimise their disruptive influence in the group.

The relationship between needs, incentives and perception is influenced by communication between the individual and the organisation. Organisations that inadequately inform their employees of opportunities for them at work are likely to demotivate them. These employees are unlikely to show much respect to their employing organisation and hence possibly only do the minimum required. However, another form of communication exists, based on the views and beliefs of individuals. Poor performance can occur if individuals do not have the same views of their jobs as their bosses. The boss may wish the individual to undertake tasks which the individual considers are not part of his workload. Equally, the boss may hold different criteria and standards of performance to his subordinate. An inability to agree on the basic principles of the subordinate's job may lead to the subordinate becoming demotivated.

An additional complicating factor is the person's level of ability. Each individual's level of ability influences his perceptions of his job as well as directly affecting his performance. Performance improves when both ability and motivation improve. Performance deteriorates when either of these variables does.

The three key variables of needs, incentives and perceptions, in addition to factors such as communication and individual ability, form the basis of the three categories of theory we are going to review in this part of the chapter. These are:

- Need theories.

- Incentive theories.

- Expectancy theories.

Need theories

What are the needs of individuals?

If an individual's motivation level is partly determined by her/his needs then we must seek to understand what needs individuals have. The importance of needs as a factor in individual motivation is that needs initially arouse and energise behaviour; they are the prime causes of individual behaviour. At least three important theorists have described the needs individuals have.

Professor Abraham Maslow believed in a hierarchy of five types of need (see Figure 5.2): physiological, security, social, self-esteem and self-actualisation. Physiological needs are those associated with basic biological requirements, such as hunger or thirst. Security needs are related to needs for protection from danger and threats, such as attaining job security. Social needs are needs for expression of friendship or love or even working with a compatible group of people. Self-esteem needs are bound up with self-respect and personal autonomy. Self-actualisation needs are the needs for realising one's own potential, more often than not through undertaking challenging work.

Maslow suggests, in relation to his hierarchy of needs, that:

- each lower order need must be satisfied before the next higher order need assumes dominance.

- when an individual need becomes satisfied, it declines in importance and the need at the next level of the hierarchy increases in importance.

- when the individual moves up to the highest level need, satisfaction of this need increases in importance (self-actualisation).

- the number and variety of needs increases as an individual's psychological development takes place.

Maslow believed in a needs ascendency process, sequential in nature, whereby one particular class of needs must reach a sufficient level of satisfaction before the next needs level becomes operational. The emphasis is on sufficiency, in that each successive level must be relatively satisfied before the next level of need becomes more important in motivating behaviour.

An alternative view is that individual needs at work do not change in quite the systematic way Maslow envisaged. Perhaps

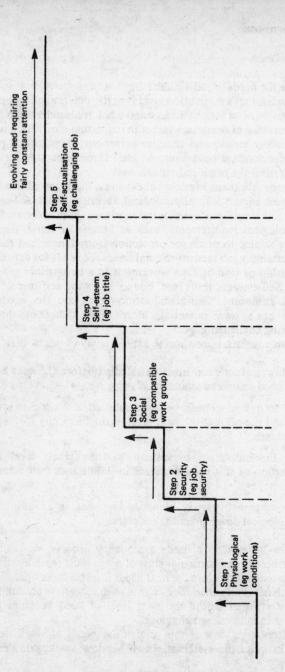

Fig. 5.2 Maslow's hierarchy of needs

Step 5
Self-actualisation
(eg challenging job)

Evolving need requiring
fairly constant attention

Step 4
Self-esteem
(eg job title)

Step 3
Social
(eg compatible
work group)

Step 2
Security
(eg job
security)

Step 1
Physiological
(eg work
conditions)

individual needs vary in relation to the incentives provided by the organisation. An individual could be involved in satisfying needs level 2 and 5 simultaneously. The attitude towards tenure in British universities and long-term employment in the public sector provide a good example. As a result of recession and the current emphasis on private sector development, job security is no longer guaranteed in such organisations. Hence, a university academic can be struggling to achieve tenure and security of employment and yet at the same time be involved in long-term, self-generated research. The academic may be satisfactorily managing both processes. Furthermore, needs can vary according to age and stages in an individual's life cycle.

The American psychologist Professor David McClelland also argues that many needs are not as universal as Maslow proposed. Many needs are socially acquired and vary from culture to culture. He defined three types of socially acquired needs: the need for achievement, the need for affiliation and the need for power. The need for achievement reflects the desire to meet task goals. The need for affiliation reflects the desire to develop good interpersonal relationships. The need for power reflects the desire to influence and control other people.

Further, McClelland argues that it is difficult for people to change their needs, once acquired. Pursuing this line of thought, it is important to diagnose needs at the selection stage. Managers can try to match individuals with particular needs to positions where these can best be satisfied. For example, an individual with a high achievement need should be in a job which offers high performance targets, like sales. A manager with a high power need should be in charge of the shop floor or a functional department – a position where he can exert control over others. A manager with a high affiliation need should be placed in a project team environment.

More recently, Professor Clayton Alderfer has developed a three factor theory of needs called ERG: Existence, Relatedness and Growth (Figure 5.3).

ERG theory relates closely to Maslow's hierarchy of needs in that existence is similar to Maslow's physiological and safety needs, relatedness is similar to Maslow's social needs and growth is similar to Maslow's esteem and self-actualisation needs. Alderfer makes three important points, which are illustrated in Figure 5.3.

• The less a need is satisfied, the more important it becomes.

• The more a lower level need is satisfied, the greater the

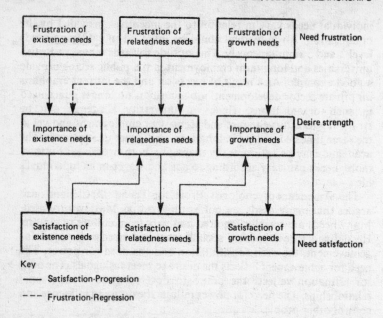

Fig. 5.3 Satisfaction-progression, frustration-regression components of ERG theory

Adapted from Steers, R. M. and Porter, L. W. (1979), *Motivation and Work Behaviour*, 2nd edn., McGraw-Hill, p. 34. Reproduced with permission from McGraw-Hill.

importance of the next higher level need.

- The less the higher level need is satisfied, the greater the importance the lower need assumes.

This last point, about need frustration, is particularly important. If individuals cannot get what they want in a job then they just demand more of what they can get. Hence employees may be disruptive at work, demanding more money, when what they really want is a more challenging job. It is important to recognise such 'displacement' behaviour if staff motivational problems are to be overcome.

Incentive theories

Whilst need theories answer the question 'What drives or stimuli cause individual behaviour?' incentive theories approach motivation from the other direction: 'What external factors influence human behaviour?' Managers have little conscious influence over the former, whereas they might have considerable influence on the latter. This is not to say that managers do not need to know about theories of individuals' needs; such knowledge is important for several reasons. A manager has only a limited number of incentives to offer employees. It is, therefore, important to select staff with needs that can be satisfied within the job/organisation. An organisation has a diversity of jobs with different sets of incentives. Needs theories can help managers identify and differentiate between individuals' needs and allocate individuals to jobs where they can best become motivated to task achievement. Lastly, whilst managers cannot directly alter individuals' needs, they can indirectly influence them by good management of the incentives through which they are satisfied.

Professor Frederick Herzberg developed his theory of incentives by asking a sample of employees, 'When you are satisfied at work, what is making you happy?' and, 'When you are dissatisfied at work, what is making you unhappy?' The result was Herzberg's famous two-factor theory (Figure 5.4). Herzberg termed the dissatisfiers the maintenance or hygiene factors, and the satisfiers the motivators. All the maintenance factors pertain to what are called the 'extrinsic' aspects of the job. Herzberg believed that if the maintenance factors were not provided to a sufficiently high standard then employees would be dissatisfied. If they were

Hygiene/maintenance factors	Motivators
Company policy and administration	Achievement
Supervision	Recognition
Salary	Work itself
Interpersonal relations	Responsibility
Physical working conditions	Advancement

Fig. 5.4   Herzberg's two-factor theory

provided to an acceptable standard employees would only 'not be dissatisfied'; they would still not be motivated. High motivation can occur only when individuals experience both maintenance factors and motivators.

The Herzberg theory is easy to appreciate and readily applicable in organisations. However, two points are not satisfactorily considered. First, certain factors, in particular money, can be both satisfiers and dissatisfiers. Second, not everyone is motivated by the intrinsic drives; someone's motivation can easily be influenced by their age and the stage of their life.

Money is a complicated motivator because it can be used to satisfy a number of different individual needs. For example, it can be used to purchase a house, thereby satisfying a basic physiological need; it can be used to give frequent cocktail parties, thereby satisfying a social need; or it can be used to buy expensive cars, thereby satisfying a need for self-esteem. Many individuals do not place a high priority on money as a work incentive, but place high priorities on items that can be purchased with money.

Despite the conceptual problems surrounding it, money plays several important roles in relation to the individual and his orientation to work. At its most basic, money is used to compensate employees for their effort in the job. There is often a 'market rate' for the job, meaning some generally agreed upon range of payment. Sometimes money is only one part of the reward package. The UK is renowned for its widespread use of fringe benefits, which can often supplement the straight salary quite significantly.

Further, money allows individuals to compare their jobs with jobs held in the past, with those of other individuals, and those in other organisations. Such comparisons can be highly motivating, for the individual can reasonably accurately attribute worth or merit to a job or organisation. Equally, money can give rise to many anxieties of inequity, since individuals can inflate their salaries when talking to colleagues. Secrecy surrounding pay policies in many companies aggravates this particular problem.

Whether money is viewed as a positive or negative motivator, it is a concrete means of measuring a job. Money is also utilised as a mechanism for indicating standards of individual performance. Merit rises, percentage increases, or incentive pay, allow managers to reward their staff for competent performance. Whether the amount offered is significant or insignificant, in absolute terms it may be a psychological boost to the individual, and so a powerful influence on him.

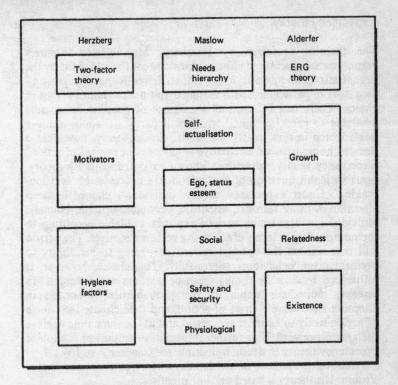

Fig. 5.5 Theories of motivation: similarities between Herzberg, Maslow and Alderfer

The need and incentive theories so far discussed can be compared (Figure 5.5). Maslow's, Alderfer's and Herzberg's theories overlap considerably. Maslow suggests that there are five needs – physiological, safety, social, self-esteem and self-actualisation; Alderfer suggests that there are three – existence (Maslow's two basic needs), relatedness (Maslow's social need) and growth (Maslow's esteem and self-actualisation needs). Herzberg, more simply, implies that individuals have only two needs: one that equates to Maslow's esteem and self-actualisation needs and Alderfer's growth need, and the other that encompasses all the lower needs identified by Maslow and Alderfer. In fact, most job attitude questionnaires in common use today reflect the need structures of all three theories.

Expectancy theory

The theories proferred by Herzberg, Maslow and Alderfer emphasise satisfaction of either extrinsic needs (provided for by the organisation) or intrinsic needs (inner drives within the person). One issue in particular that is assumed and not explained is that of choice. There can be a limitless number of possible behaviours available to each individual which will partly or wholly achieve goals which in turn satisfy his needs. Consequently, how does a person choose between alternative behaviours or courses of action? Expectancy theory, sometimes known as instrumentality theory, deals with this question of the individual's processes of 'decision-making'. Under expectancy theory, individuals choose between alternatives using rational, scientific, economic criteria. Namely, individuals will examine various rewards available according to their desirability in terms of satisfying personal motives. The person will then choose the optimal reward according to his ability to perform given behaviours successfully. This choice, however, is influenced by how he thinks these behaviours are rewarded. In essence, individuals weigh up the probabilities of success in adopting alternative courses of action, and then choose the course of action likely to be most successful and at the same time achieve the greatest reward. (For further information on the application of expectancy theory to decision-making, see Chapter 7, p. 184.)

A strong proponent of expectancy theory is Professor Victor Vroom. His theory is based on four premises:

1 People have preferences (or valences) for various outcomes or incentives that are available to them.

2 People hold expectations about the likelihood that an action or effort on their part will lead to the intended outcome or objective.

3 People understand that certain behaviours will be followed by desirable outcomes or incentive rewards, for example a pay rise or increased status.

4 The action a person chooses to take is determined by the expectancies and preferences (valences) that the person has at the time.

Vroom proposes that individuals will be highly motivated when they feel confident of achieving high performance, the attraction of the rewards is high, they feel that they are likely to receive the

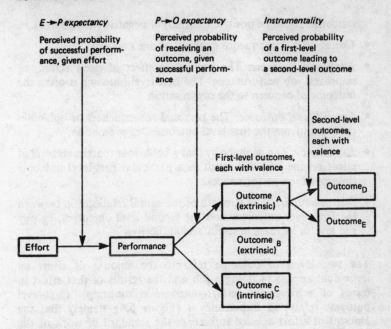

Fig. 5.6   Major terms in expectancy theory
Source: Nadler, D. A. and Lawler, E. E. III (1977), 'Motivation: A
Diagnostic Approach', in Hackman, J. R., Lawler, E. E. III and
Protek, L. W. *Perspectives on Behaviour in Organisations*, McGraw-
Hill, p. 23. Reproduced with permission from Ed. Lawlar III.

rewards if they perform highly and they feel fairly rewarded relative
to others around them.

From this basis, Vroom developed a decision tree model, whereby
the individual could attempt to quantify the degree of required
effort by being able to plot out the results of his efforts (see Figure
5.6). Utilising the decision tree, the individual could assess his
chances of meeting those task goals in relation to the amount of
effort required, and equally consider whether the likely rewards for
achieving task goals would be appropriate.

The original Vroom model has been modified by a number of
researchers. The following terms are now commonly used to
describe expectancy theory.

- *Valence*: The strength of a person's preference for a particular outcome. It can be positive (desired) or negative (not desired).

- *Outcome*: A consequence or result of one's actions.

- *First-level outcome*: The immediate effect of one's action, eg improved job performance. The first-level outcome is often the outcome of concern to the organisation.

- *Second-level outcome:* The personal consequences or outcomes that result from the first-level outcomes, eg promotion.

- *Expectancy*: The probability that a behaviour (particular level of effort on the job) will result in a particular first-level outcome (improved job performance).

- *Instrumentality*: The strength of the causal relationship between the first-level outcomes and the second-level outcomes, eg pay rise and/or increase in status and authority.

The two levels of outcome refer to the amount of effort an individual applies to doing a job and the results of that effort in terms of achievement (effort–outcome relationship). First-level outcome relates to Expectancy 1 (Figure 5.6), namely that the amount of effort applied influences the standard of work of the individual (effort–performance relationship). Second-level outcome relates to Expectancy 2 (Figure 5.6), namely that the standard of a person's work is influenced by the incentives offered by the organisation (performance–incentive relationship).

It can be appreciated, therefore, that a person's performance and preferences influence his level of motivation. Performance has been subdivided into the following characteristics:

- Productivity, ie how efficient the person is in achieving tasks

- Internal task goals, ie those goals to be achieved in doing a task that the person is internally motivated to achieve

- External task goals, ie those goals to be achieved in doing tasks that are required of the individual by the organisation and which the individual may or may not be motivated to accomplish.

An individual's preferences, namely the expected result of the application of effort, have been subdivided into:

- Intrinsic components, ie outcomes that the individual is

internally motivated to achieve, such as self-development or gaining valuable experience on the job.

• Extrinsic outcomes, ie outcomes that the individual desires from the organisation, such as increased status or promotion.

Despite all these developments the basic cores of expectancy theory (expectancy, valence and instrumentality) have not changed.

Despite the multiplicity of variables, it should be noted that expectancy theorists do not postulate that people consciously and rationally go through this process of decision making. Expectancy theory highlights the rather complicated and subjective process of reaching a conclusion to act in a particular way, emphasising the individual's assessment of his abilities to attain certain goals, the amount of effort required for particular outcomes and the probability of his effort being rewarded. All these are scrutinised in relation to personal needs and wants. Expectancy theory does not necessarily provide a model to assist individuals in the making of decisions, but examines the process by which individuals choose to behave.

WHAT DETERMINES MOTIVATION ON THE JOB?

So far, the person-oriented components of motivation have been examined. We have explained:

• Behaviour, in terms of purposeful behaviour to attain desired goals,

• Rewards and satisfaction in terms of those rewards and satisfaction that keep people working towards task goals.

• The fundamental relationship between task goals and human needs.

Needs, incentive and expectancy theories are covered by these components.

The other key variable in any discussion of motivation is the jobs that people hold.

Understanding the requirements of the job is a vital and equally complex factor in trying to improve employees' performance at work. How many individuals really understand what is required or expected of them in their job? Further, most jobs alter in terms of tasks to be undertaken, as do people's performance expectations. At times, the individual and the boss may not be aware of the implications of such changes and only understand what is happening in retrospect. Such a state of affairs has implications for the performance, rewards and satisfaction of the individual. Whilst in some cases the individual does not know what is expected of him, in other cases the problem is that the employee reports to more than one boss and they have differing views of what is required.

Equally, rewards can influence an individual's motivation to do well in his job. There are three sorts of reward: money, position (status), and fringe benefits (travel, company car, vacation paid by the organisation). The combination of rewards, the promise of rewards (incentives) and the individual's own perceived value of those rewards will influence his present and future drive and performance.

In addition, the environment and culture of the organisation influence the individual and his performance in his job. Certain basic conditions – such as typewriters or word processors not functioning properly – will, not surprisingly, negatively affect the performance of secretaries. More sophisticated factors can also influence people's performance. Devera (Case 5.1) considered that, although basically comfortable, the office was a big, impersonal, non-caring environment that was largely responsible for the absenteeism and turnover problem. He wanted to enhance the environment in order to improve work attendance and job performance.

Case 5.2 Could I just have a word?

'I'm sure the group is as frustrated as I sometimes feel. I'll ask a couple of them what they consider the problems to be! I need to give Abe Farringdon some idea of the problems in my department', thought Devera.

This Thursday morning was just like any other morning; a hot, sticky, Los Angeles traffic jam did little to improve Devera's mood.

He felt no brighter when he arrived at work. Walking towards his office, he met Kamina Fell, one of the senior ticketing clerks.

'Hey, Kamina, good to see you. Could I just have a word? I was just thinking this morning, driving to work, what is wrong with this place? What do you think?'

'You're very serious at this time of the morning but I'll tell you, it's too big; it's too impersonal. Look, Dev, I'm just off to a meeting but this is a serious problem and we need to talk about it again', responded Kamina.

'Thanks. Speak to you soon,' said Devera.

Devera asked to see some more of the clerks in his office and spoke to three more over coffee and lunch.

On his way home, he reflected on the day.

'Well the few people I've spoken to seem to be saying the same thing. The place is too big, too impersonal and people don't really know each other. One or two complained about their pay and some others talked about regrading, promotion and the social facilities provided by the company. If only the organisation would treat them better.'

Devera's brief conversations (Case 5.2) with some of his employees led him to conclude that the physical environment was the problem. Interestingly, few people gave information about their needs and desires (other than pay) and no one seems to have mentioned the content of the job. The question is, is that anywhere near sufficient information to begin to formulate any policy for increasing employee motivation?

Work design

The structure of any job can induce different expectations and behaviour patterns in each job holder. For one sort of job, the expectation could be that 'The harder I work, the more bored, fatigued, tired, depressed, I will become'. For another job, the expectation could be the reverse – self-satisfaction, a feeling of greater professionalism, accomplishment, and possibly greater extrinsic rewards (pay, status, promotion). Irrespective of extrinsic rewards, the first job is unlikely to stimulate greater effort in the individual, whilst the second is likely to induce a higher level of performance.

Thus the job itself is a vital source of expectancy, and hence motivation, amongst individuals in organisations. An individual constantly experiences the consequences of his work-related performance. The job itself is the point in the organisation where individuals are likely to see the most direct connection between how they do their work and what outcomes they receive. Hence it is important to understand how the nature of jobs and the design of work affect an individual's behaviour in organisations.

Work design has been well researched, but no one method has emerged as the best way to design work and structure jobs. Historically, one of the more influential approaches is the scientific management approach developed by Frederick Taylor (see Chapter 1). Taylor postulated that work needs to be broken down into manageable tasks. The work at hand should be quantitatively (scientifically) studied to determine how each element of work can be done most efficiently. It is then possible to develop a structured approach to task activities, which allows for precision in training to ensure that each worker masters only these skills required. Successful task completion would be rewarded by monetary bonus payments.

At the turn of the twentieth century, with the introduction of new technologies, new work processes (eg the continuous work flow principle of the production line), the emergence of new occupational groups and the dawning of concepts such as job and organisational effectiveness, Taylor's principles had, and even today have, a popular appeal. Theoretically, with Taylorism, mistakes are unlikely as each worker is only involved in part of a production process, a part in which he has been well trained. Such a system should lead to high product quality and a reduction in cost through standardisation.

For a number of decades, scientific management principles have strongly influenced management thinking in terms of task design and supervision. The subject of work study is based on Taylor's thinking. Leading international consultancy organisations, such as Urwick Orr, and McKinsey, have applied scientific management and work study as an integral part of their service, although McKinsey's have, for some time now, developed in magnitude of approaches and sophistication of application.

Although Taylor's theory is popular and simple in concept, a number of serious criticisms have been levelled against it. Research has repeatedly shown that jobs that are too simplified and routinised are likely to make workers feel dissatisfied and demotivated. Most individuals require some degree of personal growth stimulation, challenge and recognition, which will not be met under the Taylorist approach. Well documented cases show that when people's needs are not met in their job, complaints increase, people are increasingly likely to report fatigue, productivity drops (at first insidiously), absenteeism is liable to increase and even violence and sabotage occur.

Case 5.3   Just what do you know about your people?

'OK, OK, OK! Yes, I know you care about your department, Dev, but I have to ask you again - just what do you know about your people?' asked Abe Farringdon, the human resources manager of Airways International.

'I don't know what you really mean by that question! I know my people well. I know what turns them on and off!'

'Look, Dev, you're well known in this company as a good manager, but to what extent have you really tried to find out why you have an absenteeism and turnover problem?'

'Well, I've spoken to a few of the girls and one or two of the male operators and they say they just couldn't give a damn. The place is impersonal, too big, nobody knows each other, so what the hell; taking a couple of days off work now and then, who cares. The company doesn't!' responded Devera.

'Yes, but how did you talk to them? Where did you meet them? What questions did you ask? How, for instance, do you know you're not the problem? How do you know that such behaviour is problematic? Why are you so sure you've identified the problem?' questioned Farringdon.

'Hey! I just don't get you, Abe? You mean I should condone absenteeism?' responded Devera.

'No, Dev. What I'm saying is, have you really got on to their wavelength? Do you really know how they see their problems? Have you been systematic about your interviews with your staff or have you just been stopping people in the corridor? Just imagine, we'd have a real problem if you, like myself, see absenteeism as a problem but they don't,' replied Farringdon.

'Yes. I see what you mean. I've just had casual conversations with people if and when I meet them and all they seem to do when I talk to them is moan. I suppose I ask for it. All I do, most of the time, is ask them what their problems are. Yes, you're right. I'm just not sure how my staff see their situation,' replied Devera.

'Dev – I don't think your situation is at all unusual. You're running a big department. You're a busy man. Hell, how many times do I really sit down and talk to my managers?' said Farringdon sympathetically.

Pause.

'How about this for an idea, Dev? Why not let my researchers do a study on you, your department and your people. At least you'll get a more objective view of what's happening. That should help in clearing up the problem,' continued Farringdon.

'Hmm! Just wondering how my people will respond. They're busy guys. What makes it worse is that you could be seen as sneaking around for me instead of me handling the absenteeism problem,' frowned Devera.

'Don't be too worried about that. We can discuss in detail how to handle the people in your department. The best principle is honesty. But, fundamentally, you've got no objection?' enquired Farringdon.

'No, I think it's a good idea as long as we can handle it right,' commented Devera.

'OK. Then let's talk about how to get the project going,' exclaimed a delighted Farringdon.

Abe Farringdon (Case 5.3) challenged Devera's perception of the motivation problems in his department. Devera was asked to examine the sources of information and the way the information he held was gathered. The process of information gathering is as important as the information itself, for the way people are asked to provide information can influence their response. Farringdon was questioning whether the view Devera put forward was just his perception, or was really an accurate profile of the department. Not accepting Devera's view or the manner in which he communicated with his people, Farringdon suggested he undertake a study of Devera's department. Devera, recognising that he had not fully explored the views of others on the subjects of absenteeism and staff turnover, agreed to the project. More personal information is required concerning people's feelings about their job, their degree of personal satisfaction and as a result the degree to which they feel motivated by what they do.

In contrast to Taylor, two American Professors, Richard Hackman and Greg Oldham, focused on the concept of job enrichment, which is essentially a combination of scientific management principles and existing behavioural theories of motivation. From their original study examining job characteristics, three psychological states were seen as crucial to both motivation and satisfaction on the job:

1 The person must *experience the work as meaningful*, as far as his own values are concerned. If the job appears to him to be trivial and insignificant, he is unlikely to be internally motivated.

2 The person must *experience responsibility* for the results of his work, so that he is aware of his accountability for work outcomes. If he views the quality of the work done as depending more on external factors than on his own efforts, he has no reason to feel personally proud when he does well or deflated when he does not.

3 The person must have *knowledge of the results of his work*. If he rarely finds out whether he is doing well or badly, he has no basis for feeling good about doing well, or unhappy about doing badly.

The more an individual experiences these three psychological states, the more he will experience intrinsic motivation, namely motivation based on doing the job, rather than on external rewards. Hence, the person is likely to have positive feelings when he considers his work as meaningful. He is likely to have a high sense of self-regard, for he can measure his own effectiveness and in turn needs to be held accountable for the results of his efforts.

Hackman and Oldham identified a number of specific job design characteristics that, if competently managed, will stimulate these psychological states.

Experienced meaningfulness is composed of three elements:

1   Skill variety – a job which requires a person to use a number of different skills and talents to carry out a variety of different activities. A person with a job in which he has to stretch his talents, skills and abilities is likely to feel his job is worthwhile.

2   Task identity – a job which requires completion of a whole and identifiable piece of work, with a visible outcome. Doing a whole job, putting together an entire product, being able to point to an item in a shop window and say '*I* made that', is more satisfying than being responsible for only a small part of the job.

3   Task significance – a job which has a significant effect on the lives of other people. Putting drawing pins into boxes is likely to be experienced as less worthwhile than putting medical prescriptions into bottles, even though the skill levels required for the jobs may be the same; in the second case, lives may be at stake.

Experienced responsibility for work outcomes has one element, namely, autonomy and this relates to freedom, independence and discretion in scheduling one's own work and determining the procedures to be used in carrying it out. As autonomy increases, so people seem to feel more personal responsibility and involvement in the successes and failures that occur on the job, and are more willing to accept personal accountability for the outcomes of the work.

Knowledge of results of work activities is composed of two elements:

1   Feedback from the job; actually carrying out the work activities gives some direct clear information about the effectiveness of the worker's performance.

2   Feedback from others; other people, supervisors, co-workers, etc., give the worker information about how well or badly he is doing.

Feedback from the job is more immediate and more potent on the employee than feedback from other people. The individual is able to look at the work he is doing and gauge directly how well he is performing based on sound data which he can use for job behaviour change.

These core dimensions of skill variety, task identity, task significance, autonomy and feedback, influence the level of the critical psychological states (Figure 5.7) experienced by the job holder in terms of experienced meaningfulness of the work, experienced responsibility for work outcomes, and knowledge of results of work activities. High levels of the critical psychological states are likely to lead to favourable personal and work outcomes, such as high internal motivation, high work performance, high satisfaction and low absenteeism and turnover.

However, there are moderating factors related to individual differences between people. Employees have differing growth need strengths which affect the influence of the job dimensions on internal motivation and performance. People with high needs for personal growth and development will respond positively to jobs which are high on the core job dimensions; people with low growth needs will feel 'overstretched', and unable to cope with jobs which are high in these dimensions. (See Figure 5.7).

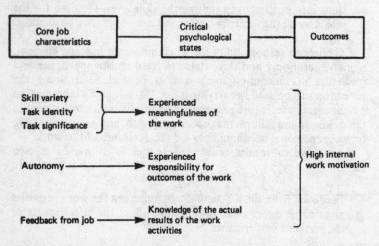

Fig. 5.7 Job characteristics that foster high internal work motivation
From Hackman, J. R. and Oldham, G. R., *Work Redesign* © 1980 Addison-Wesley, Reading, Massachusetts, p. 77, Fig. 4.2. Reprinted with permission from Addison-Wesley.

The motivating potential of a job does not directly cause employees to be internally work motivated. A job high in motivating potential creates conditions such that, if the job holder performs well, that behaviour is likely to be reinforced. Job characteristics, then, provide the framework for internal motivation. Whether individuals experience their jobs as highly motivating depends upon the characteristics of the individual.

Hackman and Oldham argue that not all jobs should be enriched or designed to be high on the core motivation dimensions. The nature of the work, the job as envisaged by management, and the particulars of the individuals holding the jobs, all need to be taken into account in determining how the job should be designed.

Case 5.4 The survey results

'The low job characteristic scores are reflected in the low scores for growth satisfaction. It seems, however, that the slightly improved evaluations of context satisfaction have somewhat counteracted perceptions of job characteristics in the rating of general satisfaction. Internal work motivation is surprisingly higher than ...'

'Hold it, Herb. Hold it. *Hold it, Herb*,' screamed Eamon Devera.

Herb Winter was not allowed to finish his sentence.

'What the hell are you trying to say?' continued Devera.

Herb Winter, a recently graduated PhD behavioural scientist from USC (University of Southern California) had been hired to conduct the staff motivation survey in the accounts department.

Silence.

Herb Winter looked around the group, somewhat on edge.

'Look, take it easy on the guy, Dev', said Abe Farringdon, finally breaking the silence.

'Let me take you through what these figures really mean. First of all your people seem to be fairly poorly motivated,' said Abe Farringdon.

'Oooeeh,' drawled out Eamon Devera.

'OK, OK. Climb up from under the table, Dev. If you look at the figures closely, there are some significant differences. Now take your five grades, C1–C5. Although motivation seems fairly low across your grades, the higher up the hierarchy (C3, C4, C5), the more motivated people seem to be. The one particularly problematic group is C1. Let's try and find out why. Any comments, Herb?' asked Farringdon.

Herb looked nervously around the room. 'I think what you are saying is right, Abe.' Pause. He continued.

'As stated, the department scores particularly low in the five job characteristic measurements. These measures fall into the lower half of the scales except for task identity. However, examination of the context satisfaction scores are slightly higher than task characteristic scores, which suggests some contentment with the extrinsic elements of work. Grade C1, in particular, seems...'

'Abe, for Christ's sake *Help!*' interrupted Devera forcefully.

'OK. Thanks, Herb,' chuckled Farringdon. 'It seems that the lower grades feel more OK with the department, the way it's administered, the pay, the bonuses and so on. Also some good news is that C1 grades identify quite highly with what they are doing, but they feel there is not much variety of work. They'd like a bit more autonomy. They feel their jobs are unimportant in terms of the rest of the work of the department and they'd like the supervisors to talk to them more on how they're getting on.'

Devera looked thoughtful. Then he said, 'So what you're saying is, basically, the problem is not so much the department or even the type of work, it's the fact that their jobs could be made more interesting. They want more of a say in what they're doing, they'd like the supervisors to talk to them more and they'd like to feel a little bit more important. Yeh?'

'Yeh,' replied Farringdon.

'You know, I thought these guys just came here to pick up the pay cheque. I just didn't know they wanted more out of life. So what do we do?' asked Devera.

The survey suggested (Case 5.4) that, for all grades, intrinsic motivation is a problem. The higher up the hierarchy, the more exciting the jobs seem to the survey participants, in terms of being better defined and of higher importance. From Devera's point of view, individuals in the lower grades had acted out behaviours, such as lower productivity and absenteeism, indicating they were uninterested in the work, so that he (Devera) did not consider them worthy of attention in terms of trying to improve their jobs. The survey crystallised the lack of understanding between Devera and his department over work needs. It is also worth noting the different styles of data feedback highlighted in Case 5.4. Terminology commonly acceptable to behavioural scientists can be unintelligible jargon for managers.

STRATEGIES FOR IMPROVING MOTIVATION

Motivation problems arise when there is a lack of fit between individual needs and work characteristics.

In exploring the choice of alternative motivational strategies, it is necessary to diagnose the problems carefully and systematically. Individuals need to be differentiated in terms of whether they hold strong needs for growth (such as needs for creativity, challenge, opportunity, further learning) or strong social needs for positive relationships with others, or just basic existence needs, such as

Needs	Incentives	Outcomes
Growth needs: Self-actualisation Achievement Challenge	Growth Opportunity Challenge Job content	A results-oriented performance appraisal Job enrichment Management training Quality circles
Relation needs: Affiliation Companionship Competition Power and status	Workgroup Leadership Supervision	Situational leadership Autonomous workgroups Organic organis- ational designs
Existence needs: Security Safety Physiological	Job security Pay Fringe benefits Working conditions	Job tenure Staff benefits Job design by accountabilities

Fig. 5.8   Alternative motivational application approaches

needs for job security and improved pay and working conditions. The need(s) to be satisfied will require different approaches (see Figure 5.8).

Intervention programmes

1   *A results-oriented performance appraisal* attempts to assess an employee's effectiveness on his job by measuring actual accomplishments. The results-oriented performance appraisal defines a set of predetermined goals against which actual performance is measured. There are a number of advantages in using this appraisal. It measures actual performance results rather than performance predictors like personality and job factors. It differentiates performance goals for different levels and functions of an organisation. Lastly, it can provide a basis for relating performance to organisational rewards. A results-

oriented performance appraisal motivates by challenging individuals and directing their energy in their jobs. (See Chapter 12 for further information on appraisals.)

2   *Job enrichment* is one way of changing the intrinsic element of a job to make it more interesting to the individual. Job enrichment, sometimes called vertical job loading, allows individuals not only to perform more task components, but also to have more responsibility, autonomy and control over the tasks they perform. Further, the range of skills the individual needs to learn is likely to increase. Hence, job enrichment is an important motivational programme because it stretches the individual more; the individual has a greater sense of accomplishment, his attitudes to work become more favourable and relationships with both higher management and subordinates improve.

3   *Quality circles* as a form of employee involvement have taken root recently in the United Kingdom and Continental Europe. The idea is quite simple. The foreman is the key. He gathers around him a small group of workers in his work area, who agree to meet regularly on a voluntary basis. Their aim is to identify and solve product and quality problems by investigating and analysing their causes using the simple techniques they learn in special training sessions. The quality circle then applies the solution if it has the authority, or presents management with its recommendations. Improved quality is the obvious result, but increased motivation also occurs through participation in decision-making and increased worker status and dignity.

4   *Management training*. Employees may be taken off the job for a formal management training programme run either inside or outside the organisation. The success of the training depends on a number of factors including the length of the programme, how the individual was nominated for the programme, the number of participants on the programme, whether the programme is residential or not, and the contents and teaching styles used on the programme. With good training programmes individuals may find themselves totally reappraising their attitudes and behaviours towards their jobs, and motivation often receives a considerable boost.

5   *Situational leadership*. The essence of situational leadership is that no leadership style is absolutely right for all situations. The selection of good leadership style depends on the characteristics of the leader himself, those of his subordinates, and the specific

requirements imposed by the job situation. An effective leader is able to adapt his style to suit the job situation and the characteristics of his subordinates. The key factors here are the motivational and task-related abilities of his employees. Reduced to its simplest terms, when an employee is poorly motivated and not very capable, the boss will need to supervise fairly closely, whereas when an employee is highly motivated and extremely capable, the boss will be more effective supervising in a much more distant manner. Thus the manager's leadership style can serve either to stifle the subordinate's motivation or to exploit and develop it. Managerial style and subordinate motivation go hand in hand. (See Chapter 7 for further information on leadership styles.)

6   *Autonomous work groups* are an essential element of work design technology. A group is given a whole task and substantial autonomy in deciding how to do the work. Consistent with this approach is that rewards are linked to the performance of the total group, rather than to individual performance. The success of an autonomous workgroup is influenced by the design of the work, membership of the group, the interpersonal skills of the group members, and the support from the organisation. Where autonomous workgroups operate well, the motivation of individuals is increased through stronger relationships with colleagues and greater challenge and fulfilment on the job.

7   *Organic organisational designs* introduce flexibility into the organisation to help it adapt to internal and external pressures. The salient characteristic is the cross-functional grouping on horizontal, vertical and diagonal levels. Under this design, members of a number of functional specialities are pulled together to work on a specific project for a finite period of time. Project structure and matrix structure are two examples of organic organisational designs. Used successfully, these designs provide employees with challenging job experiences, facilitate interactions between functional specialists and often change the traditional boss–subordinate relationship to more of a peer relationship. In addition, the individual tends to have more freedom of action in his work. (See Chapter 11 for a full account of organisation structure.)

8   *Job tenure* occurs when an individual is guaranteed a job for life in the organisation. It is characteristic of lecturing staff at

universities in the United Kingdom. The effects of job tenure on the motivation of the individual can be twofold. Individuals may tend to avoid or not undergo experiences such as stress, especially when jobs are at risk in time of recession. Under these circumstances, job tenure tends not to promote positive attitudes and performance. When it does promote positive attitudes, these tend to take the form of increased commitment to the organisation and possibly increased risk taking in decision-making. Essentially it releases individual creativity as safety/existence needs are satisfied.

9   *Staff benefits.* A number of rewards are not tied to individual performance. These vary from health insurance premiums, cars, private telephone expenses and luncheon vouchers to cut price goods manufactured by the company. Sometimes such staff benefits may increase one's reward package over and above one's straight salary by a considerable amount. Such rewards tend to do little in encouraging high employee motivation. They may induce a sense of a 'caring management' and loyalty from employees. Staff benefits, if mishandled by the company, may trap within the company the very individuals whom the company would be most pleased to let go.

10 *Job design by accountabilities.* In keeping with the philosophy propounded by Taylor, but not his recommended practice, certain companies, especially in North America, are clarifying jobs by the different accountabilities incumbent on the job holder. In high tech companies especially, where it is difficult to specify tasks and sub-tasks due to the rapidly changing nature of work patterns, people's performance is assessed by the results of their work. Hence, the objectives on which the individual is held accountable become the focus of attention. Concentrating on accountabilities has a number of advantages. The changing nature of work patterns is reflected in the programme appraisal system. The individual is likely to be motivated since he is offered the opportunity to apply his skills and creativity to solving work problems. The superior/subordinate relationship is likely to improve, as both parties have to agree the range and type of accountabilities incumbent on the subordinate. Ownership of the tasks to be undertaken is likely to be high as the person is given some choice concerning the way in which the task is completed and he is scrutinised on the results of his work.

Case 5.5 *Improving morale in the accounts department*

'So what to do?' muttered Farringdon. He continued, 'Right now let's take a real close look at these survey results, and this time listen to what Herb Winter has to say!'

'OK,' said Herb. He went on.

'Take a close look at incentives. C1 and C2 grades evaluate their jobs lowly, whereas C3-C5 employees appear to be more internally motivated by their work. O.K?'

Devera nodded.

'C1 and C2 grades report low growth satisfaction in their careers whereas C3-C5 grades are moderately satisfied with their opportunities for personal growth. You should also look at context satisfaction scores ...'

Herb smiled at Devera and said, 'What I mean to say is, let's look at the environment in which the work is done. Let's look at security, pay, supervision and satisfaction of social needs. Greatest satisfaction is with pay, followed closely by security. Just moderate satisfaction is expressed with supervision and social aspects. Supervision dissatisfaction is felt strongest by C5 workers. All staff seem reasonably OK with social relationships and training, except for C2 staff. "Being kept informed" is perceived as OK by C1 grades, whereas C4 and C5 grades indicate dissatisfaction with the information they receive,' he finished abruptly.

Devera looked thoughtful. He finally asked, 'So how do you suggest I get my people motivated?'

The ensuing discussion lasted for the next hour and a half.

'OK. So let me read out what we've agreed,' exclaimed Devera.

'First, improving the motivational levels of the staff in the accounts department cannot be done by just a blanket approach. Each particular group has to have its particular needs seen to. Second, I should examine the task, activities and jobs of C1 and C2 grades in terms of trying to make the work more interesting for them. I understand that this may have implication in terms of their pay. On this one, Herb and Abe, I'd like your help. Three, I need to examine what sort of information is required by C5 grades and see if it can be provided. Four, take one or two sections of C5 employees and restructure their work, more on a team than an individual basis.'

'Yeh, good point,' put in Farringdon. He continued, 'This is probably the best approach as we assume that the work rather than just standards of supervisor skills is the problem. But you're also going to introduce some supervisor skills training programmes, yeh?'

Devera nodded.

'Hey, guys. We've done it,' smiled Farringdon.

'Dev, why don't we start this whole thing nice and easy. Of the C5s, why not take Wilma's group and just see what we can do about improving team performance. Let's bring in Wilma from the very beginning. Then we can look at some of the C1 jobs,' finished Farringdon.

'That's fine by me!'

The motivational application approaches finally agreed to in Case 5.5 involved an examination of C1 jobs with a view to introducing a job enrichment scheme at that grade. Further, it was decided that more autonomous workgroups should be the pattern of operation at the C5 grades. In addition, it was recognised that certain basic support factors in the organisation such as improving management information systems (MIS) and basic standards of supervisory skills required attention. These strategies have been adopted because a number of jobs in the accounts department were perceived as having low motivating potential, whereas the employees indicated a high personal growth need, and the survey results highlighted low growth satisfaction. Hence, any improvements to be introduced into the accounts department needed to increase motivating potential.

Communication and motivation

The perception an individual has of himself, the job, the tasks to be undertaken, the groups with which he interacts and the overall organisation, strongly influences his level of motivation. However, in such a statement one assumes that the individual understands what incentives the organisation has to offer. It should not be assumed that such understanding exists, for low levels of motivation can be the result of misunderstanding of such important subjects as incentives. A job satisfaction survey recently conducted by Dr Susan Vinnicombe amongst secretarial staff of a large accounting practice in London revealed a great diversity of feeling towards the salary structure. On further probing it became evident that about 40 per cent of them did not know that there was an annual appraisal system from which merit rises were awarded. Here is a classic example of poor communication from management to staff which led to unnecessary frustration and demotivation. To counter this example with one illustrating good communication between management and staff, Airways International was severely cutting back on its cabin crew. Management took great pains to reassure its staff that this would only take place via natural labour wastage rather than through any redundancy programmes. This helped to maintain staff's feelings of job security, which could otherwise have been severely threatened.

Individuals can be poorly motivated not directly by the incentives or lack of incentives offered by the company, but because they have not fully understood them. Not presenting adequate information and not adequately explaining developments in the organisation can lead to low levels of motivation. As indicated in Figure 5.9, the percentage match between individual needs, organisational factors such as work conditions and relationships, salary, job design and the manner in which the two components are communicated, leads to high or low levels of motivation amongst employees.

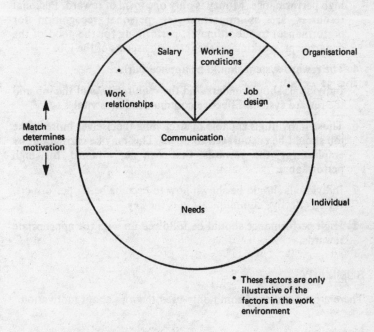

* These factors are only illustrative of the factors in the work environment

Fig. 5.9   The role of communication in motivation

Action levers

In applying motivational concepts to the work situation, a number of specific 'action levers' are available to managers:

1 It is important to diagnose needs, abilities and preferences for rewards at the recruitment stage. Not the 'best' candidate, but rather the one who most appropriately matches the job and organisation, should be hired.

2 Once individuals are in the job it is important not to assume that their needs will not change. They need monitoring, probably annually. Such monitoring can be conducted by the manager through an unstructured interview or using a structured questionnaire.

3 Managers need to understand what rewards they can give for high performance. Money is only one form of reward. Personal resources are as important (eg personal recognition for performance) to subordinates, performing for the good of the department, working on the intrinsic aspects of the job.

4 The reward system should be applied fairly.

5 Individuals should understand the requirements of the job and the reward system. Effective communication is vital.

6 Those individuals capable of stretching themselves more in the job should be encouraged to do so. This may be carried out by emphasising the rewards that can be attained for high performance.

7 Individuals should be shown how to become better performers. Again effective communication is the key.

8 High performance should be followed up with the appropriate rewards.

SUMMARY

There are a number of commonly-used theories about motivation.

Needs theory

Needs theory refers to the sort of needs experienced by individuals and highlights the importance of needs in arousing and energising behaviour. Needs act as the prime causes of individual behaviour. On this assumption, it is important to identify the variety and in-terrelationship of needs possessed by individuals.

Three influential academicians have done work along these lines. Maslow postulated a hierarchy of five types of needs – physiological, security, social, esteem and self-actualisation, in that order. He suggested that each lower need must be satisfied before the next higher order need assumes dominance. Further, when the individual moves up to the highest-level need (self-actualisation), this need increases in importance as the person attempts to satisfy constantly evolving higher order needs. Also, the number and variety of needs increases as the person attempts to satisfy constantly evolving higher order needs. Also, the number and variety of needs increases as the individual's psychological development takes place.

McClelland argues that needs are more socially acquired. They vary from culture to culture and are not as universal as Maslow suggested. McClelland identified three types of socially acquired needs, need for achievement, need for affiliation and need for power. McClelland further argues that individuals would find it difficult to alter the balance and composition of their particular needs. Therefore, attention should be given, at the recruitment stage, to establishing the strength of needs held by the individual in order to match him to a job which can largely satisfy those drives.

More recently, Alderfer has developed a three-factor theory of needs he termed ERG, ie existence, relatedness and growth, which closely resembles Maslow's hierarchy of needs and the sequential and systematic manner of needs satisfaction.

Incentives theory

Incentives theory approaches motivation from the premise that external factors influence behaviour. In Herzberg's two-factor theory, two factors – hygiene factor and motivation factor – in combination provide the incentives or disincentives to apply greater effort to work. The hygiene factor is the extrinsic aspects of the job such as money (salary, wages), working conditions, company policy, supervision and interpersonal relations.

Providing a high standard of service on the hygiene factor side would only ensure that employees would not be dissatisfied. In order for them to be motivated, sufficient attention needs to be given to the motivation factor, ie intrinsic aspects of the job, such as achievement, recognition, responsibility and advancement.

Expectancy theory

Expectancy theory concentrates on the concept of choice, namely how does a person choose between alternative behaviours and courses of action? Expectancy theory, sometimes known as instrumentality theory, looks at how individuals make decisions. Emphasis is placed on rational and scientific approaches to decision-making. Individuals will examine the various demands available according to their desirability in terms of satisfying personal motives, choose the optimal reward, and then apply behaviours that are most likely to attain the reward and, depending on how these behaviours are perceived, be rewarded. A strong proponent of expectancy theory is Vroom, who developed a decision tree model whereby the individual could quantify the degree of effort required by plotting out the paths he should take in order to achieve his desired rewards.

Work design

There are two main approaches: scientific management and the job characteristics model. Under the principles of scientific management, it is considered that work can be broken down into manageable tasks. Work can be studied quantitatively in order to determine how each element of work can be most efficiently conducted. From there on, it is only necessary to train operatives in the skills of the particular task activities they are required to fulfil. Successful task completion would be rewarded by monetary bonus payments.

In the job characteristics model, whereby research identifies three psychological states which are considered crucial to both the person's motivation and satisfaction on the job, the person must experience the work as meaningful, the person needs to have knowledge of the results of his work, and the person needs to feel the responsibility for the results of his work, so that he is aware of his accountability for work outcomes. If these three fundamental experiences are felt to be positive, then it is likely high work performance will result from high internal motivation, high satisfaction and low absenteeism and turnover. However, other factors can disturb this relationship, such as individuals having different growth needs, which could result in dissatisfaction due to being overstretched in terms of response to challenges. Further, satisfaction with the overall organisational context, such as pay, job security, co-worker and supervisor relationships, and the degree of knowledge and skills required to do the job, will all influence internal motivation.

By combining the key elements of needs, incentives and expectancy theory, it is possible to develop strategies for increasing the levels of motivation of individuals. It is necessary to question whether particular individuals or a critical number of people in the organisation have growth, relations or basic existence needs, what incentives are required to meet particular needs and, hence, what training or development approaches need to be considered. These can be broken down into ten intervention approaches, namely performance appraisal, job enrichment, quality circles, management training, situational leadership, autonomous workgroups, organic organisational designs, job tenure, staff benefits and job design by accountability.

Communication in organisations

Communications in organisations are important influences on the motivational levels of staff. Lack of effective communication can demotivate. Ineffective communication involves both inadequate and unclear transmission of information. The match between individual needs and factors such as work conditions, relationships, salary, job design and the manner in which these factors are communicated can lead to high or low levels of motivation amongst employees.

IN CONCLUSION

Motivation is a vitally important concern. Its importance arises from the simple but powerful truth that poorly motivated people are likely to perform poorly at work. Such a state of affairs is most probably undesired by both employer and employee.

Depending on what problems are perceived, it is possible to work out suitable approaches to improving the motivational levels of personnel in the organisation. Levels of motivation in the organisation can always be improved, but that really depends on management wanting to probe how people in the organisation are working, thinking and identifying with what they are doing. You see, to probe means that management are likely to find out something about themselves, as well!

6 Groups

Case 6.1 Bridge Building Company

Three months ago, Jack Grayson was on top of the world. Now he wondered why everything seemed to be crumbling around him. He turned to Dick Carroll, his main contracts manager, and whispered incredulously ...

'Tell me once again, Dick. Now you say that there's no way we're going to make the completion date for the local authority contract. You know there are penalties for over-running. You've told me repeatedly that everything was on schedule. What the hell's gone wrong?'

Jack knew this was not going to be an easy meeting.

Jack Grayson was the local general manager of the Bridge Building Company. The company had been founded by Jack's father in the 1950s. He had been a civil engineer, and the company had specialised in that type of work, cashing in on the construction of new motorways in the UK in the 1950s and 1960s. Recently the company had branched out into general construction, and particularly house building. Three months ago it opened a local office in Milton Keynes, an expanding new town about fifty miles north of London, in order to service the South Midlands area and to increase the housebuilding segment of the company's activities.

Jack himself was twenty-nine. Being the boss's son he had an advantage in his career progression in the company. He'd gone to public school, then university, where he studied geography. He wasn't particularly numerate, but he had spent five years in head office, learning the ropes, and he certainly gave people, especially clients, the impression that he knew what he was talking about. So it was natural for him to head the Milton Keynes office, and he had big plans to make it a success.

Starting up a new office wasn't all that easy, as he quickly found out. There were staffing problems. Many of the people Jack wanted didn't want to move up from London, and the office was eventually staffed almost entirely by locals, with only the finance manager being a Bridge Building Company man. Jack had in total seven managers reporting to him, and, with secretarial and service staff, the office had eighteen employees. So it was a small operation, and Jack couldn't understand how in three months his high hopes had turned into sour realities.

The local authority contract – now that was in progress when he took over the area, controlled locally by a contracts manager, Dick Carroll, and it had only five months of a one-and-a-half year contract period still to run. Bridge Building Company had contracted to build sixty-four timber-framed houses for one of the local authorities, Newton Borough Council. Competition had been fierce and there wasn't much slack in the tender price. Certaintly, there had been problems as it went along, but Dick had always managed to sort them out, and it was only in the last three months that progress seemed to have slowed almost to a stop.

Jack Grayson had instituted a weekly management meeting on Friday afternoons when he took over. He felt the only way to keep on top of things was to know what was going on, and the purpose of those meetings was to share information and report on problems. All seven of the managers attended. Jack Grayson, of course, Dick Carroll and Ben Gibson, the two contracts managers, who looked after the construction sites; Frank Warner, the finance manager; Ed Cochrane, purchasing; Angela Bader, sales and promotion; Mike Rathbone, planning; and Peter Johnson, personnel. Most of them were based in the local office anyway; only the two contracts managers worked out in the construction sites themselves. The exchange described above took place during one of these weekly meetings.

Groups and their constituent members make an organisation into a combination of interlocking and interactive systems working towards achievement of compatible goals, rather than a collection of individuals performing different activities and satisfying solely individual needs. The very term 'group' implies some form of common activity, some form of mutual collaboration, although such expressions as 'groupthink' and 'committee' raise doubts about the value of groups.

In Case 6.1, Bridge Building Company's local management team is an example of a group working in an organisation. Like all groups, it faces problems. It has not been formed very long, and is probably still trying to establish some form of identity. It is likely that personal goals and defensive/attacking behaviour characterise the interactions between members. Conflict is to be expected in this situation; each member takes their own personal values, attitudes, and objectives into the meeting. There may be some struggling for power and status. It should be expected that the group is anything but integrated.

This chapter will examine the role of groups in organisations, the influence of groups on individuals, and of individuals in groups. It will look at the uses of groups, group behaviour and dynamics, and show how groups develop norms and cohesiveness which affect their performance. It will discuss how groups make decisions, and the roles that individuals prefer to perform in group settings. Finally, it will suggest ways to good management of groups, and their role in the development of organisations.

WHAT ARE GROUPS?

A number of people queueing for a bus, the crowd watching a football team play; the main board of a professional organisation; a project team – are they groups? Professor Edgar Schein defines a group as 'any number of people who interact with each other, are psychologically aware of each other, and who perceive themselves to be a group'. Under this definition, the first two examples are not groups: they are collections of people. The third and fourth examples are likely to be groups, depending on the degree of interaction required by their tasks.

In organisations, groups are used for many purposes, and their members attempt in many cases to satisfy their individual needs through their groups. Groups can be classified in four categories.

1 *Formal groups*. These are created by design, by formal authority. A section of a department in an organisation is a formal group. The normal workgroup consists of a manager and his immediate subordinates, and the whole organisation consists of an interlocking system of such workgroups, as shown in Figure 6.1.

    The manager acts both as leader and co-ordinator for his own workgroup activities, and also as a member of the workgroup for which his boss is the leader and co-ordinator, and so on up the hierarchy of formal authority within the organisation. Formal groups are normally permanent, in that they exist and are seen to exist within the structure of the organisation as shown in the organisation chart, although their membership may change as promotion, leaving or internal movement occur. Some may be temporary, where task groups or project teams are set up to achieve specific tasks, eg a new product launch, or management of a particular contract.

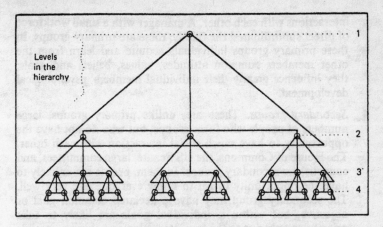

Fig. 6.1   The organisation: an interlocking of work groups
From J. Schermerhorn, *Management for Productivity*, 1984, p.
402. Copyright © 1984. Reprinted by permission of John Wiley
and Sons, Inc.

2   *Informal groups.* Within every organisation, and not necessarily
    parallel to the formal organisation structure, individuals will
    interact with others who are not necessarily members of their
    formal groups. They may form relationships with them and
    create informal groups, whose existence is the result of chance
    or of personal preference. Even within formal groups, sub-
    groups may form of individuals who like to interact with one
    another, and who share values and beliefs which may be
    at variance with those of the main formal groups. This can be
    stimulating for the organisation, especially where change is
    required and the subgroups are the agents for change; but it can
    also sometimes appear threatening to the other members of the
    main group. All groups exist to satisfy the needs of their
    members – informal groups exist to satisfy those identity, social
    and security, or task needs which interpersonal interactions
    within the formal group may not be able to achieve. They also
    act as grapevines – informal networks of communication which
    managers and individual members can use to collect
    information which they need in their work, and which may not
    be available to them through formal channels.

3   *Primary groups.* These consist of a small number of people
    performing a common task who have regular personal

interactions with each other. A manager with a small workforce
of direct subordinates; the family; these are primary groups. In
these primary groups individuals acquire and learn from the
other members common attitudes, values, beliefs and goals;
they influence greatly their individual members' psychological
development.

4 *Secondary groups*. These are, unlike primary groups, large
numbers of people who form groups, but who do not have the
opportunity to have much social interaction with each other.
The House of Commons, the US Senate, large committees, and
councils, are secondary groups. In them, people are unlikely to
have the opportunity to get to know everyone else very well.
The secondary group may have a declared common goal or
objective, but within it individual goals are likely to take
priority, mostly due to the low interaction and sharing possible
between individuals in this setting.

Within organisations, the main groups to which individuals
belong are the formal workgroups to which they have to belong by
the very positions in the hierarchy they hold. Also they may join or
form voluntarily one or more informal groups, which evolve
naturally to provide satisfaction to the congruent or related needs of
their members which are not satisfied in the workgroups themselves.

Use of groups in organisations

The management team of Bridge Building Company, in Case 6.1, is
a *formal primary group*. It was created by design, by formal
authority; and it consists of a small number of people (eight,
including the boss, Jack Grayson), performing a common task (co-
ordinating and sharing information), who have regular interactions
with each other.

With many millions of meetings occurring in organisations each
day, and with the prevalent feelings of dissatisfaction regarding
time-wasting, costs, and pointlessness of these meetings, it is useful
to identify the various functions that groups can perform. Professor
Charles Handy of the London Business School has done just this
(Figure 6.2).

Formal, permanent groups probably serve most of the purposes
described by Handy. Formal, temporary groups are more likely to
carry out tasks which fall into the last three of Handy's categories, ie

1	For the distribution of work, to bring together a set of skills, talents and responsibilities and allocate them their particular duties.
2	For the management and control of work, and to allow work to be organised and controlled by appropriate individuals with responsibility for a certain range of work.
3	For problem-solving and decision-taking, bringing together a set of skills, talents and responsibilities so that the solution of any problem will have all available appropriate resources applied to it.
4	For the processing of information; for passing on decisions and information to those who need to know.
5	For collecting ideas and information.
6	For testing and ratifying decisions; for testing the validity of decisions taken outside the group, or ratifying such decisions.
7	For co-ordination and liaison; for co-ordinating problem-solving and tasks between departments, functions or decisions.
8	For generally increased commitment and involvement; allowing and encouraging individuals to get involved in the plans and activities of the organisation.
9	For negotiation or conflict resolution; for resolving disputes or arguments between levels, departments, functions or divisions.
10	For inquest or enquiry into the past.

Fig. 6.2   The uses of groups in organisations. From C. Handy, *Understanding Organisations,* Penguin, (1976). Reproduced with permission.

innovation (R & D, product development, the raising of external captial), policy (corporate strategic planning, environmental and specific market research) and breakdown (capping an oil well blowout, managing the assets of a company in receivership).

Groups, then, tend to be used in organisations for activities which require the co-ordination of individual functions or tasks, where, in fact, the task can be carried out better by a group than by an individual. Further, where such projects require interactive behaviour and interdependence of activities and particularly the generation of new ideas or creative solutions to problems, groups bring more than an individual perspective to a problem, and by pooling ideas and perceptions are more likely to come up with the best possible solutions.

Formal groups with a high degree of formalism and structure are likely to work well on structured, routine tasks. Everyone knows his place in this type of group, knows what is expected of him, and if motivation and skill levels are adequate, high performance will ensue. Formal groups with a low degree of formalism and structure are likely to cope better with ambiguity, task uncertainty, and a changing environment. Such a group does not rely so much on specific direction and control, but each member has a degree of interdependence on the other members, and also a degree of independence of thought and actions which prevents them being tightly constrained by rules and procedures.

So organisations form and use groups to achieve certain of their objectives. But what does the individual member of a group get out of it? To a certain extent, this is determined by the size of the group and its composition.

Size and composition of groups

The larger the group, the more difficult it becomes for the organisation to achieve managerial control over group objectives. The group tends to take off on its own, to have a separate group identity, and is likely to try to determine and achieve its own objectives, which may or may not match those of the organisation. Although a large group (fifteen plus members) may have greater resources of technical skills, interpersonal skills, and cognitive abilities, there is likely to be less mutual interaction, less group process participation, than in a small group. Large groups, if not carefully managed, subdivide into smaller subgroups, which reduces the cohesions of the main group.

The composition of the group also affects the individual and organisational outcomes. *Homogeneous groups* whose members have similar backgrounds, experience, values and beliefs, eg all are from the same function, tend to produce high member satisfaction and less conflict. There is, however, a pressure for conformity which may in fact submerge overt conflict within the group, and this may surface elsewhere in the organisation, where members interact with other organisational members. Groups which are homogeneous are likely to deal well with routine tasks, whether simple or complex. In contrast, they may be less effective when faced with complex, non-routine problems which require innovative and creative approaches.

Heterogeneous groups have members whose backgrounds, experiences, values, and beliefs are diverse, eg cross-functional task teams set up to carry out specific projects. These groups are likely to be able to make higher quality business decisions which have greater acceptance among those affected by them. They are likely to display greater creativity and innovation and possess, inherently in their composition, the characteristics necessary to produce enhanced group performance. Whether or not this creativity materialises is a function of the members' commitment, willingness to manage internal conflict, the application of their technical and interpersonal skills and ability – in fact, the group dynamics which occur as a result of members' interactions.

Case 6.2 The meeting

Dick Carroll looked defiantly at Jack Grayson and replied.

'Nothing in particular's gone wrong, Jack. It's been a whole series of little incidents which have all added up to cause these delays. The weather's held us up on our outside work. I haven't been able to get the roofs on the last block of houses, and you know that was scheduled for three weeks ago. And we're held up for materials for the plumbing on the previous block too. I've asked Ed about them, but he hasn't been able to get much joy out of the suppliers.'

Jack turned to Ed Cochrane, the purchasing manager. Ed was a dour Scot who knew his job inside out; super-efficient, he was obviously going places, and earmarked for promotion. Ed said: 'Well, I'm not sure it's entirely the fault of the suppliers, Jack. They're waiting for the fittings from the manufacturers, they say. But I know their sales manager quite well, and I'm pretty sure from the hints I can pick up that the real reason we're not getting the goods is that we're behind in our payments to them.'

Jack felt himself going red. Before he could speak, Frank Warner, the finance manager, took up the point. 'Before you fly off the handle, Jack –yes, we are behind but we're only taking an extra month's credit. I've spoken to their accountant, and he understands the situation, that we're just waiting for a stage payment from the local authority and then we'll bring them up to date. You remember that when we set up this office your father said it was to be self-financing. The only way we can do that in these early days is to get the money in as quickly as possible and to avoid paying out to creditors for as long as we can. We have to finance wages and salaries too, and there's no other way we can manage.'

'But we should have had £90,000 in a fortnight ago,' stabbed Jack.

'Perhaps so, according to schedule. But we aren't working to schedule, are we', Frank smiled and turned the knife in Dick Carroll. 'And anyway, the local authority quantity surveyor is being a bit sticky about quality, isn't he, Dick?'

Frank looked at Dick and let his words hang in the air.

'That's enough.' Jack Grayson glared aggressively round the table. 'We're not getting anywhere here. This isn't a management team, a group working together, it's a bunch of crazies out on a points-scoring spree. I'm closing this meeting to let things simmer down, but I want you all back here at ten o'clock on Monday morning. We'll talk this through sensibly then. Ten o'clock will give you, Dick, and you, Ben, (the other contracts manager) time to start up your sites and get back here. Yeh, it's good to get conflict into the open, but all our jobs are on the line if we don't make this office a success. And stop smirking, Angela. I haven't forgotten how you screwed up the advertising for our last show house. We're all in this together, so let's see how we can get our energies directed into co-operation instead of in-fighting all the time.'

Bridge Building Company's (Case 6.2) local management is a formal primary, but also heterogeneous group. It was set up by design to manage the organisation as a cross-functional group. It would appear to be not too structured, but as yet is not adequately coping with the problem it faces. At present, the dynamics amongst its executives vary from defensive to aggressive. The group is not integrated and is likely to work best on routine tasks. In essence, the group needs to learn how to manage crises. As part of the process, it is up to the leader to help the group recognise that they still require further development.

GROUP DYNAMICS

Within a group context, whether it be a task team launching a new product, the members of a board in a directors' meeting, a manager with his immediate subordinates, or colleagues working in a committee, there are countless social and interpersonal interactions which make members more psychologically aware of themselves and each other, and begin to influence each other. Interaction leads to an awareness of interdependence and to the satisfaction or non-satisfaction both of the group's needs, and of those individual personal needs which each person takes with him into the group situation.

Working in a group can satisfy individual needs such as those identified by Maslow (see Chapter 5), ie:

• *Security and safety needs*: the individual feels protected within the group. The group to which he belongs is more powerful than he is as an individual.

• *Social needs*: interaction with others either with the same background and experience, or working on a common task, can give him a sense of belonging, identity, and affiliation with the other members.

• *Self-esteem needs*: where a group achieves its objectives and receives positive feedback, this recognition enhances the individual's self-concept. In turn, if the individual makes a positive contribution to the task and receives recognition for this from the other members, further enhancement occurs.

• *Self-actualisation needs*: some individuals perform best in group situations and satisfy to a large degree their needs for self-fulfilment in a group context.

• One more need can be added to the needs identified by Maslow.

• *Needs for power* can also be satisfied in groups: either power over the other members of the group, or by using the power leverage of the group to effect the changes in the organisation which individual members, by themselves, cannot achieve. Certainly working and interacting with others in groups can reduce individual frustrations and anxiety, can develop in individuals the skills of affiliating with others, and can help individuals verify or modify their individual perceptions of other people and the environment.

But what happens in groups? What happens when individuals meet and interact in a group situation? What activities are carried out, what attitudes, values and beliefs influence what occurs in the group process? A model of the group process is shown in Figure 6.3.

Not all the outputs are always achieved in the forms which the individual members, the group, or the organisation require or expect. Let us look at the group process, which moderates these required outputs into real outcomes, in the way outlined by George Homans in his classic study of group process *The Human Group*. He established that all groups have three elements in common: activities, sentiments, interaction; and that there was both the 'required' behaviour of a group and the 'emergent' behaviour which actually occurred.

Required and emergent behaviour

Required behaviour is what the organisation sees as necessary for task performance and membership of the organisation, and has informed members accordingly; in return it offers rewards and benefits for this performance and membership. These necessities may take the form of punctuality, co-operation with other members

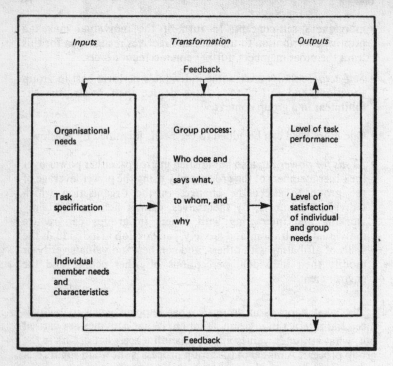

Fig. 6.3   Group process model

of the organisation or its environment, achievement and maintenance of prescribed performance standards.

Emergent behaviour is what group members actually do – either
within the organisation's prescription or as a modification or an
exception to it. This could be in the form of, say, restriction of
output where members feel they are not being rewarded equitably
by the organisation, or unprescribed social activities where
members feel a sense of belonging with the group.

Individuals make individual decisions on emergent behaviour.
Organisations make organisational decisions on required behaviour. Both can be either beneficial or detrimental to group and
organisational outcomes and effectiveness. Organisations with
cultures and climates in which emergent behaviours enhance the
required behaviours are likely to have groups which identify with
the organisation, have healthy group dynamics, and achieve their
individual and group goals.

Activities, sentiments and interaction

Activities are what people actually do in groups. Some activities are directed towards achieving the group task, some are done to satisfy personal needs, and others contribute to maintaining group harmony. These activities may be physical or verbal. They may be measured or described in terms of productivity, performance or social satisfaction. They may be prescribed by the organisation (required activities) or carried out by individual choice (emergent activities).

Sentiments are those values, beliefs and attitudes which individuals take with them into a group situation, or learn from other members in that situation. The social power of the group is such that new members may be socialised into attitudes and behaviours that they did not possess or had not clarified before entry. From an organisation's point of view, it is important that those new learned attitudes and behaviours fit in with its required behaviour.

Interactions are social transactions which occur between group members. In this definition, 'social' means 'interpersonal' and refers to behaviour between individuals relevant to both task achievement or maintenance of group harmony and morale, or directed towards achieving satisfaction of personal needs. Interactions involve communicating and receiving information on task activities or on individual sentiments (see below – Group interaction).

All these three elements are interdependent. *Sentiments*, the feelings which individuals take into the group situation, affect the behaviour, *activities* and *interactions* of members within the group itself. Changes in any one of the elements affect the other two. A group required to undertake an *activity* ie solve a problem or carry out a task, for which it has inadequate individual or physical resources may find that the *interactions* between individuals deteriorate, which may have a negative effect on the feelings which individuals have towards the group (*sentiments*), as it faces failure instead of its usual success.

Group interaction

Case 6.3   'We can work together'

At ten o'clock on Monday morning, Jack Grayson looked round the table at his managers.

'Where's Frank?' he asked.

'His wife phoned in. He's got another asthma attack,' said Peter Johnson, the personnel manager.

'OK. We'll just have to make do without him. I've been looking at the books over the weekend anyway, just to really know how things are. Now what can we do to get back to schedule with these local authority houses at Newtown? That's our main priority. Then, more important, we've got to learn to work as a team, not as eight people pulling in different directions. I spoke to Dad yesterday, and I'm under pressure to make things happen here. He's not prepared to back us much longer and says we'll pull out of Milton Keynes if it doesn't work. So, as I said on Friday, your jobs are on the line, as well as mine. Let's get down to business.'

Angela Bader (sales and promotion) spoke up. 'Dick Carroll had a rough time on Friday. We were probably being unfair on him, for the problems have only arisen recently. Looking at some of his earlier reports it looks as if the main problem has been that the Newtown Borough Council quantity surveyor, who was dealing with our contract and okayed our monthly claims, injured his back three months ago, and his job was taken over by his No. 2, this bright young kid who seems to want to make a name for himself. Dick says he's been nitpicking all the way, unreasonably so, trying to save the Council money by rejecting materials and work that would previously have been passed by his boss. Dick, would you like me to have a word with him – I've got to see him anyway as I'm negotiating for the Brown Street work at the moment.'

'That's not a bad idea, Angela,' said Dick. 'He's probably more likely to take it from you than me. I just can't seem to hit it off with him at all.'

'I've been examining the critical path analysis, too,' volunteered Mike Rathbone (planning). 'We've got a fair bit of slack on the plumbing operation, although that roofing is fairly critical. Now that the weather seems to be improving we can use the spare labour to start landscaping, which will save some time later on. And Ed,' he turned to Ed Cochrane, the purchasing manager, 'you're so on the ball that we've got plenty of materials already on site, so we won't be delayed on general progress except for those faulty chimney flue liners which the manufacturers admit don't comply with safety regulations, and have agreed they'll have to bear consequential damages.'

Ed laughed, 'Yes, I know you've all thought I was crazy to get the stuff on site too early, and sure, it caused some storage problems, and sure, it tied up money in inventory – although Frank seems to have found a way out of that by not paying our bills! But it's paid off if it's going to help us get this contract moving again.'

The atmosphere in the meeting was different from Friday. People actually seemed to want to help each other. Jack Grayson sat back and listened to Ben Gibson.

'I can reschedule some of the work I'm doing on our private housing at Wellcome Road. I'm ahead of schedule at the moment, Dick, and our sites are only two miles apart, so let me know your requirements if you want some more men, and I'll switch them over for you.'

'Thanks, Ben. I could certainly use a gang of four to start the foundations for the next block. Because we're behind, our usual subcontractors can't meet our needs this time as they've got other promises to keep. I was going to see you, Peter [personnel], but I'll certainly take up Ben's offer.'

'OK, folks,' said Jack Grayson. 'Things seem a little brighter today than they did on Friday. Mike, let me have a look at those revised schedules and we'll see if there are any other short cuts we can take. Angela, keep me posted about how you get on with the QS. And I think we've got a lot to do, so let's get on and do it. If we can work together and for each other the way we've done today we'll make a damn good team.'

In Case 6.3, the interactions which members entered into with other members have different characteristics from those in Case 6.2. On the Friday, members displayed mostly self-oriented behaviour. Dick was seeking sympathy; Frank was scoring points and defending/attacking. In Case 6.3, however, there were genuine attempts by the members of the group to address their problems and co-operate with each other. In effect, the group displayed task-oriented and maintenance-oriented behaviour. (See Figures 6.4 and 6.5.) The group climate was genuinely much more supportive. The group was developing into an integrated working unit. The interactions which took place had positive, not negative, outcomes both for task progress, and for inter-member relationships. It is also worth noting that it was Jack Grayson (group leader) who confronted the group with its poor performance. The role of the leader in improving workgroup effectiveness cannot be under-estimated.

Social interactions between members of a group fall into three main areas: task-oriented behaviour, maintenance-oriented behaviour and self-oriented behaviour.

1 *Task-oriented behaviour* is concerned with achieving the tasks or objectives of the group. It includes solving problems, initiating structures and controls, ensuring that individual members agree with what the group is trying to achieve. It is identifying and using positively the relevant skills and abilities of the individual members. It means moving forward and monitoring that progress towards task achievement. Several specific task-oriented behaviours are shown in Figure 6.4.

2 *Maintenance-oriented behaviour* maintains the morale and harmony of the group and creates an atmosphere and climate

Proposing, initiating	Initiating ideas, suggestions, courses of action relevant to the task.
Building	Developing proposals which others have initiated.
Giving information, clarifying	Offering facts, opinions, or clarification relevant to the task.
Seeking information	Asking for facts, opinions or clarification from other member(s) of the group.
Supporting	Giving a direct or implicit declaration of agreement with another member or his proposal or ideas.
Disagreeing	Giving a direct or implicit declaration of difference of opinion or criticism of another member's proposal or ideas.
Testing understanding	Seeking to establish whether or not an earlier contribution has been understood.
Summarising	Giving a summary of task progress to date.

Fig. 6.4   Task-oriented behaviours

conducive to a worthwhile contribution. It is concerned with the personal values of the members and is in many ways related to the satisfaction of the members' individual interpersonal needs – such as the needs for inclusion, control and affection (see Chapter 4). Attempts to satisfy these needs are reflected in the level and degree of interaction in the group. Several maintenance-oriented behaviours are shown in Figure 6.5.

3   *Self-oriented behaviour* aims to achieve personal, individual goals within the group situation. It is motivated by the individual's need for power or to build alliances, status and prestige, or to protect his self-concept and perceived image by others. It is sometimes difficult to see the difference between maintenance-oriented behaviour and self-oriented behaviour:

Gate-keeping	*Opening:* Positively attempting to involve others in the discussion, or
	Closing: Excluding or attempting to exclude others, cutting off or interrupting others.
Encouraging	Being warm, friendly, supportive, or responsive to others by verbal or non-verbal means.
Harmonising, reducing tension	Being prepared to compromise, and actively accommodating others, in order to preserve group harmony.
Giving feedback	Giving positive feedback on feelings and opinions contributed by others.

Fig 6.5   Maintenance-oriented behaviours

the same behaviour may be displayed, but the motive for this behaviour, eg gate-opening or closing, may be either to maintain group harmony or to satisfy personal needs. Figure 6.6 shows several specific self-oriented behaviours.

The group process therefore consists of various behaviours displayed by members to satisfy either the task or objectives of the group (task-oriented behaviour); or to satisfy the individual member's needs (self-oriented behaviour) or to maintain morale or harmony in the group (maintenance-oriented behaviour). The processes any group adopts will strongly influence the success of a workgroup as illustrated in Figure 6.7.

GROUP DEVELOPMENT

All groups go through various stages of development, and workgroup effectiveness is also a product of how the group has managed to cope with the problems it faces in each of those stages. There appear to be discrete and progressive stages in group development, each characterised by different activities and behaviours. These stages have been described in different ways by

Attacking/ defending	Attacking or rejecting others', or defensively strengthening one's own, position.
Blocking/stating difficulties	Placing blocks or difficulties in the path of others' proposals or ideas without offering alternative proposal or giving a reasoned argument.
Diverting	Moving the discussion away from areas in which you feel your position is threatened or weak.
Seeking sympathy/ recognition	Attempting to make others sorry for you, and therefore willing to support you; or actively attempting to gain positive feedback on the value of your contribution to the group process.
Withdrawing	Refusing to make a contribution.
Point-scoring	Seeking to score points off other members to enhance your status.
Over-contributing	Monopolising discussion in the group, using the group process to satisfy individual power and control needs.
Trivialising/ diluting	Picking on minor points of discrepancy of others' proposals or contribution in order to undermine their positions.

Fig. 6.6   Self-oriented behaviours

several researchers. A summary of five models of group development is shown in Figure 6.8.

From this comparison it is clear that group development is primarily concerned with the interactions between individual members which help the group to develop from a collection of individuals into a cohesive integrated unit. The five studies share certain common characteristics, such as the cautious initial interactions that group members enter into on joining a new group, the friction and interpersonal conflict that can arise as group members become acquainted with each other and the ability of group members to accept individual differences and attempt to form a cohesive group. Developing integrated and self-supporting groups will involve the four following strategies.

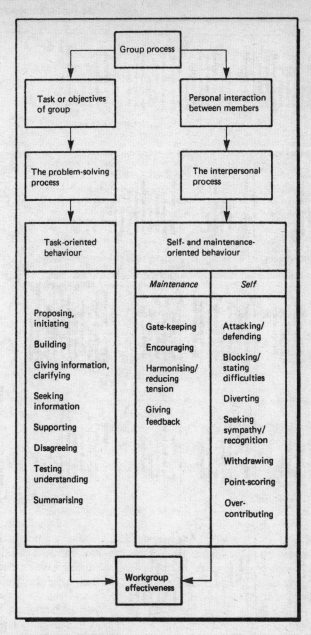

Fig. 6.7   Group processes

Fig. 6.8 Five models of group development

From J. P. Wanous, A. E. Reichers and S. D. Malik, 'Organisational Socialisation and Group Development: towards an integrative perspective', *Academy of Management Review*, Vol. 9, No. 4, 1984, pp. 670–83.

Schutz's (1958) FIRO model	Modlin & Faris' (1958) Four-stage group developmental model	Whittaker's (1970) Integrative model	Hill & Gruner's (1973) Three-stage developmental model	Tuckman's (1965) Integrative model
Stage 1: In or out Members unsure about joining group Explore boundaries of interpersonal relationships	*Stage 1: Structuralism* Establish status hierarchies based on outside roles Conform to organisation's old traditions	*Stage 1: Preaffiliation* Members unsure about joining group Engage in 'approach-avoidance' struggle Non-intimate relationships with other members	*Stage 1: Orientation* Structure sought by members Members test group's situation	*Stage 1: Forming* Establish interpersonal relationships Conform to organisational traditions and standards Boundary testing in relationships and task behaviours
Stage 2: Top or bottom Conflict among members Power struggle occurs	*Stage 2: Unrest* Emergence of friction and interpersonal conflict Personalities cause disharmony	*Stage 2: Power and control* Power struggle among members Attempt to establish status hierarchies Attempt to formalise and define relationships	*Stage 2: Exploration* Interpersonal exploration Individual differences emerge	*Stage 2: Storming* Conflict arises because of inter-personal behaviours Resistance to group influence and task requirements Group splits
Stage 3: Near or far Members make commitment to group Clarify interpersonal relationships Emotional integration of members	*Stage 3: Change* New leaders emerge Participation is balanced Groups seen as a unit	*Stage 3: Intimacy* Increase group commitment Group experiences become important	*Stage 3: Production* Definition of interpersonal relations Focus on resolution of process problems Establish group cohesion	*Stage 3: Norming* Single leader emerges Group cohesion established New group standards and roles formed for members
	Stage 4: Integration Group structure and hierarchy internalised Group's pragmatic purpose emerges Task accomplishment becomes group's goal	*Stage 4: Differentiation* Group accepts individual differences Relationships become more pragmatic Group becomes its own frame of reference		*Stage 4: Performing* Members perform tasks together Establish role clarity Teamwork is the norm
		Stage 5: Separation Group's goals accomplished Group disbanded		

1   *Help members to become acquainted.* The group members are likely to be uncertain of how they should relate to each other or even how to go about working on the tasks required of them. Each person is likely to be exploring how to form relationships and what commitments to offer to the group. A great deal will depend on the group leader to facilitate introductions between people. Further, the leaders can help matters by emphasising task achievements rather than interpersonal relationships, as working on particular jobs is less threatening to individuals and also gives each person in the group a feeling of accomplishment.

2   *Help members to offer feedback.* As the group members become better acquainted with each other's ideas and values, inevitably some friction and interpersonal conflict is likely to arise. If this is not competently managed, the group may split and disband. The reasons for such conflict may be leadership struggles or an unwillingness by members to modify their beliefs, attitudes, feelings, ideas and behaviour to suit the group's evolving organisation and culture. Under such circumstances, it is important that the group members are encouraged to offer each other honest feedback but in an open and sensitive way. Understanding how group members may feel about each other is of great help in improving interpersonal relationships.

3   *Help members to establish criteria.* As the group members attempt to find solutions to their problems an appropriate leader may emerge and group standards and norms may become established. The group is likely to become more cohesive and develop a belief in its own identity. Further, in order to attain group goals and objectives, team and individual roles are likely to be allocated for each member. Each team member will require clear criteria of performance in that role in order to be able to assess his performance. The possible criteria to be utilised should be discussed between the member in question and the other relevant members of the group. The more acceptable these criteria are to all parties, the more group members are likely to adhere to them.

4   *Members should be encouraged to take part in the running of the group and in the development of its members.* As group members have accepted each other's differences and as members have learnt to co-operate with others in the group when working on particular tasks and activities, each person is probably ready to accept broader responsibility as far as the

running of the group is concerned. Individuals could be offered particular responsibilities for the management of the group. Further, members could be encouraged to help each other in terms of each individual's personal and professional growth and development.

Developed groups are encouraged to participate with their superiors in setting their own goals, and certainly are consulted before any changes which are likely to affect them are implemented. The developed group can be a positive influence towards effective change, but if not consulted, it may consider that any change is a threat to its identity, and may thus decide to oppose it actively. See Chapter 12 for further information on how to turn a low performing group into a high performing team.

Norms

Norms are behaviours which a group expects of its members. They may be written or unwritten, explicit or implicit rules or standards with which group members are expected to comply. Norms may be positive (from an organisational viewpoint), eg punctuality, or negative, eg restriction of output. Violations of norms are not conducive to group harmony, and offenders are likely to be punished, eg a 'rate buster' could be socially isolated or ultimately expelled by the group.

Norms are developed as the group itself develops. New members are quickly socialised into these norms and are expected to comply. Group pressure is exerted if they do not. Norms are emergent behaviours which the group develops to give itself an identity and to help it to process the interactions between members to produce some form of collective progress towards task achievement and achievement of personal goals. Where these latter two elements are congruent there is likely to be a high performance norm, in other words, a desire to achieve high productivity within the group. One of a manager's prime objectives is to try to develop this congruence, this identification of the individual with the group, and of the group with the organisation.

Group cohesiveness

Groups have a high level of cohesiveness where members positively want to be and to remain members of the group. Group identity is

To increase	To decrease
Set an example on required activities and roles.	Increase role and task uncertainty.
Clarify members' role perception.	Question, criticise and stimulate disagreement on the group goals.
Give regular feedback on task and interpersonal behaviour, positively rewarding desired behaviour; these rewards allocated to the group, not individuals.	Give little feedback; structure rewards to individuals, not the group.
Give the group problems that require inter-dependent behaviour and activities.	Give the group problems that require independent, individual behaviour and activities.
Expose the group to external pressure, competition with other groups.	
Decrease group size.	Increase group size.
Increase homogeneity of members.	Reduce homogeneity of members.

Fig. 6.9   Some managerial actions to alter group cohesiveness.

clear. Interpersonal relations are good, as most members are willing to accept the group norms because of the benefits they perceive and individually value in being members of the group. Large groups, having few personal interactions between members, are not likely to be highly cohesive: individual goals may take priority over group goals. In small homogeneous groups, or where there is required to be a high level of interaction and interdependence between members, or where the group is isolated geographically or psychologically from the organisation, or where the group is perceived to have, and perceives itself to have, high status, then high levels of cohesiveness can develop. Too much cohesiveness can, however, be detrimental to group performance. A manager may have to act to reduce the cohesiveness of a group where it has low performance norms or where maintenance of group values and harmony become more important than critical evaluation of the group process or task achievement. This latter characteristic has been called groupthink: in some cases the group may lose touch entirely with reality and even consider itself above the law, as demonstrated by the Watergate affair during the US Presidential election in 1972.

Figure 6.9 shows certain actions a manager can take to increase or decrease group cohesiveness.

GROUP ROLES

The roles which individual members perform in groups have an important effect on group development and cohesiveness.

Roles are patterns of actions associated with individual members, and their positions, in particular settings. They may be, in a group situation, either

- *Formal* – the chairman, the secretary, the treasurer; or

- *Informal* – the expert, the comedian; or

- *Task-oriented* – the proposer, the analyst; or

- *Maintenance-oriented* – the encourager, the harmoniser.

Dr R. Meredith Belbin conducted a research project at the Henley Management Centre, UK, over a period of years, examining the patterns of behaviour displayed by group members participating in a management game. He sought to determine whether there were any common characteristics among groups which could be classified as either high or low performing. He used psychometric measures to analyse the sorts of people who made up successful teams. From this evidence, he established that successfully performing teams were composed of people who collectively showed a capacity to work in eight different roles. When these eight roles were truly represented, the team appeared to be balanced, for it made the best use of its resources, it was flexible and resilient, had few creative members, but was less dependent on key people than the unsuccessful teams. Eventually, Belbin considered he was able to predict success on the basis of testing and allocating individuals prior to team formation, although he does show that it is easier to predict teams that will fail than those which will succeed.

People bring into a group situation different inputs. They are individuals, with different backgrounds, experience, skills and abilities. Developing an effective group entails getting the best out of these different types of individual, who have their own preferred ways of working. In his attempt to define the eight roles which make for a truly balanced team, Belbin analysed people on four main factors – intelligence, dominance, extroversion/introversion, and stability/anxiety. He found that each person has a preferred team role, and a secondary role which they use if others seem unable to act in this role or if someone else plays their preferred role far more powerfully. These roles are: chairman, shaper, plant, monitor/evaluator, company worker, resource investigator, team worker, finisher.

- *The chairman* is the social leader of the group; he clarifies group objectives and sets its agenda. He is likely to be extrovert, stable and dominant in a relaxed, non-aggressive manner. He guides, co-ordinates, and sets criteria but it is unlikely that he is very creative in himself. He is a good communicator, who can focus people on their strengths, and is likely to have the respect of the group members.

- *The shaper* is the task leader of the group, giving shape to the application of team effort, trying to unite ideas and produce patterns. He exhibits the characteristics of an anxious, dominant extrovert, he is full of nervous energy, easily frustrated, and quick to challenge and question and to take up challenges. Intolerant of looseness in structure or ideas, he exudes self-confidence which often belies his own self-doubts. He sees the team as himself, an extension of his own ego, and wants to, and does, make things happen.

- *The plant* is the ideas man of the group, the most imaginative and usually the most intelligent. He is most likely to start looking for original, innovative approaches to the problem, but is himself more interested in fundamentals and principles than in detail. This leads him sometimes to make careless mistakes, and there is a danger that he forgets what the group is there for. He tends not to like criticism of his ideas – when this happens he may respond aggressively or withdraw. The chairman may have to work hard to get the best out of him, but careful nurturing will encourage his creativity.

- *The monitor/evaluator* is the analyst of the group, not likely to produce original ideas, but the person who is best at assimilating, interpreting, and evaluating large volumes of data: he is likely to keep the group on the rails towards its objectives and to stop it from moving in spurious directions. He tends to be cool, dispassionate, and the least motivated member of the group. This can lower group morale when he is a damper at the wrong time.

- *The company worker* is the practical organiser of the group. He turns the ideas of the plant and the shaper into manageable tasks, sorting out what is feasible and possible. He likes a stable structure and commitment to a disciplined course of action. Any sudden changes of direction may unsettle him. Extremely down-to-earth, he may be over-competitive for status in the group, within which he certainly knows what's going on.

- *The resource investigator* is the 'Mr Fix-it' of the group. He always knows someone who knows someone who can help in the situation. He tends to be immediately likeable, very relaxed and sociable, positive and enthusiastic. His enthusiasms may not last very long as he quickly loses interest in routine tasks. He works best under pressure, and helps maintain enthusiasm and morale.

- *The team worker* is the mediator within the group. He is very sensitive to atmosphere, very aware of individual needs and worries. Extremely loyal to the team, likeable and popular, he builds on others' ideas, listens and communicates well, and encourages the other members. He manages conflict, smooths out difficulties or ruffled egos, and his contribution is particularly valuable when the group is in difficulties.

- *The finisher* is the progress chaser of the group. He worries about what might go wrong and is only happy when he has personally checked every detail. He seems always to be in a hurry, working to a deadline, compulsive about order, and impatient and intolerant of the more casual members of the group. There is a danger that he might get bogged down in detail (unlike the plant), and his anxiety might bother the group, but certainly helps it keep to its task schedule.

In addition to their preferred team roles, members also take into the group situation their technical, functional and problem-solving skills and abilities. However, with respect to activities and interactions, it would appear that people prefer to work in one of those eight roles in a group situation, and that they have some long-term stability of role preference. Preferences do not change very much over time, but participation in other roles which are compatible, eg chairman/team worker, shaper/company worker, may be developed with training. There is likely to be minimal or no contribution from people who are cast in incompatible roles, eg plant/shaper, finisher/resource investigator.

Belbin suggests that groups which are formed by taking these characteristics into account are likely to have more successful outcomes than others. However, he also suggests that in different situations some roles are more important than others. In the design stage of a construction project, it may be useful to have more than one plant in the group: creativity and innovation have high priority. But this throws a heavy burden on the chairman and team worker as they strive to maintain harmony and mediate between these prickly people. In the construction phase itself, a plant may not be required at all – his job is done, and the emphasis now is on completing the project at cost and on time. The finisher and the monitor/evaluator assume the more important roles in this situation.

GROUP COMPETENCE AND EFFECTIVENESS

Case 6.4   Reflections

At the regular Friday management meeting three weeks later, everyone was heartened by the progress which had been achieved with the local authority housing contract.

'We're nearly back to our original schedule now,' reported Dick Carroll, the contracts manager. 'And the way things are going we might even finish *before* the completion date!'

'Don't let's get carried away, Dick,' laughed Jack Grayson. 'The gods have a way of pulling the carpet from under our feet when we least expect it. However, we do seem to be starting to work together quite well as a team, and we are making progress to functioning effectively. I've been talking with a friend of mine who runs a group of highly specialist computer operators. He says it takes time to really get a group motoring well. He also said that if one gets a chance, the group should talk about what's happened to them. He found it a good way of getting the group to work as a team.'

'That's not a bad idea. We've certainly raised a few storms,' chuckled Ben Gibson.

'Storms? Storms? More like bloody hurricanes,' laughed Dick Carroll.

The various members of the group laughed and joked with each other. After a while, the conversation became more serious but still quite relaxed.

'You know,' said Jack to the group, 'Ben did help us a great deal. At a time when there are problems you can be a pain,' directing his comments to Ben Gibson, 'but by God, you make sure whatever we do is word perfect, you try to help us to schedule and always keep a tight grip on contract work.'

'Thanks,' responded Ben Gibson, 'I know I'm always going on about deadlines and details and that gets on one or two people's nerves but I think they are important.'

'Another person who's always helped is Angela,' said Mike Rathbone. 'She's always ready to help you and always ready to say something nice. It's good.'

'That's right,' said Dick Carroll. 'She's always helped out when there've been problems.'

'And you, Ed,' said Ben Gibson, 'you've got such a network of contact and suppliers, I really am amazed how you manage to keep a continuity of supplies.'

'Yes, I suppose we are not a bad team really,' said Jack Grayson quietly.

The calm conversation between the management team of the Bridge Building Company (Case 6.4) suggests that they are beginning to realise what it really means to operate as a workgroup. They seem to appreciate that each of the individuals has different strengths and attributes to offer the group. Angela's willingness to help and her sensitivity to other members of the group make her a team worker, as identified by Belbin. Ben Gibson is seen more as a finisher, whilst Ed Cochrane is appreciated for his skills as a resource investigator.

Interestingly this conversation took place after the group had faced and overcome problems and conflicts. Perhaps it is the commitment to face problems and conflicts that allows a group to explore how far it can become a reasonably integrated, high performing team.

All these factors – the use of groups in organisations, the types of groups, group process and dynamics, the stages of group development, group norms and cohesiveness, the roles people prefer to play in groups – influence the degree of group competence and effectiveness. But how would one define a competent and effective group? Obviously, such a group meets its objectives and achieves its tasks – but there are other elements one can identify in a competent group.

Certain dimensions of group competence and effectiveness are shown in Figure 6.10.

Developing an effective group

Group/team building/development programmes should include the

1	The group has clearly identified its goals.
2	The group has its own identity and a sense of purpose.
3	The group is cohesive and members are involved and participating.
4	The group builds on previous ideas, results and feedback.
5	Members are strongly committed to group decisions, which are mostly made by consensus.
6	Feelings are discussed freely without judgements being made; and conflicts are overt, not covert, the objective being to resolve them as much as possible.
7	The group generates alternative ways of looking at problems and issues with the aim of improving its performance.
8	Constant analysis and evaluation of group task progress, process and interactions occur.
9	The group accepts the leadership of the person most qualified in a particular situation.
10	Group members have the expertise — task, technical and inter-personal — to achieve the group's objectives.

Fig. 6.10   Dimensions of group competence

following (see Chapter 12 for further information on team building and developing processes):

Diagnosis, which includes

- analysing and sharing each individual's style, attitudes, strengths, weaknesses, motivations, interests and satisfactions/dissatisfactions with the organisation, which could influence group performance

- analysing the team as an effective workgroup

- analysing the organisation and recognising the way its culture and the organisation potentially and actually influence different groups.

Skills development, which includes

- interpersonal skills – internally, in the group, with each other

- externally, with other managers, to facilitate eg data collection, collaboration, solution implementation

- training in particular tasks skills if required.

Problem-solving. The group should attempt to solve particular problems, to carry out particular tasks, to achieve particular objectives. In this way, the group members capitalise on their development by functioning as a working unit on important issues. Moreover, they indicate their value to the rest of the organisation.

Process review. As part of the process of problem-solving, group members will inevitably reconsider their commitment to the group. Others in the group may examine the value of their colleagues to the future success of the group. Each person will inevitably ask the question – are particular members making the contributions required of them? Considering this, and the individual's own personal needs, how much commitment should he give to the group? Although the process review could be an uncomfortable experience for each group member, the needs of the individual and the total workgroup require reconsideration before team progression.

Integration. Integration in terms of committed workgroup members, positively interacting with each other to fulfil the group's objectives, is unlikely to occur before the previous stages have been experienced. Group members need to be trained to be able to work together. They require particular problems to solve, both to gain credibility with other parts of the organisation, and in order to re-examine each others' contributions. Achieving integration indicates an acceptance of each member's strengths and weaknesses together with realistic appraisal of the achievement capability of the group.

SUMMARY

Types of group

Formal groups are created by design within the organisation. A manager's workgroup is a formal group, although membership may change with movements of individuals within, into, or out of the organisation. Formal groups may be permanent (the workgroup) or temporary (a project team).

    Informal groups are created by the needs of the individual members. These consist of members who like to interact with each other, whose values and beliefs may generate needs which cannot be met within the formal groups of the organisation.

    Primary groups are small groups where the members have many and frequent interactions.

    Secondary groups are large groups where the members do not have the opportunity to have many and frequent interactions. They are likely to be less cohesive than primary groups, and individual goals may take precedence over group goals.

In organisations, individuals tend to belong to at least one formal group (the workgroup), and also other informal group(s) which satisfy their personal needs.

Groups and their uses in organisations

Groups in organisations may be used in ten different ways. They also tend to be used in situations where the co-ordination of individual functions or tasks is required, and particularly where new ideas or creative solutions are needed. Groups bring a multifaceted perspective to situations and problems, and are useful when an individual's single perspective is likely to be inadequate for effective problem-solving.

Highly formalised groups are likely to do well with routine, structured tasks, while formal groups with low formalism and structure are likely to produce better solutions in situations of ambiguity, uncertainty and change.

Homogeneous groups, with members of similar backgrounds, experiences, values and attitudes will probably have high membership satisfaction and work well on tasks within their common experience; in these groups there is pressure for conformity to group norms. Heterogeneous groups, with members of diverse characteristics, are likely to require lower conformity to group norms and to produce more creative and holistic solutions to problems.

It may be difficult to achieve managerial control over large groups in organisations, which may also tend to split into subgroups achieving greater interactions, but which may also tend to determine their own goals which may not be congruent with those of the organisation.

Group dynamics

Individuals can satisfy various levels of need in a group situation, ie security and safety needs, social needs, self-esteem, self-fulfilment, and power needs. In addition, groups have the following common elements:

Required behaviour is that prescribed by the organisation, for the performance of which it rewards and benefits its members. *Emergent behaviour* is required behaviour which is modified by individual groups to meet their own needs, and which may be beneficial or detrimental to group and organisational outcomes and effectiveness.

Sentiments are those values, beliefs and attitudes which individuals take into a group situation. *Activities* are what people do in groups. *Interactions* are social transactions between members. All these elements are interdependent: changes in one element have consequential effects on the others.

Interpersonal transactions between group members can be classified into three types: *task-oriented behaviour*, which is concerned with achieving the tasks or objectives of the group; *maintenance-oriented behaviour*, which is concerned with being supportive to others, to maintaining group harmony; and *self-oriented behaviour*, which is directed towards achieving personal goals in the group situation.

Group development

Group dynamics plays an important part in the development of a group into an effective problem-solving unit. See Chapter 12 for a summary of the sequential stages of group development and the role of the group leader in assisting the group to develop through these stages.

Group cohesiveness, where members have a strong identity with the group, is important. High performance norms are also extremely valuable.

Group roles

Research has suggested that a balanced and high performing group is one where members are able to perform in eight separate roles. These are chairman (social leader), shaper (task leader), plant (ideas man), monitor evaluator (analyst), company worker (practical organiser), resource investigator (Mr Fix-it), team worker (mediator), finisher (details person). These roles are primarily determined by the personality characteristics of individual members. Depending on the situation facing the group, certain roles become more important than others.

Group competence and effectiveness

Individual values, group dynamics, and the group growth and development processes are all important in achieving group effectiveness.

Managers can develop an effective group using diagnosis, skills development, problem-solving, process review, and integration. At all stages, effective feedback to the group and to individuals is essential.

IN CONCLUSION

Individuals are the constituent members of groups in organisations, but the groups themselves make up the social fabric which *is* the organisation. Managers do not normally work in isolation, but are members of one or more formal and informal groups in their work environment. To be effective they need to understand the workings of groups, the differences between groups, and why individuals, including themselves, behave as they do in a group situation. They can then take action both to develop themselves as better contributors in the group process, and to make their own workgroups achieve higher performance and attain higher individual and group satisfaction.

7 Leadership in Organisations

Richard Stillman had been in production all his working life before this appointment. For this past ten years he was production manager of Diverse Products Limited, the largest company in the same group, and this was a major reason for being chosen for this position. Head office felt that Stillman, with his production background and experience, would be able to ensure that production in Complex Components Limited would be better able to meet the real requirements, particularly on delivery, of the sales department.

Stillman was proud of his record with the group. He revelled in working, as he called it 'at the sharp end of management', and had kept very close control of his previous department. He felt that people needed to be set clear targets and their progress should be constantly monitored. In Diverse Products he had always surpassed his production requirements, and this, he was sure, was because he ran 'a tight ship'. He wasn't overly impressed by his first contact with his senior staff at Complex Components. They seemed to have a *laissez-faire* attitude and kept making in-jokes at the meeting. He felt excluded, and determined to tighten things up.

In Case 7.1, Richard Stillman's leadership style displays certain individual characteristics. In the past, he has run 'a tight ship' keeping close control, with constant monitoring of performance. His style might be described as disciplinarian/authoritarian, and it seemed to work, because he achieved his department's objectives. He had been in his previous job for ten years, and thus knew his team's capabilities.

There are now three new factors, however. First, he has been promoted to general manager from production manager, and has no experience in this role, or of working multifunctionally. Second, he has no experience of working in Complex Components, which, although it is also part of the William Wade group, may have a very different organisational culture from Diverse Products. Third, he is moving, as an outsider, into an established group of senior staff, with whose way of working, and norms of behaviour, he is unfamiliar.

With these variables in the situation, the question arises – is this disciplinarian style, with tight control, little involvement of his subordinates in decision-making, and close direction, likely to work for Stillman as general manager of Complex Components?

The chairman of a company is measured by his success or failure in achieving financial and operating results acceptable to the shareholders. A divisional director is measured by how well he has been able to integrate the work of his divisional managers to make a significant contribution to the whole company's profits. A sales manager is measured by his ability to organise and motivate his sales team to meet or surpass its sales targets. The supervisor of a typing pool is measured on his effectiveness in allocating work to and ensuring that work is completed by his typing team.

Leadership in management occurs at all levels in an organisation, and the quality of a manager's performance is directly related to his management of the performance of his subordinates.

This chapter is about leadership – the abilities and skills a manager requires in order to manage people: individuals and groups at work. It will explore the development of management thought on leadership, from early studies focused on personality, to current theories of situational leadership.

WHAT IS LEADERSHIP?

The style adopted by a manager or leader is a critical dimension of his individual and organisational effectiveness, and the quality of leadership is one characteristic which distinguishes the successful company from one that is performing poorly. Many business failures can be traced back to poor or weak management leadership. It is no surprise, then, that research into the characteristics and behaviour of successful leadership has been pursued for centuries, and only now are we beginning to put together a composite picture which seems to make sense.

Studies of leadership and good leaders have often generated conflicting data, but enabled progress to be made towards understanding these phenomena more clearly. Figure 7.1 gives a historical perspective on leadership studies and the focus of research on the leader as an individual at each stage.

From early assumptions that leadership qualities were intransmutable, that leaders were born, not made; through successive studies which hypothesised that able leadership derived from an individual leader's values and beliefs, his attitudes, his behaviour, his style of leadership; today it is postulated that successful leadership is a function of an individual's skills of diagnosis of the people and tasks in a situation, and his ability to modify his style appropriately.

For a manager to be a good leader, in other words, it is not necessary to change his inner core values, but he must be able to change his style of interpersonal interaction to fit the variables of the situation.

Definitions of leadership abound, but all have three common features:

1   Leadership is an influencing process,

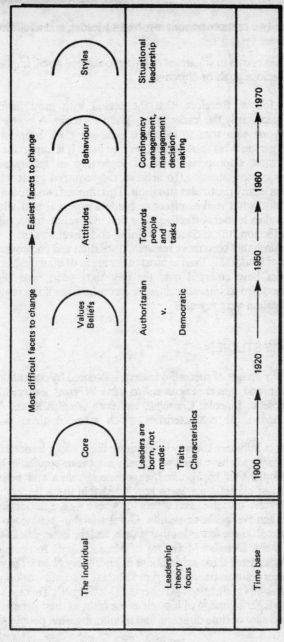

Fig. 7.1 Historical perspective: leadership theory v. level of individual involvement and flexibility

2   There are two or more persons involved – a leader, and a follower, or followers.

3   Leadership occurs in situations of trying to achieve given, implied, or unconscious goals or objectives.

It does not follow, therefore, that the person with most formal authority is necessarily the leader in any given situation. A potential leader is anyone who tries to influence someone else's behaviour, whether that person is his subordinate, peer, or boss. It is important to choose the most appropriate style of leadership in influencing, managing or communicating, to achieve the required goals with given persons in any particular situation. This implies two separate considerations: what makes effective leaders emerge, and what behaviour makes leaders effective. The first may relate to recruitment and selection, the second to training and development.

There has probably been more research, discussion and controversy on the topic of leadership than in most other areas of management. Many theories have emerged over the past sixty years, and been rejected or modified as impracticalities or inconsistencies if the results of their application were revealed.

LEADERSHIP STUDIES

We all have our images of successful leaders, influenced by our culture, our education, and our experiences. We think of great leaders like Caesar, Napoleon, Lincoln, Churchill, and even Genghis Khan. All these have individual characteristics which stamped them with greatness.

These images influence the way in which we think about leadership, and also the way we behave when we actually assume responsibility for managing people. Our background, experiences, values and beliefs generate a set of expectations as to how we should use a leadership position to involve ourselves and others for whom we are responsible in trying to achieve goals or results. Our leadership behaviour is affected by our attitudes towards other people, and the assumptions we hold about them. Douglas McGregor of Massachusetts Institute of Technology contrasted these assumptions in his Theory X and Theory Y. If a manager believes people are generally lazy, and will work only if coerced or tightly controlled and directed (McGregor's Theory X), he is likely to have an image of himself as the boss, as their superior, and will spend a lot of time directing and monitoring what people are doing. If a manager believes people are inherently good, and are willing to accept responsibility when given the opportunity for self-direction (McGregor's Theory Y), he is likely to stand back, let people get on with the task, and act more as a facilitator or co-ordinator, providing planning and services so that they can achieve the agreed targets. The manager's own expectations of leadership and leaders are vital factors in his own leadership behaviour.

Leadership behaviour and leadership effectiveness have been studied extensively from various viewpoints – personality traits, personal characteristics, attitudes, and behaviour. What has been considered a panacea at one time has been considered counter-productive at others. But the obsession with searching for, and finding, good leaders is still going on, as is the analysis of their behaviour, because leadership, or the lack of it, can make or break a business.

Trait studies

Initially, attempts to study leadership assumed that there were certain qualities of personality which were common to good leaders. Research concentrated on such factors as personal qualities (intelligence, age, experience), or personality traits (extroversion, dominance). Certain characteristics were considered inherent, unique to individuals – if a person did not possess them, he was unlikely to be a good leader. This approach meant that it would be easy to pick out potential leaders. The main purpose of training therefore would be to develop these characteristics in those who already possessed them; training would be wasted on others. The characteristics of the leader was the important factor, not the task or situation – these qualities were always appropriate, for the assumption was that a leader is always a leader!

This hypothesis that certain individuals are able to direct, control, guide and lead others because they possess certain specific qualities goes against the grain of the development of political, and particularly democratic, thought – the concept of a leadership elite perpetuated by heredity would not find much favour among the great majority of people, who thus would be perpetually led. And although research has shown some evidence that leaders, and particularly successful leaders, are more achievement-oriented, extrovert and intelligent than other people, on half a century of research and study later it has still not been possible to identify clearly and substantiate any significant traits or characteristics which are common to effective leaders.

This continuing lack of success moved attention away from the trait approach. Certainly, personal characteristics and personality factors may be some of the determinants of great leadership, but if they are not the main factors, what are? Could it perhaps be the way in which leaders behave in the process of leadership, the way in which they tackle the demands of situations in which they have to display leadership, which cause some to be better than others?

Researchers began to look more closely at *actual* leadership *behaviour* instead of what sort of people the leaders were – and also at the situations and environments in which certain different leadership behaviours appeared to succeed.

Behavioural approach

Leadership is a process whereby a person attempts to influence an individual or group towards achievement of a given goal. Capable leaders therefore help people to work successfully on a task; they are concerned with the task (production, goal achievement), and with the people doing it (relationships between the leader and his subordinates, or followers). The examination of leadership behaviour in managers and the styles they use to interact with their subordinates moves the focus of research from what leaders are to what leaders do. Leadership is viewed as a process, an activity, not as an individual characteristic or quality; leadership cannot be considered as dependent on the leader alone – it consists of interactions between the leader and his subordinates. Because leadership occurs between people, and is a process of influence, the behavioural approach assumes that subordinates will work better for managers who use certain styles of leadership behaviour than they will for others who employ different styles.

Authoritarian/disciplinarian school

Scientific management, as developed by Taylor, was concerned with increasing productivity by the use of improved techniques, work study and method study (see Chapter 1). Tasks and jobs should be broken down into clearly structured units, with specialisation of labour and well-defined and measurable performance targets. The emphasis was on direction and control by the manager, rather than on the needs of the worker. Leadership corresponded with satisfaction of organisational needs, not the needs of the individual worker. With, at this time, poorly organised workers and trade unions, power lay in the hands of management; it had sole authority for decision-making, and control of reward and punishment. Task achievement was the manager's prime concern. This style of management could be called *authoritarian.*

Unfeeling, inconsiderate and indiscriminate use of this style often leads to worker alienation and withdrawal, and also to feelings of powerlessness, which can manifest themselves in restrictions of output, absenteeism, and the development of a 'them and us' attitude which still exists today in many workplaces.

Human relations school

One of the first of a series of behavioural scientists, Elton Mayo, in the 1920s and 1930s, felt that in addition to using most appropriately designed methods to achieve productivity, management could perhaps reduce alienation and negative feelings towards the organisation by looking also at the human aspects of work. Interpersonal relations, particularly the feelings and attitudes within working groups, were considered to be important. He hypothesised that people looked for satisfaction of their social needs at work. Further, the power and influence of groups on individual members was such that organisations could develop systems and styles to try and satisfy people's social needs in their workgroups. The leader using this human relations approach would act primarily as a facilitator, sharing power and authority with the group in moving towards goal achievement. Group harmony, satisfaction of individual needs, and concern for people consequently were of prime importance. This style of leadership could be called *democratic.*

It was felt that the styles usually adopted by leaders were based on the assumptions they make about people, determined by their own values, beliefs and attitudes, and their perception of their own bases of power (see Chapter 8).

The human relations school adapted the Mayo philosophy and considered that the use of a democratic style would be more likely to motivate people to work productively than an autocratic style. By being able to participate, being involved in decision-making, having autonomy and responsibility, the individual would feel satisfied in terms of most of the Maslow hierarchy of needs and thereby release more energy and effort into getting the job done (see Chapter 5). There is evidence that democratic styles are linked to higher subordinate satisfaction, lower manpower turnover and absenteeism and less intergroup conflict, and are often the preferred styles of subordinates. The majority of research findings show a correlation between high group productivity and a democratic style of leadership. However, certain studies also indicated that productivity is positively related to

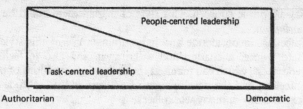

Fig. 7.2   Continuum of leadership styles
Reprinted by permission of the *Harvard Business Review*. An Exhibit from 'How to choose a Leadership Pattern', by Robert Tannenbaum and Warren H. Schmidt (May/June, 1973.) Copyright © 1973 by the President and Fellows of Harvard College; all rights reserved.

an authoritarian style – some people *do* prefer to be controlled and directed.

For some time these two styles, authoritarian and democratic, were thought to be two ends of the same continuum of leadership style, as in Figure 7.2.

Further observations of leader behaviour showed greater variations. Some leaders showed high task-directed behaviour and also showed a high concern for relationships with their subordinates. Some showed neither; some emphasised relationships but had little concern for task achievement. Some emphasised the reverse. It became evident that managers used variations of authoritarian and democratic styles.

Authoritarian and democratic styles are not two ends of the same continuum, but are in fact different dimensions of leadership behaviour.

The managerial grid

The American researchers and management development entrepreneurs Robert Blake and Jane Mouton crystallised the earlier work of the famous Michigan and Ohio State research studies with their managerial grid (Figure 7.3), which described five basic managerial styles based on the separate concepts of task achievement (production) and concern for people (relationships).

1   *Task management* (9, 1). The manager achieves high productivity by planning, organising and directing work in such a way that human variables are kept to a minimum.

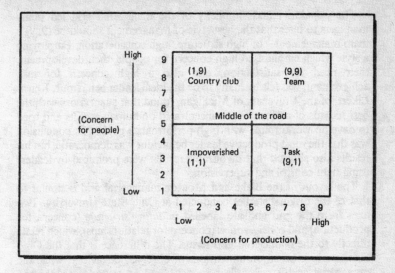

Fig. 7.3   The managerial grid
Source: *The Managerial Grid III*, by Robert R. Blake and Jane
Srygley Mouton. Houston: Gulf Publishing Company. Copyright ©
1985, p. 12. Reproduced by permission.

2   *Team management* (9, 9). The manager tries to gain commitment
    from his workers; high productivity will be achieved by obtaining
    agreement between task achievement, organisational goals and the
    satisfaction of human needs.

3   *Middle of the road management* (5, 5). Adequate performance is
    achieved by balancing and trading off production requirements
    with worker morale.

4   *Country club management* (1, 9). Satisfying people's social and
    relationship needs leads to group harmony and a comfortable
    workplace.

5   *Impoverished management* (1, 1). The manager exacts minimum
    effort to get the required work done and maintains distant
    relationships with his workers.

Looking at Case 7.1 in terms of the managerial grid, Richard Stillman
of Complex Components appears to be a (9, 1) manager – with high
concern for production and low concern for people.

The popularity and simplicity of the managerial grid led many managers to infer that the best style of management should be (9, 9) – team management – of high structure, high consideration. Employing a style which emphasised high concern for people, their development, their need for satisfaction, and also a high concern for task achievement, was felt by many to be the ideal leader behaviour. Rensis Likert, of the University of Michigan, found that supervisors with the best records of performance concentrated on human aspects and tried to develop workgroups with high performance goals. His conclusion was that the most productive leader behaviour was democratic, but his results also showed that favourable results were produced by leaders using tight control and supervision.

The layout of the Blake and Mouton managerial grid is similar to that of the original studies conducted at Ohio State University. Two axes form the grid and are labelled *initiating structure* (concern for production) and *consideration* (concern for relationships), which relate directly to the managerial grid terms. The difference is that the Ohio State study is based on dimensions of observed behaviour, while the managerial grid is primarily a model based on attitudes, values and beliefs.

In the face of this conflicting evidence, does there exist a single ideal management style? It seems unlikely. The research findings suggest that managerial competence is not a function of task-oriented or people-oriented style alone. This brings us to the third factor in the definition of leadership – the situation.

Contingency studies

The contingency model of leadership considers that leadership effectiveness is achieved when the leader's style matches the demands of the given situation, particularly the task/work group and the position of the leader with respect to the workgroup. Professor Fred E. Fiedler, a leading theoretician in this field, defined situations in terms of their favourableness to the leader. The key component of favourableness is influence over the workgroup and he argued that the influence dimension is composed of three main factors.

1   *The leader-member relationship*. A favourable relationship enables the leader to have greater influence over the workgroup.

2   *The degree of structure of the task*. The more structured the task, the more favourable the situation for the leader.

3   *The leader's formal position power.* The greater the reward or punishments the leader can award, the more influence he can exert.

The most favourable leadership situation is therefore one in which there are good leader-member relationships, the task is well-defined and highly-structured, and the leader has a high degree of formal authority. In favourable leadership situations, Fiedler concludes that a task-oriented (authoritarian) style is likely to be most successful. In situations that are neither favourable nor unfavourable, a relationship-oriented style (democratic) is preferable. In unfavourable situations, where the task is unstructured, the leader-member relationships are poor, and the leader has little formal authority – the leader is likely to achieve best results by adopting a task-oriented style. Conversely, *task-oriented leaders* are likely to achieve better results in group situations that are favourable or unfavourable to the leader, while relationship-oriented leaders tend to achieve better results in situations that are neither favourable nor unfavourable (see Figure 7.4).

Consider Complex Components (Case 7.1), and the relative weightings of the demands and constraints imposed on Richard Stillman in his first meeting with his management team:

Leader-member relationships	Good	So-so	Poor
Task structure	High	Medium	Low
Formal authority	High	Medium	Low
Leadership situation	Favourable	Intermediate	Unfavourable
Appropriate/ effective management style	Task-oriented	Relationship-oriented	Task-oriented

Fig. 7.4 Fiedler's matrix of situation favourableness/effective management style
From F. E. Fiedler, M. E. Chemers and L. Mahar, *The Leadership Match Concept*, Wiley, 1978. Copyright ©. Reprinted by permission of John Wiley & Sons Inc.

- *Leader-member relationships*. There was no attempt by Stillman or his team to develop good relationships. The in-jokes made Stillman resentful, and he disapproved of the *laissez-faire* attitude of his team. They felt they had 'a real joker here'. Relationships were poor.

- *Task structure*. The objectives were clear – to meet head office targets, but the structure was undefined; the process of achieving the objectives was still unclear. Task structure was low.

- *Formal authority*. Stillman's formal authority was defined by his job position, that of general manager. His team had been accustomed to working closely with his predecessor and had had much closer, friendly relationships with him. Stillman was a new boy and they did not fully accept the formal authority he was imposing on them.

Poor leader-member relationships, low task structure, low to medium formal authority – these, according to Fiedler, define an unfavourable leadership position. Stillman appropriately used a task-oriented leadership style.

Despite Fiedler's emphasis on managerial style, he felt that it was more practical for organisations to change a given situation than to hope that managers could adapt and change their style to fit it. In essence, task structure and formal authority were considered easier to change than a manager's natural and preferred style of leadership. Certainly Peter Drucker, a pioneer in the application of management theory, agreed that in a small organisation, training and changing managerial styles would take 1–2 years, rising to 5 years in a larger organisation. These changes need not necessarily be dramatic, for even small changes can improve effectiveness. Fiedler's conclusion also implies that leaders are more often born than made; that leadership behaviour is unidimensional in the continuum authoritarian-democratic – whereas in reality most managers' styles are combinations of these two separate dimensions.

Managerial decision-making

The researchers Victor Vroom and Philip Yetton of Yale University began with the assumption that managers learn various styles and from that basis developed a series of rules whereby leaders should modify their preferred styles to meet the requirements of given situations. They consider that there are situations where managers, in making decisions, should behave autocratically, or democratically, or should use a combination of both these styles – in effect, they identified those situations where, for maximum effect, subordinates should participate, and the degree to which they should participate, in managerial decision-making. They describe a model of three ranges of styles, *autocratic, consultative,* and *group participation.*

- *Autocratic.* The manager solves the problem or makes the decision himself on the basis of the information available to him (Style A1) or supplied to him by his subordinates at the time (Style A11).

- *Consultative.* The manager shares the problem with his subordinates, either individually (Style C1), or as a group (Style C11), then he makes the decision which may or may not reflect his subordinates' influence.

- *Participative.* The manager shares the problem with his subordinates as a group. Together they generate and evaluate solutions and attempt to reach agreement on a solution. He accepts and implements any solution that has the support of the group (Style G11).

Vroom and Yettin argue that the factors determining the best leadership style to adopt are:

1   The quality of the decision to be made.

2   The level of acceptability required by the subordinates in order to implement the decision.

3   The time scale of the decision-making process.

When making decisions, managers should assess and weigh all these factors before deciding whether, or how much, to involve subordinates in the decision-making process. The technique used in this consideration is a decision tree, applying the seven questions shown in Figure 7.5. Unlike the decision tree model which Vroom (Chapter 5) uses to illustrate an expectancy theory of motivation, this decision tree provides a model to assist individuals in the making of decisions. Using this decision tree problems can be classified as one of fourteen types defined by Vroom and Yetton.

Questions A, B and C relate to the quality and rationality of the decision required. Questions D and E refer to the acceptance of the decision by subordinates. Questions F and G concern subordinate commitment to the problem situation and the preferred solution.

Where the manager has or can obtain the information to make the

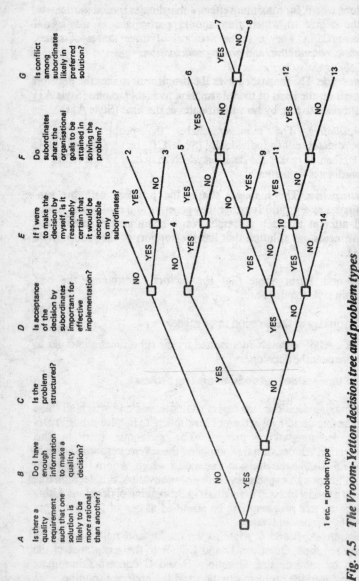

A	B	C	D	E	F	G
Is there a quality requirement such that one solution is likely to be more rational than another?	Do I have enough information to make a quality decision?	Is the problem structured?	Is acceptance of the decision by subordinates important for effective implementation?	If I were to make the decision by myself, is it reasonably certain that it would be acceptable to my subordinates?	Do subordinates share the organisational goals to be attained in solving the problem?	Is conflict among subordinates likely in preferred solution?

1 etc. = problem type

Fig. 7.5 The Vroom-Yetton decision tree and problem types

decision, or no one decision is preferable, he can make the decision himself (A1, A11). Where he does not have enough information, and acceptance is a problem, some degree of consultation and participation is needed (C1, C11, or G11).

Managers should not attempt to note or learn the model, or keep a copy of the decision tree in their desk drawer for reference whenever a decision has to be made, but it can be used in training and development to highlight the logical process of decision-making, coupled with the realisation that subordinates may have (in fact, in most cases do have!) some critical input into that process which can aid the manager in the achievement of his objectives. Each type has a range of acceptable decision methods as shown in Figure 7.6.

Vroom and Yetton clearly appreciate that good managers have to adapt their styles to match the needs and characteristics of individual situations.

Case 7.2 'We've got to introduce some better systems.'

Over the next few weeks Stillman got to know the problems he was facing. The biggest, he felt, was in production. He had been sure he would, with his experience and know-how in this field, be able to reduce lead times and schedule faster work-flows to meet sales department requirements. Mike Young, the production manager, was quite frank about it.

'There's no way we can meet these production requirements with our existing plant. It's physically impossible. These sales reps just take any orders they can get without checking to see if we can deliver when the customer requires it. As a result we've got lots of little jobs going through because there's no co-ordination to help us make up economic batch sizes.'

Stillman wasn't convinced. He felt that Mike was just making excuses for not meeting his targets, and he also knew that he himself wouldn't meet head office targets unless the company took all the orders it could get.

'You'll just have to do the best you can, Mike. I'm not satisfied that we've got the best set-up for machining or assembly. There seem to be lots of hold-ups in between operations, and our part-finished stocks seem to be completely out of proportion. We've got to get production on an even keel before I can approach head office for more investment in plant - anyway, where would we put it? Every spare place is full of unfinished goods! Report to me in two days about the progress you've made and also your plans for improvement over the next three months.'

He next saw Tony James, the sales manager. 'Tony, I know we need the orders, but the way they're coming through is causing chaos for Mike Young in production. Can't you get our most frequent customers to

> schedule their orders regularly? I've looked at your sales budget for this year and it looks as if it's been done by at best intuitive guesswork. Let's get together next week and talk about how we can smooth it out. In the meantime, let me have a report and projections on all orders and budgets for the next six months. We've got to introduce some better systems than we have at present.'

Problem type	Acceptable decision methods	Problem type	Acceptable decision methods
1	A1, A11, C1, C11, G11	8	C1, C11
2	A1, A11, C1, C11, G11	9	A11, C1, C11, G11*
3	G11	10	A11, C1, C11, G11*
4	A1, A11, C1, C11, G11*	11	C11, G11*
5	A1, A11, C1, C11, G11*	12	G11
6	G11	13	C11
7	C11	14	C11, G11*

* G11 is only acceptable when the answer to Question F is yes.

Fig. 7.6   Problem types and decision methods
Reprinted by permission of the publisher from 'A New Look at Managerial Decision Making', by Victor Vroom, *Organisational Dynamics*, Spring, 1973, p. 71. © 1973, American Management Association, New York. All rights reserved.

In Case 7.2, let us examine why Richard Stillman decided on this leadership behaviour towards the production and sales managers. Working through the Vroom–Yetton decision tree model:

- To Question A: he feels the answer is Yes – there *is* a quality requirement such that one solution is likely to be more rational than another. A balance has to be made between the often conflicting demands of both departments so that each may be performing sub-maximally but that both together are performing optimally from the whole company's point of view.

- To Question B: the answer is No – he doesn't have enough information on which to base his decision, but he has taken steps to acquire that information.

- To Question C: the problem *is* structured. It lies within clearly defined parameters.

- To Question D: Stillman is keeping tight control and direction over his subordinates. He expects their co-operation, positive response and commitment to his instructions. In his view, the answer to this question is No.

Following the decision tree, we come to the definition of the problem as type 10. The four acceptable decision methods are A11, C1, C11, and G11. Stillman decided to use method C1 – where he shared the problem with his subordinates individually, but his final decision might or might not reflect his subordinates' influence. A big factor in his decision to behave in this way was the time pressure for turnround and results from head office.

Situational leadership

Following these earlier studies, the two American consultants and academics Paul Hersey and Ken Blanchard developed a model of situational leadership. They describe four basic leadership styles, based on the dimensions of task behaviour and relationship behaviour.

- *Task behaviour* is the extent to which leaders are likely to organise and define the roles of the group (followers); to explain what activities each is to do, and when, where, and how tasks are to be accomplished; it is characterised by endeavouring to establish well-defined patterns of organisation, channels of communication, and ways of getting jobs done.

- *Relationship behaviour* is the extent to which leaders are likely to maintain personal relationships between themselves and members of their group (followers) by opening up channels of communication, providing emotional support, 'psychological strokes', and offering facilitating/supportive behaviours.

Task behaviour is, in effect, characterised by the leader's use of one-way communication in direction and explanation, while relationship behaviour opens up two-way communication through encouragement, friendliness and recognition.

Situational leadership theory suggests that there is no such thing as a common style of good leadership, no one best way to influence people all the time, but that a leader will be effective when he matches his style to his own requirements, those of his subordinates, and the task itself in the context of the situation or environment. The individual manager needs to work out which approach to use, which combination of task and relationship behaviour is appropriate, depending on the circumstances which prevail.

Hersey and Blanchard consider that the main factor determining the best management style to employ in a specific situation is the job-related development of subordinates, defined as the ability and willingness of people to take responsibility for directing their own behaviour – specifically in relation to the particular task to be performed. A subordinate or group working competently has the knowledge and skills to perform the task, is willing to take responsibility for the job, and is highly committed to achievement of the task. A developed subordinate or group can be described as 'ready, willing and able'. The relative lack of these characteristics shows the degree of underdevelopment or immaturity.

This implies that individuals may be immature with regard to certain tasks, yet developed with regard to others. In addition, when dealing with a group of subordinates, each individual may be at a different level of development in respect of each and every different task he has to perform. This means that leaders may have to behave differently (use different styles) towards individual members of their group when managing the same task, and also behave differently with the same member when he is carrying out different tasks. This is shown by Hersey and Blanchard's model (Figure 7.7), in which a curve suggests the appropriate leadership style, the best combination of task behaviour and relationship behaviour, for the job-related development (maturity) of the subordinates (followers).

When a group or individual appears to the leader to display, and be working at, a low level of development, the leader needs to provide a high degree of control, direction, role definition and structure with respect to the task, while positively reinforcing only that behaviour which shows increased motivation, job-related skills, and increased responsibility. As the level of development increases, the leader should increase this socio-emotional (relationship) behaviour while reducing the control and direction (task behaviour) given to his group or individual subordinate. As the level of task-related development approaches maturity, the leader can withdraw both task and

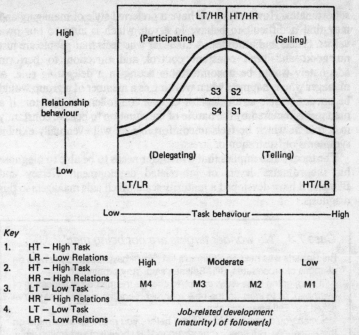

Key
1. HT – High Task
    LR – Low Relations
2. HT – High Task
    HR – High Relations
3. LT – Low Task
    HR – High Relations
4. LT – Low Task
    LR – Low Relations

Fig. 7.7   Situational leadership theory
From P. Hersey and K. Blanchard, *Management Organisational Behaviour: Utilising Human Resources*, Prentice-Hall International, 3rd edn, p. 164 (1977). Reprinted by permission of Prentice-Hall, Englewood Cliffs, New Jersey.

relationship behaviour involvement and move to a positive delegating leadership role. However, when delegating he needs to have set up monitoring systems so that he is constantly aware that this style is appropriate. If the level of development is reducing, eg if the group or individual is not achieving targets, he should move his leadership behaviour back down the curve to a participating, selling or eventually telling role. But he must beware of moving directly from a delegatory to a telling role – sudden changes of behaviour make the subordinates feel that the leader is inconsistent, and may lead to resentment and resistance to change. This may be reflected in reduced productivity and performance.

The ideal manager is one who can modify his behaviour across the four principal leadership styles to fit the job-related development of his subordinates. However, we all have a preferred style of managing and may find it difficult to behave in a role which is alien to our own values, beliefs and attitudes. A manager who feels that people are just no good and need constant control and direction to perform adequately would be uncomfortable acting in a delegating role. A manager who is happiest when working as a member of a group would be uncomfortable as a delegator or as a controller and director. If a manager is required by the nature of the situation to behave constantly in a role in which he feels uncomfortable he will eventually exhibit symptoms of frustration or stress.

The theory also implies that a manager needs to be able to diagnose his subordinates' levels of job-related development. Hersey and Blanchard have developed a maturity scale which aids managers in this diagnosis.

Case 7.3   'No wonder targets are not being met!'

Bill Roberts was next on Stillman's list. 'You'll have received my note on changes of procedures, Bill,' Stillman said. 'Any problems?'

'It's not going to be easy, or fast, to change the method of allocation of overhead, or to start up the new monthly reporting system that you've asked for,' Bill answered abruptly.

'I wish you'd had a word with me before you made up your mind on these changes. But now . . .', he shrugged his shoulders and smiled wrily, 'I'll just have to do the best I can, but don't expect miracles overnight.'

Stillman flushed and said angrily, 'Bill, the whole information processing system here and the data available to me to make decisions and exercise control are completely inadequate. It's no wonder that targets aren't being met. I shall want to be kept in the picture much more than Jack Williams was, and I expect you to get things off the ground before next month's management meeting. How the hell can I let Head Office know what's really going on if I don't know myself? You've a key role to play in all this. All the relevant data come through you and if you don't work with me and keep me informed, I'll be on your back like a ton of bricks.'

Relating Hersey and Blanchard's situational leadership model to Complex Components in Case 7.3, Richard Stillman's leadership behaviour towards Bill Roberts at this time is clearly high task/low relationship – he is telling his subordinate what to do. He determines the style to use by diagnosing that Roberts is at a low stage of development with relation to the specific task to be performed. Roberts may not have the ability and certainly isn't willing to take responsibility for his own behaviour and performance, nor is he highly committed to achievement of Stillman's goals. Consequently, Stillman is very task-oriented in his leadership behaviour towards Roberts, tightly controlling and directing him towards performance of the task.

In all his interactions with his subordinates to date, Stillman has followed up the sudden sharp shock of his initial meeting with his managers by examining closely with them their individual problems, and setting specific performance targets for them. He distanced himself personally and psychologically from his subordinates and was very task-directive. It was appropriate leadership behaviour in the situation in which Stillman found himself; his team was not meeting targets and displayed to him a low level of job-related development. They needed tight control and direction, not participative management. The previous easygoing, participative climate under Jack Williams, which led to complacency and low performance, was not appropriate for the achievement of Richard Stillman's objectives.

ORGANISATIONAL CLIMATE AND LEADERSHIP

Managers are influenced in the way in which they behave as leaders not only by the maturity of their subordinates and the job situation, but also by the constraints imposed upon them by, and the very nature of the organisation – its dominant culture and climate. In an organisation in which top management is very concerned with short-term results, managers are pressured to behave in a task-oriented, controlling and directing style – they either perform or are fired. In the short term they may achieve better results, but continuous application of this behaviour may result in worker alienation, leading to absenteeism, high labour turnover, deteriorating employee relations, strikes, etc. In an organisation characterised by participation and democratic forms of management, continuous high controlling and directing leadership behaviour is again likely to be counter productive. The culture of the organisation limits the range of management styles available to the manager. If the culture of the organisation demands continuous leadership behaviour which is counter to the manager's own preferred style, there is little person–environment fit, and stress may well be caused.

The effects of organisational culture and climate are explored more fully in Chapter 8.

IMPLICATIONS FOR MANAGERS

The bulk of research findings in the area of leadership indicates tha.
the two most important elements are task and relationship behaviour.
It is not the personal characteristics of the individual manager which
determine his success as a leader, but the way in which he uses and
integrates those two elements of behaviour to motivate his subordinates to achieve work goals.

When modifying his leadership behaviour to match the job and
needs of his subordinates, the manager should share his leadership
philosophy with his subordinates, and explain why he is behaving in
these manners. Once they understand this, they can realise that it is
their own behaviour, motivation and development which determines
their boss's behaviour, not his own preferences and personality. They
then know that they can change their boss's behaviour from tightly
controlling and directing to participating and delegating.

Douglas T. Hall carried out a study of the careers of over fifteen
thousand managers from a wide cross-section of organisations. His
findings from this very large population indicated that managers who
were successful and were more likely to rise to high positions in
organisations are indeed more likely to communicate clearly and
openly than to conceal information and play politics, and are
concerned to involve their subordinates in planning, making decisions
and solving problems in relation to their work.

Case 7.4 'We'll work together more as a team.'

Six months later, at the close of the regular management meeting,
Stillman said, 'Well, we seem to be getting close to our targets now. It's
been a hectic six months and you've worked very hard. Thank you.'

'I know it hasn't been easy for you. Here was I, a new broom coming in
after the shock of Jack Williams' death, and I made you change the ways
you'd been looking at things in this company. You may have felt that I
was being unnecessarily harsh with you at the start. This was deliberate.
You hadn't been meeting your targets, and you were all rather
complacent, blaming others for problems which you should have been
able to solve yourselves, or at least by working them out among you.
You, Mike, needed to tighten up your production line. You, Tony, needed
to organise and consolidate your sales and order system. You, Bill, were
living happily with outdated systems which didn't give the information
which was needed when it was needed.'

'We're making progress now and I feel I can relax the very tight control
I've been keeping over your work for the past six months. Don't jump for
joy, though. I shall still drop on you from a great height when you don't

perform up to standard, but I want us to work together more as a team now rather than being purely directed by me.'

Silence.

Bill Roberts shuffled his papers and coughed.

'Yes, Bill?'

'Richard, I wasn't happy about your attitude towards us when you first came, and I certainly resented the controls you put on me then. Since then, OK, I can see that you've shaken us out of our lethargy and we're performing better now.

'But six months is a long time, and I felt like leaving the company several times during that period. We got very little encouragement from you, but you might have communicated some of the reasons for your behaviour and decisions - we were mostly in the dark and we had to share information amongst ourselves to find out what was going on.'

Richard Stillman replied, 'And so you should have. There was too much compartmentalisation here. I wanted you to share information. I didn't call general meetings more than once a month because I knew they would develop into "them and us" situations. Only now are you really making progress. Perhaps I should have told you the reasons for my behaviour and style earlier. Perhaps I was wrong in my judgement of the progress and development you were making. But I hope we'll work together more as a team now. You know what the goals are, you know your own capabilities and commitment, as I do now. And I've learned a lot over the past six months about leadership, and so have you too, I hope!"

In Case 7.4, Richard Stillman has detected an improvement in his subordinates' job-related development, and is now willing to change his leadership style from high task/low relationship to high task/high relationship, which is more appropriate to the situation. Importantly, he involves his subordinates in the process. Equally, they feel they can display their resentment at the close directions and lack of communication they experienced over the past six months – continuous exposure to this style can lead to subordinate alienation, as was expressed here: Richard Stillman is not a skilful communicator. He did not explain the reasons for his behaviour to his subordinates. But the fact they feel they can talk to Stillman in this way is a sign that mutual respect and trust are being built up, that boss–subordinate relationships are becoming healthy, and that Stillman's expressed leadership style achieved its objectives – better performance.

SUMMARY

A five-fold classification of leadership is identified.

Traits approach

The early studies concentrated on trying to ascertain whether successful leaders had common personal characteristics or psychological traits. If these could be identified, the search for good leadership and management in organisations could be simplified. However, very few common factors have come to light after over half a century of research.

Behavioural approaches

Leader behaviour in relation to goal achievement indicated that jobs should be broken down into clearly structured tasks, so that it was possible to introduce specialisation of labour and well-defined measurable performance targets.

However, it was recognised that attention needed to be paid to interpersonal relationships at work as well as productivity. It was hypothesised that people expect their social needs to be satisfied at work. The human relations school of leadership considered the leader to provide a facilitative function, sharing power and authority with the group towards goal achievement.

Further, observations of management and leadership behaviour suggested that managers adopted different degrees of task-oriented and people-oriented behaviour. This concept spawned from the original Ohio studies, which revealed the relationship between a leader's concern for production and concern for people. A similar philosophy but with different styles led to the managerial grid. The styles identified are task management (emphasis on productivity), team management (achievement through negotiating commitment from others); middle of the road management (trade off between production requirements and market morale), country club management (satisfaction of social needs) and impoverished management (minimum effort to tasks and relationships).

Contingency studies

Under the contingency model, successful leadership is attained when the leader's style matches the demands of a given situation. The degree of match is defined in terms of the degree of favourableness to the leader, which in turn is composed of three elements, the leader–member relationship, the degree of structure of the task, and the leader's formal power. Assessing the situation according to the combination of these three should show the appropriate leadership style to adopt.

Managerial decision-making

In order to assist managers in making decisions, Vroom and Yetton developed a series of questions which could help leaders modify their styles to suit the circumstances of different situations. Three alternative styles were identified, autocratic, consultative and participative. Which style to use depended on the answers to seven key questions and fourteen problem types.

Situational leadership

The situational leadership model was based on the concept that good managers need to adapt their styles to meet the needs and characteristics of individual situations, it describes four leadership styles based on the two dimensions of task behaviour and relationship behaviour. Although each manager may prefer a particular combination of styles, the best manager is capable of adjusting his style to the pressures of the situation. Situational requirements are identified in terms of meeting the needs of subordinates, which is measured in terms of their psychological maturity.

IN CONCLUSION

Today's managers face demands at work which, although techno-logically more sophisticated, are little different from those faced by managers sixty years ago. They still have to achieve targets, they still have to organise work, they still have to motivate, control, and develop their subordinates. They still live in a stimulus–reactive world, driven by the demands of short-term results at the cost of reflective thinking and long-term planning. The able manager seeks to change his environment and adopt a more proactive approach: leading, and getting things done by other people, is active behaviour, not reactive behaviour. Consequently, the strong assumption underlying this chapter is that good leaders can be developed. With the growth in popularity of interpersonal skills training, it is possible to help individuals to become more self-aware, and to understand the consequences and implications of their leadership behaviour.

Good leadership style is situationally variable, but the manager leader must recognise that he is only one of many factors influencing the subordinate in his attitudes towards the job and the organisation; he must identify the other influencing factors and look for opportunities to reduce or amplify their effects on the subordinate to generate high levels of performance, such as in procedural and operating systems, departmental or organisational structure and constraints, job design, motivational hygiene factors, and personal relationships.

8 Power: a Base for Action

Case 8.1   The Dean of the medical school

The position of Dean for a world-famous school of medicine in Scotland, UK, became vacant. His colleagues had expected the incumbent to retire at fifty-five. They advised him to retire at sixty. He finally retired at the age of sixty-five.

Of the four candidates shortlisted for the position, the two strong favourites were both faculty members of the school.

This school of medicine is probably one of the more interesting of the British medical schools. Over the years, it has earned itself the reputation of being one of the foremost intellectual centres in a number of fields of medicine. It has forged strong links with other schools and medical centres in the USA and Europe. The faculty of the school hold positions of academic distinction in the university and are frequently asked to act as medical consultants to other major schools and hospitals.

The two favourite candidates have two aspects in common. Both are surgeons, although they have specialised in different areas. Second, both are intellectual supremos. Each would be considered the top brains in the country in his field. Both have undertaken extensive research, published widely, and have acted as consultants to some of the world's largest health organisations, and both could be described as workaholics. Their capacity for work has astounded even those who work closest to them.

However, there could not be two more different personalities. One surgeon is introvert, is poor at social conversation, prefers relatively solitary social pastimes such as golf or chess, and is extremely cautious on all matters. The other is extrovert, gregarious, a good mixer, spendthrift and is used to having his own way.

There are two other candidates. One is also a faculty member of the school, the other being the only external candidate. The third candidate holds the position of deputy director and is seen by his colleagues as introverted, dour, uninteresting; he has a poor research record, but is recognised as a most competent administrator.

> The tension between the two favourites has been obvious for the past few years. One has consistently opposed the other on both policy and methodology in all the large-scale projects and research programmes commissioned for or by the school. Both are feared and respected by their faculty colleagues.

Over twenty-five years ago, key writers and theorists on the behavioural sciences argued that the topic of power in organisations required further examination. They felt that motivation theory, leadership theory and even theories of organisation structure and design would not provide all the answers concerning human behaviour in organisations. Undoubtedly, the more established organisation theories on motivation and leadership were, and are, considered vital to the understanding of organisation behaviour, but there was also a suspicion that additional forces influence people's thinking, feelings and values, and lives in general within an organisational context.

Those early theorists were right to stress the importance of power in organisation psychology. Are knowledge and skills of motivation, leadership, and organisation design sufficient for high-quality executive performance? The answer is no – few organisations are that clear cut. People in organisations do not follow simple rules, such as 'because he is a good leader, I will accept him as a leader'; 'Because the organisation is appropriately structured and designed to achieve particular ends, I will comply with its present format'. No! Organisations are full of contradictions, of people acting independently, of people acting upon their own needs, of people changing their minds. These contradictions, twists and turns, and alternative behavioural patterns, need to be managed. Such breadth of human behaviour could be seen as a problem, for it does not entirely fall in any theory or conceptual category discussed this far. Alternatively all this human behaviour and passion could be turned to advantage by the organisation if it recognises that it can harness this reservoir of human energy. Case 8.1 provides an interesting dilemma. A small number of influential, respected, well-established, probably powerful people, are aiming for a top job. Would personnel selection techniques solve the problem? What is the problem? Would any of these individuals accept a standardised procedure to select the best of them? Would they attempt to influence the situation in any way? If one of them were selected, how would the others feel – but more important, what would they do? How important is the application of power in influencing what happens?

Power is a key concept in the study of human behaviour in organisations. It pervades but does not neutralise the other theories such as motivation, leadership and organisation and job design. It is rather that the other theories leave unanswered certain questions, which may be resolved through an analysis of power.

In this chapter we examine the concept of power and discuss power levers. We look at the different conceptual dimensions of power and whether different environments or cultures of organisation require different power levers. Finally, we analyse how people in organisation both adjust to and accept power plays and changes of sources of power.

UNDERSTANDING POWER

Although there are different interpretations of power, the term broadly encompasses the following characteristics at least:

- base(s) from which to act
- organisationally or individually determined
- potential for success
- influenced by organisational norms and values
- concept-based

Power is essentially a firm base from which to act. Does an individual have authority, money, and contacts with influential people? Can he use such sources of power to influence people? Such 'potential' to act can be organisationally determined, in that the individual acquires a role which allows him breadth of action, or individually determined, in that others comply because of a resource such as physical strength. It is worth stressing the word 'potential', for having acquired power, success is not guaranteed. That power has to be utilised in a manner appropriate to the situation, ie the organisation culture, norms and values: the traditions of the organisation. Certain organisations value only certain power sources, and use of a source of power considered illegitimate in that context could pose substantial problems for the power holder. Finally, power is a conceptually sophisticated topic. Recognising that various sources of power exist, identifying the sources at one's disposal, planning to use available sources and pursuing alternative power sources, is mentally taxing. Using power appropriately involves substantial thought.

Prerequisites for power

Power can be likened to a springboard, a base from which to jump, but it is a base shaped by several prerequisites. The American academic David Lawless describes three such prerequisites:

- *Resources*. Wielding power involves the utilisation of resources. The resources could be individually and/or organisationally based. A role which allows the individual to recommend somebody else's promotion or demotion would qualify as an organisational resource. Attractive looks, personal fortune or experience on the other hand, are examples of individually based resources. Whichever resource is used, it enables the person to influence the rewards offered or costs attributed to others.

- *Dependency* is coupled with the resource factor. The value of a resource is not determined solely by its possession but also by the degree of dependancy of one person on the other. A person is more powerful if he is not only in a position to determine the promotion of others, but others depend on him to do so. For example, in certain British police organisations, police officers above the rank of inspector cannot apply to be promoted to a vacant but higher status job. Only the officer's superior can recommend him for promotion. Under such circumstances, not contradicting one's superior could become a vital consideration for the individual, possibly at the expense of work effectiveness.

- *Availability of alternatives* could influence the power positions of people. If an individual is able to call on alternative resources, it is possible for him to reduce his dependancy on any other person. In a situation of labour shortage, an employer may have the resources to terminate someone's employment but would be unwise to do so, as he would be handing a skilled, experienced person, whose skills are in demand, to a competitor.

POWER LEVERS

Having established that power does not function in isolation, it is now possible to explore the various power levers (strategies) that an individual could employ. Seven power levers are identified, namely reward, coercive, legitimate, referent (personal), expert, information, and connection power.

Reward power

Reward power is used by people in a position to influence the rewards meted out to others. For reward power to be used successfully, the individual must be able to control resources desired by others.

The resources can be tangible in that they include material or non-material resources (status). The most obvious material reward, money, can be viewed as a motivator or just as a basic life commodity. Either way, a manager who can utilise money as a reward holds substantial power to influence the performance of his employees. This power increases if he is required to hire and fire. However, in larger public sector organisations that operate fixed pay scales and established conditions of employment, including procedures and agreements on hiring and firing, the power of the manager is drastically reduced. Under such conditions he has very little flexibility. The parameters of his resource power over his employees are closely defined.

Non-material-based power such as status and privilege can be a powerful lever. The headquarters of an internationally renowned UK bank has separate lifts for people of different managerial status. The high status lift has a lift attendant who allows only a few, privileged people into the lift. This low status employee enjoys a position of considerable influence in the eyes of his peers. However, he also has a high level of anxiety, for he may possibly refuse entry to a manager whose status warrants the privilege of using that lift. The lift attendant has never formally been told who has been promoted or demoted from senior management. It is assumed he knows.

Similarly, access to exclusive clubs or restaurants, the key to the executive toilet and freedom to use the company's American Express card are examples of non-material resource and material resource-based reward power.

The success of reward power depends on the rewards being desired. What one person considers 'exclusive' may well be commonplace for others. Further, even rewards that are desired may be given in a way which is disliked. Organisations that are predominantly paternalistic in nature could be held in contempt by their employees if the latter believe high rewards are offered to those who are subservient. The senior management of such organisations may find it difficult to understand why substantial rewards are at times only grudgingly accepted.

Reward power needs to be handled extremely carefully. No one likes having his behaviour constantly influenced by someone over him.

Coercive power

As the term implies, an individual adopts punishment-centred methods. The source of such power may lie in the person's role, in that he holds the authority to organise people as is deemed necessary. He may be able to fire people or move them round the organisation. The manner in which such authority is exercised will determine whether other people view such action as the rightful use of authority or as punishment.

Equally, the individual may be able to adopt a coercive power position through individual physical attributes. A big, strong man can use physical power to induce others to comply. A small man who holds a commanding position in an organisation and has characteristics that induce a fear-based response could be termed a tyrant.

Role and personal coercive power have two common elements. First, successful application of coercive power depends on others realising that the manager can or will punish (or reward). There is a significant difference between threatening to use coercive power and actually being able to use it. A common problem in larger organisations is that managers may not be able or even allowed to fire or transfer other people. Under such circumstances, power is gained from the threat of firing rather than its actual use. If others see that it is only a threat, the power base is likely to collapse.

The effect of coercion as a power lever also depends on how others have observed the use of such power in the past. The individual may hold the right (in terms of role) and the personal attributes to apply coercion. However, the actual history of application will strongly influence the response of others. If a boss threatens retribution for not meeting deadlines and it is known he can apply such measures, but in the majority of cases does not, then his capacity to influence work standards is substantially diminished. Credibility and consistency are all-important.

Legitimate power

Sometimes termed position power, legitimate power stems from organisational position or role. Hence, legitimate power is synonymous with authority and control and is based on the way a role is organised in that particular organisation. Occupying a certain role entitles the incumbent to all the benefits of the role. Managers may be allowed to redistribute work, re-set priorities and transfer personnel to various teams as needs arise. Equally, a quality control inspector may be entitled to conduct spot checks on standards of work of all operatives and supervisors throughout the company. Hence, legitimate power is an entitlement an individual obtains from the role he occupies; the entitlement ceases once he leaves that role.

What is the value of analysing a person's job or role? Such analysis is useful if the aim is to define the boundaries of activity and influence for the role holder. In other words, any one needs to know what he can and cannot do in his job. However, such analysis is of little value in terms of how the person should conduct himself in his role, without considering the current constraints and opportunities.

Professor Charles Handy poses the question: who is the guarantor of a particular position? If legitimate power is to be effectively applied, what backing does the occupant of that particular role receive? An individual needs backing from other authority figures and also needs backing in terms of resources (reward or coercive). Otherwise, legitimacy as a power base will fail.

In reality, such backing cannot be guaranteed. Too many factors are in a constant state of flux. The individual's boss may be having problems with his own boss and hence unable to back anyone. Resources promised may be unavailable or in short supply to the role holder simply due to changes in the purchase behaviour of bulk customers. It needs only one or two customers who purchase in bulk to terminate their orders to create panic in any organisation. Despite these difficulties an individual can help himself, depending on the position he holds, in three ways:

1 Information is a valuable asset. It can concern technical, product, financial or human resource issues. The greater the amount of information the individual can attain the more aware he is of developments in the organisation. In this way, potential difficulties may be foreseen and acted upon. Further, attracting appropriate information allows the individual the freedom to choose which information is released further. Hence, the legitimate power of that role is emphasised.

2 Access to other people or various networks in the organisation provides a source of further legitimate power. The individual's role may naturally allow access to personal, professional or

informal networks. Alternatively, he may have to negotiate such access and entry. Either way, legitimate power partly depends on the perception others hold of that role.

3 Setting priorities is part of a manager's job. Organising other people's work with a consistent theme and direction is a potential way of influencing others in the situation. Establishing priorities for subordinates' work, so that the success of one particular activity is emphasised, is one way of exhibiting the manager's competence. Equally, it is a reasonably good way of turning people's attention away from areas of less than adequate performance.

Case 8.2 The dinner (Part 1)

The university Vice-Chancellor invited a number of well-respected figures, including an academic in the field of medicine, high-ranking dignitaries from public service, and an influential businessman, to an exclusive dinner at the university. He hoped that the majority of his dinner guests would agree to sit on the appointing committee for the soon-to-be-vacant post of Dean of the Medical School.

'Hmmm. It's working out OK,' thought the Vice-Chancellor, as he watched his dinner guests discuss points of mutual interest. All the desired guests were in attendance at the dinner.

After further discussion, the deputy chief executive of the local authority remarked to the Vice-Chancellor, 'Well, what about Milton Aubrey? Does he stand a chance of the job?'

'I'm not sure I'm qualified to comment. I think my medical colleagues should say what they think,' responded the Vice-Chancellor.

Of the notable array of intellectual talent attending the dinner, two were faculty members of the school. 'Now. Of the insiders for the job, Milt's an outsider. He's OK, nice chap, but he hasn't done much research. He won't set the world on fire!' said one of them.

'But, I thought he'd done a lot for the school as deputy director,' commented the Dean of Humanities.

'Yes. All right. He sits on committees, he knows a few of the right people. But that's it! He's a good back-up man to Allan Ryder [present dean, about to retire],' rejoined the other faculty member.

'I don't want to hang out your dirty washing at a dinner like this, but you know the medical world, and we know too who baled Allan out,' interjected the director of another well-known medical school. He continued, 'Allan just kept on upsetting people. He made enemies. There are only two reasons people forgave his arrogance: first, Milton more than once took the heat out of the situation; second, Allan is an intellectual supremo. But, I've got to hand it to Milton, he's a good administrator who has helped the school grow and kept crises to a minimum.'

'You know,' interjected a well-known businessman,' it seems to me, the question is what sort of Dean do you want? Does a good doctor with a good research track record make a good Dean? What do you want the place to look like in ten years' time? I'll tell you something. Milton gets the system right for other people to do their job. He's not obstructive and, most of all, he's clean. If he says that's OK to do, you know it's totally legitimate.'

'You're right up to a point, but he represents the whole school to the outside world. Do you want someone who is only clean and proper running the place?' asked the first faculty member.

Everyone laughed.

In the opinion of the medical school faculty members attending the dinner (Case 8.2), Milton Aubrey should be considered the least favoured candidate as he is seen to operate only from a legitimate power base. His use of authority, control and administrative resources may have been fruitful, but that was an insufficient reason for appointment to the post of Dean. Others agreed that Aubrey's strength lay in administration, but also considered legitimate power sufficiently important to merit appointment to the role.

Another comment worth noting in Case 8.2 is the suggestion that Aubrey, as deputy director, 'cleaned up' certain problems created by the present Dean. Irrespective of Aubrey's administrative talents, had he not been deputy director, it is unlikely he would have been invited to become involved in such problems. Hence, position in hierarchy and role title are important, not only for status reasons, but for reasons of potential power. It is unlikely that in a position other than deputy director Milton Aubrey would have had the same access to his director or even have been offered information of potential embarrassment to the director. The unseen side to legitimate power, such as access to key people or valuable information, varies according to one's position in the hierarchy. It can be assumed that all organisation charts show comparable distribution of legitimate power. The hidden side to legitimate power in terms of access to people and information makes all the difference to the success, or failure, of its use.

Personal power

Personal power depends on particular individual characteristics, loosely termed personality, and physical characteristics, which make that individual attractive to others. Terms such as charismatic, popular, having panache, flair, are used to describe someone with personal power. Equally, physical attributes such as height, size, weight and strength would be considered aspects of personal power. Rather than through using role, rewards, coercion or knowledge, the person influences others by emotionally stimulating them. Hence, personal power is based on an individual's ability to make others sympathetic towards him as a person. Having stimulated such sympathy, the individual can then use the relationship to divert the feelings and behaviours of others to his own advantage. Very simply, others want to be in the presence of, or gain the favour of, or simply be liked by, the charismatic person. They will give him what he wants in order to be allowed 'near him'.

Successful application of personal power depends on two factors: first, that others are attracted to one's personality. It is easy to assume that everyone will be attracted to the same person. Such assumptions do not hold good. As academic consultants operating from a business school, we have often seen reasonably senior executives whose personal style has worked extremely well with one department, division or group, but not with another. Should one counsel the executive to adjust his style, which means maintaining a personal power base, but with a different style, or to adopt a new power base(s)? No easy solution exists. Second, charisma depends a great deal on interpersonal contact. It is difficult to feel the charisma of a person through memos or the minutes of meetings, or even through radio, book or television, although the latter two media can be happily used to project such charisma. Charisma is best experienced on meeting the person.

The failure of John De Lorean's Northern Ireland car manufacturing plant, for example, can be explained in such terms. According to reports, De Lorean is a charismatic figure, able to use his charisma as a negotiating lever. For those who only read of his negotations with, and his obtaining of grants from, the British government, it may be difficult to understand how he achieved such backing. For those who interacted with the man the story is different, for he was considered a charming, influential, and at times overpowering individual.

To apply personal power successfully in different situations requires a high level of interpersonal skill.

Expert power

A person perceived as possessing specialist knowledge or skills in a particular field is said to possess expert power. The use of expert power is especially pertinent to complex problems. An expert is called in to examine the problem, if necessary to find appropriate solutions and implement them. It is unlikely that application of expert power will be resented, as the majority of people in the situation will probably readily acknowledge that the expert has the right to offer his opinion and act accordingly. Expert power does not solely depend on qualification or other external factors. A person who is seen to have solved even one problem, or who has slightly more knowledge in a given field than others, may be labelled an expert. The halo effect applies, and people may well expect the person to solve a number of problems, and be disappointed, as the individual has never been trained to apply himself on a broader brief.

Hence, although expert power may be readily accepted, problems may arise if the individual's expertise is questioned. In that particular field of activity, the expert may be perceived as being less expert than expected. Equally, the expert may offer opinions or attempt to implement solutions outside his specialist field, which in turn would cause resentment and rejection. Further, he may offer appropriate advice and action, which interferes with the client's vested interests. Under such circumstances, the client(s) may well acknowledge the theoretical value of the expert, but reject him as a threat to their situation.

Profitable application of expert power depends a great deal on who is seen as expert at the time and for what reasons. An individual is only seen as expert until a better 'expert' comes along.

Case 8.3   The dinner (Part 2)

'All right, then. What about Irwin Selby?' asked the deputy chief executive of the Local Authority.

'Well, he's very different from Milton,' said one of the faculty members.

'He's bright. He's sharp. He doesn't write a great deal but what he writes and researches is excellent,' added the second faculty member.

'Yes, I know his reputation, but when I met him I just felt uncomfortable all the time,' commented the businessman. He continued, 'When I've talked to him, what struck me was that he's so precise in everything he says. What's more he expects you to be the same. If you haven't got your facts quite right or haven't quite used the right word to describe something, that guy just pulls you up on it and makes you, well at least me, feel that I'm stupid. What's more, most of the time he doesn't look at you when you talk to him and when he does, have you noticed, his eyes are so piercing they go right through you.'

'Look, you may not like the man! But don't you know he is a world-acknowledged expert in cancer research?' exclaimed the second faculty member.

This was the first time that one guest openly confronted another guest. Virtually everyone noticed; the room went quieter. Most felt slightly tense.

'Look, I was not commenting on the man's expertise, I know and respect that he's a world leader. I just wonder what impression he makes on other people. He left me cold. In business, it's unwise to ...', continued the businessman.

'Yes, but we're not in business - we're into teaching medicine,' interrupted the second faculty member. 'What we need as Dean is a person who has a world reputation. In that way he'll attract others with big reputations into the school, which means they bring their research money, which means we get a better school!'

'What you say is right but I think the personality of the Dean may be more important than you think. I mean, he's still going to be meeting people,' retorted the businessman.

'Interesting points of view,' said the Vice-Chancellor. He then turned to his immediate left and commented, 'Try this French wine I discovered on my recent European trip ... good eh ...?'

The conversation between the faculty member and the businessman revealed two quite divergent points of view (Case 8.3). The faculty member considered that Selby's power as an expert was sufficient to make him a strong candidate for the post of Dean. The businessman, whilst acknowledging that expert power is an important consideration, suggested that charisma could be equally worthy of consideration, as interpersonal skills play an important part in performing the job of Dean.

Information power

Information can provide an important power base. Raw data in itself means little. Information, as processed and interpreted data, used to support a point of view or to downgrade other people's arguments, can be a powerful base from which to act. The skill is knowing the information to acquire to suit the circumstances. In fact, there are three separate categories of information:

1 *Concrete information* is already compiled and dossiered information such as facts, figures, trends, projections, financial statements, reports examining the effectiveness of the enterprise or its parts or even personnel reports on particular individuals.

Most organisations generate and tabulate substantial amounts of concrete information. Such information is an important aspect of the management of the organisation. Access to the various sorts of concrete information is largely a function of role and position in the organisation. Confidential reports concerning the profitability of the enterprise are likely to be available to the chief executive and a selected few. The financial and marketing data upon which the report is based may be available to many in the sense that large numbers of clerks, secretaries and team leaders may record the performance of particular product lines or teams under their responsibility. However, as they do not have access to further information concerning the performance of the organisation, and are not in a position to discuss long-term trends, they are unable to understand the full implications of the data they hold.

2   *Process information* concentrates on the processes by which people relate to and interact with each other. Unlike concrete information, which comprises tabulated facts, figures and trends, process information is non-tabulated data concerning people's feelings about each other and the organisation. Hence, process information involves having or acquiring access to particular people or groups in the organisation, so as to influence their thoughts and actions. The secretary/personal assistant to a chief executive has potential access to process information, partly because she has greater personal contact with the chief executive and partly because most confidential concrete information is likely to be accessible to her.

3   *Self-disclosure information* is information of a personal and private nature that is freely offered by one individual to another on a basis of trust. One person trusts another sufficiently to discuss some personal and private matter that could be embarrassing if the information became public knowledge. It is important for the first person to feel that the other will listen and help if necessary, but most of all maintain confidentiality.

A vital consideration in information power is access. Access would be a function of role and position in the organisation, especially for factual and process information. Potential for access not only allows the individual to be privy to factual or process information, but, further, gives him the chance to influence the quantity or quality of that information. In contrast, self-disclosure information depends far more on the relationship between two people.

Connection power

Connection power means having both personal and professional access to a large number of people within and outside the organisation. These people may or may not have information relevant to the individual, but that is not the essential feature of connection power. Making large numbers of contacts who could be valuable is the primary concern. Making friends at conferences, getting to know people at conventions and distributing one's business card at meetings are ways of making contacts. The individual attempting to increase his connection power may not know what value each of his contacts has. Simply making contacts who could be useful at a later date is sufficient.

Two types of contacts can be defined – connectors and providers. Connectors are people who can introduce the individual to the people he wishes to meet. They provide a facilitative or linking service through their network of personal or professional contacts. Providers, on the other hand, are key contacts who provide a product or service desired by the individual. Providers may themselves be able to give a person what he wants. Connectors can only give access to providers or to other connectors. Of course, anyone can be both a connector and provider, depending on how others see him. The skills of building a wide network of contacts are discussed further in Chapter 9.

Case 8.4   The dinner (Part 3)

'Fine, we all recognise Selby's got one hell of a brain, even if he has little else, but what about Casper Grant? Now he's a real showman. That chap's got style,' chuckled the deputy chief executive of the local authority.

'Yes, he has. He's quite an entrepreneur. He was the driving force behind raising the money for the orthopaedic research unit. He generated millions of pounds,' commented the businessman.

'He's also very well connected. He really does know many people in different walks of life,' commented the high-ranking official from the Scottish Office.

'The only problem with Dr Grant is whether the faculty would accept him as Dean. He may be a showman, an ambassador or even an entrepreneur and all these may be good for the school, but not as Dean. I'm not sure he gives the right image,' commented the first faculty member.

'Charles, you should come a bit more clean!' interjected the second faculty member. He continued to talk, 'I'm not sure the faculty trust him. He's too erratic. He changes his mind too quickly. Like all good entrepreneurs he's a one man band. He wants to do things his way. The rest of the faculty just won't take to that. When he doesn't get his own way, he can be terrible to live with.'

'You certainly have some interesting internal candidates,' smiled the director of the other medical school.

'What about the external candidate?' asked the businessman.

'I've met him. Interesting man,' responded the Vice-Chancellor.

Of the numerous attributes of Dr Casper Grant (Case 8.4), connection power was seen as his predominant strength. Coercive power ('he can be terrible to live with') was another power lever he used, but, judging by the opinion offered, he used it badly. Further, Grant's individualism and flair, although respected by some, was not viewed positively by the two faculty members. His lack of legitimate power was seen as a problem.

As indicated in the cases, each of the three internal candidates was applying different power levers, which were seen as both a strength and a weakness, depending on the various individuals' point of view. Such points of view were specified according to particular criteria. One candidate was considered 'safe' for the organisation; another as a world-renowned expert who would improve the professional image of the school if he were appointed. The third was considered entrepreneurial and well-connected: he would possibly attract funds and the attention of public figures. The question is, which criteria are appropriate? The issue of establishing appropriate criteria is linked with the question of situational circumstances. Who is the right person under these circumstances, in this situation? In order to explain adequately what criteria under what circumstances, we embark on an analysis of organisation culture.

CULTURE OF ORGANISATIONS: AN ANALYSIS OF SITUATIONAL CHARACTERISTICS AND POWER LEVER APPLICATIONS

All of us have experienced cultural differences in organisations. When we move from one organisation to another, we know that simply becoming acquainted with the technical aspects of the new position will not be sufficient. If we are to be considered successful, we have to make a stringent effort to understand our new colleagues, superiors and subordinates and their attitudes towards work, supervision and the organisation in general. In our previous position we may have been hardworking, conscientious and recognised by our colleagues as making a positive contribution. In the new job, to work too hard may be undesirable and to interact too closely with colleagues and superiors may be considered 'social climbing'. After a time, all of us realise that there are certain ways of doing things; some subjects that are taboo, and there are certain people one can upset, but others one should never upset. In fact, all of us are surrounded by likes and dislikes which we must take into account in our daily work.

These likes and dislikes reveal the attitudes which determine the behaviour of people in organisations. After a time, these attitudes and behaviours can become characteristics of a particular organisation. Various organisational characteristics such as leadership, supervisory styles, organisational structure and flow of communications interact to produce the culture of an organisation.

Organisation culture is difficult to define. It is best described as a feeling which a number of people share consistently about situations in the organisation. If a sufficient number of people perceive a situation in a similar light, does it then become reality? The answer is probably yes, and if such thinking is applied to organisations, then a culture or a number of cultures may form amongst the various groups operating within the organisation. Professor Charles Handy goes further by suggesting that cultures are deeper phenomena than just commonly agreed ways of perceiving a situation. He states:

> In organisations, there are deep-set beliefs about the way work should be organised, the way authority should be exercised, people rewarded, people controlled. What are the degrees of formalisation required? How much planning and how far ahead? What combination of obedience and initiative is looked for in subordinates? Do work hours matter, or dress, or personal eccentricities? ... Do committees control an individual? Are there rules and procedures or only results? These are all parts of the culture of an organisation. (p. 177)

Culture can take on many meanings ranging from the types of buildings, offices or branches housing the organisation's employees, to the kind of people it employs, their particular career aspirations, their perceived status in society, their degree of mobility, level of education, and so on. Hence, culture refers to the way people in different (or sometimes similar) work organisations view the world, their life and the way they go about their work. Even within one organisation different cultures will prevail; different points of view exist between those working in research, administration, policy making and operational activities.

Let us now look more closely at cultures and the appropriate power levers for each one. A distinguished scholar and consultant, Dr Roger Harrison, has provided a means to help analyse the position of the individual in different cultures. Harrison distinguished four basic organisational cultures: power, role, task and person.

Power culture

A power culture provides excitement and exhilaration for some and is substantially threatening to others, for this cultural type depends on strong leadership from a central power source (see Figure 8.1). A central power figure or small group controls and manipulates all activity within the organisation. The power figures are usually accompanied by functional specialists, who provide professional advice and information to promote the image of the all-powerful.

Traditionally, the type of organisation that has held such an image has been the small entrepreneurial organisation of the nineteenth century. In the twentieth century, the industrial barons and some powerful trade union leaders have provided an equivalent image. In addition, certain key executives in import/export companies, trading and finance companies may fall into this category.

A power culture-oriented organisation functions mainly by subordinates anticipating the wishes, decisions and attitudes of those at the top. In practice, those at middle and lower levels will react quickly to rumour and use the grapevine as the main source of information.

Although regulations may be formally stipulated, in practice few rules and procedures are adhered to, as administrative procedures are viewed as more of a hindrance than a help. In-fighting at the top of the organisation can be intense and a number of casualties may result both at the top and lower down the organisation. In a power culture, decisions are largely the outcome of a political struggle rather than logical deduction.

Such a culture can be summarised by words like competitive and challenging. The actors in the fray have to be seen as strong, proud, and able to accept ever-increasing responsibility. The power holders

Reward	Rewards are offered for supporting key power figures.
Coercive	Mistakes, misdemeanours and actions are punished if they threaten key power figures.
Legitimate	Rules, regulations and procedures are likely to be in operation but unlikely to be adhered to by key power figures.
Personal	Strong, decisive, somewhat uncompromising; charismatic leader behaviour: leader tends to manipulate others to satisfy own ends. Low support for others who are not key power figures.
Expert	Knowledge and performance standards are not based on professional criteria, but on maintaining influence over others.
Information	Information desired only to help in achieving personal ends.
Connection	Attaining numerous contacts and connections is considered vital, both within and outside the organisation, tending to generate a closed shop club culture, open only to the exclusive few.

Fig. 8.1   Power culture: effective use of power levers
Adapted from A.P. Kakabadse, *Culture of the Social Services*, Gower, 1982.

must be agile and flexible in order to react to danger and change course due to unpredicted influences in the external and internal environment. Yet, whether the right or wrong decisions are made, the power holders' paramount objective is their continued success and prosperity.

People who perform well in power cultures are not professionals in the traditional sense of presiding over an area of responsibility and valuing a limited amount of technical expertise. Professional activity is seen as constraining and demotivating. In a power culture, money and status tend to be far more highly valued. Both money and status will be utilised to charm others so as to add to the powerful man's list of contacts. To this end, considerable time and effort are invested in creating and maintaining networks of potential sources of useful people, and valuable information, and in keeping an accurate diary of future events in order to extend sources of influence.

Consequently, if a person is to achieve success in a power culture, he would need to develop his personal charisma (personal power lever) and information and connection levers. To maintain a successful position in a power culture would require dexterous use

Reward	Rewards are offered for adopting behaviours appropriate to the existing rules, regulations and procedures.
Coercive	Punishment or coercive action taken if a person works outside the deemed role requirements or if existing rules, procedures and communication patterns are threatened or broken.
Legitimate	Behaviour that is in keeping with the well-defined authority relationships, rules, procedures. Task behaviour in line with existing job outlines/descriptions.
Personal	Personal power comes from the perceived rightful issuing of rules, procedures and allocation of work. Personal support offered in order to fulfil requirements of one's role.
Expert	Working solely within one's role and not threatening the existing role structure.
Information	Information flows are influenced by existing role prescriptions and need to be within established patterns and procedures.
Connection	Only contacts and connections required to fulfil role demands stipulated by rules and regulations governing performance.

Fig. 8.2   Role culture: effective use of power levers
Adapted from A.P. Kakabadse, *Culture of the Social Services*, Gower, 1982.

of reward and coercion levers. In a power culture personal success is important; charisma, intuition, constant change and risk-taking are common, everyday experiences. A successful power-oriented leader in a power culture is likely to be considered a source of inspiration. A power-oriented leader operating in any of the other three cultures is likely to be viewed with suspicion and mistrust and probably considered immoral.

Role culture

The role culture is one where functions, job specialisation, procedures and rules are seen to predominate (see Figure 8.2). Consequently, far greater attention is given to job descriptions, definitions of authority relationships, procedures for communication and rules for the settlement of disputes, and there is an urgency to establish suitable cross-over points. The principle function of senior management is co-ordination, as once direction is given each of the functions, guided by rules and procedures, will work according to the overall plan.

In a role culture, the formal definition of tasks and roles is considered more important than the individual. Individuals are selected for roles because they are thought to fit them. It does not matter so much that one individual is considered competent as that he or she is capable of working within a particular role. Performance beyond the role is not required. Indeed, performance beyond role requirement can be seen as a threat by both colleagues and superiors.

Personal power is considered immoral in organisations that are role culture-oriented, as power must be seen to emanate from the organisational role, the parameters of authority and responsibility encapsulated in the job description. Power here is acted upon in terms of the rightful issuing of rules and procedures and the appropriate allocation of work (legitimate power).

Such an organisation is synonymous with the sociologist Max Weber's ideal bureaucratic form. The predominance of rules and procedures as a form of communication, the allocation of work to roles rather than individuals and the rationality of the hierarchy are the principal features of Weber's rational–legal model.

A role culture organisation can only operate properly in a stable social environment. Either the external environment is unlikely to change, or the organisation has control of its environment through a monopoly. If one or both conditions are satisfied, then a role culture organisation may well be effective in its performance and output. The leading national banks and insurance companies operate in stable, controllable markets and hence are likely to be predominantly role-oriented cultures.

Some organisations that have held a monopolistic position for a number of years, and have developed stable, well-established role cultures suddenly face immense problems when product innovations destroy their monopolistic hold of the market. A recent example is in the telecommunications industry, where parts of the British Post Office have not only serviced the United Kingdom but installed communication systems in countries throughout the world. Innovations in America and Japan and the sudden popularity of microchip technology threw an immense organisation into a state of mild anxiety. The organisation found itself no longer in a stable environment and had to look at the right managers to manage in a crisis, product innovation issues, marketing issues.

In fact, the organisation was split up into separate and independent businesses, the Post Office and British Telecom. The principal power lever in the organisation as it existed before its external environment changed would have been legitimate power, as behaviour in keeping with well-defined authority relationships was both desirable and appropriate. However, those organisations wishing to enter into new fields of endeavour and tackle completely new problem areas (eg British Telecom in an unstable, changing environment) are unlikely to be successful with a role culture.

Similarly, creative and innovative managers are likely to suffer frustration and stress in a role culture. Actions taken in a role culture are either approved or disapproved, rewarded or punished. Not surprisingly intuitive–innovative people do not respond well to such stimuli.

It may be inevitable that role cultures form in every growing organisation as economies of scale may become more important considerations than flexibility. Managing a large number of personnel with varied technical expertise does demand clear-cut role boundaries. The price for the operation of such a system is loss of innovation within a static reward system.

Task culture

Task cultures attract people who prefer to solve new problems. Groups of experts gather to focus on a common task or problem, whether it be an organisational problem or one of a technical nature (Figure 8.3). Charisma and influence are based on application of technical expertise rather than positional or personal power.

The predominant style is to work in team settings, rather than as individuals maintaining a role within the hierarchy or pursuing personal power needs. The task culture is a group culture, where differences of individual objectives, status and style are quickly and happily sacrificed for the continued life of the team. People in task culture settings can quickly identify with the objectives of compact units (eg social work teams) but may have difficulty in respecting the overall objectives of their employing organisation.

A major advantage of a task group is its adaptability. Project teams and task force groupings can be relatively quickly formed to grapple with a problem and are equally quickly abandoned on its solution. Formal roles have little meaning in such situations, as judgement is based on expertise, control over one's work, easy working relationships and mutual respect for personal competence. Hence, the task culture and the role culture are anathema to each other: the former being based on sensitivity and flexibility to the

Reward	Rewards for high task performance, such as project leadership or responsibility for solving bigger problems.
Coercive	Coercive behaviour would focus on low task performance or differences of expert opinion. Rejection from elite group or disbandment of project is possible.
Legitimate	Solving problems at hand through application of technical expertise. Appropriate to challenge senior management if task so requires and to disband project group when it has achieved its objective.
Personal	Status and charisma from exhibiting problem solving skills.
Expert	Constant development of skills in order to solve new problems. Recognised that standards do not remain static but continuously evolve.
Information	Constant drive to acquire new information and for it to be shared amongst project group members or wider network of experts. Information to be used for problem-solving, not for personal gain.
Connection	Extensive network of like-minded experts inside and outside the organisation. Loyalty to network of experts rather than employing organisation.

Fig. 8.3   Task culture: effective use of power levers
Adapted from A.P. Kakabadse, *Culture of the Social Services*, Gower, 1982.

needs of the market and social environment, and the latter on the need to achieve somewhat inflexible long-term objectives and establish rules, procedures and roles for control purposes. The task culture thrives on speed of reaction, integrity, sensitivity, creativity as opposed to career hierarchies and role specialisation.

Control is not easy in task cultures, and large organisations especially face a number of problems. In organisations where a task culture predominates, control remains in the hands of top management by means of allocation of projects, people and resources. The actual control of projects is left to project leaders or those occupying a supervisory position and hence a decentralised task system but centralised policy system develops. When resources become scarce and project leaders have to justify their activities and ask for further resources, substantial negotiation and bargaining takes place. An immediate reaction by top management would be to control not only the allocation of resources but even daily task activities.

Such a move would be challenged by team leaders in an attempt to counteract the influence of senior management, with the result that the team leaders will be competing with each other as well as with top management. In situations of no growth, allocation of resources to one area could mean a cut for another field of activity. From a positively oriented task culture where high personal expectations and performance standards are the norm, in periods of recession morale in workgroups could begin to decline. Job satisfaction will be reduced and the workgroup will disintegrate. Individuals will begin to pursue their own objectives. In order to control the situation, management will introduce further rules, procedures and regulations and thereby begin to change a task culture into a role culture, with pockets of a power culture emerging as team leaders attempt to establish bases of power to enable them to influence top management's allocation of limited resources.

In some organisations task culture and role culture exist side by side. Such a phenomenon arises when an organisation has experienced exceptionally rapid growth. General Electric Company (GEC) grew out of all recognition due to mergers and takeovers. The social services, local government and health services had similar experiences when national restructuring changed the size and identity of the original organisations. Fundamentally, the new public service organisations were conceived and planned in terms of role structures. Little emphasis was placed during the period of reorganisation on the present and likely future needs of local communities and the task activities within the organisations. The resulting situation is that two, possibly incompatible, cultures exist within the same organisational setting. The directorate of the organisation is predominantly concerned with managing a role structure, whilst the professionals and specialists favour smaller, informal workgroups and task operations. In such circumstances, overall organisational identity is likely to be low. Task-oriented specialists are likely to perceive management as being rigid and even manipulative and untrustworthy. On the other hand, group identity is likely to be high, with substantial respect shown towards colleagues.

The task culture was championed by the behavioural scientists of the 1960s and 1970s, with emphasis on the advantages of small groups, expert and connection power between professionals and the merging of individual and group objectives. The task culture has been held synonymous with change, adaptation, democratic freedom, choice and the reduction of differences of status. Yet in periods of economic recession, stringency or even rapid growth, it is doubtful whether such a culture would predominate. Most certainly, the reason that some organisations are not influenced by a task-oriented culture is not that they are immoral or out of date, but that such a culture is inappropriate to their technology, structure and resultant group norms, in addition to the fact that the great majority of activities carried out in most organisations are routine and repetitive, and more appropriate to a role culture.

Person-oriented culture

The primary objective of the person-oriented culture is to serve the individuals in the group. Existing organisational structures, rules, procedures and roles are there to provide for the needs of individual members (Figure 8.4). The formal aspects of the organisation are prone to substantial change according to the needs and wishes of the actors in play at that time. In practice, this is the rarest of the four cultures and Harrison has suggested that it offers a higher order of moral values. For example, consideration of the other would take place amongst professional partners such as planners or architects, commune-type environments, small consultancy outfits and possibly voluntary help task forces that provide assistance and friendship to individuals in need.

Control in such organisations can only function properly by mutual consent. Each person has to have established with other

Reward	Acceptance by peers.
Coercive	Threatened by group expulsion.
Legitimate	Behaviour according to needs of individuals in the situation. Loyalty to individuals with whom one interacts. Little allegiance to the total organisation.
Personal	Personal power through sharing and partnership. Emphasis on personal growth by generating a warm and supportive environment.
Expert	Behaviour and work standards determined by individuals in the group at that time. Individuals are expected to adhere to these standards.
Information	Any relevant information to be shared amongst the group.
Connection	A personal sympathetic/emotional link with other individuals. To satisfy need of being with people one likes.

Fig. 8.4   Person culture: effective use of power levers
Adapted from A.P. Kakabadse, *Culture of the Social Services*, Gower, 1982.

group members a psychological contract (an understanding) that the individual takes precedence over the organisation. Ideally, each individual can leave the organisation when they wish and the organisation should not contain the power of eviction. In practice a compromise is often reached.

A person-oriented culture is unlikely to predominate in an organisation that is medium- to large-sized (ie over approximately 100 people). In most organisations, however, one is likely to find individuals and small groups who prefer a person-oriented approach but have to accommodate a stronger alternative culture. Some professional university staff, for example, may hold strong person-oriented values and task values, but operate in a role or task culture. Other than teaching and possibly some research, university staff tend to regard the organisation as a base from which to pursue personal professional interests which often only indirectly add to the status of the organisation. The organisation, however, operates according to quite a strict role distinction, especially between professorial and lecturing staff.

Other specialists in organisations often operate in a similar fashion: computer personnel, project engineers, hospital consultants and to an extent social workers. It is not unusual for people who hold these positions to feel little allegiance to the organisation but great loyalty to each other and to the client groups with whom they work.

Once a satisfactory conclusion has been reached with one client group and new and pressing problems appear elsewhere, the person/task-oriented professional will try to move to meet new needs. Such individuals will stress personal warmth, support and consideration towards others.

As stability of power and control depend on members' consent and co-operation, it is difficult to continue the development of a co-operative system over long periods of time. The founding member of a communal setting is likely to impose his own identity on the organisation. On his departure, the organisation will have to adjust either by developing into a different sort of culture, or by witnessing internal strife amongst potential leaders. By and large, an organisation that overcomes the difficulties of the leader's departure changes from a person-oriented culture to a task culture, or sometimes a role culture.

In person-oriented cultures which are a part of another but more dominant culture, control is always a problem. Managers within the organisation are likely to discover that person-oriented specialists are difficult to manage. To direct their activities or influence their personal values would be virtually impossible, as the normal range of sanctions brought to bear on erring individuals in organisations would be meaningless to the specialist. To begin with, many specialists enjoy tenure of employment, and those who do not will understand their position in the job market. The services of most specialists are in demand and so to move is no real problem. Hiring outside experts is unlikley to alter their opinion, and the power of a manager's personality will probably not impress the person-oriented specialist.

Case 8.5   The interviews

'Well, I think we should now make a decision. This is, after all, the third set of interviews. Of course, all three sets of interviews have been valuable in helping us decide,' commented the Vice-Chancellor.

The Vice-Chancellor was chairing the interviewing board, which comprised the deputy chief executive of the local public authority, the Director of the other Medical School, the Dean of Humanities, two officials from the Scottish Office, and a faculty member from the medical school in question, but not one of the two who had attended the dinner.

'OK. Let's see who we don't want,' responded the businessman. 'We don't want the external candidate. We got rid of him in the first round of interviews.'

'You're right, Sam. So now who do we want?' asked the deputy chief executive.

'Well, we must recognise the already significant reputation of the school,' said the Vice Chancellor.

The Dean of Humanities and the Director of the other medical school nodded. He continued, 'Numerous members of faculty are known world wide. They are highly skilled individuals who need to be allowed the freedom to do their own work. The question is, who is the most appropriate person both to develop the school and to allow individuals the opportunity to develop themselves?'

Further conversation followed.

'Oh, and also we are an international university. The medical school is only one faculty of seven. So you see, we do need someone to manage the systems and procedures that affect all faculties and be an active member of the interfaculty team of Deans and Directors. The job has quite an amount of administration,' commented the Vice-Chancellor.

The Vice-Chancellor was responding to an official from the Scottish Office who suggested an entrepreneurial director would be best and hence Casper Grant should be offered the job.

After further discussion concerning appropriate job criteria and candidate suitability, the Vice-Chancellor concluded, 'So we seem to be in general agreement. Dr Milton Aubrey should be offered the position of Dean of the Medical School.'

Most members of the interviewing board nodded. Five minutes later the meeting disbanded. The official from the Scottish Office spoke to the businessman as they walked down the corridor.

'So Steven Summers [the Vice-Chancellor] got his way. He wanted someone safe and, after two dinners and three interviews, that's what he got.'

The businessman smiled.

The criteria for appointment (Case 8.5) did not seem clear-cut. From the various comments made, the candidate required seemed to be someone suited to either a task culture or role culture. Based on the final comment, the Vice-Chancellor's real wish was to have a candidate who suited a role culture. Perhaps at such high levels criteria are never clear-cut and possibly it is a matter of who debates best, wins the day.

LEVELS OF POWER SOPHISTICATION

We have looked at the application of power and the power levers that can be used according to the various values, rituals and myths (ie organisation cultures) in any enterprise. Another fundamental issue still requires analysis: the purpose and intentions of the power holder/power wielder.

Consider what impact the word 'power' has on any individual. Probably the most common interpretation is that an individual A gets another individual B to do something, probably against B's wishes. Under such circumstances, the power levers are applied in order to achieve an immediate objective to the satisfaction of only one of the interacting parties. On this basis, power is a fairly crude, unsophisticated manipulative approach to goal achievement. But is that the only level of power play?

No! Three separate levels of power application have been classified according to their degree of sophistication by Dr Steven Lukes, the Cambridge academic.

Low level power sophistication (level 1 power)

Historically, the use of the term power has been based on the original interpretation of the German philosopher Max Weber, who suggested power was 'A having power over B to the extent that he can get B to do something that B would not otherwise do'. This interpretation was offered by the early sociologists and those researching the power of groups and communities. In fact, this is the way most people would interpret the word power. However, level 1 power is only meaningful after a careful examination of observable decisions. For example, A must know what he wants, what B can offer and how far B can be pushed. In this way, power is conflict-based and overt conflict is emphasised. Hence, decision choices are relatively clear-cut. In fact, most of the academic literature on power and politics, directly or indirectly makes a level 1-type interpretation of power.

Medium level power sophistication (level 2 power)

The view that power is simply 'A getting B to do what A wants' has been challenged, as it became evident that both crude and more sophisticated levels of power exist. Another view of power is highlighted by the question, 'What do national or local politicians do?' Politicians in western society would not survive for long if they attempted constantly to force people to do their bidding. However, politicians can be highly influential and their perceived power is probably achieved by their capacity to influence others to their own opinion on the key issues. Politicians' behaviour at election time provides a good example. Politicians argue, debate and attempt to influence the electorate as to what are the key issues. One party offers one interpretation of the primary issues whilst the other offers a different programme of policies based on different assumptions, values and issues. The ability to convince the electorate which are the most appropriate issues and policies, and that one's party has the leaders to apply those policies, wins the election. Hence, level 2 power does *not* concentrate on observable decisions and actions but on convincing others about the key issues, norms and values. In this way, certain issues are organised into the discussion, whilst other issues are clearly organised out of it. It could be argued that the Vice-Chancellor cleverly organised the interview scenario (Case 8.5) to centre on a discussion of satisfying his needs to create (or maintain) a role culture within the medical school.

It has been argued that the various financial and policy strategic planning techniques are a disguised form of level 2 power. Planning Programming Budgetary Systems (PPBS), management by objectives (MBO) and zero-level budgeting (ZBB) are undoubtedly mechanisms for making decisions, but also mechanisms for defining the key issues in the development of policy. Certain key issues may not be well understood by top management because of their complexity and technicalities. PPBS, MBO and ZBB can generate the data to assist better understanding of the problem areas in order to improve the decision-making process. Of course, everything depends on how PPBS, MBO and ZBB are applied. If these techniques have been cleverly programmed to concentrate on only certain types of data, other issues will not be highlighted. Unless people clearly understand both the technique and the way it has been applied, they will not be in a position to appreciate which data and hence which potential problems have been left out of the analysis. In fact, certain writers such as Aaron Wildavsky argue that these techniques are entirely power based, for the results of applying them vary according to who is applying the technique and his objectives.

The difference between level 1 and level 2 power is that level 1 involves action and observable behaviour, whereas level 2 may involve no action. With level 2 power, if one or more individuals can convince others that they should pursue only one particular line of argument, by simply dropping another line of argument or not voting in favour of a particular policy, they are as powerful as if they had taken some specific action.

High level power sophistication (level 3 power)

The idea that only two levels of power exist was again challenged and a third level added. Creative and farsighted people not only spot problems before they arise but are equally capable of recognising future potential issues. It is extremely difficult to be sufficiently aware and forward-looking to identify problems which may threaten one's interests, but without this ability one will never know whether one's interests are threatened until time passes and those issues turn into more concrete problems. Those people who have the capacity to examine short-, medium- and long-term trends, analyse the myths, rituals, norms, values and cultures of their organisation and then predict the likely impact of economic and social trends on their organisation hold the potential to utilise level 3 power. Sir Geoffrey Vickers termed this ability 'systemic wisdom': in other words the wisdom to foresee how their organisation's structures and systems are capable of meeting future potential challenges. If certain individuals are so talented, then major fire fighting problems need not arise.

Potential problems can be spotted, and acceptable courses of action taken which most others would recognise as a benefit not a threat, even though they may not realise the implications behind such moves. It is the ability to understand potential issues through an understanding of organisational norms that distinguishes level 3 power from the other two.

Case 8.6   Another dinner

The port was passed. The table broke up, and small groups formed.

'That was an excellent meal, wasn't it? Now we have discussed research contracts, but what is the real reason for this meal?' asked the businessman.

Pause.

'Well,' said one medical school faculty member looking at the other. 'We also want to know how Milton Aubrey got the job!'

The businessman chuckled.

'I thought as much! Can't you guess? Hmm... Well, what happened was that Steven Summers got his way. But don't think it was as simple as that,' smiled the businessman.

'I thought as much!' exclaimed the second faculty member.

'But how come every one of you let Summers have his way?' queried the first faculty member.

'Well, most of us didn't realise we were. I think I was one of the first to spot what was happening. One or two of the others still haven't realised what happened,' finished the businessman.

'What *did* happen?'

'Summers hardly mentioned Aubrey's name. He kept talking about criteria; yes, criteria; criteria for assessing which of the candidates should be chosen. Then before anyone could reply, he seemed to wander off the point and talk about the long-term trends and future potential challenges for universities. The discussions kept chopping and changing between appropriate criteria for candidates and the future challenges to be faced by universities. Do you see what was happening?'

Pause. The businessman looked quizzically at his two dinner companions.

'Not only was the candidates criteria question linked to the future trends for the universities ... you're right, that was obvious ... but his view of the future of universities. You see, nobody was discussing the future of universities. Most of us, without realising it, were discussing the Vice-Chancellor's view of the future of universities. He didn't say what the future would be. He just led us down a certain path by asking the right sort of questions,' chuckled the businessman.

'All right! Even so. But why Aubrey?' asked the second faculty member.

'Simple. Summers wants no problems in his team of Directors and Deans. Second, he wants to control the medical school. You see, in the future, funds from government are going to fall. So Summers wants to be in complete control of his university. The medical school will always be rich, so with Aubrey there, he can cream off some of the revenue into central funds. Also, and I know you two won't like this, but isn't Aubrey the best for the job in any case?'

The two faculty members looked at him in disbelief.

'What the future wants is a good administrator. Some one who can control overheads and costs. Look, the guys with the scientific or even entrepreneurial talent shouldn't be hindered. Let them do their own job. But not spend money. Grant will still bring in funds but can he manage the whole school? Selby will still write papers and go to conferences. Do you see the point?' questioned the businessman.

'I hear what you say but I don't like it,' commented the first faculty member.

'You know, you people should try running a business. That'd teach you a thing or two. Look at me with my companies. I'm doing exactly the same,' laughed the businessman.

The businessman (Case 8.6) highlighted the Vice-Chancellor's capacity to implement level 2 and level 3 power. By concentrating on particular issues the Vice-Chancellor managed to influence the appointing committee's thinking as to the likely future issues that would directly affect the university. Whether the Vice-Chancellor is proved right or wrong is irrelevant. What is of concern is that he has recognised that a change of leadership is required in the medical school to meet future needs. Further, as reported by the businessman, by adopting a selective question and answer approach, the Vice-Chancellor was able to crystallise future potential problems into present possible action. By clever application of level 2 and 3 power, the Vice-Chancellor successfully negotiated for Aubrey's appointment.

SMOOTHING OUT POWER STRUCTURE CHANGE

Certain changes, such as changes of leader and leadership style, new acquisition, growth, contraction, reorganisation, singly or in combination can alter the cultural norms in the enterprise. As a consequence, the fundamental structure of relationships will alter. Changes of important cultural features will alter the power structure. If an organisation is very much driven by one man, then that change of leadership will have substantial repercussions in the rest of the organisation. Those previously in favour may fall out of favour and vice versa. What is considered legitimate or illegitimate behaviour may change according to the style and philosophy of the new leader.

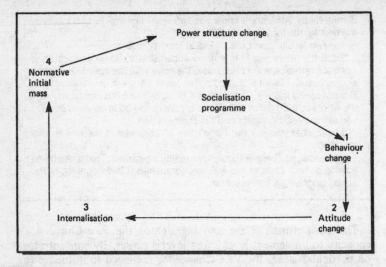

Fig. 8.5   Assimilating power structure change into the organisation

However, whether the changes are minor or major, whatever is new must be consolidated into the fabric of the organisation. A programme of socialisation needs to be introduced to ensure that changes of power structure are accepted by a critical mass in the organisation (Figure 8.5). Socialisation (as described in Chapter 2) is a process by which individuals accept changes of organisation and eventually consider them natural. Essentially, whatever discomfort the individual may have experienced, a well-managed programme of socialisation should enable him to feel more amenable and further capable of interacting well in the new environment. There are four stages of socialisation.

Behaviour change

Behaviour change means individuals doing something which could alter a previous acceptable behaviour pattern. If people discover for themselves that they can cope at work if they adopt new behaviours, then the links with the past are substantially weakened. Attempting to change people's pattern of behaviour may mean introducing induction programmes providing formal instruction in the new and desired practice and structures of the organisation. Induction programmes could be formal training programmes lasting one day or more. Equally, an induction programme could consist of informal chats between individuals and a series of small groups, comprising those people whose acceptance of change is critical for future success.

Alternatively, project groups or working parties could be formed, with the specific brief of examining better ways to introduce change. The project groups should comprise people for and against the changes of power structure. The findings of these groups are likely to be of some value, not simply because a number of influential people are talking about how to improve the situation, but the groups also provide a sufficient critical mass to begin to sway opinion in the organisation.

Equally, coercion can be applied in addition to a co-operative approach. People may be allocated tasks they dislike or be harassed, punished for errors. Those who feel they cannot conform will probably leave the organisation. Those who adjust to the new power structures will probably feel affinity with the new norms of the organisation.

Attitude change

A change of attitudes will slowly come about as people adopt new behaviours and discard old practices. Either by support or by coercion, as soon as people adopt different styles and approaches and practise them for a while, their attitude towards the new power structure begins to alter. Constantly practising new behaviours psychologically reinforces the need to change one's views. If the behaviour change inputs are successful, then in time the resultant attitude changes are likely to be successful. However, one factor that can hinder attitude change even though the behavioural programme may be appropriate is dissonance.

Dissonance is a state of psychological discomfort that an individual is likely to experience as a result of two or more substantially different influences which he cannot accommodate. Most people experience mild forms of dissonance quite often. A fashion-conscious girl finds a dress in a shop attractive, asks her friend's opinion of it, hoping for confirmation of her view, only to hear her friend criticise the garment. The girl is likely to experience dissonant discomfort between acting on her own opinion and rejecting the dress in concert with her friend's opinion. A great deal will depend on the extent to which she values her friend's opinion or even the friendship. If the friend is just a casual acquaintance, the person is likely to experience little dissonance. If her friend is a well-known fashion model, then the dissonance could be high.

Managing change in organisations involves attempting to reduce dissonance in others. Attempting to change behaviour by action groups, project groups or redesigning jobs can reduce dissonance. If people can do a new job or activity well, then they receive positive feedback about their skills and capabilities. Knowing that one can perform well relieves some of the anxieties concerned with change. The more positive the feedback, the more the person will be sympathetic to the changes of power structure.

Apart from restructuring the work of groups and individuals, the initial training could be organised to be tough and punishing. As long as a sufficient mass survive the training, then the likely outcome is that those who succeed value what they get, and in turn attempt to influence others on the value of such endeavour.

An alternative approach is simply to allow time for discussion. The opportunity for people to talk to each other and exchange views and experiences of recent problems can be valuable. If the majority in a discussion group agree that the changes are valuable, then those not in favour of change will often alter their attitudes in line with the majority, or leave the group, or even the organisation. However, it is important to be fairly sure of the direction the discussion will take, for if the majority reject the new changes, then the new power structure may collapse. In order to obtain the desired view, either the discussion in the group needs to be controlled, which can lead to further alienation if discovered, or the members of the group need to be vetted.

Finally, asking particular individuals publicly to commit their support to the new changes can be a powerful tool. Offering commitment publicly is synonymous to an admission of ownership which is difficult to disclaim. If a number of people publicly commit themselves to support a particular view or action, then it is impossible for them to say they are merely carrying out someone else's orders. In fact, they are likely to be seen as the order givers rather than the order receivers.

Internalisation

Internalisation is the result of an individual having undergone behavioural change, attitude change and dissonance, and emerged from the experience with reshaped values, norms and practices. The person finds the changes acceptable and willingly attempts to promote further the changes of power structure. The person identifies with (has internalised) the new norms and practices.

Normative initial mass

This phrase is used to denote that initial mass of people who support the changes of power structure and view the new norms and practices as an acceptable, natural part of the culture of the organisation. Once such a critical mass of people has been achieved there is no further need to emphasise approaches to behaviour and attitude change as the change of power structure has been achieved.

Case 8.7   Talking in the corridor

'Well, thank you, gentlemen. That brings this meeting to a close,' said Milton Aubrey bringing the meeting to an end in his role as chairman.

The faculty attending the meeting left the room. The first faculty member caught up with the second faculty member in the corridor.

'Well, it didn't take you long, did it?'

'What do you mean?' asked the second faculty member.

'You were the one who criticised Milton most. Now you're supporting these changes within the school,' responded the first faculty member.

'I'm afraid you're way behind. You see, I recognised some of the issues that Aubrey has been on about when I sat on the working party examining the structure of the school. We do need these changes. Oh, and all credit to Aubrey, he spotted the need for them and stuck to his guns all this time. My respect for him has grown appreciably during these last couple of months,' said the second faculty member.

'That's obvious,' commented the first faculty member, now clearly irritated. He went on, 'What about all those ideas about having a world expert or even an entrepreneur as dean? What about all those suggestions that if things didn't work out you'd resign?'

It was the second faculty member who now expressed his irritation. 'Look, things change. The fact that you can't go with change is not my problem,' he snapped.

He quickened his pace leaving his colleague behind. As he did so, he turned his head and said to his colleague, 'I don't think resignation is an issue which concerns me as much as you, wouldn't you say?'

The second faculty member (Case 8.7) seems to have undergone behaviour change and attitude change and has come to terms with and supports the new dean and his policies. The first faculty member does not seem to have undergone a similar experience and holds on to his original views. Interestingly, people are not fully aware of the changes of attitude they have experienced, which is evident when confronted by someone who holds an 'outdated' view. The response for challenging the new power structure is, so often, primitive.

SUMMARY

The analysis of power covers five different aspects:

Power definition

Power is equated with potential; potential to do something, ie a firm base from which to act. In effect, the application of power relies on the fact that an individual can (or cannot) muster sufficient resources to influence people to behave in particular ways. The concept of resources is crucial to the analysis of power. Resources can either be organisationally determined, ie role-bound, or personally determined, ie a feature of that individual's personality, skills, and physical characteristics. Further, the degree of dependency of others on these resources and the person wielding the resources will strongly influence how well the resources are utilised.

The power levers

The manner in which an individual applies power is termed 'a power lever': in essence, the approaches to power application. Seven power levers are identified.

- *Reward power*: the capacity to influence the material resource and non-material resource based rewards offered to others.

- *Coercive power*: a punishment-centred approach to power utilisation, which can be organisationally or individually based.

- *Legitimate power*: in effect, the application of appropriate authority and control stemming from the individual's organisational position or role. The application of legitimate power is influenced by the role holder's access to relevant information, access to relevant others and networks and approaches to priority goal setting.

- *Personal power*: involves the application of personal characteristics which can be personality-based (charm, charisma, flair) or physical attributes such as strength, height, size and weight.

- *Expert power*: specialist knowledge or skills can be attributed as possessing expert power.

- *Information power*: the ability to utilise information to support a particular point of view or alternatively downgrade other viewpoints.

- *Connection power*: access to relevant others within and outside the organisation.

Power lever application and organisation culture

The shared attitudes, behaviour, beliefs and values of people are considered to form the culture of any organisaiton. There are four separate organisation cultures, power, role, task and person cultures. A power culture depends on strong leadership from a central power source such as one person or small group who controls and manipulates virtually all activity in the organisation. A role culture is based on the concept of legitimacy in that the procedures, rules and control, authority and information systems are considered right and proper and not to be broken or transgressed. A task culture is one where problem-solving, application of expert knowledge, working in teams and individual and group adaptability are highly valued. Person-oriented culture develops when the existing structures, rules and procedures are interpreted as existing only to provide for the needs of each of the organisation's or group's individual members.

The behaviours, values and attitudes of each individual need to change and adapt when moving from one organisation culture to another, if the individual is to be perceived as performing effectively in the new culture. Equally, the seven power levers need to be applied in a manner that is acceptable to the predominant culture in a part, or whole, of the organisation.

Levels of power sophistication

The analysis of application of power levers is not only related to culture of organisation, but further, to the purpose and intent of the individual power holder. Level 1 power concentrates on observable decisions and actions. Level 2 power emphasises the key issues, norms and values but does not necessarily concentrate on immediate behavioural patterns. Level 3 power concentrates on latent issues and how an organisation's structure, systems and employees are capable of meeting future potential challenges.

Approaches to managing power structure change

In order to assist people to accept change, a four-stage socialisation programme is offered. Stage 1 involves inducing behaviour change in individuals in order to show that people can work just as well if they adopt new behaviours. If the new behaviours are found acceptable, then at stage 2 attitude change will slowly come about as people adopt new behaviours and discard old practices. It is common for the individual to experience dissonance at this stage. At stage 3, he emerges with reshaped values, norms and practices which he tries to implement. This process is known as internalisation. A person at this stage is likely to find the changes acceptable and may willingly attempt to promote further changes of power structure. If a sufficient number of people undergo internalisation, then they are the critical mass (stage 4) who are likely to support the changes of power structure and wish to make any new norms and practices an acceptable part of the culture of the organisation.

IN CONCLUSION

Power is by no means a 'black art'. It is an integral part of life in organisations, and practising managers and students of organis- ation theory alike will find an understanding of it extremely valuable.

Just as with politics in organisations (Chapter 9), the issues are not black and white, but delicate shades of grey.

9 Increasing Personal Influence

Case 9:1 Quality Systems Inc.

Quality Systems Inc. is a rapidly growing, USA-based multi-national information and network systems company, specialising in communications networks (telephone switching telecommunications) and software systems. In fact, the hardware side of the business, the communication networks and the software side of the business have been kept as two separate organisations.

For Mary Kinns, the Vice President, (VP) Human Resources, the separation of the two sides of the business from each other was seen as a problem. That was not all. Mary identified other problems facing Quality Systems (QS). She perceived the company as too product/specialist oriented. The company hired highly qualified engineering and computer specialists to service the ever changing products and services offered by the company. For the more ambitious, the career route to pursue was into management, with the result that most managerial roles were held by former engineers and programmers. Mary recognised the benefits that such a career pattern generated; quality of product or service was paramount in the minds of managers. The drawback was that management as a whole was insensitive to developments in the market place, and that for Mary was a pressing concern. She once said at one of the regular board meetings, 'We keep talking about the improvements and developments to our products and services. I really don't think that is the issue! I think the issue is that we don't really know what our customers are likely to want. Hell, we're OK this year but this is a fast moving business. What will the market want in two years' time? What are our competitors doing? How forward thinking are we?... are we really?'

Her colleagues listened. They liked her and respected her as an executive. She always got the feeling that they were polite and listened. Little else seemed to happen.

Mary's notions were not just conjecture. She deeply believed that the company would face a major problem over the next two to three years. She felt that the two sides of the business should be better co-ordinated. Customers required integrated communication networks. There seemed

249

to be little point in one half of the company providing the customer with the necessary hardware with separate negotiations having to be conducted for the software. A number of QS customers would offer the contracts for software to competitors. Others would purchase appropriate software resource packages but might then find integrating with the communications network a problem. Mary considered that few customers were satisfied with the total package offered by QS.

Something had to be done! Mary had spoken to some of the more influential managers on both the hardware and software sides of the business. Some listened; some disagreed with her; most told her that they did not see a problem. Mary then approached Karl Rode, General Manager, Business Development Systems (software). Karl was one of the few senior personnel in QS who held similar views to Mary. He too was convinced that the company would lose market share unless a more integrated total service, which the customer wanted, was provided. 'Look, Mary! it's no use just holding one to one meetings with a few senior managers. Nobody really knows what the hell you and I are talking about. We've really got to influence a few people. How the hell are we going to do it?'

Working in an organisation does not just involve developing effective business and/or professional skills, chairmanship skills, counselling and motivational skills, or even knowing how to restructure and integrate the various parts of the organisation. Each single problem facing any manager may be, in itself, not too complex and solutions should, in theory, be easily forthcoming. However, managers do not face problems one at a time. They often have to handle numerous issues at the same time. As portrayed in Case 9.1, the mix of problems, issues and constraints can stimulate considerable anxiety, for no clear solution may seem to emerge.

In this chapter, ways of increasing personal influence are equated with politics in organisations. Organisational politics is examined because conflict and contradiction are normal, everyday occurrences which require particular strategies if any manager is to manage such a situation properly.

This chapter lays special emphasis on how politics arise in organisations. In particular, it highlights the way in which differences and problems arise between people. The concepts of shared and unshared meaning are discussed as the foundation stone for political behaviour. From there on, seven action strategies are offered as political skills for managers to adopt. Throughout, it is stressed that politics in organisations is a natural process that all will experience. Politics should be managed rather than viewed as something unpleasant and not to be discussed.

EXAMINING POLITICS IN ORGANISATIONS

Professor Lyman Porter of UCLA (University of California, Los Angeles), at one of his international lectures, reported a study he had recently conducted examining successful and unsuccessful promotion bids by management executives. Porter discovered that:

- Those successfully promoted attributed their success to their various personal skills and abilities.

- Those whose promotion bids failed attributed their lack of success to politics; they thought either that they were out of favour or that someone else was more in favour than themselves.

Those unsuccessful saw politics as an unpleasant, negative but most powerful experience. Porter concluded that politics in organisations is probably the most important influence on a manager's development.

There can be little doubt that Porter's conclusion is accurate. Most people in organisations recognise that simply doing a good job is not sufficient. For people who are more ambitious, attaining professional competence is only the first step. To achieve high office quickly requires skills in negotiation, skills in forward planning, skills in making projects work, skills in getting on with people; in fact, skills in being different, and yet ironically in being able to fit with superiors, colleagues and subordinates. Others not so fortunate who are at the forefront of the promotion stakes may spend their time at work vying for limited resources simply to get a good job done, competing for limited status positions or just attracting the attention of a senior executive. It is easy to see how politics comes to be perceived as negative.

Consider the situation at the group level. Certain groups or group leaders in organisations may wish to preserve a certain identity based on a professional ethos, geographic location or previous traditions; all of which may be without the knowledge , or in direct conflict with the wishes, of corporate management. Other groups may attempt to preserve their values and identity but have no wish openly to confront their superiors. They may seem to accept new systems of working but covertly tamper with those systems to meet their needs.

If the actions and intentions of others can be easily misinterpreted; if groups and individuals confront and oppose one another; if the skills of negotiation and manoeuvre are as important as task skills for promotion to senior management; why then is politics in organisations not given greater attention in the training of managers? After all, politics seems to pervade our lives.

There are two reasons:

1   Writers, researchers and managers are not able to agree the true meaning of the terms power, politics and influence (see Chapter 8). Despite this, it is clear that politics involves characteristics such as interpersonal influence, the skills of negotiation, a means to an end. In other words, politics is action-based, it is individually determined and the actions can be practised in any organisational setting, limited only by the norms, values and foresight of each individual. However, certain actions, such as influencing others principally for self-gain or deliberately withholding information from others, are likely to be considered unethical. Hence an inability to agree on basic principles, coupled with the taboo nature of the subject, has made politics an underexamined area of study.

2   Writers, researchers and managers have not quite come to terms with the fact that life in organisations has as much to do with differences as with similarities between people. Theorists and practitioners alike have preferred to believe that similarities bond people together, for example, believing that managers have the right to manage; that managers should be sources of energy and inspiration (ie motivators); in other words, that the most appropriate way to live our lives is to accept the principle of *downward influence*. Yet all too often the strife and conflict of life have shown that downward influence is supposition rather than fact.

Politics is an integral part of life in organisations. Differences, rather than similarities, between people form the reality of life. As a prelude to understanding politics in organisations, it is necessary to establish what sort of differences exist in organisations.

DIFFERENCES IN ORGANISATIONS *

How do differences arise? In all organisations, individuals and groups compete for resources, for attention, for influence; there are differences of opinion as to the priorities and objectives to be attained; clashes of values and beliefs occur frequently. All these

---

*This chapter is based on A. P. Kakabadse, *The Politics of Management*, Gower, 1983.

factors lead to the formation of pressure groups, vested interests, cabals, personal rivalries, personality clashes, hidden deals and bonds of alliance. Probably managing conflict, competition and the formation of alliances forms part of most people's workload. The first step to the successful management of differences is to understand how differences arise, as described in Professor Andrew Kakabadse's book on politics in organisations.

Grand strategy v local identity

All organisations are involved in some form of planning for the future. The greater the perceived need for effectiveness, the greater the need to plan on a broad scale. As part of the planning process, managers may decide on policies for change; new areas of investment; there may be a need to change the location of plants and offices. Equally, a new senior executive recently appointed may feel it necessary to stamp his authority on the organisation, thereby introducing changes which represent his unique contribution.

Grand strategy	Local conditions
Policies for change	Identity with existing group patterns
New product lines	Identity with existing work patterns
New investment	New developments of little interest to locals
New technologies	Certain skills no longer required
Re-training personnel	People identify with old skills
Closure of plants	Redundancy
Opening new plants	Transfer of personnel

Fig. 9.1   The contrast between grand strategy and local conditions
From A.P. Kakabadse, *The Politics of Management*, Gower, 1983.

Whatever the reasons for change, major changes are likely to disrupt local conditions (Figure 9.1). Reorganisation of systems and structure, the introduction of new technologies or product lines and the lack or increase of investment are at best likely to disrupt existing groupings of people and patterns of friendship, and at worst could mean moving to another area or redundancy. There is little doubt that changes at the policy level do disrupt people's lives.

As one group of people identifies with the need for change and the future, another group's concern centres on the negative effects of change upon their locality. Mistrust and serious differences of beliefs and values develop, irrespective of how sensitively management attempts to implement its change strategy.

Superiors v subordinates

The superior/subordinate relationship has attracted substantial attention in the study of organisations. As early as 1911, Frederick Taylor considered this relationship crucial to developing a successful organisation. These writings concentrated on establishing the key factors in the roles people held that would lead to an efficient and workable relationship.

Other researchers and writers have examined the superior/ subordinate relationship from the point of view of the manager learning to collaborate with colleagues, superiors and subordinates; from the point of view of appraising individuals in their current job in order to identify those suitable for further training and promotion.

The underlying characteristic of the vast majority of the studies has been the search for ways in which the relationship can be made to work better. Rightly so, for the superior/subordinate relationship frequently leads to serious differences between people in organisations. Such differences emerge between people in the organisation hierarchy for two reasons (see Figure 9.2):

Superior	Subordinate
May or may not be given adequate authority in role to manage	May or may not respect authority
Belief in the right to manage	May or may not respect the individual manager
Increased salary and status	Conscious of salary and status differences
Try to motivate subordinates	Subordinates may see attempts to motivate as manipulation

Fig. 9.2   Different viewpoints in the superior/subordinate relationship
From A.P. Kakabadse, *The Politics of Management*, Gower, 1983.

- Role reasons: the manager may not be given sufficient authority to carry out the duties required of him.

- Personal reasons: the manager may not be sufficiently skilled to establish a positive and comfortable working relationship with his subordinates. The subordinate, for example, may be obstructive towards the superior due to the superior's lack of social skills, technical skills or planning and administrative skills. It becomes that much more difficult to stimulate a genuine productive working relationship when, from the subordinate's view, someone of lower ability but earning more money has the right to direct other people as he desires. People may eventually oppose and undermine the individual manager and further offer little commitment to the organisation.

Although managers may be appointed to pull people together and develop good teams, the superior/subordinate relationship can generate more differences than similarities.

Management v operatives

In the superior/subordinate relationship, both parties are likely to share the same beliefs – an identity with organisations – and pursue the same rewards – promotion, status, recognition. Differences mostly arise out of dislike or disrespect. In contrast, conflicts between management and the shop floor are due to basic differences of belief as to how people should conduct themselves at work and at home.

Consider how differences of beliefs, values and norms arise (Figure 9.3). Although both groups fall into the category of employees, managers tend to conform to the myth of acting as the owner. Understandably so, for the decisions a manager makes and his style of operation would be identical to any owner/manager.

Hence, for any manager to operate competently, it is important for him to identify with the norms and values of his employing organisation and feel that he has a reasonable chance of receiving substantial reward for his endeavours. That is not the case with the workforce. Due to the nature of the tasks they are asked to perform, they can provide work to a reasonable standard and not necessarily identify in part or whole with their employing organisation.

The tasks of the manager will include planning, product and market development: tasks that require a longer-term futuristic time

Manager	Operative
Myth of owner	Reality of shop floor employee
Works on longer-term time span	Works to short-term objectives
Allocating resources	Responds to management's allocation
Hires/fires	Maintains a steady job
Promotion upwards	Negotiates for increased pay
Individualistic work style	Accepts workgroup norms
Salary	Wages
Suit as the working garment	Overalls as the working garment
Various social interests	Local community interests

Fig. 9.3   Different viewpoints in the manager/operative relationship
From A.P. Kakabadse, *The Politics of Management*, Gower, 1983.

span. Operatives complete reasonably well specified subtasks to a required standard; the attitude an individual develops towards his work under such circumstances is short-term – finish the job.

In preparing for the future, the manager will need to consider the way resources (including people) are allocated and who to hire for a job in order to achieve optimum results. Shop floor operatives are required to respond to the manager's direction. Whereas a manager stands or falls according to his own performance, workforce operatives form a group culture, partly as a defence against management and partly in an attempt to stimulate satisfactory working relationships.

Even socially, great differences arise. In terms of dress, individuals in each group will have accumulated a different wardrobe for work. Managers wear the higher status suit, operatives the lower status overall or casual dress such as jeans and tee-shirts.

Where groups of people think, feel and conduct their work and social life so differently to one another, stereotypic beliefs develop. From the manager's point of view, such beliefs could be *the manager's right to manage; the manager's right to control.* From the shop floor operative's viewpoint, a widespread belief may be that *management is uncaring or not responsive to employee needs.* Although these are stereotypic, people do conduct their work lives according to such values.

Professional v administrator

With what do people identify other than hierarchical or shop floor values? An additional strong determinant of beliefs is the profession. Consider the factors that determine professional action and identity.

The professional will place great emphasis on the quality of work he produces. He may see each new task as a challenge to his professional expertise. The task may have to be tackled slightly differently from all other previous tasks. Consequently, the professional, whether engineer, doctor, lawyer, teacher or social worker, would probably attempt to tackle each job as he sees fit in professional terms and not refer to the organisation for guidance.

In contrast, the administrator would not hold dual allegiances. His work performance and career aspirations would be directed by the demands of the organisation. The classic image of the administrator, if not entirely accurate, is of a person who only identifies with his employing organisation – do no more or less than what is required of you; preserve the hierarchy; actions should be determined by your role requirements – all of which are the antithesis of the values of professional practice (Figure 9.4).

Not conforming to organisational norms can lead to a lack of trust between the line manager and the specialist, especially in each other's ability to manage work problems. With the growth of specialisation, line managers should be able to delegate certain tasks to specialists. For delegation to take place, line management must have sufficient confidence in the ability of the specialists and vice versa. Such trust, however, may be difficult to generate. Where the professional holds little influence over his employing organisation,

Professional	Administrator
Emphasis on professional quality of work	Doing no more or less than required
Actions determined by the professional ethos	Actions determined by role requirements
Often a strong team identity	Preserve the hierarchy
Low identity with any one organisation	Career development seen as promotion up the hierarchy

Fig. 9.4   The attitudes of the professional and the administrator
From A.P. Kakabadse, *The Politics of Management*, Gower, 1983.

he is at a distinct disadvantage for he is just one more resource to be developed or discarded according to the current objectives of the organisation. Certainly, professionals in R and D units and training personnel have traditionally been vulnerable. During times of stringency, training and R and D are among the first to have their budgets reduced, irrespective of how well or badly they have accomplished their tasks in the past. Such conditions do little to endear the professionals to the organisation.

It is unlikely that we will ever escape the classic professional/bureaucratic conflict.

Planning v execution

The theme of the professional and the administrator is continued.

The specialist will design a particular product. The line manager will attempt the manufacture of the product according to the limitations of his budget Figure 9.5).

Planning	Execution
Professional specialist	Line manager
Market-oriented	Product-oriented
Control of expenditure	High capital outlay
Future long-term policies	Acting on present contingencies
Meeting future market needs	Restrictive work practice

Fig. 9.5   Differences between planning and execution
From A.P. Kakabadse, *The Politics of Management*, Gower, 1983.

The process of product design and manufacture may not be well aligned. Much will depend on the clarity of the detailed plan of the product. Much will also depend on the personal relationship between the designer and manufacturer. How will problems that arise on the spot be handled? Will one or both groups blame the other, or have they developed a sufficiently strong relationship to be able to solve problems jointly?

Much the same considerations apply to relationships between those who are market-oriented and those who are product-oriented.

Marketing departments, as part of a product development campaign, may take advance orders and promise deadlines on certain goods. Production departments may be unwilling, or more likely unable, to fulfil marketing departments' promises to clients. The result is that disagreements, loss of face and poor relationships between units in the organisation can easily develop. Such negative interactions can after a time become part of the tradition or culture of the organisation, which makes improving relationships an almost impossible task. It is so easy for deviations of some magnitude to occur between what is supposed to happen and what actually happens. In the end both organisation and client suffer.

CRISIS OR INAPPROPRIATE THEORY?

With such differences between people who need to work together simply to achieve ouputs, are we in a permanent state of crisis? Is it merely a dream that we can live, work and share problems and personal experiences with each other?

The answer is partly yes and partly no. Yes, differences do exist; yes, people think, feel and see the same situation differently. However, that does not have to be a serious constraint.

The problem is that managers have been fed with inappropriate theory. Consider certain basic values which many managers hold:

- Managers have the right to manage.

- It is a manager's job to motivate his people.

- It is a manager's responsibility to get others to work to common objectives.

- Good middle managers are the backbone of any company.

The common theme underlying the above values is that of *shared meaning*; people sharing similar norms, attitudes, values, views of the world, feelings about situations; the sharing of a common experience and viewpoint for people in the same situation. Unfortunately for management theorists, people do not behave in such a predetermined manner; individuals do not pursue the same objectives; stability and equilibrium are not necessarily the norm. In fact, there is as much *unshared meaning* as *shared meaning* in organisations. There are as many differences between middle and senior management as between management and workforce operatives.

A shop steward may not recognise that managers have the right to manage. In complete contrast, a shop floor operative may prefer managers to manage, as his own concern is to maintain a steady and secure income. A middle manager may think managers have the right to manage, but consider his own boss incapable. He may try to undermine and usurp his boss's position and yet still believe in the structure of the hierarchy.

People in employment are led to believe in shared meaning, and nowhere more than in management training. Managers who attend management training programmes find strong pressures brought to bear on them in terms of – get involved, take part, make a contribution, work with your study group. The underlying dynamic is to achieve *best fit*, ie you come to terms with the environment and the people around you.

Let us not swing to the other extreme. Notions of shared meaning are valuable. The 'pulling together' philosophy, especially when a group or organisation faces difficulties, is necessary and vital. But so often shared meaning becomes compulsive and enforced. What happens to the idiosyncratic and creative person? History shows that creativity stems from the unusual person, the mutant gene, the persistent lone voice.

Living and interacting with other people has as much to do with unshared meaning as it has to do with shared meaning. Understanding politics in organisations involves analysing how people manage both shared and unshared meaning.

Case 9.2   The politics of planned change

Mary knew that Karl was right and that something more than just talking to a few line managers had to be done.

Mary held further discussions with Karl and then involved certain members of her own human resources team. As a result of their discussions, it was agreed that if change was to be properly introduced, the human resources function had to become the champions of change. The company faced a people problem. It *had* all the specialist expertise and equity capital it needed. The problem was that senior management were not responding to changes in the market place.

However, despite Mary's energy and foresight she doubted the ability of a number of her human resources specialists to act a catalysts for change within quality systems. In the past, all the human resources function was required to do was provide an efficient personnel administration and remuneration service. The development of people at work was under the overall responsibility of the two Vice-Presidents who managed the two sides of the business. The challenge of acting as change agents would require an attitude of mind and skills that Mary considered was not abundant among her staff.

With Karl's support, Mary decided to hire a consultant, as much to stimulate the need for change in her own department, as for helping her with introducing change into the rest of the organisation.

After an extensive search process, they identified a highly recommended consultant whose speciality was the management of change.

In situations where there exists substantial unshared meaning, it may be necessary to utilise external catalysts, as indicated in Case 9.2.

POLITICS IN PRACTICE

Politics in organisations means bridging the gaps between the individual and his motivation (the needs of the person), the group he deals with and their norms and behaviour (the shared attitudes of people), the general situation in which the individual finds himself and the acceptable and unacceptable ways people interact with each other.

One way of bridging the gap is to understand politics as the process of influencing individuals and groups of people to one's own point of view. The individual may wish others to accept his ideas, do what he wants them to or simply get them to re-examine what they are doing so that they can improve their performance. Holding a position of formal authority is not sufficient. All too often an unacceptable boss finds that he is blocked, outmanoeuvred or even out-talked by smarter subordinates. What is required is to influence others sufficiently for them to accept one's own ideas and efforts.

Here are seven approaches to fruitful interpersonal influence:

1 Identify the stakeholders
2 Keep the stakeholders comfortable
3 Fit the image
4 Use networks
5 Make deals
6 Withhold and withdraw
7 If all else fails ...?

Identify the stakeholders

The stakeholders are the people who have a commitment to act in
particular ways in a situation. They have invested time, effort and
resources to ensure that their objectives are adopted by the others in
the situation. The stakeholders are likely to influence what should
be done and how it should done. They are the key to the pressures
and strains in a situation. How influential they can be depends on
their own skills of interpersonal influence and their determination
to pursue certain issues. It is not important that the stakeholders
hold formal role authority, for pursuing particular objectives is a
matter of influence and not command. Further, it may be difficult
to recognise the stakeholders. They may take refuge behind others,
especially those who hold formal role authority. People who wish to
have their view adopted do not necessarily have to make themselves
visible to show their hand.

Case 9.3   Identify the stakeholders

Herb Maulden, the consultant, recognised that the first step in his
assignment would be to stimulate the managers in human resource
functions to become more pro-active as agents of change. His
ultimate objective would be to help the line managers and top
management on the main board become more aware and respond
appropriately to market conditions.

After consultation with Mary, Herb began the assignment by talking
informally to the managers in the human resource function about
their work, ambitions and the role of the department in the future. It
quickly became clear that the majority wanted no change. They were
content to continue administering the function. How then to go about
the change programme? In fact, should Mary Kinns' function be the
central impetus for the management of change?

Herb confronted Mary with his reservations. She agreed with him
but also asked him how to overcome these problems. Herb
recommended a series of 3-day management of change workshops,
where in-depth analyses and training to address the problems of
change management could be provided. Mary agreed to the
recommendation but stated that she would require feedback as to
who in her department seemed most suited to the catalyst role and
who did not.

'Mary, I understand your problems, but what you are asking me to
do is not honest' commented Herb.

Mary agreed, but wondered what the alternative was. She needed a
team that could help line management confront the problems it faced.

Herb organised and ran the 3-day workshops.

The participants reported that they found them to be beneficial and a success. Mary and Herb held a number of discussions concerning the members of Mary's department. Slowly, the nucleus of a team of internal consultants began to take shape.

For the others that were considered unsuitable for the consultant team, certain strengths and attributes were identified in the workshops which helped Mary, through discussions with her subordinates, to identify appropriate career paths for them.

A few were identified as unsuitable for human resource work. Mary began holding discussions with each of them in order to identify jobs or career direction that would suit their attributes.

Herb provided further training for the internal consultants: he suggested that the next step, in order to capitalise on the training, would be to initiate a number of small projects whereby people would be given an opportunity to apply their newly trained skills. Herb acted as advisor to most of the project teams.

As time passed, the intervention seemed to work out well. Other departments saw the human resource department as providing useful helping service. In addition, it was still able to provide for the administration needs of the company.

The consultant (Case 9.3) was able to identify the stakeholders who were worthy of further development and those who seemed unlikely to fit in the 'new look' human resource department – he mapped them out. However, the consultant was not comfortable in holding 'covert' conversations with Mary Kinns about the workshop participants. He recognised that Mary needed to nurture a team that could effectively interact with line management but, at the same time, he and Mary needed to be cautious as to what they disclosed to the members of the human resource department. People would not have attended the workshops if their suspicions had been aroused. The case highlights the tensions of introducing change into an organisation and in particular identifies the problems of honest disclosure of intentions. It is a common experience for management to be cautious and guarded in what they disclose during periods of change.

Keep the stakeholders comfortable

Helping an individual to feel comfortable involves concentrating on those behaviours, values, attitudes, drives and ideas that the person in question can accept, tolerate and manage, ie their comfort zones. The reason the 'comfort zones' are emphasised is that every person has developed a range of values and behaviours which they find acceptable and wish to put into practice. The range of values and behaviours is their identity.

People will pay attention to the concerns of others as long as their own are not threatened. Once an interaction with another concentrates on the issues important to only one party, and is threatening to the other party, that interaction is likely to be terminated. And why not? People interact sensibly only when they have sufficient interest in a situation.

People hold two interests in any situation:

- the final objective, ie what is in it for them,

- the manner in which the final objective is achieved, ie the process.

By handling the interactions so that the receiving party feels comfortable, outcomes can be managed so as to satisfy both parties.

Working on 'the comfort zones' is synonymous with positively stimulating people and gaining their trust and confidence. Different people require a different approach. Each person should develop some idea as to what other individuals can and cannot accept, otherwise a sincere attempt to help and act positively may be interpreted as manipulation.

Case 9.4   Working on Jim Criddle

Mary Kinns learned a great deal from the intervention by the consultant. She began to understand her strengths and weaknesses as well as those of others in her department. She really appreciated how necessary it was to be skilfull at influencing others without being identified as a threat. She was about to put those lessons into practice in her dealings with Jim Criddle.

Jim was the President of Quality Systems Inc. Jim, an engineer by background, had worked his way up the organisation. He had experience of most functions in the business. Mary perceived Jim as a low risk-taker, a person uncomfortable with ambiguity and someone who needed a structured and systematic approach to work. Mary wanted Jim to confront the problem of lack of co-ordination between the network and software businesses. She surmised that Jim would not feel comfortable in addressing that issue with the members of the board.

On that basis, Mary considered the best way to influence Jim Criddle would be to gather information identifying customer satisfaction with the total service, provided by both sides of the business, but contract by contract, Mary's team interviewed customers and some of the engineers working on the programmes. Karl Rode supported Mary's efforts by giving her direct access to various customers. Mary fed this information

through, contract by contract, with recommendations on how to
improve the situation.

  These data stimulated a series of discussions on the main board and
within a six month period the board decided to review the current
structure of the organisation. A project team was formed, chaired by
Karl Rode, to examine the structural needs of the organisation.

The new scheme was accepted based on what the President of Quality
Systems Inc. could tolerate. The Human Resources VP in Case 9.4
had effectively played the politics of management.

A word of warning; by all means work on the comfort zone of the
stakeholders, but there is always the danger that meeting the needs,
whims and fancies of others involves relegating your needs to second
place. In the case above, the Human Resources VP lost ownership of
her ideas, as Karl Rode was placed in charge of the team examining the
needs for re-organisation. Although the Human Resources VP
achieved what she desired, she could experience frustration in that her
efforts might not be acknowledged.

There is a fine dividing line between working on the comfort zone of
the other person and ensuring that others recognise and reward one's
own contribution to the situation.

Fit the image

By working on the comfort zones, it is possible to influence the
stakeholders to one's own way of thinking. However, to gain the
recognition and acceptance of superiors or individuals considered
powerful and influential, it is necessary to work continuously on
their comfort zones. As a result, one becomes aligned to the
powerful other; one fits his image.

Maintaining that image is no simple task. Rather than becoming
a fallen star, it is important to consider what one requires from the
powerful other, how long it would take to get it, and whether
realigning with another powerful individual may be required.
Working on the comfort zones and fitting the image of an influential
person is only likely to be effective in the short to medium term.
Plan ahead for when the relationship ceases to be fruitful.

Use networks

Most people in organisations hold a number of identities. First, all
employees have a job or role. All job holders are held accountable

for certain tasks and authority responsibilities inherent in their role. In addition, most individuals belong to certain interest groups which are formed for non-organisational reasons and may attract members from a number of separate organisations. These interest groups are termed networks.

The network gains its identity from the values and objectives of its members. Essentially, a sufficient number of like-minded people gather to debate, exchange information and achieve consensus about the issues that concern them. Depending on the prevailing issues and the dominant personalities in the network, a network can be a more powerful determinant of the objectives to be pursued and how they are to be acted upon than the formal organisation.

Consequently, attempting to influence people who belong to networks is as necessary as attempting to influence particular individuals in an organisation. The principle of working on the comfort zones has to be extended to influencing individuals and groups. The key to networking is to establish the dominant core values of the network, identify the individuals who are generally seen as upholding the values of the network and influence them by working on their comfort zones.

Entering the networks

Getting yourself known and becoming recognised as someone who has a worthwhile contribution to make is achieved by entering one or more networks. To enter a network and be seen to make a contribution quickly requires that the individual be aware of the following processes:

1 *Identify the gatekeepers.* The gatekeepers are individuals who are influential in the network and trusted by the network members, but spend as much time outside the network as within. Naturally, they meet with others who may wish to join the network or have a contribution to make to the network. The gatekeepers will assess whether the individual is worthy of introduction to the network. If a gatekeeper acts as a sponsor to an individual, then that person will have saved considerable time and effort, for he will become acquainted with the senior network members.

2 *Adhere to network norms.* Once inside the network, it is important to recognise that it has certain sacred values and norms of behaviour which should not be challenged. Whether one intends to sponsor one's own career through the network, or

to introduce or even prevent changes in a particular profession or the community at large, one should not introduce too many issues too quickly. Each network has its own way of doing things. To raise too many issues in too short a time could upset the other members. It is as important to fit into the network as it is to do anything new.

Case 9.5 The new network - people

Karl Rode invited a number of influential managers to sit on the team. He, with Mary's agreement, used the Human Resources consultant team as specialist advisors when required.

The Karl Rode team soon identified that Mary's arguments concerning the poor customer service and the need for re-organisation held weight. They made a number of recommendations concerning organisation and structure to the main board, including the need for management and customer service training, which should start almost immediately. 'Whatever structure we put into practice, I think our people need to be better at managing or handling customers,' remarked Karl Rode to Jim Criddle.

After further discussions involving Mary, it was decided that the training programmes should proceed. Herb Maulden was invited back to run the programmes. A series of 3½-day programmes was structured, for middle and senior managers. The senior management seminars included training in managing teams, decision making skills and managing change. In addition, a main board vice-president would make a lengthy presentation on the future strategy and structure of the company. Finally, the last two hours of the fourth day would be devoted to action planning whereby the senior managers would be split into pairs, helping each other draw up a six month action plan, which each senior manager could implement on his return to work. It was hoped that enabling senior managers to generate action plans would commit them to doing something positive within the organisation. Furthermore, by talking through key issues with colleagues during the process of action planning, the managers would form close working relationships and hence help each other implement their action plan.

The seminars for the middle managers would concentrate more on team building, providing effective customer service and the generation of action plans. It was considered that the middle managers would benefit more from team development and interpersonal skills training as most of their time was spent within team settings.

The senior and middle managers considered their seminars tremendously successful, as it was widely felt that their needs were met. It quickly became clear that the senior managers had little knowledge of subjects such as strategy and structure. Gaining more knowledge helped the senior managers understand how and what to improve. The participants on the programmes further considered the process of

action planning to be invaluable. Most stated that they never realised
that others were facing similar problems. Using each other to talk about
work problems, and from there to identify solutions, helped the different
levels of management to form positive working relationships. Mary
Kinns later discovered that many of the senior managers continued to
meet and share problems with each other on a fairly regular basis. Six
months on, one senior manager commented to Karl Rode:
  'Your programme helped our managers really talk to each other. We
are getting far better co-operation across departments although we still
have some way to go.'
  Mary smiled.

For the senior and middle managers, (Case 9.5) the opportunity to
meet and exchange views and ideas about their work and the
organisation, proved to be a valuable experience. Such an
experience allows for the building of relationships in order to
continue the education process once the workshop or management
programme have finished. It should be recognised that such
processes, which are essentially the formation of networks, help
managers to address managerial problems as more open, informal
patterns of relationships are formed. Under such circumstances
people feel more comfortable in discussing sensitive issues!

Make deals

Making a deal with other individuals or groups is common practice
in most large organisations. Whether resources are limited or not,
different individuals or groups may agree to support each other to
achieve a common purpose as long as there are benefits for them. It
is realistic to expect individuals and groups in the organisation to
wish to promote their own goals, which may be at the expense of
others. Consequently, coming to some sort of agreement about
common policies, or at least not disturbing each other's aims, may
be necessary.
  The way deals are made is as important as the actual deal itself.
For some a deal is seen as a gentleman's agreement which has to be
kept and honoured. For others, it is a different matter: agreements
may not be adhered to in the future. Either party may willingly
break the agreements if they see this to be to their advantage. More
probably however, circumstances change, so people's needs alter
and new agreements need to be negotiated. If both parties are aware
of the new developments, then change can be negotiated openly. If,

however, one of the parties is unaware of new developments, or finds that changed circumstances are not in his favour, he may then attempt to hold the other party to the agreed arrangement. Even if the other party is willing to stand by the agreement, it is unlikely he will do so for long. He will simply cease to adhere to the agreement without informing the first party.

Whenever deals are struck between two or more parties, it is worth considering the true intentions of the other party and for how long one could realistically expect the arrangement to stand.

Withhold and withdraw

It is impossible to satisfy the needs of all parties in any organisation. One way of ensuring that certain groups do not over-react to issues which they see as important is to withhold information. By preventing certain information from becoming common know-ledge, the manager is able to achieve his objectives without facing opposition that could destroy his plan. In such circumstances, the manager should be fairly convinced that his plan is valuable, but that others have not, or will not, recognise its worth. To withhold information constantly is not recommended, for such behaviour is symptomatic of a manager who cannot confront certain problems. Continuously withholding information protects the manager and not the policy.

Withdrawing from a situation may also be necessary at times. Sometimes the presence of a manager in a dispute or negotiations is of no help. It is common practice to withdraw and allow the different factions to negotiate their own terms, or for management to withdraw an unpopular policy and shelve it for the time being. The larger and more diverse an organisation becomes, the more important is the timing of actions, the introduction or withdrawing of plans and information.

Case 9.6   'Karl isn't with us anymore'

Mary was pleased with the new developments in Quality Systems. A plan for re-organisation had been drafted and accepted by the main board. Two of the General Managers were working hard on identifying the details of the merger and decentralisation of telephone networks and software. The training programmes run by Herb Maulden were rated highly by the participants.

Karl Rode, however, was not satisfied with the situation. He was completing a major part of the re-organisation plans whilst still maintaining a similar workload in his line management capacity. The pressure was beginning to show on Karl. In addition, Karl disagreed with recent developments concerning the impending re-organisation. He did not approve of certain of the departments planned to emerge from the re-organisation nor the manner in which particular plans for re-organisation were being implemented. He felt that customer service was not being given top priority and that the managers in his department were being overloaded with tasks others did not want.

Karl complained to Jim Criddle. Others complained about Karl's complaints but also complained that the service his department was supposed to be providing was poor. Mary considered that Karl was isolating himself. Even her working relationship with Karl had deteriorated.

Unexpectedly, Jim Criddle called Mary. 'Can we meet to discuss Karl Rode?' questioned Criddle. A meeting was arranged later that afternoon. At the meeting, Criddle quickly came to the point.

'I'm having real problems with Karl. He and I can't agree on even the smallest details. We argue too much and I'm getting complaints about him.'

Mary listened. It soon transpired that Criddle had never really appreciated Rode and had considered him over-promoted. Jim Criddle wanted a way out, preferably for Karl to leave the company.

Whatever problems there were with Karl, he still held a reasonably good reputation in the company. It would be difficult for Criddle just to fire him. He needed the support of some of the VPs before Rode could go. Mary knew why she was at the meeting; Criddle was sounding her out.

In her own mind, Mary weighed up the alternatives. Karl had contributed a great deal to the company. On the other hand, this was a sensitive period in the company's development. The key and influential managers had to pull together to make the changes of structure and systems work. It would be difficult to make the re-organisation work if one of its proponents opposed any further plans. Mary spoke softly: 'Karl isn't with us any more'.

Criddle looked at her and nodded. Soon after, Mary left Criddle's office. Criddle picked up the phone and dialled a three digit number.

'Karl, I wonder if you and I could meet some time today?'

The issues facing Jim Criddle and Mary Kinns (Case 9.6) were numerous, complex and contradictory. Both recognised the poor relationships stimulated by one key manager in the organisation. The company was undergoing re-organisation and poor relationships between key managers could have prevented the effective implementation of the re-organisation. The one person who would most probably have been able to manage that re-organisation, Karl Rode, was held in low esteem by powerful and influential executives, namely Jim Criddle and Mary Kinns. With so many conflicting pressures,

Criddle managed the situation by reaching an understanding with Mary Kinns but without fully discussing the situation with Rode. Criddle withdrew from confronting Karl Rode about the problems he was generating in the company. The case highlights the sensitivity involved in dealing with issues of motivation and executive performance at senior management levels. Addressing problems openly is in itself problematic.

When all else fails ...?

Of course, these strategies to increase one's personal influence do not guarantee success. Things go wrong and situations can get out of hand. What to do then, when all else fails?

The range of options is limited. The most obvious is to leave the job, situation or organisation. However, suitable alternative employment may not be easy to find. Job searches take time. Further, any individual would require a reference from his previous boss for a potential new employer. If the interactions between boss and individual have not been successful, then obtaining a worthwhile reference may not be possible. In fact, it may be more difficult to leave than to stay.

The second alternative is stick it out. Working in an unpleasant environment is, however, no easy option. It is both distasteful and demoralising to continue interacting with others who do not appreciate one's contribution and who may wish to prevent one's further growth and development. The only real advantage in trying to stick it out is the chance to reassess one's own values, beliefs and action strategies. Was one trying to do too much too quickly? Were the underlying issues that important? Certain uncomfortable experiences simply have to be lived with and accommodated. It is possible to use the time to re-examine one's own purpose and objectives, if for no other reason than to prevent similar uncomfortable experiences in the future.

The third alternative, if adopted, is a high-risk strategy. It involves getting rid of the stakeholders. A superior putting pressure on one person in the hope that he leaves makes others uncomfortable. They wonder when it will be their turn next. Trust, respect and work performance are likely to drop sharply.

For a subordinate to try and get rid of his boss is equally dangerous. The only realistic way is to conspire with the boss's boss in order to remove the troublesome superior. However, the boss's boss may feel uncomfortable, for he is having to relate to a

272   PEOPLE, JOBS AND RELATIONSHIPS

subordinate operating outside his role boundary.

The individual may be successful in getting rid of his boss, but there is always the danger that he may be next!

Case 9.7   Reflections

'She knew. Yes of course she knew!', remarked Karl Rode. It was 11pm and Karl was at home, talking to his wife. Karl had spent a particularly harassing day at a meeting with Jim Criddle in the chair, a group of network managers and Mary Kinns. At the meeting, whatever suggestion Karl offered was criticised and finally rejected. Further, Karl was heavily criticised for not 'sorting out' the integration plans for Canada. Karl knew that effective integration would take another nine months. He had been only three months in the job.

'Mary did, at times, try to support me today, but she was just too quiet', reflected Karl.

'That does not sound like Mary Kinns. I always thought she was a straightforward sort of person. I also thought you two get on so well', said Evelyn Rode.

Pause.

'Just shows you how wrong anyone can be. What a situation. Mary Kinns working against one of her supporters who took a risk in backing her at the beginning' continued Evelyn.

'I'm not sure that Mary is that political. I think she's just stuck. I created a problem in the organisation. I believed things should have have been done differently. I reckon those guys came to see me as a problem. I suppose you've got to have the team pulling together. I just couldn't agree with their views and ideas', said Karl.

Pause.

'I just don't think Mary Kinns is that political', finished Karl Rode.

Silence.

'Forget Mary. What about you? What are you going to do?' enquired Evelyn.

'You remember my telling you that I met someone from Syntax Systems about two weeks ago. Well, he kept telling me that a senior position was about to become vacant, but he did not say what. I wonder if that was a hint', said Karl.

'Give him a ring. Invite that chap to dinner here at home. You certainly have nothing to lose', said Evelyn.

'Quite right! Time I did something about my situation'.

Karl Rode (Case 9.7) slowly recognised the tensions and pressures he was having to contend with and realised the difficulties that Mary Kinns faced. Mary's lack of support for Karl seems to have disappointed him but under the circumstances, Karl wonders how else Mary could have behaved. Hence, he does not seem to blame her for the way events have turned out.

Perhaps the most obvious solution is best – leave!

SUMMARY

Politics in organisations has been examined from four angles –

Importance of politics in organisations

Politics is equated with the way life in organisations is managed: in effect the way matters are really discussed and affairs conducted. In order to analyse how managers in organisations handle their actions and interactions, it is assumed that both similarities and differences between the individual and others influence their behaviour.

Differences in organisations

There are five types of difference:

1   Grand strategy v. local identity, ie the different values and approaches of macro and micro organisational functioning;

2   Superiors v. subordinates, ie the differences that can emerge when one individual holds authority over another. This relationship is prone to tensions, mistrust and at times an inability to confront such problems.

3   Managers v. operatives, ie those who identify with organisational values, and work to medium- to long-term horizons, and operatives who respond to management's initiatives and work to much shorter time horizons;

4   Professional v. administrator, ie those who identify with a strong professional/expertise ethos and those who preserve and defend the systems and mores of the organisation;

5   Planning v. executive, ie the differences in attitude and style between those involved in design of goods and services and those involved in the manufacture or service provision of goods and services.

Shared and unshared meaning

Shared meaning involves people identifying with similar norms, attitudes, values, views of the world, feelings and sentiments. Unshared meaning denotes an inability or unwillingness to hold similar views, values, sentiments or pursue comparable objectives or work towards stability and equilibrium by generating shared meaning.

There is as much unshared as shared meaning in organisations. Differences and similarities, side by side, are considered natural, inescapable experiences.

Politics and interpersonal influence

How can people influence each other? Politics is a process, ie a means, or a way, of influencing other individuals or groups more to one's own views. Hence, politics involves skills in negotiation in order to increase one's own interpersonal influence. Seven approaches to increased interpersonal influence follow:

1 Identify the stake holders.

2 Keep the stakeholders comfortable.

3 Fit the image.

4 Use networks.

5 Make deals.

6 Withhold and withdraw.

7 If all else fails...?

IN CONCLUSION

It is necessary to be political!

Understandably many people fear the politics played in their organisation. Equally, many people do not wish to play politics. Whatever each individual decides, there are times when it is necessary to behave politically. But politics is not all negative and bad.

What is the difference between motivation and manipulation? The answer is the interpretation the receiver puts on attempts to influence him. If he is influenced in a positive and favourable way, the person may consider himself motivated. If, however, attempts at influence are not well planned or well conducted, the other party may feel himself manipulated. Undoubtedly, most people at work will find stress, discomfort and manipulation a common experience. Such situations can be managed and turned into positive experiences.

Politics is nothing more than getting what one wants done, preferably with the full permission and approval of all others in the situation.

WORKING THE ORGANISATION

INTRODUCTION TO PART II

In Part II we examine organisations from a broader perspective. We identify the characteristics that influence both the patterns of relationships within the organisations and the key issues that are likely to determine the future direction, survival and prosperity of the organisation.

The three chapters cover organisation strategy, organisation structure and mechanisms for integrating people, strategy and structure to achieve the organisation's objectives.

Strategy involves identifying and pursuing particular goals and objectives, taking into account the state of the market; the financial position of the organisation; the past, present and likely future behaviour of competitors, government, unions, federations, employees, interest groups; the costs and availability of raw materials and services. More than likely, organisations pursue a number of strategies. However, for the strategies of the organisation to be meaningful, they need to be in keeping with the mission, purpose and values with which that organisation identifies. Tensions within any organisation may make it difficult to generate an acceptable mix of mission, purpose and values. For this reason, three alternative forms of strategy are described which highlight the difference of views and values in the various parts of the organisation.

Whereas strategy is concerned with goals, objectives and direction, structure provides the mechanism to help attain those goals and objectives. Structure involves establishing role hierarchies; introducing controls and appropriate information and administrative systems; utilising necessary resources such as appropriate technologies, and being aware that external market, economic, or societal changes may require alteration of organisational structures and systems. Before any alteration of internal structures takes place, an examination of the organisation's history, the predominant attitudes amongst personnel, the influence of geographic location on various parts of the organisation, the size of the organisation and the technologies employed is required, for these are the factors that determine what can and cannot be changed.

If internal changes are necessary, how can they be effectively applied? A great deal depends on the mechanisms for integrating the constituent parts of the organisation in order to provide clarity of purpose. Mechanisms for integration involve the application of techniques such as management by objectvies (MBO), appraisal systems, the managerial skill of the organisation's general managers; and the manner in which teams perform.

By pursuing certain strategies, by establishing appropriate structures, and by introducing relevant mechanisms for integration, the organisation generates for itself a coherent purpose and direction.

10 Mission, Strategy and Organisation

Case 10.1 The Boxmakers

The great period of growth and expansion in the boxmaking industry in the USA was in the late 1960s and early 1970s. Goods were placed in boxes to transport to another locality for sale or further distribution. The introduction of containerisation of goods on shipping, roads and rail systems induced further demand for strong, robust boxes as packaging materials. Large amounts of purchased goods could be stocked in large containers relatively cheaply and efficiently transported to other foreign or national localities. Customers could receive their purchases fairly quickly, and, most important, undamaged and in good working order. The boxmaking business was effectively responding to the packaging needs of industry.

The oil crisis of 1974 disrupted this happy state of affairs for the boxmaking industry as for so many other industries. Fuel costs rose and products became more expensive.

At the time, key decision-makers in the boxmaking industry showed little concern. Yet, their products, like most others, had become dramatically more expensive. Like everyone else, the boxmakers passed their increasing costs to the customers. Most companies in the business considered they would not be seriously affected by what was (or so it was thought) Arab retaliation for Israeli military successes. It was thought that the crisis would pass without seriously affecting profit margins. Market place performance for 1974 to early 1976 seemed to justify this view. Most boxmaking companies were holding to their previous profit margins despite rising costs and inflation.

There were, however, certain individuals who did not accept the predominant view that market stability and prosperity would return. The chief executive of one subsidiary company of a US multinational argued that the bottom had fallen out of the market. He was convinced that the market had matured. The prospects for the future were only those of a declining market. Such decline would not be entirely due to rising oil costs but more to technological advances that had gone unnoticed. For certain industries, packaging goods in a box was now a redundant concept. It would be more efficient and in the long run cheaper to utilise new stacking and distribution methods that required no boxes.

The boxmakers knew of such developments but did not consider them a threat. Prior to 1974, it was still cheaper to pack goods in boxes. The chief executive prophesying market decline stated that rising fuel costs would make boxes more expensive. Valued customers would switch to alternative forms of stacking that were more economically viable. In the longer term, certain valued customers would probably, in any case, have switched to alternative forms of packaging. Rising oil costs had merely accelerated that process.

Most influential decision-makers in the boxmaking industry took little notice of this lone chief executive. Most sincerely believed it was simply a matter of surviving the storm and waiting for the return of a profitable, stable market.

The survival, growth and prosperity of any organisation depends on the quality and viability of the strategy the organisation is pursuing. Almost inevitably, the longer-term decline of any organisation can be directly attributed to poorly developed strategies for the future.

It is difficult to develop consistent, relevant, all-embracing strategies because of:

1   *The large number of factors that have to be considered.* In Case 10.1, these factors include changes of technology, ever-changing market needs and demands, actions of competitors, costs, world politics, social tensions. Managers in the organisation need to have sufficient information and knowledge on each of these factors to try and weld them together into an overall plan.

2   *The problems of strategy implementation.* No matter how well thought-through and valuable one's plans, implementing them requires particular skills and approaches to ensure their success. Strategic plans, by their very nature, upset the status quo, unless the explicit intention is to maintain current conditions. Implementing new strategies may require a re-organisation of management structures and systems. As a consequence, people with certain skills or experience may no longer be required and hence be voluntarily or forceably retired. New people with fresh ideas and experience may be hired. Therefore, in the implementation of a strategy plan, resistance is common; strife, conflict and disagreement abound; uncertainty for the future increases. That uncertainty has to be successfully handled in order for the organisation to progress. The chief executive in Case 10.1 was making himself unpopular by offering a view that

was feared and unacceptable. Although they rejected his statements, other people's uncertainty as to future developments grew. Simply by talking, the chief executive was upsetting the status quo.

In this chapter, we concentrate on the processes of strategy generation and strategy implementation. Three categories of strategy are examined and the relationship between them is discussed.

GENERATION OF STRATEGY

Every organisation pursues some sort of strategy. Key decision-makers in the organisation will make choices, act on contingencies and further attempt to consider developments in the external environment which could influence their final decisions. Whether such choices, action and understanding form a sensible strategy depends on three separate issues:

1 factors influencing strategy

2 key elements of strategy

3 approaches to formulating strategy

The combination of these three issues determines whether appropriate or inappropriate strategy is generated.

Factors influencing strategy

Many factors influence the development of a strategy for any organisation. These factors, as shown in Figure 10.1, are arranged in four categories:

- government
- external business influence
- special interest groups
- internal organisational influences

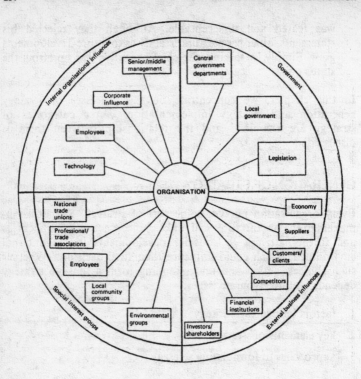

Fig. 10.1   Factors influencing strategy

Government

Government, in the form of central government departments, local government departments or legislation, can influence the strategy of an organisation in two ways:

1   *as a watchdog*, specifying which activities and services can or cannot be pursued; advising on desired standards of goods or services; regulating the strategic options available to any organisation, such as ensuring monopolies are not formed by large powerful organisations or ensuring adherence to trade embargoes.

2   *as a customer*, purchasing goods or services. Central government and local government departments make attractive

customers. Contracts with government are likely to be bulk orders with the possibility that business (whether it be goods or services) will be repeated at regular intervals in the foreseeable future.

Case 10.2   The spider, the web and the fly

The operations vice president of the subsidiary box company was concerned that the company was holding too great a stock for sale. This company had been making a small loss for the last three years which the parent company absorbed. Such a state of affairs could not be allowed to continue.

After numerous discussions between the operations vice president and sales, marketing and manufacturing vice presidents, it was decided that a consultant should be hired to examine the situation. A suitable consultant was hired. His first recommendation was that he hold individual discussions with each of the vice presidents, sales managers and if necessary salesmen.

After a number of interviews a fairly clear picture emerged. The sales vice president had, over the years, developed a strong network of customers and clients. In the early to mid-1970s, the most attractive customers were large companies and state and federal government departments. The large bulk customers tended to reorder the same sort of quantity annually. Selling to large customers required little effort; they merely had to be wined and dined. As a result, the numerous smaller customers were ignored. A centralised sales organisation had evolved with the sales vice president at the centre of a web of contacts of bulk customers.

However, the recession disrupted this comfortable network of customers. Government budgets were slashed. Large companies closed down parts of their own organisation in order to remain solvent. The last thing in the mind of government officials, and the purchasing managers of large companies, was boxes. Orders for boxes fell dramatically.

This information was fed back to the operations vice president. 'We should have been chasing the small customers!' he exclaimed. He thought for a while.

'Hell, the sales organisation is far too centralised for that to happen,' he said. 'Yet, I cannot blame the sales vice president. We all fell into the same trap. Government was the spider, we were sucked into a web of relationships throughout all these government departments and now we are the fly just about to be eaten!'

Government (state and federal) became an increasingly important customer to the boxmakers. The degree of dependence on government as a customer only became clear through recession. Case 10.2 shows how easily an organisation can find itself in difficulty if strategy is not clearly discussed and formulated.

External business influences

The state of the national economy is one factor which influences strategy but over which no one organisation has any control (Figure 10.1). Organisations mostly respond to economic conditions. With all other factors, organisations can exert far greater influence.

Certain groups can directly affect the long-term growth and development of any organisation. Suppliers, by maintaining or increasing their prices, will directly influence the pricing and marketing policies of any manufacturing organisation. Customers and clients influence the longer-term profitability of the company. Changes in market demands may mean losing well-established customers and having to find new ones. It is so easy to be unaware of new trends, and therefore not make adjustments to the strategies being pursued. In Case 10.2, the boxmakers had not fully appreciated the changes in customer demands. They are faced with the prospect of not only rethinking their sales strategy but reorganising their sales organisation, in the hope that they can dramatically capture new market segments.

One way of keeping up to date is to be aware of the actions and intentions of competitors. However, relationships with competitors are sensitive. The fear of giving something away from which competitors may profit, possibly to the detriment of one's own organisation, is understandable. On the other hand, people who face similar problems gain from discussing, analysing and sharing experiences about common strategic issues. Organisations do not lose credibility and/or market share simply because of the actions of others. They lose largely due to their own poorly-thought-through actions or inactions.

Financial institutions as guarantors of loans or as investors are becoming increasingly involved in the activities of private and public organisations. Small to medium-sized organisations are dependent on loans from banks. Larger organisations have attempted to gain the financial support of a consortium of financial institutions.

Debt rescheduling is no new development, but is now through necessity becoming an increasing popular way of ensuring the continued existence of the organisation in the short term to medium term. However, for the organisation in question, new strategies for the future have to be approved by a by no means silent partner.

Financial institutions are a significant influence in the strategy formulation of any organisation. In the past, financial institutions were silent partners who provided some form of fiscal backing. Not

any more; financial backers are demanding a more active role, or
have the ultimate authority to determine strategy as major
shareholders in the organisation.

Special interest groups

Special interest groups can have a direct or indirect influence on the
organisation's strategy formulation process (Figure 10.1). Environ-
mentalist groups concerned with the protection and care of urban
and rural areas can influence such strategic choices as the siting of
plants, expenditure and pollutant controls and landscaping. Local
community groups can influence organisations on local environmental issues and on local employment policies.

National trade unions may set guidelines or stipulations as to
how local pay and condition negotiations should be conducted.
Similarly, professional/trade associations may prove to be a strong
influence on how certain groups of technical specialists should be
managed in the organisation. Even the employees of a particular
department, division or plant may influence the management of that
particular unit to suit their needs with little reference to overall
strategies.

Internal organisational influences

Strategies for the future must take account of the internal
organisational influences (Figure 10.1). Accurate forecasting of the
market trends, identifying new areas of activity and maintaining
those activities considered valuable, is insufficient in terms of
strategy generation.

It is necessary to assess how influential individuals and groups in
the organisation will respond to new ideas and changes of policy.
For example, introducing new technologies to improve work
efficiency is only fruitful when the policy has the support of most
key groups in the organisation.

The directors of the organisation should also be aware of the
industrial relations climate in the region. If similar ventures have
been accepted or approved in other organisations in the locality,
that will influence, positively or negatively, the introduction of new
technologies into the organisation.

If the organisation is a subsidiary company of a larger
corporation or one department of government, it is necessary to
take account of the views of corporate headquarters. Introducing
new services or work systems or closing down unprofitable

operations may mean confrontation with unions or with heads of
other subsidiaries or heads of other government departments. For
the unit in question, such actions may be justified. From the point
of view of corporate headquarters, strike and conflict in one
company could quickly spread throughout the group. Corporate
directors are likely to oppose any strategy that could threaten the
corporation as an entity.

Any changes of strategy require the support of key senior and
middle managers. If these management groups are not in favour of
new policies, then whatever decisions are taken at meetings are
unlikely to be implemented to any great extent. The strategy makers
in the organisation need as much to negotiate with key managers as
with union representatives for new strategies to be accepted, as
outlined in Case 10.3 below.

Case 10.3   The Maryland boxmakers

The subsidiary box company has an unprofitable plant in the state of
Maryland. Until recently, the senior management of the company made
no real effort to improve the situation.

Finally the president and his vice presidents decided to close down
the plant. In anticipation of such a move a number of senior and middle
managers, a large number of supervisors, trade union officials and
operatives signed a joint petition demanding that their jobs be
safeguarded by keeping the plant operational.

The senior management of the company responded by attempting to
negotiate with the various groups of employees in the plant. The
employees would not compromise their objective that the plant would
remain operational. Fearing disruption in other plants, top management
agreed to keep the plant running in return for certain productivity
improvements.

It is unusual for management and workforce to unite against top
management (Case 10.3). However, when they are under threat and
located away from corporate headquarters, such unity can develop.
See Chapter 11 on the impact of geographical dispersion on
organisation structure and individual behaviour.

Key elements of strategy

Identifying the factors that will positively or negatively influence
strategy is the first step. The next step is to ensure that strategy
incorporates the four key elements that will lead to the success of
the enterprise:

1   *Selection criteria.* In developing the strategy, the relevant issues
    and choices should be singled out in order that the most
    appropriate policies can be selected. It is as important for top
    management to understand why they are selecting or rejecting
    actions for the future, as is their successful implementation.

2   *Life cycle sensitivity.* It is necessary to estimate the life span of a
    particular strategy. Such thinking allows for a smoother
    transition from one strategy to the next.

3   *External/internal integration.* Strategy must take into account
    external developments, such as changing market place trends
    and the behaviour of competitors and investors, as well as
    internal organisational influences such as the skills level of
    employees, the attitude of employees to the organisation and the
    organisation's financial health.

4   *Actionable focus.* The strategy must be realistic in that it
    provides a valuable guide to action. An effective strategy is one
    that can relatively easily be translated into objectives, activities
    and tasks that others in the organisation can identify with and
    implement.

Appropriate terminology

Any sensible debate on strategy will involve a re-examination of the
fundamental purpose and mission of the organisation, even though
the final decision could be to maintain present strategies. Strategy
therefore is quite different from tactics or short- to medium-term
plans, which may change in order to preserve current strategies. Use
of the appropriate terminology prevents misunderstanding.

Discussions on strategy involve the use of seven key words which
could lead to some confusion largely due to their overlap of
meaning. These words are: mission, objectives, strategy, plans,
tactics, activities and tasks. Let us be specific as to their usage.

Mission refers to the fundamental reason why the organisation
exists – what is the organisation there to do? Objectives are the
targets to be achieved in order to satisfy the mission of the
organisation. Strategy is a comprehensive, specific plan of action
which takes mission statements and objectives and turns them into a
co-ordinated series of plans for actions. Plans can be broken down
into activities, which can be further subdivided into particular tasks
to be carried out by certain individuals or groups in the
organisation. Tactics are the means of implementing plans by

establishing the relevant activities and tasks and the manner in which they will be pursued.

At times it is difficult to distinguish between strategy, plans, activities and tactics, especially if substantial changes are taking place in the external environment which require a re-examination of current strategies. It is important however, to distinguish between strategies and tactics so that key decision-makers in the organisation feel confident that they are dealing with the fundamental problems facing the organisation.

Formulating a strategy

How do strategies develop to form cohesive longer-term policy? Is the process of strategy formulation a well-thought-through, shared experience by the key decision-makers in the organisation?

The answer is that it depends. It depends on the particular approaches to problem-solving of those involved in the process of strategy formulation. Three basic approaches to strategy formulation are discussed.

Vision, belief and intuition

Certain powerful, dominant entrepreneurs have created successful organisations by their foresight and virtually unshakeable belief in their intuition, for example, the nineteenth-century English shipping magnate Sir Alfred Jones, Henry Ford in the USA, and Konosuke Matsushita, founder of the Matsushita Corporation in Japan. All three displayed similar approaches to strategy formulation in their organisations. The strategy for the future depended on their intuition. Few deviations from the strategy were tolerated. Even though all three entrepreneurs were running large, well-established organisations managed by professional executives, they themselves decided the way ahead.

Often their ideas and approaches were unconventional and involved big risks. Matsushita, for example, followed none of the rules by which Japanese business was conducted. He promoted his products through advertising instead of using the customary networks of independent sales representatives. He dealt directly with retailers and forged a close, supportive relationship with them, offering financial incentives and assistance. Further, Matsushita believed in the importance of market share. He offered customers reduced prices if sales volumes reached a point where they were reducing production costs.

Analysis approach

Committing any organisation to a particular strategy based on the vision of one man is risky. The problem lies not so much in identifying the strategy as in the dependence on that one man's awareness of all potential developments that could endanger, enhance or facilitate that strategy. A great deal can change within two to five years: market conditions, the policy of financial institutions, actions of competitors, restrictions on world trade – can one man be omniscient?

A thorough analysis of all the forces impacting on the organisation will reduce the risks involved in implementing particular strategies. Three separate areas should be examined:*

1   Industry – as a first step it is necessary to examine the broader industry perspective; † to find out what influences the industry, in order to predict the sales volume and profitability of the company, by looking at industry growth potential, industry medium-term viability, and degree of competitiveness in the industry (Fig. 10.2). Once the longer-term industry trends are clear, the organisation can set realistic and achievable targets for its products. Achieving these targets will depend on the health and strength of the organisation.

2   Organisational health – what are the organisation's strengths and weaknesses? It is important to appreciate strengths and limitations. The areas of market share potential, supply predictability, and organisational response capability (Figure 10.3) require examination.

3   Key person analysis – who are the individuals who could stimulate changes? Every organisation has to interact with a number of key people – suppliers, financiers, competitors, distributors, customers, local and national politicians. Each of these individuals will be pursuing his own objectives. The demands of one may contradict or directly conflict with the ambitions and values of another. Further, certain of these

---

*The ideas on analysis of strategy are based on the work of Newman and Logan (1981) and Newman, Warren and Schnee (1982).

†For the term industry, substitute external environment when analysing public service organisation. Similar issues concern external demand.

1 Growth potential

Market maturity:	new; experimental; high potential; declining; new or old production technologies in use; specialised or flexible use of products.
Stability of demand:	necessity or luxury; low or high fixed demand; durable or consumed when used; number, size and type of consumers; degree of risk and uncertainty.
Market segmentation:	geographical; usage; customer type; quality level; dependent on the success of other industries.

2 Medium-term viability

Capacity of industry:	present estimated capacity; future likely demand; fixed and variable costs; speed of entry; ease of exit.
Degree of technological change:	product improvement needs; production process improvement needs; needs for investment in R & D.
Constraints:	environmental; social; operative welfare; difficulties in hire and fire; redundancy payments; product safety.
Availability of needed resources:	specialised labour; specialised equipment; energy; raw materials; substitutes; alternative sources for resources.
Market pricing policy:	cost; sales prices; inflation vulnerability; timing changes; consumer expectation of prices.

3 Degree of competitiveness

Industry structure:	few or many competitors; small, large or powerful competitors; trade associations, 'old boy' networks; openly competitive.
Government intervention:	subsidies; tariffs; protectionist against foreign competition; monopoly laws; tax policies.

Fig. 10.2 Total industry perspective. From Newman, W.H. Warren, E.K. and Schnee, J.E., *The Process of Management: Strategy, Action, Results,* © 1982 pp. 26–28. Reproduced by permission of Prentice-Hall Inc., Englewood Cliffs, New Jersey.

individuals may be required to respond in a manner acceptable to the managers in the organisation.

When analysing key individuals it is necessary to predict who they are, what they want, what they are capable of doing, and what the organisation is capable of doing (Fig. 10.4)

1 Market share

Relations with competitors: performance by key competitors; past trends; need for change; potential for increased share; strength of distribution systems.

Company image: quality v quantity as seen by users; relative appeal of company services; product/service leadership; price setting in relation to competitors.

2 Supply fluctuations

Resource utilisation potential: comparative access to resources (availability and price); management and union relations; aid from government or financial institutions.

Productivity potential: geographic location; new or old plant and machinery; optimum size; productivity quota.

R & D tradition: creativity tradition; competitive or co-operative work styles; short- or long-term thinking; ability to manage interdepartmental projects; sensitivity to explore new areas; leadership style.

3 Organisational response capability

Financial stability: present cash flow; future financial commitments; freedom to sell assets; high overhead costs; ability to borrow; profit margins; inhibited or supported by government regulations; customer loyalty.

Strengths and weaknesses of management: abilities, attitudes and values of managers; risk-takers; company men; adaptable and flexible.

Organisational structure: flexible/inflexible structure, centralised/decentralised structure, product, functional, divisional based structure affects attitudes of managers and their ability to respond to market place needs.

Fig. 10.3 Organisational health. From Newman, W.H. Warren, E.K. and Schnee, J. E., *The Process of Management: Strategy, Action, Results,* © 1982 pp. 26–28. Reproduced by permission of Prentice-Hall Inc., Englewood Cliffs, New Jersey.

Step-by-step realisation

How is strategy generally formulated in practice – through the vision and entrepreneurial flair of one man or by a logical, systematic analysis of all aspects of the situation by various people, or a combination of both?

1 Who are they?

Suppliers: bankers; financiers; raw materials or semi-
                                    finished product suppliers.

Customers: large, influential customers; low consumer
                                    customers; market penetration.

Competitors: for resources; for labour; for finished products.

'Watch dogs':   government agencies; commissions; professional
                                    associations; licensing authorities; the press;
                                    special interest groups; union leaders.

2 What do they want?

Mission: what are their purpose, aims and objectives;
                                    status; power; market penetration?

Styles: particular ways of doing things; past action
                                    which led to success; tried and tested methods.

3 What can they do?

Areas of influence: customers; suppliers; competitors; product
                                    substitutes; alternative sources of finance.

Use of power: retaliation; dependence on us; willingness to
                                    reach agreement with us; reserve for future.

4 What can I do?

Collaboration: aid; merger; joint agreements; accommodate
                                    certain wishes.

Develop coalitions: scope of activities; member satisfaction; pay-off
                                    for members; common interests.

Individual relations   co-operative; conflict; demanding.

Fig. 10.4   Key person analysis. From Newman, W.H. Warren, E.K. and Schnee, J.E., *The Process of Management: Strategy, Action, Results,* © 1982 pp. 26–28. Reproduced by permission of Prentice-Hall Inc., Englewood Cliffs, New Jersey.

Probably the generation of strategy involves both basic processes. Certain individuals in the organisation may hold particular views on which strategies to pursue. In their debates with colleagues, working parties may be formed and/or individuals offered the responsibility of further examining the proposals. Once a certain amount of data has been gathered, further debate is likely to ensue, probably in both an overt manner involving all interested parties and in a covert manner whereby small cliques or pressure groups form in support of, or opposition to, the original proposals.

Such a process means individuals taking sides, changing their opinions, or even consciously standing back from the process until outcomes are agreed. Igor Ansoff describes this process as involving a cost/benefit/risk analysis and at the same time gaining commitment, understanding and support from all parties in the organisation. In essence, individuals form their views, recognise strengths and weaknesses in the strategies proposed and offer their commitment to the strategy and their colleagues only when they are satisfied that it is valuable. The process of strategy generation involves a step-by-step realisation, in terms of the identification of appropriate strategies and personal commitment to implement them.

Case 10.4   The survival of the boxmakers (part I)

The chief executive of the boxmakers recognised the problems faced by his company. The drop in demand for boxes had already meant that substantial cuts in costs had had to be implemented. The training and reinvestment budgets were slashed. Redundancies had taken place, concentrating at the shop floor and supervisory levels. However, the pressure was on to introduce further cuts. The president of the multinational demanded that each of the subsidiaries return a profit or even greater profit; a motion supported by the corporate executive committee of which the boxmakers' chief executive was a member.

After initial discussions with his own board colleagues, the chief executive decided to seek the aid of consultants again and invited a well-known consultancy to conduct a feasibility and profitability study of the boxmaking industry in general and the boxmakers in particular. The consultants interviewed all of the vice presidents and senior managers of the boxmakers. The consultants spent most time with the chief executive, discussing his ideas for the company in the future.

The consultants' report concurred with the views of the chief executive. Market demand for boxes had dropped and was unlikely ever to return. It was expected that at least 25 per cent of the companies in the business would become bankrupt. Reorganisation and cost-cutting were essential for the survival of those that remained.

In a separate report, the consultants made a number of recommend-ations for the survival and growth of the boxmakers. Basically, it was recommended that the organisation be decentralised into a number of regions, each under a general manager. Each general manager would have full responsibility and be held fully accountable for production, marketing and sales. In this way, each regional organisation would be geared to meet the needs of its region. Each region would in effect become a profit centre. Further, in order to have some control over costs, purchasing of raw materials and capital investment should be firmly identified as the chief executive's responsibility.

The report was placed unedited before the board. After substantial discussion, the majority on the board concluded that the consultant's recommendation made eminent sense, and decided to accept it.

However, during the discussion it became clear that the Maryland plant did not easily fit into the agreed regional distribution. Some of the board recognised this as an opportunity to close down what they considered an inefficient, poorly-run and conflict-ridden manufacturing entity. However, the operations vice president disagreed.

'Hey! Hold on! You guys want to go regional in order to meet customer needs. Part of that means meeting customer orders on time. Already the Phoenix and Bute plants are working to full capacity. We need at least one plant to take on board and service the increased orders. Don't laugh. Don't laugh. We will receive increased orders. After all, that's the whole point of going regional!'

The debate continued with no final conclusion in sight. The chief executive agreed to put the future of the Maryland plant to the main board. It was the operations vice president who gave a warning.

'Look! Whatever you do, don't close that plant too soon. It needs to be operational for another 3–4 years in order to provide for the capacity that I suspect we'll need.'

The chief executive smiled and nodded in response.

In Case 10.4, strategy was formulated by analysis of market trends, reaching a conclusion as to appropriate organisational structure. However, in the discussion on structural re-organisation it became clear that the organisation faced a crucial strategic decision, the closure or continuance in operation of one plant. The importance of this decision was realised step by step, despite the fact that the strategic analysis did not highlight the future of the Maryland plant. Henry Mintzberg, one of the more recent and probably most influential writers of management, considers that most strategy is formulated in a somewhat haphazard and incremental manner. According to Mintzberg step-by-step realisation is a more powerful process than rational analysis.

IMPLEMENTATION OF STRATEGY

To implement any strategy successfully, one must confront two crucial problems:

1 Can the organisation call upon the necessary resources for effective strategy implementation?

2 Will key people in the organisation support the strategies?

The issue of resources is relatively easily resolved. Resources could be bought in, by hiring new labour or purchasing equipment, or borrowed from banks. The decision to generate additional resources or utilise existing resources in a different way will depend on the market and industry trends, and hence on the expectations for the organisation's future performance in the market place. In this way, the generation and the implementation of strategy, although separate issues, are inseparable processes.

Whether strategies really have the support of key people in the organisation is an entirely separate problem and often overlooked. Problems of strategy implementation can be underestimated because the process of implementation is by nature 'political'. (See Chapter 9 for a discussion of organisational politics.) Political interactions do occur, largely due to the various differences and frictions in any organisation, such as differences between particular individuals' beliefs, values, and attitudes, frictions between departments, lack of understanding between superiors/subordinates etc. Consequently certain people in the organisation may agree with strategies in theory but consider them impractical to implement. Some may not support the new strategies as they hold a vested interest in maintaining the status quo. Others may find it difficult to identify with one or more of the people who generated the strategies and so provide opposition on more personal grounds. Further, people may feel that there is a covert reason why a particular strategy has been generated. Although the strategy itself could seem reasonable, the grounds for its proposal may induce a feeling of mistrust. The end result could be little or no support for, or even opposition to, the proposed strategies.

It is important to recognise that the implementation of strategy involves overt and covert behaviour; at times sharing one's intentions and at other times not revealing one's true objectives. Yet whatever the feelings, views and attitudes of people in the organisation, strategies still have to be implemented. Below, five approaches to effective strategy implementation are described.

Map the issues

Individuals and groups need to feel at ease before they will talk to each other about matters that are important to them. In order to find out and understand the issues that dominate people's attention, then, it is necessary to talk to them in informal, relaxed surroundings.

Under more relaxed circumstances it is easier to build trust and rapport so that people share information and views. Further, people can explore concerns without having to take a stand. Often when people face problems at work they feel pressurised to take a definite view even when they do not fully understand the issues. Part of the process of exploring problems in a non-stressful environment is to help people understand the broader influences on their work environment.

The mapping process can be conducted by holding confidential one-to-one meetings, informal small group meetings, lunches and brainstorming sessions. Each approach could work depending on the objectives being pursued.

Just one problem to start with

Map out all you want, but at least test your ideas before putting the map into action. Mapping is a theoretical process. It only becomes real when applied. Until application, it is impossible to know that the most relevant data have been gathered, that people's reactions to change have been well understood, or even that the changes proposed are what the populace want or will tolerate.

Further, to put a complete map into action could easily alienate those at the receiving end. A workable rule is that people are not fond of change until they recognise the advantages for them. To introduce too much too quickly is to overwhelm; to overwhelm is to blind all to what they can gain.

The cardinal rule is – just one problem to start with! If the problem is successfully managed, success will lead to success. Others will wish to be associated with the successful, even if experimental, venture.

If it is not successful, all is not lost. An unsuccessful experiment will provide valuable data for the map. The change agents may lose some credibility and be required to slow down temporarily, but they will still be able to continue with their long-term plans. The worst possible course is to introduce too much too quickly, invest highly, allow the situation to deteriorate and hence stimulate a climate of anti-change that will allow no further developments to take place. The first steps to implementing change will strongly influence people's opinions on change for years ahead.

Once the issues and key people's opinions are well understood, it is possible to place the necessary actions in order of priority.

Break down old identities

Well-established departments, plants, divisions and even whole organisations are likely to have developed identities or cultures supportive of their own people but possibly suspicious of all new influences that could be disruptive to their groups. Both management and workforce may make no allowances for changes to work patterns and work practice to cope with external market conditions. Traditional values are likely to predominate.

Under such circumstances it is necessary to break down old identities. The situation may be remedied fairly simply by retraining programmes for key groups and individuals. In addition, managers or operatives who have remained too long in the situation or are too influential may need to be transferred to other positions in the organisation.

If neither retraining nor job transfer is appropriate then redundancies or early retirements must be considered. It is no use blaming shop floor operatives for adopting restrictive work practices. Management are just as guilty in having allowed the situation to deteriorate. Under such circumstances, cutting back has to apply to both management and the shop floor.

An alternative and potentially powerful means of changing organisational identities is to make alterations to the structure of the organisation. For a full discussion of the issues concerned with structural change, see Chapter 11.

Confront conflict

As new strategies are implemented in any organisation, tensions and conflicts are likely to arise. Most certainly, work practices will change. Further, traditional groupings of people may need to be disrupted, some made redundant and others transferred to other parts of the organisation. Such conflicts must be confronted, no matter how uncomfortable it may feel to operate in such a situation.

Those backing new strategies should recognise that they must gather support for their cause. Even senior managers in the organisation could harbour doubts and anxieties about actively supporting a policy that involved direct confrontation even if no feasible alternative exists. The situation could so easily get out of their control.

Support may be offered for new strategies but not necessarily given when required. It is necessary to negotiate continuously with colleagues to ensure their backing.

Allow others to catch up

Once plans for the future have been made; once opposition to the plans has been dispersed and support gained to implement them; once pilot projects have been introduced and corrections and alternatives made to the fundamental strategy, others must be allowed to catch up.

Individuals, especially those in key operational positions, have to be given time to identify with the new strategies. People have to become accustomed to new ways of doing things. They may need to develop some different on-the-job skills; training requires time. Most of all, people need to become involved in implementing any new strategy in order to become committed by their contribution to making the strategy work. The more substantial the changes, the greater the time people require to identify with, and work towards successful implementation of, strategy.

Case 10.5   The survival of the boxmakers (Part 2)

The chief executive of the box company and his boss, the president of the multinational, met for lunch.

'You don't seem too happy about the decision, Hal,' commented the president.

'You mean closing down Maryland? ... Yeh. You're right. It's going to cause a lot of problems in the company. Some of the boys are really going to be mad over this one. Some, like Ritch Johnson [operations vice president], honestly believe that we won't be able to cope with the extra capacity,' replied the chief executive.

The conversation continued as the meal progressed, and broached topics other than the closure of the Maryland plant. Shortly, however, the discussion returned to it.

'Hal, you've got to accept there's going to be opposition. Not all of your boys appreciate the true nature of the problems at Maryland. The fact that you and I are two steps ahead of them is not your fault. OK?' said the president.

'Yeh, but what do I do? How do I tell them and keep them all fired up to make the regional structure work?' asked the chief executive.

'At your next board meeting, just announce the closure of the Maryland plant. Say this was a majority main board decision and you were outvoted. Tell them that this decision has my full backing. In effect, blame me! ... Oh and by the way, tell them the true reason for the closure was the new performance criteria which will be applied to all plants. Maryland just did not match up to what we want our boys to be doing in the future,' finished the president.

'Yeh. The boys will probably buy that!' smiled the chief executive.

Both men (Case 10.5) recognised that the implementation of strategy is not straightforward. It was considered important that the Maryland plant be closed down. It was equally considered imperative that any opposition to the Maryland closure be kept to a minimum, as substantial effort and will were required to ensure a successful reorganisation to a regional structure. Both the president and chief executive recognised the importance of the politics of strategy implementation.

TYPES OF STRATEGY

Strategy is an all-embracing term. We need to distinguish between three different types of strategy – unit strategies, corporate strategies and functional strategies.

Unit strategy

Specific, identifiable organisations, or in the terms of the three distinguished American writers Newman, Warren and Schnee, business units, adopt unit strategies. A business unit is an identifiable, single-product (or related multi-product) organisation such as an independent company, subsidiary or division of a diversified corporation, or a single service public organisation (eg social service or education department of a local authority). The essential feature of a business unit is that the organisation is identified with a single range of products or services so that its mission is quite clear.

All strategic action depends on the performance of the business unit. The ultimate success or failure of any large diversified multinational depends on its business units.

Elements of unit strategy

1   Company philosophy/structure/degrees of freedom/employee attitudes to change.

2   Product portfolio. How wide a range of products has the company developed and are those products attractive to consumers?

3   Competitive position of the business unit in the market.

4   Market sensitivity and degree of market penetration.

The way in which the company structures its activities is an important concern. The flexibility of its people to adapt to changing market conditions and the resources that are directed towards R and D are issues dependent on the philosophy of that business unit. If the philosophy of the organisation is to generate business and pursue profit, then flexibility of structure is likely. If, however, the philosophy is more concerned with internal organisational matters, then the structure is only likely to alter in response to 'internal' organisational issues, and individuals would be more concerned with maintaining their role and status than responding to market changes.

Equally, for a subsidiary or division of a large corporate organisation, the degree of freedom the business unit can negotiate from the parent company will directly influence the unit's performance. The greater the freedom of the subsidiary the greater the chances for the unit to respond directly to market conditions, the better the chances for improved performance.

What of product portfolio? Has the business unit generated a comprehensive product portfolio to attract the necessary attention from the market? Offering just a few, or a poorly related range of, products or services is insufficient, as customer needs change and the products offered may shortly no longer be in demand. A well-matched product portfolio is required which takes account of likely changes in the short to medium term.

From the consumer's point of view, a well-developed product portfolio is an aid to decision-making. It should not be assumed that consumers, in general, have clearly identified the product(s) or services that will satisfy their needs. Examining a broad but integrated range of products or services allows the consumer to work out what he really wants and to choose one of the products in the range. A poorly-developed product portfolio will still allow the consumer to establish his needs but unless they are specific to their limited portfolio, he may reject the products or services and possibly purchase from competitors.

A comprehensive product portfolio depends on two factors – the resources given to R and D and the degree of market penetration. In the long term, the competitive position of the business unit in the market reflects a strong or weak R and D function. As R and D is unlikely to produce short to medium-term results, the very survival and growth of R and D is determined by the attitude of senior managers in the organisation. In a culture of short-term thinking, R and D is unlikely to prosper. It takes strong, determined, far-seeing management to back a function that does not directly contribute to immediate revenue.

The flipside to development is market awareness. Successful unit strategy depends on the accuracy of information on market trends. What is the total market size? What percentage of market share can the business unit realistically expect to maintain? What does the business unit need to know to increase market share?

An impressive business unit currently is Corning Medical and Scientific, a division of the American multinational Corning Glass. Corning, originally one of the largest glass product manufacturers in the world, has since diversified into various fields, one of which is medical and scientific equipment. Of the various business units, the medical and scientific division is a growing and highly profitable part of the corporation. It operates under its own structure and philosophy. The structure is matrix-oriented, whereby managers will hold particular line roles but also belong to product/development teams. Hence, colleague relations and superior/subordinate relations are equally emphasised. The division is highly competitive, offering a well-thought-through product portfolio, and has invested substantially in R and D. The philosophy of the division seems to be 'sensitivity to change,' which is hardly surprising as both the product technology and market demands change at an astounding rate.

Case 10.6 The survival of the boxmakers (Part 3)

'You said that damn stupid decision wouldn't work out. And it hasn't!' shouted one of the regional general managers.

'Damn right,' commented two or three others. The operations vice president looked at the group he was chairing.

The venue was a hotel near Aspen, Colorado. The meeting was one of the regularly monthly one-and-a-half-day business meetings to discuss short- and medium-term business performance. The group consisted of the operations vice president's team, which included the VP's assistant and the regional managers.

'We all made the regionalisation policy work. We increased our competitive position in the market place. We are far more customer needs-based. We know our customers better. We've even taken some customers from some of the big boys in the game. Jim, Allen and Warner (three of the regional managers) worked hard on their change programmes, especially in their plants. What looked like dead losses 14 months ago are now regions that are breaking even and would have been profitable had those bastards not closed down Maryland,' continued Roger Katz, one of the more assertive of the general managers.

'Yeh, we've increased our business without having to invest extra in increasing our product range. It's been a cheap reorganisation,' responded a somewhat sullen operations vice president.

'And what's the problem now?' asked another of the general managers. 'Having got the business, we can't give what the customer wants, when he wants it! And why? Because we do not have that extra production capacity facility. That's why!'

'OK. So Maryland was one of the worst. So at the time you could say that we needed to cut overheads. But that has not happened. We cut Maryland, sold off the site, made people redundant and what happened? We started hiring more people to the existing plants in order to cope with the increased demand. We've had to contract work out to other manufacturers. So at a time when we are growing, we've cut skilled labour, paid out extensively in redundancy money, hired the same amount of labour in other plants, labour that has to be trained up to do the job well and is as yet not trained up, and subcontracted large blocks of work to manufacturers not used to our standards. We've done the very thing we said we'd never do - cut quality and what's more, during our growth period!' commented another general manager.

Another of the general managers asked, 'What the hell did Hal Springer [chief executive] think he was doing when he allowed the main board to close down Maryland? Sure the plant was poor quality, but it was obvious to anyone that we needed that plant to remain operational more than ever before ...'

Pause ...

'And those guys on the main board call themselves strategists!'

Other critical comments were made. The operations vice president looked round at his team, said nothing and continued to listen.

The general managers energetically and openly displayed their dissatisfaction at one of their regular business meetings (Case 10.6). Understandably, for they had, as a team, generated a highly successful unit strategy to increase their market share of a declining market. Without any change to their product portfolio, the general managers considered that they had improved the competitive position of the subsidiary (business unit) in the market place by concentrating on satisfying customer needs. Now they had achieved an increased order book, it was felt that such demand could not be met when required or at the right standards due to limitations in the production facility. The general managers, taking a unit strategy perspective, found it impossible to understand why the decision was made.

Corporate strategy

Corporate strategy relates to organisations which control a number of business units, such as multinationals or multipurpose local government organisations as in the UK. The ultimate aims of such organisations would be two-fold:

1   To stimulate a corporate identity and improve the performance of the number of different business units under the one corporate umbrella

2   To be sensitive to developments in the market place so as to be able to focus on new areas of business activity.

It is rare that any major corporation only conducts business in a narrowly defined field of activity. Corporate strategy involves different considerations from unit strategy.

Elements of corporate strategy

1   Spread of business areas. How many separate businesses fall under the corporate umbrella? How many separate types of business are covered within this spread? Do conflicts of interests exist between the business units?

2   Strategic thrusts. In which area are future strategies to be concentrated?
    • Are improved/increased results expected from the existing business units?
    • Have new areas of business been identified, through acquisitions, mergers and sales?
    • How has capital been allocated amongst the business units – has greater capital assistance been offered to others? Is the capital moved to the business units congruent with the strategic thrusts?

Whereas unit strategy is geared towards achieving business results, such as profitability, effective provision of services or reducing costs, corporate strategies do not directly share such aims. The objective of corporate strategy is the survival and growth of the corporation as an entity, through the increased performance of the business units, through finding new areas of business or through reallocating capital assistance to the business units.

Understandably, the interests of the corporation and of the business units do not always coincide. The provision of capital support for one part of the corporation may undermine the profitability of one or more other business units. Corporate headquarters could consider the undermined business units

expendable or able to survive with reduced profitability. The
relationships between corporate headquarters and the business units
has never been comfortable with such a diversity of objectives.

Case 10.7   The survival of the boxmakers (Part 4)

'So the general managers were not at all happy, Ritch, huh?' asked the
chief executive.

'That's what I said, Hal,' replied the operations vice president. He
continued. 'Just take me through again why Maryland was closed.'

'OK! First, we all know it was unprofitable. The place was going to be
shut sooner or later. The question was when. When, it was decided,
should be at the time of reorganisation to a regional structure. Don't look
at me like that, Ritch. I know we cut the production facility, but look at
the problem from a corporate point of view. Maryland had survived more
years than it should, largley because of the power of the trade unions.
Secondly, just imagine what could have happened if the regions became
dependent on Maryland. Those guys would have had us over a barrel.
Maryland just could not be relied on. Third, the policy was that each
region should become a profit centre. In the long run it is imperative that
each of the general managers develop his own strategy for his region.
Having Maryland would have delayed that strategy being fully practised.
It is a bit unfortunate that they are just putting their regional strategies
into operation at a time of rapid growth through increased orders. The
next ten months will be frustrating for them but they should have the
situation sorted out by this time next year. Finally, the main board has
got the whole group to think about. Maryland has become a joke
throughout the group. You know the policy, we're going for increased
market share with no major change to our product portfolio, not just in
our company, but throughout the group. That means we entirely depend
on the commitment of senior and middle management in each
subsidiary to produce results. Nothing could demotivate more than if the
main board said, "We want results, we reward high performers, won't
tolerate poor performance" and allowed Maryland to survive. The whole
increased market penetration policy for the group would become a joke.
For everyone's benefit, Maryland had to be closed down when it was,'
finished the chief executive.

The operations vice president smiled and said, 'Yeh, from head office
point of view, what you say makes sense. But that doesn't help me with
my regional managers.'

'Don't moan, Ritch. Like me, you're a board director and these are
fairly commonplace problems. You're part of managing the whole
business and not just bits of it. That's why you've got more status and
earn more money that those other guys,' said the chief executive.

The operations vice president smiled.

From a corporate point of view, the closure of the Maryland

plant made good strategic sense (Case 10.7). As the chief executive indicated, the future corporate thrust was increased market penetration with the same product portfolio coupled with a policy of decentralisation/regionalisation on a profit centre concept. The success of the corporate strategy was strongly influenced by the attitudes, energy and commitment of managers of the subsidiary organisations. The continuation of the Maryland plant could have upset the commitment required from lower level management in other business units. Although there was a conflict of interests between unit and corporate strategy, neatly encapsulated by the dilemmas faced by the operations vice president, the chief executive rightly pointed out that such tension was commonplace in most businesses.

FUNCTIONAL STRATEGY

Functional strategy relates to particular plans of action adopted by the various functions in a business unit, such as production, marketing, finance and personnel. The various functional strategies support unit strategy. Functional strategy cannot be formulated until unit strategy is decided.

Elements of functional strategy

1 Working towards fulfilling the mission of the business unit.

2 Influencing the direction of the unit strategies through identifying particular problems of introducing new initiatives.

3 Providing performance feedback in order to influence the direction of unit strategies.

It is important that in bringing together the various functional strategies a culture of collaboration and co-operation is stimulated in the organisation. If the strategies of the functions do not knit well together, a possible end result is an ineffective business unit. It is no easy task to combine the energies of the various functions, for each may hold different short- to medium-term objectives. For example, in a manufacturing organisation production departments manufacture goods according to set specifications; sales departments are required to sell the goods and respond to customer needs; a sales department may accept orders and deadlines which production cannot meet.

Such friction between various departments is common in most organisations. Should lack of co-operation and poor cross-functional relationships become the norm rather than the exception, management training and development techniques (as outlined in Chapter 6) have to be utilised to improve relationships amongst key personnel within the organisation.

SUMMARY

In this chapter, we have analysed the concepts of organisation mission and strategy.

Strategy generation

The issues concerned with the generation of strategy are outlined in Fig 10.5.

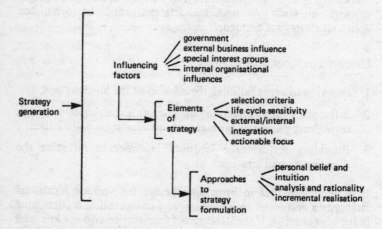

Fig. 10.5   Strategy generation

In the analysis of strategy generation, a sequential perspective is taken whereby influencing factors, elements of strategy and approaches to strategy formulation are considered in a stepwise fashion. The first step in the analysis involves taking into account all possible influencing factors, such as the impact of central (federal) and local (state) government, external business concerns, the power of special interest groups and the needs and demands of forceful individuals and groups in the organisation that could provide shape and direction to the range of alternative strategies.

Having identified, analysed, and weighed the effects of the influencing factors, it is necessary to examine the elements (components) of any strategy. The elements comprise selection criteria (reasons why particular actions for the future are rejected or selected), life cycle sensitivity (an estimation of the life span of a strategy), external/internal integration (an understanding of the impact that changes in the market place/society/general environment will have on the organisation), and actionable focus (an appreciation that strategies need to provide a soluble guide for action).

The third aspect of strategy generation is the manner in which particular strategies are formulated, namely, personal intuition, rational analysis and incremental and often disjointed realisation. Personalised intuition is dependent on the drive, flair, beliefs and capacity of single, powerful individuals who can create new and vibrant organisations and/or alter the market place, according to their views and ideals. A rational-based analysis approach takes three separate areas into account:

1   A broad industry/external environment perspective, identifying those factors that influence the industry/community in terms of demand, sales, volume, profitability, cost effectiveness, for goods or services.

2   Organisation health factors, the strengths and limitations of the organisation.

3   Key person analysis review, an assessment of those individuals who could influence and change the scenario.

According to a step-by-step realisation process, people learn of the strengths and weaknesses of the strategies they formulate through practice, discard elements they find unfavourable and change according to circumstances. Although strategists may at times be perceived as contradicting themselves in terms of words and actions, the learning required for strategy formulation takes place in cumulative but haphazard manner.

Strategy implementation

The pursuit of certain strategies affects, positively or negatively, the interests of all people in the organisation and some in the external environment. No matter how well considered or appropriate are particular strategies, if people's interests are threatened they are likely to argue for alternatives. Hence, the process of strategy implementation is 'political' in nature. On this basis, five approaches to strategy implementation are suggested:

- map the issues
- just one problem to start with
- break down old identities
- confront conflict
- allow others to catch up.

Types of strategy

There are three types of strategy: unit, corporate and functional.

Unit strategies are adopted by identifiable business units, such as independent companies, subsidiary companies, largely self-determining divisions of diversified corporations, or service supporting or service providing departments of public sector organisations. The key concerns for unit strategy are the product/service portfolio offered by the organisation, the competitive position of the business unit in the market, the degree of market/external environment sensitivity and the overall organis-ational capacity to manage change.

Corporate strategy relates to organisations which control a number of business units and who intend to improve the overall performance of separate business units which may or may not hold conflicting objectives. The key concerns for corporate strategy are the spread of business areas and whether and what sort of conflict of interests exists within this spread; and further, what should be the strategic emphasis of the future, bearing in mind the convergence or divergence of separate business unit interests.

Functional strategy relates to the objectives, plans and actions adopted by particular functions in the business unit, such as marketing, personnel, production. The aim of functional strategy is to support business unit strategy and so it cannot be formulated until business unit strategy has been established. The key concerns for a functional strategy are to work towards fulfilling the mission of the business unit through identifying particular problems or introducing new initiatives and through providing performance feedback which could influence the future direction of unit strategies. Unit strategy depends a great deal on the ability of the various functions in the organisation to collaborate and co-operate, even though each may hold different short- to medium-term objectives.

Terminology

The term 'strategy' can be used to represent various different decision making and decision implementation processes in an organisation. Consequently, clarity of meaning is crucial in any debate concerning organisational strategy. For this reason, seven key words are offered – mission, objectives, strategy, plans, tactics, activities, tasks – in order to show the developmental relationship between broad-based statements of philosophy and fundamental purpose and those activities which cumulatively are the basis of strategy.

IN CONCLUSION

Clear, comprehensive strategy is the link between mission statements and the effective implementation of particular tasks; the link between the desired and the attainable. Strategy has to account for projected external influences such as company image, sources and availability of funds, consumer habits, market trends, material costs, cost and availability of energy sources, legislation and international politics. Equally, internal organisational influences need to be considered, such as resource allocation, fixed costs, product range, marketing, quality of R and D, employee attitudes, management/union relations, the degree of collaboration and conflict between particular individuals and groups.

Future strategy which has been clearly thought through acts as a unifying process, clarifying what is and is not feasible in any situation.

11 Organisation Structure

had sent over its own top executives to run the clothing company. The cultural differences have become an additional irritant.

Currently most managers consider the company to be too unstable and in desperate need of an opportunity to consolidate its position.

Structure is immediately noticeable to anyone who has anything to do with organisations. For a new employee, structure could be viewed as an imposed condition as soon as he is told to report to his supervisor. Working for a supposedly 'bureaucratic' organisation could mean that most people in the organisation associate structure with repetitive tasks and inflexible managers. In so-called loose structures, such as academic institutions, a career promotion structure exists based on publications, expertise and seniority. Customers or clients dealing with an organisation are confronted by structure when they select goods to buy, or request a service to meet their needs. They may be seen by one organisational employee, referred to a second, who it is thought can better satisfy their needs, and possibly charged for the service by a third. Inevitably, every organisation operates under some sort of structure. The value of that structure to the organisation in terms of harnessing resources to meet goals and the impact it makes on attitudes and work performance are primary concerns in any debate on organisation structure.

In this chapter, we explore why organisation structure requires analysis. To provide a broad-based perspective of structure, we examine the factors that have influenced the organisation to be what it is today, the various alternative blueprints of organisation structure, and the likely impact of applying a particular form of structure in an organisation, bearing in mind the influences that have shaped the organisation to its present state. A narrow examination of structure is considered unwise, as one needs a general view of the organisation in order to appreciate how well the structure is operating. An underlying assumption throughout this chapter is that organisation structure should be seen as a means to an end, ie structure is the means by which strategy is pursued and resources harnessed so that goals, objectives or outputs may be achieved (ends).

ANALYSING ORGANISATION STRUCTURE

To understand why any organisation operates and develops the way it does, it is necessary to analyse structure. There are four reasons for this:

1 *Need to organise resources.* All organisations aim to achieve certain goals and objectives by generating plans and attempting to organise available resources. Structure provides the mechanism for the implementation of plans and the controlled usage of resources. Particular resources can be allocated to people who are then required to carry out certain tasks, and who in turn are likely to be supervised and monitored by others in the organisation. This aspect of structure involves organisation charts (to show reporting relationships), the mechanisms of boards, committees and working parties and the use of job descriptions to specify task responsibilities. The shape and pattern of organisation charts and committee mechanisms will depend on the size of the organisation. The clothing manufacturers in Case 11.1 are considering reorganising and need a structure that is more suitable to a smaller organisation.

2 *Clarification of job activities.* People need some idea of what is expected of them in their job. Where a task can be well defined, devices such as standing orders or operating manuals provide a step-by-step procedure for the completion of that task. Where a task does not easily lend itself to detailed definition, standards of performance can be established by incorporating criteria such as output or quality of achievement. Hence, people's expectations about their jobs are formed by the established control procedures, the reward and appraisal systems, the planning schedules and the systems of communication in practice.

3 *Decision-making/information processes.* Decision-making and the dissemination of information must be provided for within

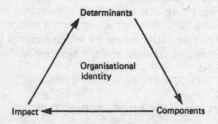

Fig. 11.1   The elements of organisation structure

the framework of the organisation's structure. Adequate information is vital for practical decision-making. Arrangements have to be made for relevant information to be collected from inside and outside the organisation. In addition, information needs to be evaluated as part of a standard process. In this way, valuable information can be made available to decision-makers on a regular basis in response to new developments. The process of decision-making can be assisted through programming, ie specifying key stages in the process and allowing information to be fed back in order to review the original decision.

4 *Determination of attitudes.* The structure of an organisation is a strong determinant of the attitudes commonly held by its members. Such attitudes have been termed the 'culture of the organisation'.

For example, the larger the organisation the greater the physical and psychological distance between top level management and operatives. Under such circumstances middle management may feel themselves unable to influence decision-making at senior levels, thus possibly developing an attitude of resignation, and may feel they do not have sufficient challenge and responsibility in their jobs. Operatives may not identify with the organisation at all, as they may see themselves as the expendable element of a large bureaucracy. Hence, from middle management downwards, people may feel demotivated and performance standards and output expectations are reduced.

The employees of Rayon Designs Inc. in Case 11.1 are demoralised because they perceive their environment as unstable. Too many changes of structure in too short a time period have generated passive and negative feelings amongst a large number of the people employed in the company.

Whether the resultant attitudes are positive or negative, structure undoubtedly influences culture.

In order to analyse structure, three elements must be taken into account – determinants, components and impact (Figure 11.1). Each of these factors influences the other so that the combination provides the organisation with a particular shape, culture and identity that distinguishes it from all others.

Determinants are influences or forces that determine the current and future shape, size and structural pattern of the organisation. Determinants act as a link between the past, present and future and strongly influence what changes are feasible.

There are seven key determinants, size, technology, historical background, geographic dispersion, external environment, people and their attitudes, and management information systems (MIS).

The *components* are those aspects of structure with which most managers are familiar, the role hierarchy or organisation tree, the hierarchical placement of roles in the organisation. Four blueprints of hierarchical role placement are identified. Changes of organisation structure will inevitably influence the patterns of decision making in the organisation. Hence, an analysis of the pros and cons of centralisation and decentralisation is undertaken.

The *impact* section deals with the manner in which, and the reasons why, any organisation is likely to react to the introduction of change or maintenance of current conditions. Impact is concerned with how new or historically based developments will manifest themselves in the organisation. In effect, what are the likely reactions in the organisation to change or no-change. In particular, managerial span of accountability and control and culture of organisation are examined.

The determinants, components, impact model is dynamic. It is important to recognise the key determinants that have influenced the organisation to its current shape and identity; what structural alternatives exist and how the maintenance or change of the present structure can be enhanced through centralised or decentralised decision-making processes; and finally, what effect any desired or undesired change will have on the organisation. The impact of these changes will, over time, become further determinants of what can be altered in the organisation. On this basis, change and structural reorganisation are a never-ending process, interrupted by periods of maintaining existing structural conditions (the length of the maintenance periods will vary from organisation to organisation). Structural reform and change introduced now will, in the long term, be a reason for further reform and change. Today's reorganisation could end up being tomorrow's problem and hence a stimulus for further reorganisation.

DETERMINANTS OF ORGANISATION STRUCTURE

Size of organisation

Size, as a determinant of organisation structure, has received substantial attention from researchers and management writers alike. The existing evidence indicates that size is probably the most important variable influencing the structure and shape of an organisation. The following conclusions can be drawn:

- Larger organisations usually have more formalised systems and procedures.

- Larger organisations tend to develop a network of complex interrelations between a number of different specialist groups.

- Larger organisations require extensive systems of co-ordination as much as of control.

- Size, in itself, does not seem to determine either efficiency or quality of output.

- Size is an important determinant of the predominantly held attitudes amongst employees (culture of organisation).

As we saw in Chapter 8, organisation culture refers to the attitudes, feelings and norms of behaviour shared by most personnel in the organisation. Size strongly influences the structural design which in turn helps to shape the underlying shared attitudes and behavioural pattern that people accept and practise in the organisation. For Rayon Designs Inc. in Case 11.1, the systems and structures in operation were appropriate to an organisation of a far larger size – established by the previous owner. The company faced a major structural reorganisation to ensure it complemented the new parent company.

The relationship between structure and culture is further explored in the section of this chapter entitled 'Impact' (for a fuller discussion of organisation culture, see Chapter 8).

Technology

Although management theory developed amidst the manufacturing industry, little mention was made of technology until the late 1950s/early 1960s. The researcher Joan Woodward asserts that the technology of production utilised is a fundamental determinant of organisation structure. From her studies Woodward concludes that issues such as the length of line of command, spans of control, white collar/blue collar staff turnover and the ratio of managers to operatives vary according to the technology of production in use. Woodward hypothesises that efficient organisations are those where the structure fits the norm for their technology.

The Tavistock group, operating from the Tavistock Institute in London, consider that changes of technology which also involve a substantial change of work pattern for people disrupt the relationships of those involved in the work, hence potentially reducing productivity. The phrase 'socio-technical systems' is used to demonstrate that the structural design of the organisation must take into account the nature of the work and its impact on people.

Other researchers have taken quite different views. For example, the American, Charles Perrow, suggests that several factors influence the impact of technology on the different aspects of organisation structure and goals. No one technology strongly influences the total structural configuration. The two British researchers, Derek Pugh and David Hickson, conclude that only a combination of technology and size is an important determinant of organisation structure. Alternatively, it can be argued that little reliable evidence shows that structure is strongly affected by technology, as technology and structure are multidimensional concepts and cannot be expected to relate in a simple manner.

With such divergence of view, developments in the 'new' technology of micro-electronics have not clarified the relationship between technology and organisation structure. Various terms are used to describe recent advances in technology, but all refer to miniaturised electronic circuitry employed to process information. Such technology reduces reliance on clerical support. In addition, miniaturised electronic circuity and mechanical technologies can be combined to allow programming of machinery for computer-controlled industrial processes, generally termed automation. The applications of micro-electronics have ranged from completely new or substantially improved products such as calculators, electronic games, digital watches, electronic typewriters, programmes for washing machines, remote control and teletext facilities for television, to processes in manufacturing such as CAD/CAM (computer aided design/manufacture) applied in aerospace, architecture and building, robots, flexible manufacturing systems, computerised stock control and warehousing; to the provision of commercial and social services such as electronic cash dispensers, electronic funds transfer, or applications in medicine such as computer diagnosis or intensive care monitoring or in libraries through computerised information systems; to office work in terms of word processing, electronic filing and speedy communication systems such as electronic mail and facsimile transmission, teleconfering and networking. Micro-electronic technology is cheap, reliable, compact and accurate and affects every aspect of our lives.

The issue for debate is: how will such developments affect organisation structures, employment patterns and work-oriented behaviour? Once again, various views are offered. Professor Charles Handy predicts smaller organisations, run by a professional elite along less bureaucratic lines, with the greater proportion of employees being hired on short-term contracts with no guarantee of contract renewal. Professor John Child of Aston University similarly predicts a contraction process in organisations, as advances in information technology will stimulate:

• reduction in operating costs

• increased flexibility

• improvement in the quality of product or service,

• increased control and integration.

Child foresees smaller, highly centralised organisations where managers in the centre will be able accurately to control and integrate the various operational and support service activities. Child labels the process 're-centralisation' and argues that the impact of such a process on the majority may be negative and demotivating.

If anything, the literature on new technology and organisation has polarised. At one end of the continuum, some optimistically argue that, in terms of profit maximisation and cost minimisation, the application of micro-electronics is a most potent force. Others see a future scenario involving shrinkage in opportunities for employment and centralised, even 'elitist' controlled, organisations. It is worth bearing in mind that the predictions made in the 1950s and 1960s about the impact of computers on work and organisations did not materialise, and if anything employment opportunities increased. Similarly, with the current rapid advances in information processing technologies, it is possible to paint a more favourable picture of the future, whereby organisations pay less attention to the activities of the centre and far greater attention to their operating business units (see Chapter 10 for an explanation of business unit strategy), with the centre merely providing an information processing service.

Whatever view is adopted, one fact is clear – technology is, and will be in the foreseeable future, a powerful determinant of organisation structure.

Historical background

The organisation's historical development, especially over issues such as ownership and control, will influence the present structure, culture and performance. Families who own and manage an organisation will probably maintain control over resources and distribution. Employees in the organisation may become too dependent on the key decision-makers in the organisation and hence find it difficult to think and act independently.

Large decentralised organisations may allow their divisions and subsidiaries substantial freedom. Such an organisation may be a combination of different cultures.

Morale and motivation amongst employees will be influenced by the management style of yesterday's as well as today's top management. Rayon Designs Inc. (Case 11.1) has been sold and bought five times within seventeen years. No wonder they find it difficult to share the new owner's aspirations. A commonly held attitude that has developed in that organisation is: 'Why bother; whatever you do won't make any difference!'

A history of takeovers and too much change combined with an inability to define or control future direction or purpose can lead to despondency and low morale amongst the personnel.

Mergers equally induce a particular structure/culture configuration. Historically, some mergers have involved a more aggressive organisation combining with a slower-moving, less energetic entity. Yet, a decade later, employees may identify with their original organisations. In fact, the systems procedures and structures may never have been fully integrated, with the result that two separate systems are in operation. Under such circumstances, the organisation is unlikely to utilise its full potential.

Irrespective of size and technology, the history of the organisation must be taken into account, especially if changes of structure, products and systems are contemplated. People's response and capacity to accept change are partially determined by history.

Geographic dispersion

Size and the structural configuration of an organisation are further complicated by geographic dispersion. An organisation whose units are geographically widely dispersed may generate different structures and mechanisms for co-ordination and control from a similar-sized organisation operating within one locality.

Case 11.2   Invoicing the customer

Particular frustration arose over the question of sales invoicing. The USA parent company wished to introduce their system of sales invoicing to the UK subsidiary. Although there was a system of sales invoicing within Rayon Designs, each area sales office had developed its own method and practice.

The newly appointed senior sales manager wanted to revise current practices. He introduced a scheme whereby all sales invoices were issued at the end of the month. After a three-month trial period, the sales manager called his area sales managers to a meeting to discuss the development of the scheme.

'I must tell you, I don't think the new system is operating too well. The sales accounting procedures are still in a mess,' commented the sales manager.

Silence.

'Well, I'm not surprised,' responded one of the area managers.

'This new system takes no account of our customers' needs, it costs too much money and it is too difficult to understand,' he concluded.

The meeting continued for another hour and a half. The opposition to the manager's experimental system was universal. He was accused of not understanding the needs of customers, which varied throughout the country, and that simply introducing a centralised system would not do. It was finally decided that the senior sales manager would re-examine the experimental system in detail and present new proposals at the next sales meeting.

Today, the sales manager is not feeling too comfortable, for tomorrow his US boss is coming to see why a new scheme of invoicing is not fully operational.

Case 11.2 outlines a particular problem arising from geographic dispersion. The sales managers, in an attempt to meet customer needs and requests, found it difficult to comply with head office requirements. Equally, problems arise when a company is spread out within one country. The structure, systems and attitudes amongst employees vary according to market demands and local environmental conditions. One motor manufacturing organisation in the UK recently transferred the whole manufacturing operation producing a particularly high status vehicle from the Midlands to the South of England. The cost of such a move was enormous. Labour in the new locality was less militant, so that in the long run greater stability of output would be achieved from the transfer. The move was made after systems and structures aimed at generating greater control and co-ordination of output in the original site had been unsuccessful.

Structures and systems of operation need to be geared as much to local conditions as to head office requirements.

External environment

External environment, although closely linked to geographic dispersion, covers additional factors such as:

- current market situation
- competitor behaviour
- national and world political and economic environment.

Changes are constantly taking place in the external environment, changes that directly or indirectly will affect the organisation's efficiency and productivity. Awareness of external changes is all-important. Acting on such data determines the organisation's future prospects. The ability to perceive and act upon changes in the external environment is indicative of any organisation's ability to manage change.

People, positions and attitudes

People can act as a determinant of organisation structure in the following ways:

- placing people in appropriate roles,
- contingency management,
- overmanning,
- interpersonal friction,
- *ad hoc*ery,
- predominant shared attitudes.

All organisations need to be sufficiently flexible to be able to switch people from one role to another according to circumstances. Such moves do not necessarily involve promotion, but simply transferring a person who is recognised as 'expert' to work in an area that requires his skills. Such mobility means that lines of accountability need to be redrawn to accommodate such people. Each individual's responsibilities within the role structure may need to be reassessed in the light of the new demands made on that work unit. In a well managed transfer the incumbent and his new colleagues, subordinates and superiors have all been briefed as to the reasons for the move, identify with the new structure and give it their commitment and support and meet each other before he starts his new appointment.

Certain organisations whose product life cycle is short and who therefore need to re-examine their structures constantly, or large organisations who make it policy to transfer managers to various parts of the organisation in order to develop their managers on-the-job, may appoint key people on a contingency basis to manage particular projects or assist line managers with a particular problem. Other large organisations may appoint internal consultants who can assist line managers with specific problems or even be seconded to particular departments or divisions for agreed periods of time. The internal consultant is a full-time employee of the organisation, but is not appointed to a particular position within an established line hierarchy. Again, the introduction of new projects or consultants may stimulate a minor reorganisation within a specific part of the organisation.

Any organisation can face problems of overmanning, at shop floor and managerial levels. Although most organisations do discard labour, they are unlikely to do so to any extent until they are better able to predict trends in the market or external environment. Consequently, people need to be found jobs, roles and titles within the organisation's structure. The problem is more acute in larger organisations which are well able to carry excess labour, especially managerial personnel, or in organisations which have agreed to tenure of employment. Individuals who do not make any substantial contribution to the organisation still need to be accommodated in the short and, at times, longer term. Hence, people who have to be placed somewhere in the organisation can strongly influence the structural configuration. In public service organisations, where security of employment is a predominant feature, role structures may be changed purely to accommodate particular people.

Friction between managers can act as a determinant of structure. Individuals who make a worthwhile contribution but find it difficult, or refuse to negotiate, a reasonable working relationship with colleagues, subordinates or superior(s) may well be moved to another part of the organisation on a temporary or permanent basis. The organisation wishes to retain their services but does not know where to place them and so makes changes to a unit's structure (ie department or division).

People can be moved around the organisation for any of the above reasons, but also on an *ad hoc* basis that makes sense to managers at the time. It may be felt that an individual merits further on-the-job development. The most appropriate way to achieve that is to expose the person to the activities of various functions, departments or divisions in the organisation. Equally, individuals may be moved around the organisation in response to expected demands which never materialise. Senior management may also move individuals to different parts of the organisation because they do not know where best to place them. These individuals may not be valued, but on the other hand, senior management does not wish to retire them or make them redundant. *Ad hoc*ery in people placement can help to determine structure.

The way an organisation manages its people can stimulate strong opinions amongst its personnel. People may feel that their organisation requires its managers to be competitive and assertive and rewards high performers. As a result, the employees in the organisations may share certain attitudes, such as 'negotiate for what you want', 'you can always get what you want' or 'it does not matter how you get it – just get it'. Alternatively, people may feel that it is important to be supportive and helpful to one another, or more negative attitudes may predominate. The attitudes shared by personnel generate an organisational identity.

Every organisation has some sort of identity: something that makes it different from any other organisation even in the same industry. Anyone new to the organisation will quickly realise that he has to learn a number of unwritten acceptable dos and unacceptable don'ts. Such dos and don'ts are, as previously stated, the culture of the organisation, in fact the sum of all the people and their attitudes. Cultures are the product of the combination of determinants and components of structure, ie the impact that such a combination has had on the employees of the organisation. Although cultures are further discussed under the 'Impact' section of this chapter, it is worth noting that the people and their attitudes become a determinant as well as an outcome of structure, in that the predominant attitudes and patterns of behaviour may act as strong determinants to adopting a particular structural configuration.

Case 11.3 The feelings within Rayon Designs

As outlined in Case 11.1, the morale of management and workforce had reached an all-time low. People generally felt that they did not know what the future held for them.

In the business operations division in particular, anxiety about current performance and future prospects was particularly great. Sales were decreasing, the marketing forecasts turned out to be inaccurate and the director of business operations (DBO) was finding it difficult to motivate his salespeople to sell existing stocks, let alone new fashion lines. Some of the better salespeople (in terms of product sales) were negotiating contracts with competitors, and some had already left the organisation.

The position of director of business operations became vacant. The newly appointed director, an individual with many years' experience in the fashion industry, was astounded at the level of demotivation in the business operations division. He quickly realised that a reorganisation and restructuring of business operations was vital. He also recognised that an extensive on- and off-the-job training programme was needed to improve morale amongst managers, sales force and administrators. Restructuring without any motivational stimulus would mean that in reality nothing would change.

The newly-appointed DBO wondered whether he had made the right choice.

'What sort of organisation is this?' he pondered by the end of his second week. 'Shall I look for a new job; am I going to do anything here; am I even going to survive?'

An individual newly employed by an organisation, as the DBO in Case 11.3 discovered, needs to pay attention to the culture he perceives. Work satisfaction and future promotion are substantially influenced by the perceived match between organisation culture and personal needs. Culture is unlikely to alter unless the determinants and components of structure are changed. Consequently, it is up to the individual to select and utilise those aspects of the culture he finds valuable, or find alternative employment, if the culture is not compatible with his needs.

Management information systems (MIS)

It is important for any organisation to ensure that the activities of its units/departments/divisions are well co-ordinated. The process of co-ordination can only be satisfactorily achieved by installing an adequate communication and information system. Hence, it is important for any medium- to large-sized organisation to develop an effective MIS. MIS thus becomes a determinant of organisation structure, even though its prime aim should be to improve the quality of decision-making and problem-solving.

An MIS should be the linking mechanism in organisations where diversity predominates. Diversity could relate to the different functions and activities that are performed, as well as to differences of values, attitudes and norms held by individuals and groups within the organisation. Four objectives can be achieved by introducing an MIS to the organisation:

1 *To improve long-term planning*. In an industrial organisation, the data for long-term planning are more accessible; sales data, for example, can be broken down by the sales in each geographic area, or time taken for a range of products to be sold. In public service organisations the situation is different. The data required for future planning are difficult to define and always open to question. Yet, even in the field of social work, brave attempts have been made to develop systematic recording and review systems, providing important information on social worker activities, which senior management could easily utilise for their long-term planning.

2 *To improve managerial control*. In certain situations, the speed of provision of information may be more important than its accuracy. Probably a major problem for any organisation is that information needed quickly by management is not rapidly forthcoming from those operating lower down in the organisation. An efficient MIS will provide management with the information it requires and will also be seen by those lower down the hierarchy as useful instead of yet another interference.

3 *To reduce conflict*. An information system that binds disinterested parties to each other is likely to reduce the potential level of aggravation between the groups. First, all interested parties will know what is required of them and why. Second, individuals can plan their workload, for they know what type of information they have to gather and refer upwards. A nagging frustration at work is that people at all levels in the hierarchy may be asked to provide or find information without any prior warning. Sometimes they do not know where to begin to search and often do not know why the information is needed. Working to a common information system will reduce the level of frustration.

4   *To improve motivation.* People who know what is expected of
    them can plan for future events and know that what they are
    doing is purposeful. They are motivated to work within
    specified boundaries where they are more certain of their
    position. The more people know what is required of them, the
    less the need for continuous supervisory attention.

Case 11.4   Reshaping Rayon Designs (Part 1)

The director of business operations (DBO) decided he must actively
initiate the restructuring of the company. He called together some of his
managers for an informal day-long meeting to discuss some of the
problems in the division. At the start of the meeting, DBO outlined his
view of the problems of the division, the poor sales performance and the
vulnerable position of the organisation, and firmly stated that the future
success of the organisation depended on the ability of business
operations to sell the company's products. Although they were polite
and seemingly co-operative, DBO felt that the managers were not really
forthcoming in their views. DBO learnt little more from the meeting than
he knew already.

As time passed DBO resolved to investigate further the views
of different managers in the organisation. He organised a series of semi-
informal one-to-one meetings and invited some of the more senior
managers to dinner and others to lunch. On each occasion he steered
the conversation towards a discussion of the fashion design business,
Rayon Designs Inc. and business operations in particular. On more than
one occasion, people mellowed and offered fairly forthright opinions of
the problems and opportunities of business operations.

As time passed DBO formed his view of the chief problems in Rayon
Designs. He noted:

1 Most of the managers implied that the present organisation structure
  was not working.

2 Most managers had developed often overlapping contacts with
  numerous customers and clients, and had not informed each other who
  their contacts were. Any one customer could be negotiating with two or
  three separate managers.

3 There were few effective co-ordination and control mechanisms.

4 The lack of control and co-ordination meant that managers were not
  informing each other whom they visited, how many times and with what
  outcomes.

5 The majority of Rayon's good managers were demotivated. If they
  could find another job and leave, they would probably do so.

As a result of these findings, certain bulk customers were approached

> to ascertain their views. They revealed their dissatisfaction with the
> present state of affairs. Most did not know who to relate to in the
> company. Equally, most attempted to use the current situation to their
> own advantage. If a bulk customer was unable to negotiate something in
> his favour with one manager, he would merely contact another person
> he knew in the company and attempt to negotiate a more favourable
> outcome with him, thereby reversing any previous decision.
>
> DBO re-read his notes on all these points, then called his secretary.
> 'Avril. Would you type up these notes, please. I'll check them and then
> could you give a copy of them to each member of the executive
> committee, with a short note attached saying we need to meet just to
> discuss organisation structure. Thank you, Avril.'

A number of problems have been highlighted in Case 11.4, such
as a need to re-examine the present structure, the largely negative
attitudes towards work and the company held by many of Rayon's
employees, the ill-co-ordinated contact with clients and poor co-
ordination and control systems in general. The key decision-makers
in the organisation must debate these problems with the intention of
finding a structural solution suitable for present and future needs.

However, remember that the structural shape of the organisation
will depend on the configuration of the determinants of structure
and the tasks the organisation has to accomplish to fulfil its mission
and objectives. The total size of the organisation and the
technologies utilised as part of the work process are strong
determinants of the shape of the components. Equally, the degree of
geographic dispersion, the organisation's history and background,
the predominant attitudes of its personnel, and the need for a
particular MIS will influence the extent to which the organisation is
capable of changing from one structural pattern to another.

ORGANISATION STRUCTURE, DECISION-MAKING AND PROBLEM-SOLVING

It is uncontroversial to say that the allocation of responsibilities, the
grouping of responsibilities, decision-making, co-ordination and
control are all fundamental to the continued operation of an
organisation. What is hotly disputed is their combination, for from
that derives the basic quality of an organisation's structure, which in
turn affects its daily functioning and long-term development. That
quality is established by examining the components of organisation
structure.

The components of organisation structure are the organisation charts/role hierarchies and decision-making patterns in practice in the organisation. Two questions need to be asked:

- Is the organisation organised according to product, functional, divisional or matrix structure?

- Is it possible to distinguish a pattern of decision-making?

Role hierarchy

In a small organisation, employing just a handful of people, there is little need to arrange people's roles and relationships formally. Individuals will conduct their business with each other face to face, especially the allocation of task responsibilities. Equally, the process of quality control is personalised as individuals are likely to praise or criticise one another's performance as the occasion arises.

The need to design formal structures increases with growing size and complexity. The formal structure refers to role structure, namely the manner in which people's roles are structured within a particular work unit. Management is required to control and co-ordinate the various activities conducted in the organisation to be able to achieve targets and outputs. The larger an organisation becomes, the more difficult it becomes for any one individual or group to control the activities of others. As direct control becomes problematic, then people pay greater attention to co-ordination. The work of Professor John Child shows that the larger an organisation, the greater the need for co-ordination. Child suggests that four levels of hierarchy are the average from about 200 employees (this includes the chief executive, departmental heads, supervisors and operatives) and six at around 1,000 people. From there on, the rate of hierarchical levels is not in proportion to increases in growth. At 10,000 employees the norm indicates about seven or eight levels.

To account for the determinants of structure, and to facilitate control and co-ordinate processes, four alternative models of role hierarchy are described:

1 Functional structure.

2 Product structure.

3 Divisional structure.

4 Matrix structure.

Functional structure

A functional structure is normally adopted once an organisation
develops beyond the small group size.

Essentially, activities are grouped into departments, with a
departmental head, all contributing to a common mission. The co-
ordination of these departments is achieved through the
appointment of an overall director, often backed by an executive
committee or board (Figure 11.2).

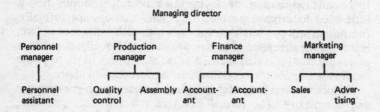

Fig. 11.2   Functional structure

If the organisation is not too large, there are advantages in
employing a functional structure.

- There is less need for a large number of managers. Because of the
  relatively simple structure, co-ordination of activities is left to top
  managers.

- If experts are required to cope with certain problems, it is simpler
  and cheaper to request assistance from a single department.
  Grouping specialists together in one department increases the
  potential for the efficient utilisation of personnel across the whole
  organisation.

- There are easily recognised career paths for specialists. The
  specialist enjoys the satisfaction of working with colleagues of
  similar interests. For the organisation, the management of such
  specialists is relatively simple. The opportunities for increased
  pay and status are already provided for in the career hierarchy
  and little else needs to be done to hire and retain the services of
  specialists.

Problems occur in utilising a functional structure once the organisation grows further or diversifies into new products, services or markets.

Product structure

With growth and expansion, the functional structure is unlikely to meet the demands placed on the organisation, which will probably diversify into new products, markets and services. Individuals with product or service responsibilities need to be appointed to champion the development of individual products or services. Managers operating under a functional structure are unlikely to be sufficiently motivated to make an impact with new products or services. Further, the market or service in question will not be the functional manager's prime area of responsibility and hence he will be unable to devote the necessary time and energy to managing its potential growth. Under these circumstances, the functional structure will be far less effective.

Fig. 11.3 Product structure

The solution is to create a separate entity to manage each of the new processes. The product structure (Figure 11.3) is a more appropriate approach to grouping activities where an organisation has developed two or more ranges of products or types of service. Adopting a product structure will involve a duplication of services, as each particular range will have available its own specialists to service it. The advantage is that the greater the need for change on the products or services offered, the greater the pressure to respond to the external changes by the managers and specialists of the organisation. Sufficient attention can be given to the needs of each product or service range according to market demands. With a greater number of specialists being available to service a particular product or service, the demand for co-ordination and control will increase. Specialists will need to meet at regular intervals to examine the operational management and strategic development of each product range. Should, however, market demand for any product range dramatically decrease, then the organisation will be faced with the problem of maintaining a superfluous workforce (often comprised of technical specialists).

Switching from a functional to product structure makes sense under growing market conditions. Problems arise when the market stabilises or declines as the organisation is no longer sufficiently flexible to find alternative employment for its line managers and staff specialists.

Divisional structure

Divisionalisation involves splitting the organisation into separate and at times virtually autonomous units where each division provides a total service for any one client. In effect, a number of smaller units are created within the organisation, and these are termed divisions (Figure 11.4). Each division has at its head a divisional director. Below the divisional directors may be functional, product or even matrix structures. Each separate division may have a different structure.

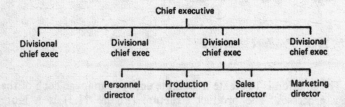

Fig. 11.4   Divisional structure

A divisional structure holds a number of advantages:

- Cost and profit issues are the direct responsibility of the divisional directors. The overall director of the organisation (ie chief executive) is not concerned with the daily finances of the division.

- The main function of organisational headquarters is strategic planning, appraisal of policies and projects, and overall financial control. This process involves planning for the future, which would be impossible if too many people became involved. Only the divisional directors and possibly corporate planning specialists, in conjunction with the chief executive of the organisation, are involved in considering future developments.

- Corporate and future planning would be committed to the development of the overall organisation rather than any individual division. It is inappropriate to identify only with the development of any one division, often to the detriment of other divisions. Hence, it is necessary to have a corporate structure above the divisional structures.

- The ability of a division to respond more freely to particular needs in certain local areas. In essence, self-contained units operating within particular geographic localities can meet specific community requirements, bearing in mind the budgetary constraints under which they operate.

Matrix structure

Matrix structure management is needed when an organisation has developed a somewhat unresponsive and inflexible culture, possibly through ever-increasing growth leading to a product structure or divisionalisation, but finds that various specialists need to be incorporated more closely into the day-to-day operation of the organisation. Matrix management is a way of generating greater flexibility over task activity and more market responsive attitudes amongst managers and specialists in the organisation (Figure 11.5).

Matrix structure management arose from the development of the aerospace industry in the USA. The US Government had begun to demand that numerous companies work on large project contracts that required substantial co-ordination and intricate interrelationships within and between firms. Countless management and organisation consultants were hired to develop human relations training and form organisations into more closely-knit teams, thereby promoting a more open climate for the workforce. It was

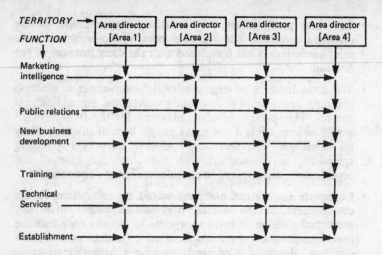

Fig. 11.5   A Matrix structure: for example, a bank

recognised that serving two masters, each with quite different objectives and personal values, led to a number of dilemmas within the operating entity and a substantial degree of personal stress for individuals. Professor Ralph Kingdon calls it:

> An attempt to combine the advantages of functional specialisation with those of project management recognising that lateral negotiated relationships, complementary to superior–subordinate authority relationships, are essential for the performance of highly complex and interdependent technical tasks and for the promotion of organisational adaptiveness and flexibility. The key problem is, to derive ways of implementing such relationships and reconciling them with the hierarchical order. (p.1).

For some, the matrix management approach may seem contradictory. On the one hand, people require control and co-ordination in order to work together on quite complex tasks. On the other hand, control can no longer be applied through hierarchical authority. In an attempt to increase co-ordination at the expense of control, certain private and public service organisations have introduced an additional role in the structure – the internal consultant. Their purpose is to respond to requests for assistance from persons of any level or organisational unit, if the problem area in question lies within their field of competence.

Whether internal consultants are utilised or not, the distinction between a matrix organisation, a complex organisation and a 'badly' organised organisation is fundamentally one of attitude, as held by both management and lower level personnel, rather than the presence or absence of rules and regulations. Most organisations function in a matrix manner, but it is the degree of recognition given to matrix development by senior management that is crucial. If higher level management is attempting to impose an authority structure on what is essentially a matrix pattern of work relationships, then the matrix style will predominate but work performance will be poor. There will be subversive activity at lower levels. Senior management will feel its plan is being sabotaged by those beneath and attempt to introduce further controls to, in its terms, rectify the situation. Eventually, even middle management will only pay lip service to formal procedures imposed from above.

People at lower organisational levels will continue to interrelate on a colleague basis in order to meet the requirements of their everyday tasks. The formal procedures imposed from above will be seen as hindrances to be bypassed. A substantial amount of time will be lost as senior management hold numerous meetings to find ways in which they can, in their eyes, regain control. Those at the lower levels will be meeting to look for ways of continuing their work without management interference. In addition to loss of time, trust between persons at different organisational levels will diminish and conflict-oriented relationships may become the most common form of interaction. Effective matrix organisations are as much a sign of the maturity of the personnel in the organisation as they are a type of organisational structure.

Decision patterns

Most managers find themselves continually redesigning the structure of their group, section, department, division or organisation. Organisational charts may be drafted and redrafted, individual areas of responsibility and authority are often redefined and budgets for additional personnel and equipment are usually under constant scrutiny. In this way, managers in the organisation are able to argue for the continued development of their establishment. The arguments and points of view may be many and varied and at times in direct contradiction to each other.

The reason such differences of view are offered in any organisation is that external conditions change and various managers hold different views as to how to respond to change. In addition, in trying to get the structural design right, management is juggling with two conflicting policies simultaneously – the need to standardise and the need to diversify. The reasons for standardisation are threefold; reduction of costs; ease of communication by working to a common set of proceedings; control over work, so that both the way work is done (the process) and the results of that work (quality of products or service) can be monitored.

Equally, senior management has to allow sufficient flexibility in the system for it to be able to respond adequately to external changes.

The degree of flexibility within the system depends on the goals of the organisation. Certain goals can be clearly established. For example, Rayon Designs Inc. has to sell more clothes; the system needs to be sufficiently flexible for the salesman at the lower end of the organisation to be able to feed information to senior management so that they can re-evaluate their goals.

However, other goals are an expression of identity and cannot be introduced or taken away according to changes of policy. These are the goals of individuals, teams or groups, especially if backed by a strong professional ethos, which can be different to the intended goals of the organisation. The goals of a professional and the goals of the organisation may not be the same.

There is a danger that the greater the range of goals within the organisation, the more senior management would wish to gain control over both resources and people. This may undermine the role of managers in outlying areas as control remains at head office. Middle managers occupying a geographically peripheral position may then strive for a redistribution of control over resources.

The arguments for greater conformity of procedures or greater diversity of goals and action have been couched in the centralisation/decentralisation arguments. As centralisation and decentralisation are important structural design issues, it is worth examining them further. Professor John Child neatly summarises the points in favour of each option.

For centralisation

1   Simplicity of co-ordination will occur if decisions are made at one point or amongst a small group.

2 Senior management will have a broader perspective on developments within the organisation and maintain conformity of already established policies. In terms of keeping up to date with recent developments, they are better able to adjust to any changes in order to provide for the interests of the organisation. This will avoid loss of control to people at lower levels who would be making decisions which are optimal for their group or sub-unit but less than optimal for the organisation as a whole.

3 Centralisation of control and procedures provides a way of helping the various functional areas in the organisation – research and development, production, personnel, finance and administration – to maintain an appropriate balance. This occurs by centralising decisions on resource allocation, functional policies, targets and human resource matters.

4 Centralisation can economise on managerial overheads by avoiding duplication of activities or resources if similar activities are being carried out independently in divisions or subunits.

5 Because the segmentation of management to the lower levels of the organisation is prevented, there is greater justification for the employment of specialists who can act as consultants to the various functions and levels within the organisation. This service would be difficult to account for, expenditure-wise, in a decentralised system as there could be substantial duplication of consultant resources.

6 It is commonly held that top managers have proved themselves by the time they reach a senior position. Although a point in favour of centralisation, there is a danger that management can adopt the attitude that purely because they are at the top, they are right.

7 Crises often require strong leadership to cope with external and internal pressures. Centralisation of power and control of procedures focuses on a key person or group. Thus arises the opportunity for speedy decision-making and control over communication and co-ordination.

For decentralisation

1 Delegation can reduce the amount of stress and overload experienced by senior management, especially when operating

in large-scale, complex organisations. It is well understood that when senior management becomes overloaded, then the exercise of control becomes diminished. Delegation can remove some of the burden from senior management, allowing it to spend more time on policy issues and long-term planning. Delegation is not simply a clear-cut decision by senior management to increase the number of decision-making tasks of managers at lower levels. It is more a process of sharing responsibility by inviting other members of the management hierarchy to participate in decisions that senior management used to make.

2   It has long been held by behavioural scientists that the motivation of employees will increase the higher the degree of discretion and control they can apply to their work. The opportunity to make decisions and be involved can help to provide personal satisfaction and commitment for the individual. An assumption is made that with greater personal freedom, individual goals will broadly be in line with those of the corporate entity. In situations of delegated power, the matching of personal goals and corporate goals is more likely, but delegation can be severely tested in situations where people's work is independent of each other. The problem there is to motivate people sufficiently to co-ordinate their activities without too much central direction.

3   Organisations that are too large or growing need managers who are able to cope with uncertainty because of the immense number of complex tasks that have to be performed. It is impossible for one person or small groups of people to supervise such complex activities simultaneously. Delegation, therefore, can assist the development of management by widening the on-the-job-skills of managers and hence develop a number of people capable of undertaking senior management positions.

4   Delegation generally allows for greater flexibility by providing for less rigid responses to change at the operative levels in the organisation. Decisions do not have to be referred up the hierarchy.

5   By establishing relatively independent subunits within an organisation where middle management and supervisors are held responsible for operations, delegation can result in better controls and performance measurements. Separate spheres of responsibility can be identified and control systems applied to

these units in order to provide adequate feedback to higher management. Costs can be allocated to particular operations, rendering specific responsibility to specific persons or units. Greater self-responsibility and self-direction are required of people in such circumstances.

A simple decision to centralise or decentralise is impossible, for the choice can only be made in the light of specific conditions and circumstances. These conditions will vary from:

- the overall purpose of the organisation
- the capacity of senior management to conceive a new type of organisation
- the skills and attitudes of subordinates
- the overall size, divisional size (if applicable) and geographic dispersion of the organisation
- the efficiency and accuracy of the organisation's planning, control and information systems
- the time restrictions that accompany decisions made in the field or within the organisation. For example, is it appropriate for a decision to be made on the spot based on professional judgement, or is the situation sufficiently flexible to allow time for a decision to be referred upwards to senior management?
- the degree to which subordinates can accept and are in turn motivated by making their own decisions
- the conditions external to the organisation that will strongly influence its operation, such as government requirements, trade union objectives and local community conditions.

Case 11.5 Reshaping Rayon Designs (Part 2)

'Hmm. We've known it for some time but not really confronted the problem. You've spelled it out in black and white,' said the chief executive officer (CEO).

This was the second meeting of the executive committee. At the first meeting, it was eventually decided that DBO should chair a project group to examine the organisation structure problems of Rayon Designs and make recommendations for improvement. The second meeting of the executive committee had been called to discuss the findings of DBO's project group.

'It's not just the fact that everyone's pissed off, but we've even got problems, like none of the directors at any moment has an accurate breakdown of the sales figures,' commented DBO. He continued... 'Well, anyhow, here are the recommendations. I'll take you through what you have in front of you.

1   What we have in operation is an old-fashioned functional structure, which is no longer useful for what we are doing.

2   We recommend that the organisation be restructured according to key product lines. That means certain of our factories must specialise in particular lines. John West's function as director of manufacturing operations will still be represented on the board. However, he should have underneath him two or three general managers who will take charge of complete operations. That means John loses some direct contact with his plant managers.

3   In order to support such a structure, my marketing and sales part of the business needs to be organised in a slightly different way, not as a direct line function, but more as a support service. It should look like more of a matrix. In essence, the marketing and sales boys will have two bosses, their marketing and sales managers and the general managers under John West.

4   Sounds a complex proposal, but what are the advantages? Let's go through them.

    ● Higher volume sales by focusing our people's attention on the particular needs of each market sector. The marketing and sales focus will be strongly determined by the needs of each particular product line under the general guidance of each of the general managers. In this way, marketing and sales should improve. Further, because marketing and sales will be providing a concentrated but varied service according to the needs of each general manager, we on the executive committee should receive far more accurate information concerning sales performance, short-term trends and long-term design trends.
    ● Discarding jobs we don't need. Because the structure was wrong, we made jobs for the boys because we did not know what else to do with our people.
    ● Breakdown of the old rivalries in this organisation between market and sales and between production and everyone else.

Well, what do you think?'
   Silence.
   'These are the basic principles. I suppose you'll look at jobs and departments in greater detail?' asked the company secretary.
   'Yes, we will. What we need is permission to go ahead with this basic blueprint and come up with more detailed proposals for the next meeting,' responded DBO.

Further discussion ensued. Eventually it was agreed that a detailed organisation structure plan for Rayon Design should be drafted by the project team.

The project group spent the next two weeks drafting a detailed organisation structure blueprint. It became clear that the senior marketing, sales and plant managers would lose a certain amount of status and influence in the proposed reorganisation. In essence, they would drop one level in the hierarchy. Equally, their influence would diminish as they would be required to report to two bosses, their line boss and a functional specialist.

A final report was drafted and placed before the executive committee for their consideration. Although one or two details in the plan were changed, the key elements of the proposals were accepted. DBO and the director of personnel (DOP) were charged with implementing the reorganisation.

DBO recommended (Case 11.5) a more decentralised structure which encompassed both product and matrix structure principles. He hoped to establish clear lines of accountability, and a strong sales and marketing awareness in the organisation by ensuring that sales and marketing personnel reported to a functional boss and an overall business general manager. Such a structure should break down the old, traditional rivalries that had dominated the decision-making process in the organisation and so information would be far more freely available to all managers. In essence, DBO recommended that his business operations division should provide an essential support service to the production and design processes. The newly recommended role structure is based on four essential determinants – people, management information systems, historical background and need for decentralisation to stimulate greater product, product design and marketing awareness.

IMPACT

The combination of the various determinants and the particular components of structure that are implemented will make an impact on the organisation. The impact will be either to strengthen the current identity of the organisation or to change it, through accident or intent. Whether maintenance of current conditions or change is the outcome, two areas in particular will be affected:

1 Spans of accountability and managerial control

2 The culture of the organisation

Spans of control and accountability

Span of control refers to the number of subordinates reporting to any one manager or supervisor. The greater the number of subordinates reporting to any one manager, the greater the span of control. Span of accountability refers to the total number of subordinates for which any manager is ultimately held accountable. Span of accountability is a broader concept than span of control.

Any alteration to the composition of the components of organisation structure will affect the spans of accountability and control. A tall structure, involving numerous levels of hierarchy, is likely to reduce the span of control and may or may not increase the total span of accountability. A flatter structure will widen the span of control and, again, may or may not increase the total span of accountability. Numerous organisational theorists such as Franz Schumacher of 'small is beautiful' fame, and Professor Reg Revans, the Action Learning advocate, argue strongly that flatter structures offer greater advantages than taller structures. Taller structures can lead to communication problems and a dilution of managerial control. Administrative overheads may be raised and certain tasks, activities and duties may overlap substantially from one level to the next. In addition, taller structures may have a negative impact on subordinate motivation by reducing the scope to exercise responsibility.

However, difficulties do arise from widening spans of control. First, managers and supervisors alike need to be skilled in managing individuals and groups. Managers need to motivate and stimulate their subordinates through the use of their interpersonal skills. The manager cannot rely on the authority in his role to induce compliance with his requests. Second, by widening spans of control, greater reliance is placed on co-ordination as opposed to control mechanisms, to integrate the activities of various managers and group levels. In practice, this would mean attending more meetings and a greater commitment on the part of individuals to share and collaborate. If such commitment is not readily forthcoming, senior management can easily lose control over short- to medium-term operations, and may be tempted to narrow the spans of control and revert to a direct control as opposed to collaborative structure.

Whether management decides to opt for taller or flatter structures, the period of greatest stress and tension is at the time of change. Structural reorganisation is a period fraught with anxiety and ambiguity for two reasons:

1   *Motivational impact.* Reorganising structures involves reorganis-
    ing people's job content and their position in the hierarchy.
    Inevitably, some get a better deal than others as a result of
    reorganisation. Certain individuals will be required to
    undertake more interesting work involving an increased number
    of duties with greater pay, enjoying a wider span of control.
    Their status, pay and job motivation have improved. Others
    may feel themselves to have been demoted, by having their span
    of control narrowed and being required to administer less
    interesting activities. Those who consider themselves not to
    have benefited from the reorganisation either stay and come to
    terms with the new structure (an uncomfortable process) or
    leave and find another job.

2   *Stakeholders' response.* Stakeholders are those people who have
    a strong interest (ie stakeholding) in a situation (see Chapter 9
    on stakeholders). The stakeholder could be a person who has
    built up a department, nurtured a group of clients or developed
    a new product or process. At the time of reorganisation, it is
    necessary to be sensitive to the response of stakeholders in the
    organisation. Rearranging structures will undoubtedly impinge
    on the 'empire' of key stakeholders. Their reaction to reorganisa-
    tion is likely to be an important determinant to the success of
    that reorganisation. Stakeholders are more likely to react
    negatively to a major reduction in their total span of
    accountability than to just changes of span of control. Any
    stakeholder could react negatively to their empire being
    dismantled.

Case 11.6   Reshaping Rayon Designs (Part 3)

DBO was worried! 'How the hell am I going to do it? he thought. 'After
all, O'Riley was my appointment,' he muttered to himself, mouth curling
bitterly at one end. 'Best get O'Riley in and have it out with him!'

The appointment was made. O'Riley was to see DBO in two days'
time. In the intervening period he was told to prepare a future
organisation plan for his department.

'Hi, Ed, come in,' said DBO rising from his chair. Ed sat down. The two
men talked. It became clear to DBO that O'Riley was not going to be
easy to handle. 'I was right,' thought DBO, 'O'Riley is doing too much!'

O'Riley's title was senior marketing manager. In fact, O'Riley was
managing marketing, marketing planning, sales, after sales service,
advertising, promotions and publicity.

There had been complaints about O'Riley. Decisions that should have
been made were not being made, or were made late, or the decisions

were poor, usually because the implications had not been fully thought through. The complaints made it easier for DBO to take a hard line.

'Look, you know there have been complaints and you also know why – YOU are doing too much!' stated DBO. 'In the new structure, all the managers are really going to be held to account. Your performance must be good. You simply cannot be doing everything, Ed!'

Ed was going to fight this issue as hard as he could.

'I built up these various functions from the mess they were in when I first came here, to something reasonable. This is what I get for effort – a stab in the back!' he growled. 'Right, you bastard,' he thought, glaring at DBO, 'if I'm going to lose some of my patch and some of my people, I'm going to give you a hard time in the process!'

As is shown in Case 11.6, no matter how well-thought-through or appropriate any structural reorganisation, the probable response of any stakeholder to loss of span of control and accountability can so often be negative and uncooperative. It is vital to have accurately predicted the response of stakeholders to any structural redesign if the new structural arrangements are to have any chance of succeeding.

Culture of organisation

Culture of organisations is a crucial feature of organisational life. Culture refers to the shared values, attitudes, styles, manners of behaviour, mores and norms in any organisation. It is unlikely that any one organisation has only one prevailing culture at a time. In Chapter 8, culture was analysed from the point of view of appropriate means of applying the seven power levers. Below, culture is discussed in relation to organisation structure.

Of the various organisational characteristics that determine a particular culture, the strongest of the determinants is the role hierarchy. The application and maintenance of a particular role hierarchy will induce particular views, feelings and attitudes amongst the people employed by the organisation. A tall hierarchy with limited spans of managerial control will probably stimulate a formal, controlling leadership style amongst managers in their relationship with their subordinates. Equally, many employees may feel that the degree of challenge and responsibility in a large number of jobs is limited, for people need do only what is required of them. Yet, for those who find such a culture acceptable, the degree of identity with the organisation is likely to be high. People adhere to the existing rules and systems, and may genuinely direct their loyalty to the organisation rather than to their group or particular individuals.

In a matrix structure, people may adopt different attitudes. They may feel the degree of challenge and responsibility in their jobs is high, and as a result the quantity and quality of work completed is equally high. The leadership styles may be more open, informal and confronting, but that is largely due to the fact that managers cannot rely solely on the authority in their role in their efforts to organise people to complete certain tasks. In a matrix structure, individuals interact with many other people through membership of various teams and possibly by changing jobs at reasonably frequent intervals. Under such circumstances, people will simply not tolerate an authoritarian style of management. Managers will have to use their interpersonal skills to influence their bosses, colleagues and subordinates.

Case 11.7 Reshaping Rayon Designs (Part IV)

Whatever DBO did seemed to go wrong. First, O'Riley really let him down. Shortly after the interview with DBO, O'Riley spread a rumour that the imminent reorganisation was a way of getting rid of or demoting some senior managers. Karlson leaked his new job responsibilities to Fry. Fry became so hostile that he went to see DoP to establish whether this was a way of easing him out of the company and what his redundancy terms were likely to be. John Conner liked the job he was offered, partly because he would no longer report to DBO. He went round boasting that, if you try hard enough, you can get out of DBO's organisation. Shortly after, Henderson and Tims went to see DoP to see if they could negotiate their way out of DBO's division and into another part of the organisation.

'What the hell is going on?' exploded DoP, charging into DBO's office. 'What are you doing? Why are so many people coming to see me, telling me they are pissed off with your part of the organisation? What is happening here?'

DBO tried to explain the problems of introducing reorganisation into the division; how untrustworthy and dissatisfied people were; how they had broken promises to maintain confidentiality; in fact, how impossible was the whole situation.

'You mean you blew it – right, we're going to see the chief exec!' said DoP, diving over to the phone and dialling the CEO's number. The CEO, disgruntled, cancelled an appointment in order to see them.

DBO first gave his version of the story. Then DoP offered his views on the current reorganisation. The CEO listened, eyes ꞷwing. 'If what he (pointing to DoP) says is true, you (pointing to DBO) know what this means for you personally!' he said calmly.

'But you don't understand the place or the people. You don't understand what it's like to handle business ops or production ... you just don't,' shrugged DBO.

'Listen, you (pointing to DBO) will work with him far more closely (pointing to DoP) from now on. The two of you will make sure that business ops especially is reorganised; the right people are in the right jobs; the people are trained up and the place is selling clothes. Do you get me?' he said icily to DBO.

DBO nodded; the interview ended; the two men got up and walked out.

DoP conducted most of the interviews that were basically DBO's responsibility. Although less direct and confronting, he was more successful. People listened to what he said and did not break a confidence once given. Very soon, most of the top managers were appointed with the minimum of fuss.

DoP recognised that some sort of management training programme was required to help the newly appointed managers understand their new roles and the skills required, and develop a willingness to work more closely in a team setting. He found appropriate professional management trainers, and hired them to run the programme.

Over the next four months, four four-day training programmes were successfully conducted. Within eighteen months, the company broke even and was looking forward to profitability. DBO remained very much in charge of business operations. However, his colleagues and most of the senior managers consider it was DoP who masterminded and introduced fundamental changes to the company. DBO is dissatisfied with his position in the organisation. He is now looking for a new job.

Attempting to change the structure will inevitably involve changes of attitudes, beliefs and feelings on the part of the employees towards their work and the organisation. In fact, structural reorganisation in itself is a relatively small exercise. To induce employees to accept the new structure and to work well within the new parameters is the real challenge. In Case 11.7, DoP was determined that he should be in control of the inevitable attitudinal change, through training. However, whatever structural reorganisation does to the culture, elements of the old culture remain. Technological/structural change takes place far more quickly than social change. In Case 11.7, the company kept DBO in post, even though it was clear to most that he had lost some control as head of business operations. The irony of the situation was that it was DBO who really introduced the changes in the first place. However, he had not accurately predicted the stakeholders' response, nor adjusted his behaviour accordingly. In the end, it was DoP who was seen as the positive force in introducing change in the company.

SUMMARY

In this chapter, the analysis of organisation structure has covered four areas.

The analysis of structure

1 Structure strongly influences the way in which resources are organised;

2 Jobs need to be structured so that people can appreciate what is expected of them in their work;

3 Decision-making and information processes need to be structured in such a way that relevant information is fed to appropriate personnel to enhance the decision-making process;

4 Structure can act as a powerful determinant of organisation culture.

Determinants, components, impact model

Determinants are those elements that have strongly influenced the organisation's current shape and identity. Components refers to four alternative role hierarchy blueprints as well as to centralised/decentralised decision-making processes. Impact is the manner in which an organisation reacts to the introduction or prevention of structural change.

Determinants

The determinants are:

• size, ie the effect and requirements of large, medium and small organisations on systems and procedures, group inter-relationships, co-ordination and control systems, efficiency and effectiveness of outputs of products or services and employee attitudes

• technology, such as socio-technical systems and micro-electronics

• historical background, ie the impact of the past on the present functioning of the organisations in terms of ownership, control, motivation of employees, culture and flexibility to change

- geographic dispersion and its influence over control and co-ordination mechanisms

- external environment, ie current market situation, competitor(s)' behaviour and national and world political and economic environment

- employee attitudes ie people's response to changes within and outside the organisation, over- or under-manning, crisis management and the manner in which interpersonal relationships are conducted

- management information systems, ie the way in which information is processed and distributed in the organisation.

Components

In a *functional structure*, all the key functions (ie marketing, sales, production, personnel) are grouped into separate departments and each of the functions is represented at the strategic decision making levels.

A *product structured* organisation places the organisation's outputs (ie products or services) as the prime focus. Hence, each major product line will form a branch of the organisational tree hierarchy with a director or general manager at its head. Each branch should have available each of the major functional services to service that product line. A duplication of functional services is likely to occur.

A *divisional structure* involves splitting the organisation into separate units, whereby each one provides a total service to the client(s) according to its mission and product or service range. Each division has at its head a divisional director and underneath that can adopt a functional, product or matrix structure.

A *matrix structure* is a means of generating greater support for task activity and market responsiveness in medium to large organisations. In practice, a matrix manner of operation is more concerned with the attitudes of middle and senior management in the organisation. If senior and middle management do not wish to manage their work and interrelationships in a more flexible, problem-responsive way, but are more role- and status-oriented, then a matrix structure will not function. In fact, it is somewhat

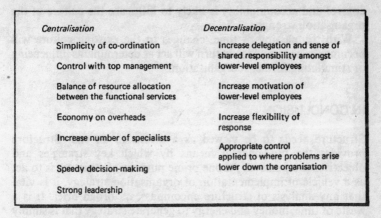

Fig. 11.6 The arguments for and against centralisation

misleading to talk of matrix structures, for the issue is really whether managers can adopt a matrix style of operational behaviour.

The debate on decision patterns revealed two conflicting issues that often need to be taken into account simultaneously – the need to standardise and the need to diversify. These are summarised in Figure 11.6.

Impact

Changing the configuration of the components of organisation structure will increase or decrease managers' span of control and accountability. Such an alteration will have a motivational impact on individuals. Those with narrow and limited spans of control and accountability that increase in width and depth are likely to see such a change as a challenge, an increase in their status possibly accompanied by increases in pay and a change of job title, and as a sign of confidence by the organisation in their skills and abilities. Those whose spans of control and accountability contract in both width and depth are likely to view such a change negatively in terms of challenge and status (possibly pay) and as a sign of lack of confidence in them by the organisation.

Finally, the combination of changes of determinants, components and the reaction of individuals to changes of their span of control and accountability is likely to influence the culture of the organisation strongly.

With the passing of time, changes to the existing culture will become the norms which in turn will act as determinants influencing or stimulating further reorganisation.

IN CONCLUSION

Structure needs to be viewed as a means to an end. Structure provides the fundamental means by which key strategies and objectives are pursued. As one prime purpose of structure is to act as a vehicle of implementation of organisation strategy, it is vital that any analysis of structure encompasses a broad brief. It is a waste of time, money and energy to generate strategy that is simply inoperable within the existing structure of the organisation and yet is implemented without any accompanying structural change. However, if changes of structure are contemplated, then it is necessary to assess the likely success of change realistically. Successful structural change involves an analysis beyond the narrow confines of role hierarchy.

12 Managing People, Managing Pressures

Case 12.1   The big bang

'Big Bang' is the term applied to a revolution that has occurred in the financial heart of London, namely The Stock Exchange. Big Bang refers to de-regulation, a far-reaching and fundamental change that confronted the financial business community in the UK in 1986. De-regulation addressed three key changes in the rules of The Stock Exchange:

- the end of fixed scale commissions, namely the fee charged by stockbrokers when doing business on behalf of their clients.

- the introduction of dual capacity, namely the capacity to act both as a *broker* (an agent for other people) and a *jobber* (a person trading on his own account).

- the newly won approval for outside institutions, such as clearing banks or foreign banks, to own Stock Exchange businesses.

The implications of such new practices were sweeping. Jobbers and brokers were acquired by UK and USA financial houses, termed merchant banks in England. Stockbrokers had, for the first time in their history, to consider client needs because of the two most important reasons imaginable: their fees could be undercut; other financial businesses could provide a far better client-oriented service. Probably the biggest change was that de-regulation allowed the Americans into the bastion of the British financial market. Soon merchant banks, clearing banks, jobbers and brokers were to learn that they had been protected by a set of artificial rules. For the first time, British financial institutions were facing real competition, and the Americans showed just how competitive they can be.

For one well known merchant bank, Thomas and Timms (T&T), 'Big Bang' represented just one of many problems. They had recently acquired two jobbers and one broker. They were considering the acquisition of a second broker. Integration of these three new organisations into the parent was an important concern. The post of

Director of Administration and Services had been vacant for a month after the sudden collapse and immediate hospitalisation of its former incumbent. The information network improvement programme, which the former director had initiated, halted. The bank was really experiencing what it meant to attempt to provide professional services without adequate information services in an increasingly competitive market. Worst of all, the organisation had appointed, chewed and spat out two chief executives in the last twenty months. The appointment of Simon Adams to Chief Executive Officer (CEO), poached from another bank, added to the turmoil experienced by managers and professional financiers alike. Under such circumstances, gossip was rife –

'He's a real bastard!'

'You know what really happened: he got the push and that's what he'll get here!'

'Good banker, hopeless manager! That's what they say at Corinthia ... you know, where we got him from!'

Simon's progress in the City from his humble clerk beginnings in the Bank of England was written and re-written numerous times.

However, a person like Simon Adams pays little attention to such idle talk. He needed a Director of Administration and Services. He cast his net worldwide and found Walter McKenzie, Senior Manager Administrative Services, in the Sidney office of a competitor.

Simon arranged an informal meeting on one of his numerous trips to Hong Kong and Japan. The two met for over two hours in Simon's room in an upmarket Sidney hotel.

'... and I would sit in the 'Cabinet'?' questioned McKenzie.
Adams nodded.
'From what you've said, the organisation really needs pulling together. It's quite a challenge.'
Adams nodded.
'OK with me, if it's OK with you', said McKenzie.
Adams nodded and then stated, 'You're now Director of Administration and Services. I'm not looking around any more. I've not got the time. I've also not given you any bullshit. You've got about as much chance of surviving in T&T as I have'.

Integration is a vital issue in any organisation. Clarity of both strategy to pursue and structure to implement does not ensure effective organisation performance. The people in the organisation need to identify with their tasks and feel that they are making a worthwhile contribution. It is of prime importance that individuals are motivated to pursue the various activities in their jobs. Effective job performance is a major step towards achieving the organisational strategy.

Adopting a positive view of the work each individual has to undertake, of the structure and of the various supervisors, subordinates, and colleagues with whom the individual interacts, does not simply happen by chance. Integrating the individual with the organisation needs to be a planned policy which complements the strategy and structure of the organisation. In this chapter, the various pressures that can lead to excessive disharmony and poor performance are highlighted. Differences between departments; personal enmity between a manager and a subordinate; differences of view between fully qualified professionals and line managers; the disruption that changes of organisation strategy can have on particular localities: all these uncomfortable forces create pressure in the organisation which needs to be managed in a systematic and logical way.

Thomas and Timms (Case 12.1) are facing the challenge of great changes in their markets: the need to improve their information systems, the integration of three new businesses into the parent organisation, and substantial changes in the top management team. It is insufficient to draft a sensible organisation structure whereby line and support service roles are clearly and appropriately identified. Particular mechanisms for integration have to be introduced so that individuals can identify with the new structure, have trust in their top management team, generate balanced workloads and know that they are being appropriately assessed on their performance through the introduction of meaningful appraisal procedures. In this way, the needs of the individual and the demands made by the organisation can be reconciled.

There are four possible mechanisms for organisational integration:

1 The use of performance appraisal.
2 Effective team development.
3 Management by objectives (MBO).
4 The role of the general manager.

PERFORMANCE APPRAISAL

Dr Shaun Tyson and Alfred York give five reasons for conducting performance appraisals:

1 To determine the suitability and potential of people for particular types of employment.

2   To determine the developmental needs of individuals in terms of job experience, training and education.

3   To identify those who are apparently suited for promotion.

4   To develop motivation and commitment by giving feedback on performance and discussing individual needs.

5   To provide a basis for the allocation of rewards.

From the organisation's point of view, performance appraisal provides an opportunity for assessing the value of each individual's work contribution. What aspects of the individual's workload have been well conducted? Should the individual receive greater attention from his boss, or off-the-job training, or a move sideways, or upwards, or an increase in pay, or maintain his present level of pay? From the individual's point of view, performance appraisal is an occasion to discuss the problems he has faced, the achievements he has attained and the rewards he expects. The performance appraisal process provides a forum to debate the requirements of the organisation and the needs and aspirations of the individual.

Part of the success of the appraisal process depends on what is discussed. The individual being appraised will hardly identify with the organisation if only the requirements of the organisation are addressed and little mention is made of their own needs, points of view or problems.

Of equal importance with *what* is discussed is *how* topics are discussed. The staff appraisal process, particularly the appraisal interview, has to be not only conducted, but perceived to be conducted, efficiently, effectively, and equitably. In the process – which should not consist simply of an annual ill-prepared interview between boss and subordinate to measure the subordinate's achievement against targets set a year ago, but which should be part of continuous performance management process – both managers and individual employees are attempting jointly to evaluate those employees' contributions to organisational achievement. The employees need to feel confident that the performance appraisal process is being handled competently in a climate of openness, trust and mutual respect, because they are disclosing to their managers personal and confidential information which will be relevant to, and may influence, their future in the organisation.

Three separate approaches to conducting performance appraisal are possible:

1 *Informative.* The boss informs his subordinate as to how he sees his performance. In addition, he may indicate the level of reward and promotion potential that he is likely to recommend. Under such circumstances the subordinate is only likely to influence the appraisal process by querying the issues raised by the boss.

2 *Consultative.* The boss offers his views on the individual's performance, potential and reward over the last period of time. The boss then invites the subordinate to comment, query and generally become involved in a discussion about himself. Both agree on certain outcomes concerning rewards, performance and on- or off-the-job training and development which will form the objectives the individual should pursue until the next appraisal.

3 *Participative.* The boss and the individual meet to discuss the individual's performance. Both offer their views and attempt to build up a picture from their discussion. In certain organisations that practise participative appraisal, it is recommended that boss and subordinate separately write down their views on the individual's performance, potential and likely reward. The appraisal recommendation will emerge as a result of the agreement reached between appraiser and appraisee. This approach also generates a climate within which it is possible for the manager to receive feedback on his own leadership performance in relation to his employees. Whatever formal approach is utilised, it must be recognised that the assessment of performance also occurs informally. All managers are constantly reviewing their subordinates by direct observation and indirect reports, or taking part in a process of joint work planning and integrative performance management. Such evidence colours the view of the boss prior to the formal appraisal of his subordinate. Hence it is necessary to be aware that the ultimate value of the system, no matter how theoretically sound, depends on the values and integrity of those who apply it in practice.

The details and methods of the approach used for staff assessment will vary according to the functional and cultural differences of organisation. However, Shaun Tyson and Alfred York suggest that there are certain basic requirements which should be considered in any system of assessment. The system of assessment should:

1   cover all aspects of work performance, needs for training, education, job experience and suitability for promotion.

2   be uniformly applied throughout the organisation.

3   be co-ordinated by formal arrangements between personnel staff, line managers and subordinates.

4   include arrangements for formal feedback to subordinate staff about performance, needs and opportunities for training, education, employment and promotion.

5   be understood by all employees.

6   include arrangements for training personnel staff and line managers in the administrative and interpersonal skills needed to apply the system sensibly.

Case 12.2   Examining payment and performance

Simon Adams had commissioned McKenzie to improve the information systems in the bank. Both Adams and McKenzie recognised that outside consultants would have to be hired, and budgeted appropriately. Simon had now been four months in the job.

'Hell!' I'm just firefighting!' thought Simon. He had just lost a deal to an American competitor. Why? The competition had more up-to-date information which could be easily accessed, due to effective information networking in the company.

'Was it just information?' contemplated Simon. 'They presented well, but so do we. It's just that I got the feeling that, overall, they were better managed'.

Simon decided to talk, informally, with his main Board directors and a sample of other senior managers and team heads about managerial issues rather than about clients, deals, bulls or bears. So Simon 'went walkabout'.

The views, challenges and problems presented to him in his informal chats were interesting but not sufficiently substantial to satisfy Simon's curiosity. For the CEO to go 'walking the floor' in a British merchant bank was unprecedented, but for him openly to ask intimate questions about how people felt about the bank and its manner of management, and to say he expected honest answers, was just unpalatable. That is, of course, until Simon met George Jefferson III, the American-born Human Resources manager. The conversation with George lasted over two and a half hours.

However, it was an hour before George spoke without inhibition.

'This bank is filled with market makers, deal getters and accountants. This place is filled with entrepreneurs and administrators. The last thing they know about is managing!'

George catalogued his view of the problems in the bank. He stated that the role of the manager was poorly defined. All too often, individuals were being held accountable as a manager, but not given the authority to service the role fully.

As George indicated, 'Merchant banks are flat structures by nature. Intelligent, quick thinking and experienced in the subtleties of their markets, merchant bankers do not easily identify with managerial authority or accountability'.

'Certainly few rewards are given for being an effective manager. Rewards are attained for negotiating deals', commented Simon.

If managerial authority and accountability are poorly defined, and little reward is offered for effective managerial performance, other problems naturally arise. Appraisal of subordinate performance tends to be conducted poorly. Also, most managers would probably have little commitment to use the appraisal mechanism to help subordinates improve work performance. Under such circumstances, the managerial skills and sensitivities of individuals are low.

Not surprisingly, few bankers are trained in management.

Simon listened and knew that George was right. The problems of Thomas and Timms were the common experience of most UK merchant banks. However, that was of little comfort to Adams. Personnel in T&T were demotivated. Simon wanted his organisation to be fully prepared for the impact of 'Big Bang' in the next financial year.

Simon had just completed discussions on bonuses for staff. Across the board, percentage increases, which varied from department to department, had been negotiated between him and his functional directors. Really, little effort had been made to link pay to performance. He knew that few openly questioned why they received a bonus and whether it was too little or too much. He also knew instinctively that for some, being awarded a bonus 'out of the blue' would act as a demotivator. He could hear the comments:

'If we don't know how to solve a problem, we throw money at it!'

Simon decided that a programme of re-structuring and re-training had to be introduced into T&T.

Performance appraisal is a two-way process. The subordinate's performance needs to be linked to the wider performance of the whole group, department or division. Undoubtedly, the boss's performance will also influence his subordinate's performance. If relevant, both should be considered in the appraisal process. With the various issues to consider, the depth of feeling of one or both parties concerning the prevalent issues and the manner in which the appraisal is conducted, effective appraisals are not easy to conduct. Case 12.2 highlights that managerial jobs need to be adequately structured, appropriately rewarded, and managers need to be sufficiently skilful, in order to conduct effective appraisals. Conducting appraisals is a sensitive process and, if badly managed, it can lead to the demotivation of staff. Offering bonuses is no remedy.

EFFECTIVE TEAM DEVELOPMENT

Some issues in the organisation may require the attention of more than one person from more than one department. These could include exploring new market opportunities, working out a sales strategy for a new product or improving the production quality of certain products. Whatever the issues, one of the best ways of handling them is the use of teams. (See also Chapter 6 for an examination of alternative models of group development.)

Simply placing a number of skilled professional individuals in a group and expecting them to perform as a team is unrealistic. For teams to perform reasonably takes time: time for people to become better acquainted with each other, to assess each other's strengths and weaknesses and to reflect whether they can identify with the values, beliefs, attitudes and general style of their colleagues, individuals or the whole group.

Because of this, teams and team development have come under considerable scrutiny. Many aspects of team performance and development have been analysed, such as individual team or organisational values, group dynamics, approaches to training and team building and group learning processes, ie how individuals learn to work together in a team setting. One area of research crucial to both understanding and developing effective teams is how a disparate group develops into an efficient working team. The Human Resource group at Cranfield School of Management examined the problem of how to develop and stimulate productive teams and has adopted the team development wheel as a means of training managers to perform as team members. It was concluded that teams experience four distinct learning stages in their development from a group of individuals to a more cohesive unit. These four stages are outlined in the team development wheel (Figure 12.1).

Forming

At the forming stage, the individuals in the newly established group need to become acquainted with one another, understand each other's views, expectations, ideas and stated objectives. Quite naturally, at this point the people in the group are likely to feel somewhat inhibited. The behavioural pattern is likely to be polite

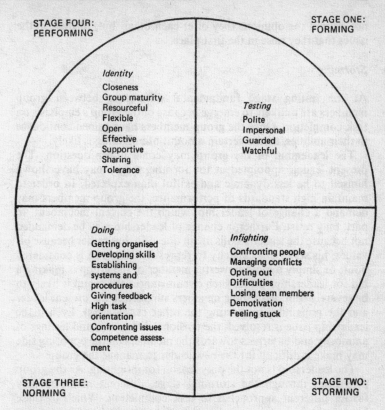

STAGE FOUR:
PERFORMING

STAGE ONE:
FORMING

Identity

Closeness
Group maturity
Resourceful
Flexible
Open
Effective
Supportive
Sharing
Tolerance

Testing

Polite
Impersonal
Guarded
Watchful

Doing

Getting organised
Developing skills
Establishing
systems and
procedures
Giving feedback
High task
orientation
Confronting issues
Competence assess-
ment

Infighting

Confronting people
Managing conflicts
Opting out
Difficulties
Losing team members
Demotivation
Feeling stuck

STAGE THREE:
NORMING

STAGE TWO:
STORMING

Fig. 12.1   Team development wheel*
From Tuckman, B. W. 'Developmental Sequences in Small
Groups', *Psychological Bulletin*, 1965 Vol. 63, No. 6, pp. 384–399.
Copyright 1965 by the American Psychological Association.
Adapted by permission of the author.

and probably impersonal in conversation, guarded in disclosing
personal or work-oriented information or even in offering opinions
on certain issues and watchful of each other's behaviour and
conversation. In essence, the individuals in the group are testing
each other out. They test each other as individual personalities, as
professionals and as people holding views concerning how the
group should be run in the future. People are likely to be guarded

*The Team Development Wheel is based on the work by Tuckman (1965).

not only in the opinions they offer each other, but, further, in the issues that they raise in the first place.

Storming

At the testing stage fundamental differences between group members are unlikely to emerge because of the group's emphasis on task completion. Once the group members have gained confidence in their abilities, then a certain amount of infighting is likely.

The leadership of the group may come under question. The present leader, appointed at the forming stage, may have shown himself to be less dynamic and skilful than expected. In order to maintain high standards of performance, the group members may demand a change of leadership, which the current incumbent, in part, may resist. Further, a change of leadership may be demanded not because the leader's skills are in question, but rather because his values, his styles, his capacity to represent the group is considered poor; or simply a more powerful member of the group is making a bid for leadership. Under such circumstances the group is likely to be severely split, with some members supporting the present leader and the remainder supporting the other candidate(s). Even if the leadership issue is resolved, the tensions, differences and feelings of animosity and bitterness towards the members on the opposing side may make it difficult for the new leader to manage the group.

The leadership is not the only reason for infighting. As the group progresses through the storming stage, different members may favour different approaches to task completion. Which of these fundamental work approaches should be adopted can become an inflammatory issue, for it affects not only how people work on jobs, but also what sort of people with what sort of skills will be required in the group in the future, and by default certain present members of the group could feel threatened as they may accurately predict that they are likely to be no longer required.

A further reason for conflict between group members is personality differences. Individuals in the group may find it difficult to accept another person's approach to handling problems, people or tasks. Such differences in beliefs and values may lead one group member to be antipathetic towards others. Although the conflict may initially be confined to two or three group members, the resulting interactions and tension may influence all of the members. The two or three warring members may seek support from the remaining members of the group, which could split the group. Alternatively, the tension in the group could spark off other interpersonal conflicts amongst the other members of the group. Further, if the tensions between some members are not resolved, then conflict and confrontation could become normal behaviour in the group.

Whatever the cause of the infighting, the behavioural pattern in the group is characterised by conflicts and divisions: individuals feeling demotivated leave the group and some of the ones who remain may feel trapped. It is also likely that certain group members may opt out of these processes altogether and simply concentrate on tasks and not the relationship side of group activity.

Norming

The storming stage may be quickly overcome or the group may be stuck there for some time. A great deal depends on the style and personality of the group leader and on the pressures facing the group to produce work outputs (results). The sooner the group attempts to fulfil certain task goals, the sooner it will break out of the infighting stage. The group organises itself to achieve particular goals, appropriate systems and procedures are established, work issues are confronted and the group needs to establish the skills level and competence of each of its members. Hence, observation of each member's performance is likely to take place and the individuals are likely to give each other feedback on what they see and assess. By doing tasks, norms of behaviour and professional practice begin to be established. The interpersonal barriers between people begin to dissipate as a result of exchanging views, ideas and experiences on professional problems.

Despite progress on task issues, the group may regress to stage two and then fluctuate between stages two and three. Having initially developed beyond the infighting stage possibly by having established a new leader or lost certain group members, and recruited new people, the group through attempting to reintegrate may begin once more to challenge practices, values and ideals. Such confrontation is likely to take place through attempting to achieve goals. The new leader or group members may find some procedures or norms of behaviour inappropriate or too limiting. It is unfortunate that, after the group has experienced tensions in stage two and progressed to stage three, any new members of the group may need to progress through stage two, and influence the group to 'slip back'. From stage one, whether it takes a short or longer period, groups are likely to progress to stage two. Unfortunately, there is no reason to assume that a group will break out of the stage two/three cycle into stage four. Many groups keep fluctuating between stages two and three, with the group members knowing there is something wrong, but being unable to break out of the storming/norming cycle.

Performing

Breaking out of the storming/norming cycle is no easy matter. A great deal will depend on the skills of the leader to assist the group members to identify with each other enough to move to stage four. The leader needs interpersonal, counselling and listening skills, so that he can act as a third party (ie consultant) to two or more warring group members. In situations where no reconciliation seems likely, the leader could use these skills to help the members talk through their problems with him so that the group develops some sort of cohesion through the members becoming close to the leader. In addition, the group members need to identify with a mission or purpose which will provide some bond in the group. A sense of mission or purpose may emerge from the debates and discussions during the storming/norming phase. Equally, it may be incumbent on the leader to help the group find, or even impose, an acceptable mission and purpose. A skilled leader realises that shaping a meaningful identity for the group is the most likely way to carry it into stage four.

Once in stage four, the group becomes more cohesive. Group members are more supportive of each other, sharing information and ideas and tolerating each other's differences. A greater professional closeness begins to emerge. As a result of utilising each other's strengths and talents to a greater degree, the group is more resourceful and flexible in its approach to problem-solving and task performance. The group has matured and is performing as a genuine team.

Once having entered stage four, the team could remain there for a substantial period of time or may well fall back into any of the stages of the team development wheel. A great deal will depend on whether a substantial number of team members leave the team over a period of time, and the degree of integration of the new members. If the new members do not integrate well, then the team may find itself back at the forming stage. Equally, a substantial change of direction, objectives, mission and purpose may force the team to rethink the manner in which it conducts its work and the skills required of its team members. Changes of longer-term strategy may lead to the disbandment of the team and formation of a new one.

However, a change of leadership is unlikely to push the team into stage one. If the leader integrates well, the team is likely to remain at stage four. If work difficulties or interpersonal tensions arise, the team may slip back into the storming/norming cycle.

Factors influencing progression through the team development wheel

The length of time it would take a newly-formed group to go through the team development wheel and emerge as a team or simply remain as a group, stuck in stages two and three, depends on four factors: values, group dynamics, the impact training and team building, and group learning processes.

Values

Workgroups and teams cannot be satisfactorily explained unless the values of the individual team members, the group, and the whole organisation are taken into account. Values, which can be broadly described as the underlying drives which influence the attitudes and behavioural patterns of individuals, groups and even organisations, strongly influence whether certain outcomes are desirable or undesirable. Hence, values are a key consideration in analysing the differences between intended outcomes and actual performance. The values that will influence the performance of a work team can be divided into three sections: the values of the workforce, the values of the managers and the predominant values of the organisation.

Research by Dr Bob Cummings has shown that two kinds of values determine workforce reactions to work:

1   growth needs, ie the desire for achievement and personal development

2   social needs, ie the individual benefiting from interacting with others to complete tasks as opposed to working alone.

A manager needs to take into account both growth needs and social needs in the design and formulation of task teams. Equally, the values of the manager (and/or team leader) must be considered in terms of team formulation or performance. The overwhelming evidence in the literature is that growth and social needs can only really be satisfied in participative, self-regulating groups. If the values of the managers or team leaders are not supportive of such processes, then groups are unlikely to function well. Further, the manager or team leader must consider whether his values are synonymous with the broader values of the organisation. If the values of the manager are not in keeping with certain of the shared beliefs in the organisation, then team performance may be affected, even though the manager and his team may hold similar beliefs and views. Teams are more likely to progress through the team development wheel and emerge performing better if the ideals of the group, the beliefs of the manager and the fundamental values of the organisation are in keeping with each other.

Group dynamics

Group dynamics refer to the various interactions that individuals enter into within a group setting. A number of factors could promote or upset the relationships and interactions within a group. The time, effort and energy required by individuals to achieve positive interactions within a group can be most easily influenced by the perceived positive/supportive or negative/destructive behaviour of one or more individuals in the group. The skills and influence of the group leader and the degree of compliance or proactivity between the group members and the leader influence the performance of the group. Equally, changes of tasks, work distribution or pattern or the impact of new technology can influence any group's performance. Finally, changes external to the organisation which may cause instability in the work environment, and the ability of the group to introduce measures to cope with change, will strongly influence group dynamics.

Training/team building techniques

A valuable means of improving group dynamics and assisting teams to proceed through the team development wheel is the application of training and team building techniques. Team training and team building involve attempting to both improve and make more disciplined the performance of that team in order that outcomes are more predictable. In this way, it is easier to estimate what is required, the time it takes and the likely impact of the demands made on team members in the attainment of group objectives. Towards this end, team development requires attention to four separate sets of needs; those of the individuals, the leader, the group and the organisation. Depending on circumstances and the particular requirements of these four separate areas, the techniques of training and team building need to suit the situation.

It should not be assumed that team needs and organisational needs are the same. Researchers have shown that well-applied team development programmes increase the loyalty the individuals feel towards the group, but this may occur at the expense of organisational loyalty. The group members may collectively pursue their goals, but view the wider organisation as a constraint. Hence improving team performance does not necessarily increase organisation effectiveness.

Consequently, in situations where team performance and organisational effectiveness are integrally linked, it is necessary to introduce relevant team and organisational issues into a team building programme. In this way, managers are being prepared to face important and sensitive concerns within their teams and possibly in a wider organisational context, but within the relative safety of a team building experience. In addition, it may be necessary to hire consultants to help with issues of team performance, team development or organisation development, thereby helping individuals and groups reach realistic and workable decisions. A skilful consultant in such a forum does not lay down what his client(s) should do, but facilitates a process whereby the client reaches his own conclusions about his behaviour and performance.

Appropriate and sensibly applied team building/development techniques should assist groups to reach stage four of the team development wheel.

Group growth and development processes

The experiences that group members need to undergo in order to emerge as a working team is the least explored area in the field of the social psychology of groups. Different conceptual models are utilised to examine group growth and development processes. In terms of examining whole groups, the team development wheel is a powerful example of group growth and development process analysis. At the individual level, certain writers offer a sequential, step-by-step process model, showing the stages of individual growth and development in attempting to achieve interdependence between individuals and group integration. Frequently quoted is Kurt Lewin's seminal work, describing the three learning stages of freezing (clinging to what one knows), unfreezing (exploring ideas, issues and approaches) and refreezing (identifying, utilising and integrating values, attitudes and skills with those previously held and currently desired).

An alternative design is offered by Professors Chris Argyris and Donald Schon, who consider that people need to be helped to learn and term the 'learning to learn process' double loop learning. Essentially, for any person to examine how they are operating and attempt to alter patterns of work behaviour, they need to develop new attitudes, skills and ideas. In order to achieve that, they have to spend time learning how to learn new things and re-examine their learning from the past. Naturally, a great deal depends on the group leader stimulating a learning climate within the group.

Training the team members to learn to work together, mature as a group and successfully negotiate the four growth stages is far more desirable than leaving the workgroup on its own to become a team. Training in team development does not remove any of the four growth stages, but rather assists individual members to develop from one stage to the next in a more controlled manner.

Case 12.3   'Birth of a management team'

Simon considered various alternatives: bringing in consultants to examine the pay and promotion issues; forming a team of committed T&T employees, headed by George Jefferson, to examine and recommend approaches to the training and development of staff. Simon concluded that his first priority was the 'cabinet' that had to be turned into an effectively performing management team. There seemed to be little point in improving the managerial performance of the levels below, if top management were not prepared to improve. Simon decided to invite the 'cabinet' to a weekend away, for all to discuss informally and openly the issues each individual considered important. A charming hotel well outside London but on the River Thames was chosen as the location.

'At least the surroundings are conducive to talking things through', muttered Simon.

The 'cabinet members' were booked in from Friday evening to Sunday, late afternoon. By the early evening of Saturday, the strongly felt issues were being addressed. Some argued with Simon that the management and integration of departments, divisions, and the newly acquired businesses were an immediate challenge. Others considered that fighting off the American challenge in the Big Bang market environment should be the vital issue. For that, improved information systems were needed. Clark Dobré, in particular, spoke against Simon's ideas on improving the management of the organisation.

'We have highly professional deal seekers, not clerks. Our problem is that we cannot match the six, and now recently seven, figure sums that the Americans pay to hire good players. Forget all this management stuff!'

'That's right, Clark. We will never be able to compete with the Americans in this way. That's why our management has to improve!' responded Simon.

Clark Dobré headed Capital Markets, generally considered 'prima donnas' in the fast moving world of merchant banking.

The discussions were interesting, heated, but most of all meaningful. Even Dobré stated that the group had really got to the heart of particular problems. Decisions were made at the weekend. The structure of the organisation and a drive to improve the managerial skills of middle and senior management were agreed as issues requiring immediate attention. It was also agreed that McKenzie's brief on the information systems restructuring should be broadened. Directors should give McKenzie access to their departments in order that McKenzie could structure information systems to meet departmental needs fully. Other decisions concerning capital markets and corporate finance markets were made.

Most of the directors agreed that they were now more like a management team.

The cabinet of T&T (Case 12.3) are about to embark through the stages of the Team Development Wheel. The question is, will this group of individuals be able to emerge as an effective working team? The issues facing the group concern the lack of co-ordination, and poor managerial practices in the organisation. If the group focused only on poor management systems, an improvement in administration would overcome these problems. The group would then probably progress beyond stage two of the Team Development Wheel. However, it seems as if the problems facing the 'cabinet' are far deeper cultural issues of professional practice within the organisation. Such fundamental tensions and rifts could prevent the team from progressing. In order to improve the situation, a planned and on-going team development intervention should be seriously considered. Even with the benefit of team development, the team may be caught in the storming/norming cycle.

The following guidelines will assist in the process of team growth and development:

1 Encourage persons of different professional backgrounds to become team members where relevant, eg chemists, physicists, engineers, accountants.

2 Ensure that the team adopts a positive attitude towards the task(s) at hand by giving it sufficient freedom to make decisions

and act with a degree of independence of the parent organisation.

3   There should be only one accountability line within the team. The person at the head of the team is accountable for the practices and activities of all personnel within the team.

4   Teams should be relatively small to allow for greater interpersonal understanding and team cohesion.

5   Attention needs to be focused on the differing demands made on individuals by their acting in a line capacity and as team members.

6   The team should operate as a multi disciplinary unit, in an interdisciplinary style, and co-operate with relevant outside agencies.

A big problem facing most project team members is the potential incompatibility between line and team responsibilities. A line manager may have to undertake a cost-cutting exercise in a period of reduced sales. Additionally, he may be a member of a product development team which concludes that further investment is required on particular products as part of a product redevelopment campaign. Subordinates asked to implement cost-cutting measures could easily lose faith in their boss, should they witness him spending on product development but depriving his own department of particular facilities.

MANAGEMENT BY OBJECTIVES (MBO)

If organisational strategy is to be carried out, operating objectives have to be specified which are in keeping with the strategy defined. An MBO type approach can help in laying down and achieving operating objectives. Three issues need to be considered:

1   *Interpretation.* When breaking down strategy into smaller attainable objectives, it is important that people understand what they are trying to do and why. MBO can help in this process. Further, it is necessary that those responsible for attaining those objectives be identified within the organisation.

2   *Establish identity.* Management must believe in the objectives so that it works towards their accomplishment. MBO is a valuable technique here.

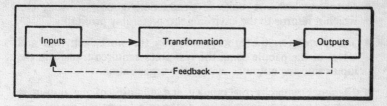

Fig. 12.2   A simple organisational system

3   *Flexibility.* As external/market conditions change, so operating objectives need to be adjusted to accommodate such changes. Again MBO is a valuable tool.

Specifying practical shorter-term objectives is the first hurdle. The second hurdle is to motivate and induce both managers and operatives to accomplish those objectives. MBO is not simply an approach to motivating and leading others to achieve objectives: it represents a series of different management techniques, activities and skills concerned with planning, organising, leading and controlling.

A widely read book by George Odiorne suggests that MBO is more a philosophy than a set of rules for running a business and that purposes and aims are important in determining the quality and style of life in an organisation. If this is so, and MBO is introduced and maintained with commitment to this philosophy, then it can be a very effective means of integrating the individual with the organisation and developing more competent managers. MBO can, if there is commitment to this philosophy, increase the levels of two of the three critical psychological states described in the job design model – responsibility for work outcomes, and knowledge of results – and so generate a higher level'of internal motivation in individuals in an organisation (see Chapter 5).

What is MBO?

An organisational system consists of four elements (Figure 12.2):

- *Inputs* such as people and resources which it acquires from its environment.

- *Outputs* which are units of production, goods, services, etc. which it returns to the environment, preferably profitably.

- *Transformation* the process whereby the work, activities and effort of the people using the resources acquired transform the inputs into the outputs – within the organisation.

- *Feedback* whereby the quality and quantity of the output is assessed and changes in inputs or the transformation process can be made where necessary.

Life becomes simple if we look at the organisational system in these terms. All we have to do is to define the outputs we want (for an organisation, and its objectives), then use these to assess the quality of the transformation process and the inputs. Then we break down the organisational objectives into departmental and individual objectives and follow the same process. But that is not all. As organisations become more complex so does this process, but not linearly – exponentially! Subobjectives overlap; their achievement depends on achievement of other subobjectives. It is important to appreciate that the whole system is interdependent. The simple process of a manager and his subordinate discussing and agreeing objectives for a period, and then at the end of the period jointly assessing progress against those objectives, can often be frustrating and alienating experience. Small wonder that organisations frequently fall back on a structured, systematic approach to the process, where goals become paramount, and people are simply factors in the input–output equation; where people strive to become more efficient in their work activities rather than identify with their work goals; where the humanistic, developmental aspects of MBO are submerged in an impersonal, mechanistic performance appraisal system whose objective seems to be to generate forms and still more forms.

But MBO can work if the underlying philosophy permeates the organisation.

The principles of management by objectives

As management by objectives is primarily a system of defining goals, measuring performance against goals, and using those measures to modify and redefine the goals for the future, it seems natural that the system should start at the top – by clearly identifying the objectives of the organisation, and particularly the goals and objectives of the chief executive of the organisation. The goals and objectives set for his subordinates must, within the hierarchy of responsibility, be congruent with, and actively progress, the achievement of the chief executive's goals. These subordinates then continue the goal determination process downwards through the managerial hierarchy. So the system contains these downward stages.

1   The chief executive determines his objectives for the coming period and decides on measures of organisational, and his individual, performance.

2   The chief executive and his subordinates discuss and agree on their objectives for the coming period, and establish measures of individual performance.

3   This process of goal setting and performance measurement for the coming period is continued down the managerial hierarchy.

The whole process thus consists of two separate but interdependent activities.

1   At the beginning of each period (budget year, calendar year, etc.) boss and subordinate agree on subordinate's goals for the coming period and on measures of his performance during the period.

2   At the end of each period, boss and subordinate discuss and agree on subordinate's performance against these goals, and set and agree his goals and performance measures for the next period.

Three words are important – goals, performance and agreement.

Goals

Agreed goals need to be realistic within the context of the environment, the organisation, the department, and the manager's position within that department. Goals may be financial, or relate to service levels or development. They need to be set high enough to require high effort and motivation by the job holder, but not so high that he feels he has little chance of achieving them. If they are too low he will feel no sense of achievement when he has reached them. They also need to be within the controllable area of responsibility of the manager concerned.

Performance

Goals need to be measurable, for how else can one measure performance against targets? Further performance should not just be monitored at the end of a period, but a joint work planning and review system needs to be in continuous operation. Performance appraisal and goal setting once a period is not the end of the operation. During the period the manager needs to be reviewing, with the individual subordinate, how he is progressing towards his objectives, how and why subtargets are being achieved, or not achieved, whether targets should be amended in the light of progress or changed situations. Performance is not something which happens once a period, it is continuous, and the manager needs to be aware of what is happening from day to day.

Agreement

Agreement between boss and subordinate is vital to the success of management by objectives. A boss who sits down and dictates his subordinate's next period's goals without consultation and discussion negates the philosophy of the process. For a boss simply to tell a subordinate how he has performed over the past period, to chronicle his successes and failures without giving the subordinate an opportunity to discuss and agree them, is to induce defensive behaviour in the subordinate and negative attitudes towards the whole process. The subordinate might rightly remark, 'It's just another system for keeping us in line.'

Agreement can lead to improved boss–subordinate relationships, particularly if the boss is prepared to disclose his own objectives. Too often a subordinate's objectives are set and agreed without the subordinate being very clear about the *purpose* of his objectives, without him knowing how they fit into the whole picture of the boss, the department, or the organisation, so that he feels he is working in the dark, and his commitment is likely to be less than 100 per cent.

Causes of over- or under-performance against objectives need to be analysed carefully. Was it due to factors outside the job holder's control, or was it due entirely to his own contribution, or was it, perhaps, due to the manager as his boss: managers are often blind to the effects of their behaviour on their subordinates.

Passing from the subordinate's performance in his past period, agreement on future goals can then be achieved. His development needs emerge as a result of this process. Perhaps he will not be able to achieve future targets without some development or training? Perhaps he has some individual career development needs which cannot be met while working to achieve the required targets, or while working in his present job? Can the organisation and the individual find some way of meeting those individual needs while still achieving organisational objectives? Can these personal development objectives be included in the set of objectives to which the subordinate and his boss commit themselves? The answers to these questions depend a great deal on the quality of agreement between superior and subordinate.

Management by objectives can, and does, work in many organisations. One might think that it is more suited to organisations in stable environments where it is easier to set goals. But it works just as well in high technology companies where the environment is changing rapidly. Hewlett-Packard (HP) has a system of MBO to which its management is highly committed. It incorporates the philosophy that 'managers, given the right support, guidance and objectives, are better able to make decisions about the problems with which they are directly concerned than some executive up the line – no matter how able that executive may be'.

This philosophy places great responsibility on the managers concerned, but also tends to make their work more interesting, varied, significant, motivating and challenging. It makes those managers feel that what they do has a direct effect on the performance of the company, and helps them to see that there is considerable congruence between satisfaction of their own individual needs and achievement of organisational goals. HP managers are truly committed to 'the HP way' – management by objectives.

Case 12.4   'Making bankers managers!'

Simon asked George Jefferson to draw together a small group to examine and recommend improvements on the current structure and managerial practices within T&T. Although George was at a lower level than the directors with whom he would inevitably have to interact, Simon trusted George's ability to handle the situation. George was an extrovert, related easily to people, was popular in the bank, but most of all was respected by most of senior management. George chose his team members carefully, from corporate finance, administration and services, capital markets and business development.

Within a month, George reported to Simon and presented him with a plan for management training and job structuring. After some alterations to the plan, it was approved by Simon for George to implement. The plan consisted of generating a series of in-house, coupled with external, management programmes that would directly address the performance issues at particular managerial levels. One hundred and sixty managers were earmarked to attend one or more of these programmes. Over the next seven months, 70 per cent of the managers attended more than one programme. All had attended a short two-day programme on the nature of the manager's job and managerial responsibilities. On that two-day event, the fundamental tasks of, and skills required for, organising, appraising others, managing subordinates, meeting deadlines and running meetings effectively, were taught. By the end of that seven-month period, most senior managers indicated that improvements in the workplace, were visible. Most reacted positively to such developments; one or two did not!

The tensions within the Cabinet erupted during 'any further business' at one of the cabinet meetings.

'How do you feel all this management training is going then, Simon?' asked Dobré.

Simon sensed that this was not just one more question.

'As far as I can see, very well. Do you want to make a comment on this, Clark?' questioned Simon.

'Yes, I do. You may remember that I was never in favour of this whole programme. I said as much at our weekend away. But, congratulations, Simon. It's working' commented Dobré sarcastically. He continued. 'So you're getting good managers spending all their time listening and talking to subordinates. You know what's happening; that drive and cutting edge you need to make it in the markets is no longer being valued. We're slowly becoming less competitive!'

As Dobré continued, Simon's mind wandered. He had never really understood Dobré; he had considered him rather a shallow but arrogant individual. For Simon, this was the first time Clark Dobré was sincere, even though he was opposing Simon's policies.

Dobré stopped talking. No-one spoke. Simon finally broke the silence. 'You really feel strongly about this, don't you, Clark' said Simon softly. Dobré had not expected such a response from Simon.

'Yes, I do!'

'Clark, once the meeting is over, can you and I talk in private?'

'Is there any point, Simon?'

'Yes. There is!'

The other cabinet members exchanged glances.

In Case 12.4, the programme of training provided an MBO approach to addressing the management problems of T&T. In order for the training to be successful, the role and objectives of managers had to be identified and then appropriate training mounted, to improve line management's skills. If the initial survey and subsequent training had been well conducted, the likely response from the participants would be positive and motivated.

If people feel that their problems are being attended to, they are more likely to identify with senior management. As a result, their contribution to the organisation will probably increase, which will add to the motivational stimulus, especially if that extra effort is recognised.

Ironically, MBO for the cabinet proved to be a valuable exercise, for it highlighted the differences between individuals. Such differences can undermine the commitment in terms of implementing top management decisions. If one of the top managers who approved the decision is perceived as not committed to acting on the decision, how can one expect lower level management to be committed to decision implementation? Whether the group, as a result of discussing differences, can knit itself more together as a team, is another issue. At least the MBO approach has helped the group members discuss underlying tensions. Case 12.4 indicates that MBO can be considered as much an approach to on-the-job people development as a device for increased organisational performance.

THE GENERAL MANAGER

The general manager (GM) serves a practical, vital function in any organisation. He acts as the bridge between operation and strategy; he decides on what is appropriate or inappropriate information for top management; he can make the difference between a motivated and demotivated middle management and workforce. The relationship the GM has with his/her subordinates and the relationship the GMs have with each other are likely to have a substantial impact on the whole organisation. Policies decided at the top need to be implemented through the GMs. The GMs, as a group, need to have good working relationships with each other in order to apply policies uniformly. At the same time, each GM is required to interpret broad strategy into action plans that suit the culture of his/her division or department. Inevitably, substantial differences between the actions and activities of various divisions or departments will arise. It is the function of the GM to act as a link-pin in the organisation. Depending on the organisation, a GM could be a senior manager responsible for a division, possibly a subsidiary company or a large department in a public service organisation.

A number of recent studies, largely championed by the milestone work of Professor John Kotter of the Harvard Business School, show that the personality characteristics of the GM are all-important. John Kotter explains: 'The basic personality themes that one finds in a group of successful general managers relate to power, achievement, ambition, emotional stability, optimism, intelligence, analytical ability, intuition and a personable style.' (p. 6).

Kotter puts substantial emphasis on the personality characteristics of GMs. He concludes that potentially successful GMs exhibit such characteristics as ambition, achievement and power orientation, have developed a balanced temperament and are interpersonally skilful. Competent GMs hold a detailed knowledge of their business and organisation. Further, good GMs have deliberately attempted to fit and be seen as credible in their context, culture and overall organisation. Such a wide range of personal and interpersonal skills has not developed by accident. The original sample of fifteen GMs studied showed that they held a lifelong concern for their professional development.

Kotter considers that high-performing GMs possess three sets of skills. First, they need agenda setting skills, so that when new in a job or project they have the capacity to identify and convince others of the primary concerns and objectives of the project or enterprise. Setting appropriate agendas which will be accepted by others is likely to be a time consuming process. In addition, GMs need to develop networking skills. In effect, good GMs deliberately attempt to develop contacts with influential people within and outside the organisation. Such a network of contacts means that the individual is likely to be aware of pertinent issues and act on them in good time. To develop agenda setting and networking skills GMs need to be interpersonally skilful, especially since they spend most of their time with others such as peers, superiors, subordinates and people outside the organisation.

In terms of work, tasks and attitudes, Kotter, in keeping with Mintzberg's findings (see Chapter 1), shows managerial work to be erratically (but effectively) conducted in short bursts, with managers working on numerous activities which may at times hold conflicting objectives. Kotter also discovered that successful GMs discuss a wide range of subjects often in a disjointed and unplanned manner. They tend to ask questions rather than give orders. The reason for this is that GMs, to perform well, seem to require large amounts of potentially relevant information. The work of senior managers is conducted in environments characterised by uncertainty and diversity so that the approach and style of the individual has to vary according to the setting in which he is operating.

Finally, Kotter concludes that, as high performing managers

implement policies, objectives and activities through a diverse number of individuals and groups, they are complex people undertaking complex work. Such a conclusion holds profound implications for the selection and development of such personnel.

Case 12.5 The reconciliation

'Thanks for agreeing to talk, Clark', said Simon, closing the door to his office. 'I'll just ring Maureen for two coffees. Take a seat.'

Dobré sat himself down in one of four easy chairs in Simon's compact office. Not all bankers have large, luxurious and spacious offices. Simon put the 'phone down and faced Dobré.

'Did you really mean what you said in the meeting, Clark?' asked Simon.

Dobré nodded.

Silence.

'What are you going to do, Simon? Ask for my resignation?'

'No. I want directors to feel strongly about what they do. We need strong leadership!' responded Simon.

Dobré looked surprised.

'Look, Clark, we have a number of regional offices on the capital markets side throughout the world. Administration and Services has to administer for a number of different departments and whole divisions right across the board. Corporate finance is similarly regionalised. You know what all that means?'

Dobré shook his head.

'It means that we need intelligent, energetic bankers who have experience of market making and negotiating deals, living and working side by side with good all-round managers who have an independent office or an "across-the-board" service to administer in T&T. We need top money men at director level. We also need good general managers at probably one or more levels below director. Good management practice has been our headache for some time. As bankers, however, we pay little attention to such problems. You said it yourself, Clark, we cannot afford to buy in the players as the Americans can. We have to try to keep our good people by other means.'

Dobré said little throughout the conversation. He listened, and nodded occasionally.

'At the end of the day, we are not doing anything so new. Having general managers and professional bankers side by side has been tried in some of the American investment banks'.

Pause.

'When it comes down to it, you more than anyone, have to support this policy, Clark. As Head of Capital Markets, you are going to be managing these new general managers in your regional offices', stated Simon.

The conversation continued into the evening. Finally.

'OK, Simon. Let's give your policy a go! You're right, we have to improve somehow', said Dobré.

Simon (Case 12.5) considered that managers who are required to run multi-functional offices or departments should be recognised as general managers (GMs). The GMs would have to be highly skilled in agenda setting and networking, to enable them to manage specialist unit heads successfully. Dobré's support, however, was crucial, for the GM role had to be introduced in his division. It was important for Simon to convince Dobré of the value of the policy, for the GMs would provide the necessary integration at the sub-unit strategy level. (See Chapter 10 for sub-unit strategy.) The professional specialists could remain in charge of the whole organisation as long as the necessary integration of managerial services and human resource management could take place. Simon's vision of the GM role was to introduce it to those services that have a high customer profile but require the input of different specialists in order to provide a professional service to the market.

SUMMARY

Performance appraisal

Performance appraisal provides an opportunity for both the individual and the organisation to assess the performance and value of the individual's work contribution. If well conducted, performance appraisal sessions can largely determine the suitability of personnel for particular types of employment, their training, the longer-term development needs and possible potential. It can further act as a motivational stimulus by generating feedback on performance and also provide a basis for allocating rewards. Three separate approaches to performance appraisal are possible; informative, whereby the boss informs his subordinate as to how he sees his (the subordinate's) performance; consultative, whereby the boss invites the subordinate to comment, query and generally become involved in the boss's views concerning the individual; participative, whereby the boss and individual meet to discuss the individual's performance.

Effective team development

For a newly formed group of individuals to perform as a team, four distinct stages of team growth and development are experienced, namely forming (the formation of the group), storming (questioning of group members' values, attitudes, skills and behaviour), norming (the generation of group norms) and performing (maturity of interpersonal relationships and effective task performance). In addition, four factors increase or impede the group's development through the team development wheel. These four are personal and group growth needs and social interaction needs (values); internal group dynamics, such as leadership influences, the impact of technology, stable and unstable work environments and ability to react to change; training and team building techniques; and the growth and development individuals need to undergo in order to emerge as an effective team.

Management by objectives (MBO)

MBO is a way of specifying operating objectives that are in keeping with the broader strategies of the organisation. An MBO-type approach to objective-setting can assist in the following ways: it can help break down broad strategy into smaller achievable objectives; it can help individuals identify with these objectives; it can help people cope with the processes of change and the need to specify new operational objectives. MBO consists of four elements, inputs (people and resources), transformation (the process of changing resources into goods or services), outputs (goods or services), and feedback (assessment of output which can lead to changes in inputs). In order to put any MBO system into practice, it is necessary to agree goals and appropriate performance measures.

The role of the general manager (GM)

The role of general manager serves an important bridging function in an organisation, for the GM acts as the link between operation and strategy. The GM can influence the quality and content of information processing systems and can make the difference between a motivated and demotivated middle management and workforce. As the GM can have such an influence on the performance of units within the organisation and eventually the whole organisation, the characteristics that make for a successful GM have become crucial. Personal characteristics, such as achievement orientation, need for power and good interpersonal skills, are vitally important.

IN CONCLUSION

Finding appropriate ways of integrating the person with the organisation is of vital concern to the long-term future of the organisation.

It is unrealistic to expect people of managerial standing to identify with any organisation simply because they receive salaried payment from it. Ambience, organisational culture, ways of doing things, managerial style and status are all relevant to whether good managers stay or leave, perform to expectations or below par. Similarly, those employed on operative tasks will be positively or negatively influenced by the style(s) management adopts. Running any business (in the broadest sense of a private or public organisation) is as much an emotive as it is an analytical experience.

Strategy provides mission and purpose to an organisation. Structure is the medium by which strategy is implemented. Mechanisms for integration are the means whereby people identify with the structure in order to contribute toward strategy. In essence, mechanisms for integration are a way of rounding off the organisation.

PART III
GUIDE TO
FURTHER READING

INTRODUCTION TO PART III

As stated in the Preface, our intention throughout the text has been to concentrate on the key issues and not to divert the reader's attention with references, footnotes and insertions. The few references provided in each chapter, in addition to references for further reading, are now presented as Part III of the book.

The references and brief outlines act as a guide through the labyrinths of management articles and research and conference papers. In addition, we acknowledge that it is impossible to write a value-free, unbiased chapter. We, probably no differently to other writers, have stamped our values, ideas and beliefs on the material in this book. Although we consider these views pertinent and valuable, they are nevertheless our own.

Consequently, each of the sections in Part III contains a brief explanation for the philosophy, structure and reasoning underlying each chapter. Alternative ways of examining each subject area are also briefly discussed.

II. INTRODUCTION TO PART III

SECTION 1

The question, 'What is a manager's job?', has been debated for over fifty years. Early writers such as Taylor (1911) and Fayol (1916) established an area of enquiry that is much researched to this day. An examination of the literature reveals numerous approaches to this issue. They fall into two broad categories:

The manager's job

Mintzberg (1973) and Stewart (1976) have made a considerable contribution with their studies of managerial work. However, other exploratory studies are also worth reading, such as that of Horne and Lupton (1965), who studied the work activities of middle managers.

Pavett and Lau (1983) examine the nature of managerial work as it is influenced by hierarchical level and functional speciality. They suggest that the nature of managerial work changes according to functional specialisation and position in hierarchy. Further references are Alexander (1979), Paolillo (1981) and McCall and Segrist (1980).

One reason why hierarchy and function may affect the nature of managerial work is discretion. Jaques (1961) suggests that discretion is a measure for indicating the maximum period of time that an individual can apply choice to a range of diverse activities and alternative actions. His thesis is that jobs of greater seniority in the hierarchy have wider spans of discretion. See also Montanari's (1978) discussion of managerial discretion.

An equally interesting perspective of the manager's job is an examination of the stages or cycles that managers' jobs go through over time. Smith (1985) considers that managers' jobs do change over time and outlines the stages that managers commonly pass through. Further, training and appropriate development vary according to the stage of the manager's job, and this in turn affects the criteria that need to be applied at each stage. Other references in this field are Katz (1980) and Nicholson (1984).

For a sound overview of work on managerial jobs, see papers in Dreuth et al. (1984) and Nystrom and Starbuck (1981).

Managerial performance

Great attention has been given to the question, 'What is effective management performance?' At senior management levels, recent work by Kotter (1982) and Margerison and Kakabadse (1984) is worth perusal. Further discussion on effective managerial performance appears in Boyatzis (1982), Copeman (1971), Ghiselli (1971), Reddin (1970) and McCall and Lombardo (1983).

An interesting paper is that of Morse and Wagner (1978), who attempted to develop a questionnaire to evaluate what managerial behaviour succeeds best.

In contrast, Marshal and Cooper (1979) provide an easy-to-read analysis of how executives' work performance respond to pressure. Anderson, Hellriegal and Slocum's (1977) study has a similar theme.

Suggestions as to how executives should be developed are provided by James (1980) and Reynolds and Tramel (1979). In fact, there are a great many books and articles about managerial development. For further references, read journals such as *Organisational Dynamics, Journal of Management Development, Leadership and Organisational Development Journal, Journal of Organisation Development* and *American Society for Training and Development Bulletins*. For a good source of references for books and articles in this area, read Kakabadse and Mukhi (1984). See also the further reading section for Chapter 12 (p. 443).

Concluding comments

A recently emerging area which is likely to make a powerful impact on concepts of managerial work and performance is the subject of values and personal beliefs. Kakabadse and Parker (1984) refer to this. Boulgarides, Fisher and Gjelten (1984) directly address the topic, and consider that the personal values and beliefs of the individual manager are an important influence on managerial performance. See also the study by Watson and Sampson (1978).

However, as this topic is only just emerging, it was not explicitly covered in the chapter, which focuses on two key concerns for managers: the nature of their jobs and the different views on managerial performance.

References

Alexander, L.D. (1979), 'The Effect Level in the Hierarchy and Functional Area have on the Extent Mintzberg's Roles are Required by Managerial Jobs', *Academy of Management Proceedings*, pp. 186-9.

Anderson, C.R., Hellriegal, D. and Slocum, J.W. Jr (1977), 'Managerial Response to Environmentally Induced Stress', *Academy of Management Journal*, Vol. 20, No. 2, pp. 260-72.

Boulgarides, J.D., Fisher, M.A. and Gjelton, E. (1984), *Are You in the Right Job?*, Monarch Press.

Boyatzis, R.E. (1982) *The Competent Manager*, Wiley.

Copeman, G. (1971), *The Chief Executive and Business Growth*, Leviathan House, London.

Dreuth, P.J.D., Thierry, H., Williams, P.J. and De Wolff, C. J. (eds) (1984), *Handbook of Work and Organisation Psychology*, Vol. 2, Wiley.

Fayol, H. (1916), *Administration Industrielle et Générale*, Dunod, Paris.

Gant, H.L. (1919), 'Work, Wages and Profits', *Engineering Magazine Company*, New York.

Ghiselli, E. (1971), *Explorations in Managerial Talent*, Goodyear, Glenview, Illinois.

Gilbreth, F.L. (1941), *Motion Study*, Van Nostrand, New York.

Horne, J. and Lupton, T. (1965), 'The Work Activities of Middle Managers: An Exploratory Study', *Journal of Management Studies*, Vol. 1, No. 21.

James, K. (1980), 'The Development of Senior Managers for the Future', in Beck, J. and Cox, C., *Advances in Management Education*, Wiley.

Jaques, E. (1961), *Equitable Payment*, Wiley.

Kakabadse, A.P. and Mukhi, S. (eds) (1984), *The Future of Management Education*, Gower; Nichols Publishing Co., New York.

Kakabadse, A.P. and Parker, C. (eds) (1984), *Power, Politics and Organisations: A Behavioural Science View*, Wiley.

Kotter, J.P. (1982), 'General Managers are not Generalists', *Organisational Dynamics*, Spring, pp. 5-19.

Margerison, 'C.J. and Kakabadse, A.P. (1984), 'How American Chief Executives Succeed: Implications for Developing High Potential Employees, An American Management Association Survey Report.

Marshall, J. and Cooper, C.L. (1979), Executives Under Pressure, Macmillan.

Mayo, E. (1945), The Social Problems of an Industrial Civilisation, Harvard University Press.

McCall, M.W. Jr and Lombardo, M.M. (1983), 'What makes a Top Executive?' Psychology Today, February.

McCall, M.W. Jr and Segrist, C.A. (1980), In Pursuit of the Manager's Job: Building on Mintzberg, (Technical Report No. 14) Greensboro NC: Centre for Creative Leadership.

Mintzberg, H. (1973), The Nature of Managerial Work, Harper and Row.

Montanari, J.R. (1978), 'Managerial Discretion: An Expanded Model of Organisation Choice', Academy of Management Review, Vol. 3, No. 2, pp. 231–41

Morse, J.J. and Wagner, F.R. (1978), 'Measuring the Process of Managerial Effectiveness', Academy of Management Journal, Vol. 21, No. 1, pp. 23–35.

Nicholson, N. (1984), 'A Theory of Work Role Transitions', Administrative Science Quarterly, June, Vol. 29, No. 2, pp. 172–91.

Nystrom, P.C. and Starbuck, W.H. (eds) (1981), Handbook of Organisational Design, Vol. 2, Wiley.

Paolillo, J.G.K. (1981), 'Role Profiles for Managers at Different Hierarchical Levels', Academy of Management Proceedings, pp. 91–4.

Pavett, C.M. and Lau, A.W. (1983), 'Managerial Work: The Influence of Hierarchical Level and Functional Specialities', Academy of Management Journal, Vol. 26, No. 1, pp. 170–7.

Reddin, W. (1970), Managerial Effectiveness, McGraw-Hill.

Reynolds, H. and Tramel, M.E. (1979), Executive Time Management: Getting 12 Hours' Work out of an 8 Hour Day, Gower.

Smith, P. (1985), 'The Stages in a Manager's Job, in Hammond, V. (ed), Current Research in Management, Frances Pinter.

Stewart, R. (1976), Contrasts in Management: A Study of Different Types of Managers' Jobs, their Demands and Choices, McGraw-Hill. See also Stewart, R. (1982), Choices for the Manager: a Guide to Managerial Work, McGraw-Hill.

Taylor, F.W. (1911), *The Principles of Scientific Management*, Harper and Row.

Watson, J.G. and Simpson, L.R. (1978), 'A Comparative Study of Owner–Manager Personal Values in Black and White Small Businesses', *Academy of Management Journal*, Vol. 21, No. 2, pp. 313–19.

Weber, M. (1947), *The Theory of Social and Economic Organisation*, transl. by A.M. Henderson and T. Glencoe Parsons III, Free Press.

SECTION 2

Although this section brings together four distinct topic areas, it is impossible to discuss fully the type and variety of readings under this umbrella, as no one subject, as such, exists. Hence, the four areas of recruitment and selection, induction and socialisation, careers and work and family are treated here as separate.

Recruitment and selection

Thomason's (1975) comprehensive text on personnel management adequately covers the processes of recruitment and selection. See also Tyson and York's (1982) easy to read but comprehensive analysis. In fact, most standard texts in personnel management cover the steps and stages of recruitment and selection.

Induction and socialisation

The processes of induction and socialisation have only recently come under scrutiny. Van Maanen (1978) and Schein (1978) take a longer-term career focus for their research. It was Van Maanen (1978) who made the statement, 'Socialisation shapes the Person'.

In contrast, researchers such as Nadler, Hackman and Lawler (1979) and Hackman and Suttle (1977) adopt a 'motivation to work' perspective to these processes (see Section 5 for further information on job motivation). Their view is that particular work characteristics, such as having a challenging job, a good boss and a supportive workgroup, initially influence the induction and socialisation process. Studies such as the one conducted by Louis, Posner and Powell (1983) support this argument. A particularly interesting study is that by Feldman (1981), who presents an integrated model of socialisation, namely the development of work skills and abilities, the acquisition of a set of appropriate role behaviours, and the adjustment to workgroups' norms and values.

In contrast, the Human Resources group at Cranfield School of Management, championed by the Lewis and Parker (1980) study, have adopted the view that, irrespective of work characteristics, all individuals experience a transition, in effect a process of relearning, in that the individual is attempting to understand what high performance means for him in his new job and/or organisation. The transition work emanated from the Kubler Ross (1969) study on the successful means of counselling terminally ill patients. The Leeds University group of Adams, Hayes and Hopson (1976) further developed the concept in their work on helping individuals manage personal change.

Career development

Career development has been viewed from different angles. The McCall and Lombardo (1983) and Margerison and Kakabadse (1984) studies adopt an effective management performance basis. These two studies attempt to identify the necessary skills required for various levels of management and follow this by recommending the sorts of development opportunities managers would need to make full use of their skills. Boyatzis' (1982) work offers a similar contribution. In contrast, McClelland (1965) and Kotter (1982) consider that personality and need for power are more important than managerial skills or development opportunities.

In contrast, Schein's (1978) work on career anchors is of particular interest, for it assumes that individuals adopt certain attitudes to their work and career which may become so deeply ingrained that they cannot adjust their views. On the topic of career anchors in particular and personal work needs in general, see also Schein (1982), Vardi (1980), Louis (1980) and the original study conducted by Super (1957).

In addition, certain studies have dealt with career mobility, describing the prerequisites and blockages to lateral and upward mobility. See Verga (1983), Gould (1979) and Karman, Wittig-Berman and Lang (1981).

Work and family

The conflicting demands of work and home life have recently attracted attention. The Bartholomé and Evans (1979) study is a milestone. The Cooper and Davidson studies are neatly encompassed in their 1982 text. See also Bailyn (1980), Hall and Hall (1979) and Rappaport and Rappaport (1978), explaining the problems and life styles of dual career families.

From the point of view of how people's needs change over time and the impact that has on work and family life, see Gould (1972) and Sonnenfeld and Kotter (1982). See also Pym (1980), examining the negative reactions of people who have been mismanaged.

Concluding comments

The Human Resources group at Cranfield School of Management have long been concerned with people's development in an organisation from the point of entry onwards. Recognising that no one text covers all aspects of entry, socialisation, career progression and the work v. family interactions, this chapter is a compilation of separate topic areas concerned with issues influencing career progress.

References

Adams, J., Hayes, J. and Hopson, B. (1976), *Transition Understanding and Managing Personal Change*, Martin Robertson.

Bailyn, L. (1980), *Living with Technology*, MIT Press.

Bartholomé, F. and Lee Evans, P.P. (1979), 'Professional Lives Versus Private Lives – Shifting Patterns of Managerial Commitment', *Organisational Dynamics*, Spring, pp. 3–29.

Boyatzis, R.E. (1982), *The Competent Manager*, Wiley.

Cooper, C. and Davidson, M. (1982), *High Pressure: Working Lives of Women Managers*, Fontana.

Feldman, D.C. (1981), 'The Multiple Socialisation of Organisation Members', *Academy of Management Review*, Vol. 6, No. 2, pp. 307–18.

Gould, S. (1975), 'Adult Life Stages, Growth Towards Tolerance', *Psychology Today*, February.

Gould, S. (1979), 'Characteristics of Career Planners in Upwardly Mobile Occupations', *Academy of Management Journal*, Vol. 22, No. 3, pp. 539–50.

Hackman, J.R. and Suttle, J.L. (1977), *Improving Life at Work*, Goodyear, Glenview, Illinois.

Hall, F.S. and Hall, D.T. (1979) *The Two Career Couple*, Addison-Wesley.

Kakabadse, A.P. (1983), *The Politics of Management,* Gower; Nichols Publishing Co., New York.

Kanter, R.M. (1977), *Men and Women of the Corporation,* Basic Books Inc.

Korman, A.K., Wittig-Berman, U. and Lang, D. (1981), 'Career Success and Personal Failure: Alienation in Professionals and Managers', *Academy of Management Journal,* Vol. 24, No. 2, pp. 342–60.

Kotter, J.P. (1982), *The General Managers,* Free Press.

Kubler Ross, E. (1969), *On Death and Dying,* Macmillan.

Louis, M.R. (1980) 'Career Transitions: Varieties and Commonalities', *Academy of Management Review,* Vol. 5, No. 3, pp. 329–40.

Louis, M.R., Posner, B.Z. and Powell, G.N. (1983), 'The Availability and Helpfulness of Socialisation Practices', *Personnel Psychology,* Vol. 36.

Margerison, C.J. and Kakabadse, A.P. (1984), *How American Chief Executives Succeed.* An American Management Association Survey Report.

McCall, M.W. Jr and Lombardo, M.M. (1983), 'What makes a top executive?' *Psychology Today,* February.

McClelland, D. (1965), 'Achievement Motivation can be developed', *Harvard Business Review,* November/December.

Nadler, D.A., Hackman, J.R. and Lawler, E.E. III (1979), *Managing Organisational Behaviour,* Little Brown and Company, Boston, Toronto.

Parker, C. and Lewis, R. (1980), 'Moving Up...How to Handle Transitions to Senior Levels Successfully', *Occasional Paper,* Cranfield School of Management, Cranfield, Bedford.

Pym, D. (1980), 'Professional Management: The gentle wastage in employment', *Futures,* April, pp. 142–50.

Rappaport, L.R., Rappaport, R. and Bumstead, J. (eds) (1978), *Working Couples,* Harper and Row.

Schein, E.H. (1978), *Career Dynamics,* Addison-Wesley.

Schein, E.H. (1980), 'Career Theory and Research – some Issues for the future', in Brooklyn Derr (ed), *Work, Family and the Career,* MIT Press.

Sonnenfeld, J. and Kotter, J.P. (1982), 'The Maturation of career theory', *Tavistock Institute of Human Relations Journal,* pp. 19–46.

Super, D. (1957), *The Psychology of Careers,* Harper and Row.

Thomason, G. (1975), *A Textbook of Personnel Management,* Institute of Personnel Management.

Tyson, S. and York, A. (1982), *Personnel Management Made Simple*, Heinemann.

Van Maanen, J. (1978), 'People Processing: Strategies of Organisational Socialisation', *Organisational Dynamics*, Vol. 7, pp. 8–36.

Vardi, Y. (1980), 'Organisational Career Mobility: An Integrative Model', *Academy of Management Review*, Vol. 5, No. 3, pp. 341–55.

Veiga, J.F. (1983), 'Mobility Influences During Career Stages', *Academy of Management Journal*, Vol. 26, No. 1, pp. 64–85.

SECTION 3

Personality is a controversial subject. Cooper and Makin (1981) offer a twofold classification of personality formation, the nature and the nurture schools. According to the naturalist school, personality is due to the genetic and physiological make-up of the individual. According to the nurture school, personality is the result of an individual's interactions with his environment. For further general reading on personality, glance through the very readable text by Helgard, Atkinson and Atkinson (1971). Eysenck (1964), although dated, still makes interesting reading. As there are different interpretations of the terms 'personality' and 'perception', the guide to further readings will follow the structure of Chapter 3.

1. *Personality*

Personality is divided into four areas.

Instinct and physical characteristics. Instinct refers to behaviour that is not learned but is inbred in particular species. Lorenz (1966) showed animals have mental mechanisms for preventing fights to the death between members of the same species. Similarly Sheldon (1954) insisted that personality formation is beyond the individual's control, and argued that certain personality stereotypes develop characteristics based on physical build.

Psychoanalytic theory. The Freudian hypothesis that personality formation is the result of early experiences plus the operation of a basic drive for pleasure has been adopted in a number of fields. In the area of management, read De Board (1978), and Loevinger and Knoll (1983) for a general view relating Freudian concepts to management. For a Freudian interpretation of aggression, read Kohn (1972). For those interested in the life of Freud and his work, the entertaining paperback by Wollheim (1975) is well worth the investment.

Type and trait theories. Type and trait theories hold that particular personality characteristics are common to all, but each person encompasses these characteristics to varying degrees. However, type and trait theories do not explain how character is formed. The difference between the two theories is their level of generality. One of the best-known type theorists is Carl Gustav Jung (1923), who coined the commonly-used term extroversion. For a good overview of Jung, read Storr (1973). The contribution of Myers and Briggs is based on the work of Jung. For further information on the Myers Briggs indicator, see Myers Briggs (1962), Stricker and Ross (1964a; 1964b; 1966). Two excellent texts emerge from the Myers Briggs typologies: Margerison and Lewis (1981) and Keirsey and Bates (1978).

It is worth noting the percentage distribution of Myers Briggs types offered in this section (80 per cent traditionalist/visionary; 10 per cent troubleshooter/negotiator; 10 per cent catalyst) of managers attending business school programmes. These data were gathered at Cranfield School of Management and as yet have not been published.

Type theories have been criticised as too simplistic, not capturing the complexity of human development. Trait theorists believe that a greater number of characteristics or traits exist and that personality can be measured and described by a score and scale. Eysenck's (1970) work is particularly interesting. Read also the popular texts by Eysenck, such as Eysenck (1977) examining neurosis and the easy guide to personality by Eysenck and Wilson (1978). Specifically in the management area, read Eysenck (1967). The paper examining personality, stress and disease (Eysenck 1983) is especially relevant.

Eysenck has, however, been considered more of a type than trait theorist as his work has concentrated on two major dimensions of personality – introversion/extroversion and neuroticism/stability. For a first-hand overview of personality and personality theorists, read Pervin (1980).

Cattell et al. (1970), based on Allport and Odbert's (1936) original work, developed the now famous 16PF-16 Personality Factor questionnaire. Using a statistical technique known as factor analysis, Cattell reduced 171 variables to 16 workable traits.

A recent interesting and well-referenced management study utilising a trait classification is Kim (1980), examining the relationship between personality and stimulating and non-stimulating tasks.

Social learning theory. Bandura (1977) and Mischel (1977) consider that people are capable of choice and self-discipline. In this way, they have legitimate control over themselves for, although they are influenced by environmental forces, they are also capable of choosing how to behave. People are responsive to situations but are able to influence them. In effect, people learn how to cope and interact well in situations, a process which Kakabadse and Parker (1984) term 'cognitive competencies'. For further information and readings on social learning theory, see Section 9's guide to further reading, as one interpretation of politics in organisations is based on a social learning theory framework.

A number of reviews and interesting research publications have emerged in the area of social learning theory in the two journals, the *Academy of Management Review* and the *Academy of Management Journal*. See, for example, Barclay (1982), Brief and Aldag (1981) and Jones (1983).

Perception

Perception as a topic has been linked to personality and to the social skills of individuals. The references on interpersonal skills provided in Section 4 will cover perception. However, for an explanation of the term, see Cooper and Makin (1981) and Hilgard, Atkinson and Atkinson (1971). Also see the chapters in Part III of Leavitt and Pondy's (1973) book, *Readings in Managerial Psychology*. Leavitt and Pondy have collected papers which relate perception to managerial situations.

Managerial mapping

The expression 'managerial mapping' has been popularised by Margerison and Lewis (1981) from their original and interesting work utilising Jung's theory. The process involves identifying the Myers Briggs type for each individual manager in a group, team, department, division, etc., and then laying open the likely implications of having that combination of managers in the particular group in question. Read also Jung (1923) and Margerison (1983). An interesting and entertaining book examines mapping from a different perspective, that of relating geography to people's expectations and choices – see Gould and White (1974).

Concluding comments

Although psychological testing, as a professional service, has been utilised by managers for some time, theories of personality have not been discussed in any depth in management texts. Leadership and styles of management have been far more popular areas of debate. However, it has come to be recognised that the underlying personality characteristics of an individual as well as the styles he learns to apply in managing situations are an important area to explore. Greatest attention has been given in this chapter to Jungian psychology as it is a model which managers can easily understand and utilise for managerial mapping. However, for those interested in the subject, equal attention needs to be given to the other areas of personality theory, especially social learning theory, which assumes that individuals continuously learn and develop but without being hampered by having to 'break out' of one set of personality characteristics and adopt new ones.

References

Allport, G.W. and Odbert, H.S. (1963), 'Trait-names: a psycholexical study', *Psychological Monographs*, Vol. 47, No. 211.

Bandura, A. (1977), *Social Learning Theory*, Prentice-Hall.

Barclay, L. (1982), 'Social Learning Theory: A Framework for Discrimination Research', *Academy of Management Review*, Vol. 7, No. 4, pp. 587–94.

Brief, A.P. and Aldag, R.J. (1981), 'The Self in Work Organisations: A Conceptual Review', *Academy of Management Review*, Vol. 6, No. 1, pp. 75–88.

Cattell, R.B., Eber, H.W. and Tatsuoka, M.M. (1970), *Handbook for the System Personality Factor Questionnaire* (16 PF), NFER Publishing Co. Windsor, Berks.

Cooper, C.C. and Makin, P. (1981), 'Personality and Individual Differences', in Cooper, C.C. and Makin, P. (eds), *Psychology for Managers*, Methuen.

De Board, R. (1978), *The Psychoanalysis of Organisations*, Tavistock.

Eysenck, H.J. (1964), *Uses and Abuses of Psychology*, Penguin.

Eysenck, H.J. (1967), 'Personality Patterns in various groups of businessmen', *Occupational Psychology*, Vol. 41, pp. 249–50.

Eysenck, H.J. (1970), *The Structure of Human Personality*, Methuen.

Eysenck, H.J. (1977), *You and Neurosis*, Fontana.

Eysenck, H.J. and Wilson, G. (1978), *Know Your Own Personality*, Pelican.

Eysenck, H.J. and Wilson, G. (1983), 'Stress, disease and personality: the innoculation effect', in Cooper, C.C. (ed), *Stress Research: Issues for the 80's*, Wiley.

Gould, P. and White, R. (1974), *Mental Maps*, Penguin.

Hilgard, E.R., Atkinson, R.C. and Atkinson, R. (1971), *Introduction to Psychology*, Harcourt Brace Jovanovich, New York.

Jones, G.R. (1983), 'Psychological Orientation and the Process of Organisational Socialisation: An Interactionist perspective', *Academy of Management Review*, Vol. 8, No. 3, pp. 464–74.

Jung, C. (1923), *Psychological Types*, Routledge and Kegan Paul.

Kakabadse, A. and Parker, C. (1984), 'The Undiscovered Dimension of Management Education: Politics in Organisations', in Cox, C. and Beck, J., *Management Development: Advances in Theory and Practice*, Wiley, Chapter 2.

Keirsey, D. and Bates, M. (1978), *Please understand me*, Promethean Books Inc., California: Del Mar.

Kim, J.S. (1980), 'Relationships of Personality to Perceptual and Behavioural Responses in Stimulating and Non-Stimulating Tasks', *Academy of Management Journal*, Vol. 23, No. 2, pp. 307–19.

Kohn, H.A. (1972), 'The Incidence of Hypertension and associated factors: The Israel ischemic heart disease study, *American Heart Journal*', Vol. 84, pp. 171–82.

Leavitt, H.J. and Pondy, L.R. (1973) (eds), *Readings in Managerial Psychology*, University of Chicago Press, 2nd ed.

Loevinger, J. and Knoll, E. (1983), 'Personality: stages traits and self', *Annual Review of Psychology*, Vol. 34, pp. 195–222.

Lorenz, K. (1966), *On Aggression*, Methuen.

Luft, J. and Ingham, H. (1955), 'The Johari Window: A graphical Model of Interpersonal Awareness' *Proceedings of the Western Training Laboratory in Group Development*, Los Angeles UCLA.

Margerison, C.J. and Lewis, R. (1981), 'Mapping Managerial Styles', *International Journal of Manpower*, Vol. 2, No. 1, Monograph.

Margerison, C.J. and Lewis, R. (1983), 'Mapping Managerial Work Preferences', *The Journal of Management Development*, Vol. 2, pp. 36–50.

Mischel, W. (1977), 'Self Control and the Self', In Mischel, T. (ed), *The Self: Psychological and Philosophical Issues*, Rowman and Littlefield, New Jersey.

Myers Briggs, I.B. (1962), *The Myers Briggs Type Indicator*,

Educational Testing Service, USA.

Pervin, L.A. (1980), *Personality: Theory, Assessment and Research*, Wiley.

Rogers, C. (1951), *Client Control Therapy: its Current Practice, Implications and Theory*, Houghton Mifflin.

Sheldon, W.H. (1954), *Atlas for Men: A guide for somatotyping the male at all ages*, Harper, New York.

Storr, A. (1973), *Jung*, Fontana Modern Masters.

Stricker, L.J. and Ross, J. (1964a), 'An assessment of some structural properties of the Jungian personality typology', *Journal of Abnormal Psychology*, Vol. 68, pp. 62–71.

Stricker, L.J. and Ross, J. (1964b), 'Some correlates of a Jungian personality inventory', *Psychol Rep*, Vol. 14, pp. 623–43.

Stricker, L.J. and Ross, J. (1966), 'Intercorrelations and reliability of the Myers-Briggs Type of Indicator Scales', *Psychol. Rep*, Vol. 12, pp. 287–93.

Wollheim, R. (1975), *Freud*, Fontana Modern Masters.

SECTION 4

The subject of managing personal relationships at work has attracted considerable attention since the 1950s. Popularised in the USA, various trends in interpersonal behaviour have begun and swung into decline. In the field of organisation development, characteristics such as openness, trust and caring (Cole 1981; Bridger 1980) have become the predominant values. Institutions such as the National Training Laboratories (NTL) in the USA adopted a philosophy of openness and caring in their interpersonal skills training. However, whatever the underlying philosophy, the three key areas are interpersonal communication, interpersonal needs and styles of interpersonal communication. Consequently, this guide to further readings will follow the chapter structure.

Interpersonal communication

Two interpretations of interpersonal communications are offered: first, the dynamics and mechanics of personal communication. Two texts in particular stand out in this field, Argyle (1979) and Collett (1978). Second, interpersonal communication from a personality angle, such as provided by Duck (1973) and Harré and Secord (1972).

Interpersonal needs

Schutz (1958) provides a milestone work in the area of interpersonal needs, for he recognised that individuals hold different expectations of others. Also see Laing, Phillipson and Lee (1966), who adopt a similar attitude to Schutz, but from a psychiatric point of view. Alternatively, Berne (1967) has taken a Freudian base in his examination of interpersonal needs, tensions and behaviours. Berne's work has provided the stimulus for the series of excellent texts that followed, such as Berne (1972), Harris (1979), Meininger (1973) and James and Jongeword (1971). All fall under the heading of transactional analysis.

Styles of interpersonal communication

Writings on management styles, personal and interpersonal styles of communication are legion. An exceedingly good book is Robert Bolton's (1979) *People Skills.* Apart from concentrating on the skills required for effective interpersonal communication, Bolton provides excellent references to other texts. In particular, read Kogan (1975) on listening skills, Cotler and Guerra (1976) on assertion skills and, for an old favourite, Carl Rogers (1961). In addition, see Cooper's (1976) collection of readings, examining advances in group training. Rather than provide a whole series of references, the following journals regularly publish articles on 'people skills': *Journal of Organisation Development* (USA published), *Journal of European and Industrial Training, Journal of Management Development, Leadership and Organisation Development Journal* and *Personnel Review.* The last four are published in the UK by MCB who, at selected intervals, publish a valuable selected annotated bibliography of these and other journals – see Petman (1983).

Concluding comments

In writing Chapters 3 and 4, we originally felt that they should be collapsed into one. From the point of view of managing interpersonal relationships, it is important to understand people in terms of their personalities, the way they view situations, their personal needs and how processes of communication actually work. Once the 'whole' person is understood, it is easier to know how to handle them! However, the subject matter is too great and, therefore, two chapters had to be written. Also, Chapter 9 on the politics of interpersonal relationships is closely linked with Chapters 3 and 4, for again the theme is that the person one is addressing needs to be fully understood, so that interpersonal skills can be applied in such a way that the individual is not unduly threatened. In fact, Chapters 3 and 4, and then 9, are perhaps two sides of the same coin. The coin is the individual and the two sides are understanding him and then managing him.

References

Albrecht, R.G. and Boshear, W.C. (1974), *Understanding People: Models and Concepts*, University Associates Inc Press.

Argyle, M. (1979), *The Psychology of Interpersonal Behaviour*, Penguin.

Berlo, D.K. (1960), *The Process of Communication*, Holt, Rinehart and Winston.

Berne, E. (1967), *Games People Play*, Grove Press.

Berne, E. (1972), *What Do You Say After You Say Hello?*, Corgi.

Bolton, R. (1979), *People Skills*, Prentice-Hall.

Bridger, H. (1980), 'The Relevant Training and Development of People for OD Roles in Open Systems', in Tresbech, K. (ed), *Organisation Development in Europe*, Paul Haupt, Berne.

Cole, D.W. (1981), *Professional Suicide: A Survival for You and Your Job*, McGraw-Hill.

Collett, P. (ed) (1977) *Social Rules and Social Behaviour*, Blackwell.

Cotler, S. and Guerna, J. (1976) *Assertion Training: A Humanistic Behavioural Guide to Self Dignity*, Champaign Ill., Research Press.

Duck, S.W. (1973), *Personal Relationships and Personal Constraints*, Wiley.

Harre, R. and Secord, P. (1972), *The Explanation of Social Behaviour*, Basil Blackwell.

Harris, T.A. (1979), *I'm OK – You're OK*, Pan.

James, M. and Jongeward, D. (1971), *Born to Win: Transactional Analysis with Gestalt Experiments*, Addison-Wesley.

Kogan, N. (1975), *Interpersonal Process Recall: A Method of Influencing Human Interaction*, Ann Arbor, Michigan State University Press.

Laing, R.D., Phillipson, H. and Lee, A.R. (1966), *Interpersonal Perception*, Tavistock.

Meininger, J. (1973), *Success Through Transactional Analysis*, Signet.

Pettman, B. (1983), 'Management: A Selected Annotated Bibliography', *Management Bibliographies and Reviews*, Vol. 9, No. 2/3, MCB University Press.

Rogers, C. (1961), *On Becoming a Person*, Houghton Mifflin.

Schutz, W.C. (1958), *FIRO: A Three Dimensional Theory of Interpersonal Behaviours*, Holt, Rinehart and Winston.

Shannon, C.E. and Weaver, W. (1949), *The Mathematical Theory of Communication*, University of Illinois Press.

SECTION 5

The discussion and further references concentrate on the two key aspects of motivation identified in the Chapter, namely person-centred motivation and job-related motivation.

Person-centred concept of motivation

The principal motivation theories in this area are the need satisfaction models (Maslow 1965), expectancy/volume theory (Vroom 1964) and goal-setting theory (Locke 1968). The underlying notion is that individuals are composed of complex internal psychological mechanisms which strongly influence their behaviour. Subsequent elaborations to these assumptions are made by Porter and Lawler (1968), who postulated that individuals develop subjective probability estimates of the extent to which a given level of effort leads to a certain standard of work performance, and in turn the extent to which given performance levels lead to a particular outcome. The assumption is that the greater the certainty in these two links, the stronger the predictability of work motivation or expected effort.

In addition to the references mentioned above or in the text of Chapter 5, read also Vroom and Deci (1970) for a perceptive and easy-to-read overview of psychology, paying particular attention to the Brayfield and Crockett article in this book.

Recent research or concept/model development publications include Fedor and Ferris (1981), who attempt to show the link between behaviour modification and cognitive theories of motivation. In a similar vein, Latham and Steele (1983) attempt to measure the motivational effects of participation in decision-making as opposed to goal-setting as a mechanism for improving task performance. In this article, the authors draw mainly on the early field studies on the effect of goal-setting on performance, such as Cock and French (1948), Meyer, Kay and French (1965), as well as more recent work, such as Latham and Marshall (1982), Tolchinsky and King (1980) and Latham, Steele and Saari (1982).

Alternatively, a number of research publications have emerged over the last decade examining the impact on intrinsic motivation of certain extrinsic factors. Pate (1978) thoroughly examines this whole area of debate in his literature review of motivation: an article well worth reading as much for the references as for the concepts offered. In the same vein are the research of Sherman and Smith (1984) as well as Daniel and Esser (1980) and Calder and Staw (1973).

Job-related motivation

Since the 1950s considerable research has been conducted into employee response to the design of jobs. Early research, such as that conducted by Shepard (1964), assumed that tasks could be designed by objective criteria such as functional specialisation. Later, it became recognised (Blood and Hulin 1967) that the design of tasks needed to take into account the job holders' perceptions, so that the job would be motivating. Much of this work was contained in the original Hackman and Lawler (1971) paper, which drew mainly from the original Turner and Lawrence (1965) research describing measures for six particular tasks attributes. Revised versions of Hackman and Lawler work were produced by Sims, Szilogyi and Keller (1926) and Hackman and Oldham (1975), the latter attaining notable popularity for their job diagnostic survey (JDS) instrument. For further information on the JDS in particular and task design and employee motivation in general, read Aldag and Brief's (1979) excellent work on task design and employee motivation.

In contrast, other writers and researchers have extended the concept of task-centred motivation to have broader organisational implications. London (1983) attempts to develop a theory of career motivation by considering it a multidimensional construct encompassing individually based characteristics as well as decisions about careers and personal behaviour. Miner (1980) explores the sources of professional motivation of management professors by examining an individual's capacity to identify with organisational hierarchies or professional values.

Other researchers have related motivation to even broader concepts, such as motivation and national characteristics, work epitomised by Tung's (1981) recent study of patterns of motivation in Chinese industrial enterprises. In contrast, Mills, Chase and Margulies (1983) relate concepts of motivation to workforce productivity in service organisations. They conclude that productivity can be improved by viewing the client/customer as a 'partial' employee, and extending conventional motivational concepts to include him.

Concluding comments

The subject of motivation is enormous. It has been widely researched and interpreted in numerous ways. Lawless (1979) indicates the breadth of the subject in his introduction to motivation by considering personality theories, cognitive theories, drive theories, instinct theories and even the philosophy of hedonism are all aspects of motivation. Consequently, an all-embracing review of the literature has not been attempted. The focus has been on practicability, emphasising individual drive and job characteristics.

References

Aldag, R.J. and Brief, A.P. (1979), *Task Design and Employee Motivation*. Glenview, Ill., Scott Faresman.

Alderfer, C.P. (1972), *Existence, Relatedness and Growth: Human Needs in Organisational Settings*, Free Press.

Blood, M.R. and Hulin, C.L. (1967), 'Alienation, Environmental Characteristics and Worker Passages', *Journal of Applied Psychology*, Vol. 51, pp. 284–90.

Calder, B.J. and Staw, B.M. (1975), 'Self-Perception and Intrinsic Motivation', *Journal of Personality and Social Psychology*, Vol. 31, pp. 599–605.

Cock, L. and French, J. (1948), 'Overcoming Resistance to Change', *Human Relations*, Vol. 1, pp. 512–32.

Daniel, T.L. and Esser, J.K. (1980), 'Intrinsic Motivation as Influenced by rewards, task interest and task structure', *Journal of Applied Psychology*, Vol. 65, pp. 566–73.

Fedor, D.B. and Ferris, G.R. (1981), 'Integrating OB Mod. with Cognitive Approaches to Motivation', *Academy of Management Review*, Vol. 6, No. 1, pp. 115–25.

Hackman, J.R. and Lawler, E.E. III (1971), 'Employee Reactions to Job Characteristics', *Journal of Applied Psychology*, Vol. 55, pp. 259–86.

Hackman, J.R., Lawler, E.E. and Protek, L.W. (1977) (eds), *Perspectives on Behaviour in Organisations*, McGraw-Hill.

Hackman, J.R. and Oldham, G.R. (1975), 'Development of the Job Diagnostic Survey', *Journal of Applied Psychology*, Vol. 60, pp. 159–70.

Hackman, J.R. and Oldham, G.R. (1976), 'Motivation through the Design of Work: Test of a Theory', *Organisational Behaviour and Human Performance*, Vol. 16, pp. 250–79.

Hackman, J.R. and Oldham, G.R. (1980), *Work Redesign*, Addison-Wesley.

Herzberg, F., Mausner, B. and Snyderman, B. (1959), *The Motivation to Work*, Wiley.

Latham, G.P. and Marshal, H.A. (1982), 'The Effects of Self-Set, participatively set and assigned goals on the performance of government employees', *Personnel Psychology*, Vol. 35, pp. 399–404.

Latham, G.P. and Steele, T.P. (1983), 'The Motivational Effects of Participation Versus Goal Setting in Performance', *Academy of Management Journal*, Vol. 26, No. 3, pp. 406–41.

Lawless, D.J. (1979), 'Organisational Behaviour: The Psychology of Effective Management', Prentice-Hall.

Locke, E.A. (1968), 'Toward a theory of task motivation and incentives', *Organisational Behaviour and Human Performance*, Vol. 3, pp. 157–89.

London, M. (1983), 'Toward a Theory of Career Motivation', *Academy of Management Review*, Vol. 8, No. 4, pp. 620–30.

Maslow, A.H. (1954), *Motivation of Personality*, Harper and Row.

Maslow, A.H. (1965), *Eupsychion Management*, Irwin-Dorsey.

McClelland, D.C. (1953), *The Achievement Motive*, Appleton-Century-Crofts.

McClelland, D.C. (1962), 'Business Drive and National Achievement', *Harvard Business Review*, July–August, pp. 99–112.

Meyer, H.H., Clay, E. and French, J.R.P. (1965), 'Split roles in performance appraisal', *Harvard Business Review*, Vol. 43, No. 1, pp. 123–9.

Mills, P.K., Chase, R.B. and Margulies, N. (1983), 'Motivating the client/Employee System as a genuine production Strategy', *Academy and Management Review*, Vol. 8, No. 2, pp. 307–10.

Miner, J.B. (1980), 'The Role of Management and Professional Motivation in the Career Success of Management Professors', *Academy of Management Journal*, Vol. 23, No. 3, pp. 487–508.

Nadler, D.A., Hackman, J.R. and Lawler, E.E. III (1979), *Managing Organisational Behaviour*, Little, Brown and Co.

Pate, L.E. (1978), 'Cognitive Versus Reinforcement Views of Intrinsic Motivation', *Academy of Management Review*, Vol. 3, No. 3, pp. 505–14.

Porter, L.W. and Lawler E.E. III (1968), *Managerial Attitudes and Performance*, Richard D. Irwin.

Shepard, J.M. (1964), 'Functional Specialisation, Alienation and Job Satisfaction, *Industrial and Labour Relations Review*, Vol. 23, pp. 207–19.

Sherman, J.D. and Smith, D.L. (1984), 'The Influence of Organisational Structure on Intrinsic versus Extrinsic Motivation', *Academy of Management Journal*, Vol. 27, No. 4, pp. 877–85.

Sims, H.P., Szilogyi, A.P. and Keller, R.T. (1976), 'The Measurement of Job Characteristics', *Academy of Management Journal*, Vol. 19, pp. 195–212.

Taylor, F.W. (1911), *The Principles of Scientific Management*, Harper & Row.

Tolchinsky, P.P. and King, D.C. (1980), 'Do goals mediate the effects of incentives on performance?', *Academy of Management Review*, Vol. 5, pp. 455–67.

Tung, R.C. (1981), 'Patterns of Motivation in Chinese Industrial Enterprises', *Academy of Management Review*, Vol. 6, No. 3, pp. 481–9.

Turner, A.N. and Lawrence, P.R. (1965), *Industrial Jobs and the Worker: An Investigation of Responses to Task Attributes*, Harvard University Press.

Vinnicombe, S. (1980), *Secretaries, Management and Organisations*, Heinemann Educational Books.

Vinnicombe, S. (1984), 'Communications and Job Satisfaction: A Case Study of an airline's cabin crew members', *Leadership and Organisation Development Journal*, Vol. 5, No. 1, pp. 2–7.

Vroom, V.H. (1964), *Work and Motivation*, Wiley.

Vroom, V.H. and Deci, E.L. (eds) (1970), *Management and Motivation*, Penguin.

SECTION 6

The two key areas are the function of groups and the powerful impact group processes can make on individuals. This distinction is a difficult one to make, and most texts would cover both areas.

The function of groups

This heading covers certain basic issues, such as the different sorts of group; the functions served by groups in organisations; the value of groups to individuals and organisations. Two texts are particularly valuable, Cartwright and Zander (1968) and Chapter 6 of Nadler, Hackman and Lawler (1979). Some early work is also interesting: read Homans (1950) and also Krech, Crutchfield and Ballakey (1962), Leavitt (1951 and 1975) and Davis (1969). Mayo (1945) is essential reading in order to appreciate the development of thinking in this area.

In addition, three interesting articles have recently appeared in the *Academy of Management Journal*, exploring the functional usage of groups in organisations. Stumf, Freedman and Zand (1979) examine the impact of interactions amongst group members on decision-making. Blumberg (1980) explores alternatives to job design in teams of autonomous workgroups, focusing on a Pennsylvania coal mine. Fry and Slocum (1984) study the effectiveness of workgroups as affected by organisational factors such as technology and structure. In addition, see an excellent article by Cummings (1978) discussing self-regulating workgroups as an alternative to traditional forms of work design.

Power of group processes

Writers and researchers have paid greatest attention to the topics of group dynamics, group processes and the impact these processes have on individuals and organisations. The early studies of group processes, in particular Bales (1950) and the methodologies he adopted for recording group interaction, are particularly interesting.

Especially interesting is the group dynamics school, based on the concepts of Lewin (1947). From these ideas emerged the group training and developing techniques and philosophies such as the T-group of the National Training Laboratories in Washington, USA or the Group Training Relations Association in the UK. For further references on using groups for organisation development purposes, see the references on teams in Section 12. See also Beckhard (1969), Beer (1976), Warner Burke (1974) and Bridger (1980).

Alternative areas of enquiry have been studies of social pressures brought to bear on individual members by group members. Early work by Festinger (1950) provides some basic reading. For those interested in group dynamics, it is also worth paying attention to the use of group processes for therapy. McCullough and Ely (1968) explore the use of groups in social work, whilst Walton's (1971) collection of papers outlines the value of small group psychotherapy. Two fascinating non-academic texts on individual and group interaction are John De Lorean's (1981) memories of his days at General Motors, and Kidder's (1981) revelations of the problems, pressures and interactions of installing computer and information systems in an organisation.

A good overview of groups and group processes is furnished by the interesting but now dated collection of readings edited by Peter Smith (1970). See also Berne's (1963) explanation of groups from a Freudian standpoint.

Group dynamics concepts have also been applied in industrial relations. The growth in popularity of quality circles is one such example; see Mohr and Mohr (1983) and Werther (1983). The other example is in the area of worker participation in managerial decision-making; see Wall and Lischeron (1977).

Concluding comments

As Handy (1976) points out, any discussion of groups immediately raises questions of leadership and motivation. Although leadership and motivation are discussed in this section, their involvement has been kept to a minimum so as to focus attention on the functions groups serve in organisations and also the power of group pressures in influencing individual behaviour.

References

Bales, R.F. (1950), *Interaction Process Analysis*, Addison-Wesley.

Beckhard, R. (1969), *Strategies of Organisation Development*, Addison-Wesley.

Beer, M. (1976), 'On Gaining Influence and Power for O.D.', *Journal of Applied Behavioural Science*, Vol. 6, pp. 44–51.

Belbin, R.M. (1981), *Management Teams: Why They Succeed or Fail*, Heinemann.

Bennis, W. (1966), *Changing Organisations*, McGraw-Hill.

Berne, E. (1963), *The Structure and Dynamics of Organisations and Groups*, Grove Press, New York.

Blumberg, M. (1980), 'Job Switching in Autonomous Work Groups: an Exploratory Study in a Pennsylvania Coal Mine', *Academy of Management Journal*, Vol. 23, No. 2, pp. 287–306.

Bridger, H. (1980), 'The Relevant Training and Development of People for OD Roles in Open Systems', in Tresbesch, K. (ed), *Organisation Development in Europe*, Paul Haupt, Berne.

Burke, Warner W. (1974), 'Managing Conflict Between Groups', in Adams, J.D., *New Technologies in Organisation Development*, Vol. 2, University Associates.

Cartwright, D. and Zander, A. (1968), *Group Dynamics: Research and Theory*, 3rd ed., Harper and Row.

Cummings, T. G. (1978), 'Self-regulating Work Groups: A Socio-technical Synthesis', *Academy of Management Review*, Vol. 3, No. 3, pp. 623–34.

Davis, J.H. (1969), *Group Performance*, Addison-Wesley.

De Lorean, J. and Wright, J.P. (1981), *On A Clear Day, You Can See General Motors*, Sidgwick and Jackson.

Festinger, L. (1950), *Social Pressures on Informal Groups: A Study of Housing Project*, Harper.

Fry, L.W. and Slocum, J.W. Jr (1984), 'Technology, Structure and Workgroup Effectiveness: A Test of a Contingency Model', *Academy of Management Journal*, Vol. 27, No. 2, pp. 221–46.

Handy, C. (1976), *Understanding Organisations*, Penguin.

Homans, G. (1950), *The Human Group*, Harcourt Brace Jovanovich.

Kidder, T. (1981), *The Soul of a New Machine*, Penguin.

Krech, D., Cruchfield, R.S. and Ballackey, E.L. (1962), *The Individual in Society*, McGraw-Hill.

Leavitt, H.J. (1951), 'Some Effects of Certain Communication Patterns on Group Performance', *Journal of Abnormal Psychology*, Vol. 46, pp. 38–50.

Leavitt, H.J. (1975), 'Suppose We Took Groups Seriously', in Cass, E.L. and Zimmer, F.G., *Man and Work in Society*, Van Nostrand Reinhold, New York.

Lewin, K. (1947), 'Frontiers in Group Dynamics', *Human Relations*, Vol. 1, No. 1, pp. 16–40.

Mayo, E. (1945), *The Social Problems of our Industrial Civilisation*, Harvard University Press.

McCullough, M.K. and Ely, P.J. (1968), *Social Work with Groups*, Routledge and Kegan Paul, Library of Social Work.

Mohr, W.L. and Mohr, H. (1983), *Quality Circles: Changing Images of People at Work*, Addison-Wesley.

Nadler, D.A., Hackman, J.R. and Lawler, E.E. III (1979), *Managing Organisational Behaviour*, Little Brown and Co.

Schein, E.H. (1969), *Process Consultation*, Addison-Wesley.

Schermerhorn, J. (1984), *Management for Productivity*, Wiley.

Smith, P.B. (ed) (1970), *Group Processes*, Penguin Modern Psychology Readings.

Stumf, S.A., Freedman, R.D. and Zand, D.E. (1979), 'Judgemental Decisions: A Study of Interactions Amongst Group Membership, Group Functioning and the Decision Situation', *Academy of Management Journal*, Vol. 22, No. 4, pp 765–82.

Tuckman, B.W. (1965), 'Developmental Sequences in Small Groups', *Psychological Bulletin*, Vol. 63, No. 6, pp. 384–99.

Wall, T.D. and Lischeron, J.A. (1977), *Worker Participation: A Critique of Literature and Some Fresh Evidence*, McGraw-Hill.

Walton, H. (ed) (1971), *Small Group Psychotherapy*, Penguin Science of Behaviour Series.

Wanous, J.P., Reickers, A.E. and Malik, S.D. (1984), 'Organisational Socialisation and Group Development: Toward an Integrative Perspective', *Academy of Management Review*, Vol. 9, No. 4, pp. 670–83.

Werther, W.B. Jr (1983), 'Going in Circles with Quality Circles? Management Development Implications', *Journal of Management Development*, Vol. 2, No. 1, pp. 3–18.

SECTION 7

In this section we did not attempt to explore all existing theories and models of leadership and management style. That would have required a book on its own. Instead, we concentrated on the way in which the views of leadership as a characteristic of the individual manager have changed; from theories that leadership is an inherent personal quality, to recent theories which indicate that, to be an effective leader, a manager requires primarily to develop two basic skills: those of diagnosing situations, and those of varying his leadership and interpersonal styles to match the requirements of those situations.

Within this context, four approaches to the study of leadership emerged: trait theory, behavioural theory, contingency theory, and situational leadership theory. Stogdill (1984) provides a survey of the research on personal factors associated with leadership, and Ghiselli, (1971) outlined particular qualities important for successful leadership. See also Campbell et al. (1970) for a good overview of leadership thinking.

Trait theory

See references on trait theory in Section 5. From a leadership interpretation point of view read Stogdill (1974).

Behavioural theory

Read Taylor (1911) for an excellent treatise on scientific management. In order to appreciate the historical growth and development of the human relations school, read Mayo (1945, 1947). Also read the two McGregor texts (1967a, 1967b). The work of Taylor and Mayo helped define two aspects of leadership behaviour – autocratic and democratic, a theme further expanded by McGregor. For a good practical summary of democratic/autocratic leadership read Tannenbaum and Schmidt (1973). In keeping with the behavioural approach, Likert (1961, 1965) and Blake and Mouton (1964, 1978) wrote seminal works on the two-dimensional leadership behaviour theories (ie concern for task; concern for people) which emerged from work commenced at the Ohio State University and the University of Michigan in the 1940s. Likert's last book before his death (Likert and Likert 1976) maintains a similar theme.

Contingency theory

In the section and generally in the literature greatest attention is paid to contingency theory and situational leadership theory. The underlying assumption is that there is no universal ideal style of management. The difference between the two theories lies in the notion of managerial success and effectiveness. For further reading purposes, the Vroom–Yetton model is placed under the banner of contingency theory. Read Vroom and Yetton (1973) and Vroom (1976). For an evaluation of the Vroom–Yetton model, see Jago and Vroom (1980). The Fiedler work is especially worthy of attention. See Fiedler (1967); Fiedler and Chemers (1974); Fiedler, Chemers and Mahar (1978).

Situational leadership

The most popular and widely-read proponents of situational leadership are Hersey and Blanchard (1976, 1982). A number of recent research publications in this area are also worth a mention. See McFillen and New (1979); Bartol, Evans and Stith (1978); Volenzi and Dessler (1978); Smith, Carnon and Alexander (1984).

Concluding comments

Seven other leadership theories lie outside the scope of this book. Two main ones are path–goal theory and action-centred leadership. House's (1971) path–goal theory considers that good managers identify and clear the paths subordinates require to take to achieve work and personal goals. Adair (1979) argues that leader effectiveness depends on the leader fulfilling the requirements of the task, team maintenance, and individual needs of group members. Sayles (1979) asks what will be the new areas of focus in leadership research and, interestingly, considers that personality theory will become an important concern (see Section 3). Sayles highlights Jungian theory as a source of further exploration. Ironically, Sayles implies that trait theory may re-emerge as a focal area of research. For a further view on where leadership research should go, read Karmel (1978).

References

Adair, J. (1979), *Action-centred Leadership*, Gower.

Bartol, D.M. Evans, C.L. and Stith, M.T. (1978), 'Black Versus White Leaders: A Comparative Review of the Literature', *Academy of Management Review*, Vol. 3, No. 2, pp. 293–304.

Blake, R.R. and Mouton, J.S. (1964), *The Managerial Grid,* Gulf Publishing Company.

Blake, R.R. and Mouton, J.S. (1978), *The New Managerial Grid*, Gulf Publishing Company.

Campbell, J.P., Dunnette, M.D., Lawler, E.E. III and Weick, K.E. (1978), *Managerial Behaviour, Performance and Effectiveness*, McGraw-Hill.

Drucker, P.F. (1974), *Management: Tasks, Responsibilities, Practices*, Harper and Row.

Fiedler, F.E. (1967), *A Theory of Leadership Effectiveness*, McGraw-Hill.

Fiedler, F.E. and Chemers, M.E. (1974), *Leadership and Effective Management*, Scott Foresman and Company.

Fiedler, F.E., Chemers, M.E. and Mahat, L. (1978), *The Leadership Match Concept*, Wiley.

Ghiselli, E.E. (1971), *Explorations in Management Talent*, Goodyear, Glenview, Illinois.

Hall, D.T. (1976), *Careers in Organisation*, Goodyear, Glenview, Illinois.

Hersey, P. and Blanchard, K. (1976), *Situational Leadership*, Centre for Creative Leadership, USA.

Hersey, P. and Blanchard, K. (1982), *The Management of Organisational Behaviour*, 4th ed., Prentice-Hall.

House, R.J. (1971), 'A Path–Goal Theory of Leadership Effectiveness', *Administrative Science Quarterly*, Vol. 16, No. 3, pp. 321–8.

House, R.J. and Mitchell, T.R. (1974), 'Path–goal theory of

leadership', *Journal of Contemporary Business*, Autumn, pp. 81–97.

Jago, A.G. and Vroom, V.H. (1980), 'An Evaluation of Two Alternatives to the Vroom/Yetton Normative Model', *Academy of Management Journal*, Vol. 23. No. 2, pp. 347–55.

Karmel, B. (1978), 'Leadership: A Challenge to Traditional Research Methods and Assumptions', *Academy of Management Review*, Vol. 3, No. 3, pp. 475–82.

Likert, R. (1961), *New Patterns of Management*, McGraw-Hill.

Likert, R. (1965), *The Human Organisation*, McGraw-Hill.

Likert, R. and Likert, J.G. (1976), *New Ways of Managing Conflict*, McGraw-Hill.

Mayo, E. (1945), *The Social Problems of an Industrial Civilisation*, Harvard University.

Mayo, E. (1947), *The Political Problems of an Industrial Society*, Harvard University.

McFillen, J.M. and New, J.R. (1979), 'Situational Determinants of Supervisor Attributions and Behaviour', *Academy of Management Journal*, Vol. 22, No. 4, pp. 793–809.

McGregor, D. (1976a), *The Human Side of Enterprise*, Harper and Row.

McGregor, D. (1976b), *The Professional Manager*, McGraw-Hill.

Sayles, L. (1979), *Leadership: What Effective Managers Really Do ... And How They Do It*, McGraw-Hill.

Smith, J.E., Carson, K.P. and Alexander, R.A. (1984), 'Leadership: It Can Make a Difference', *Academy of Management Journal*, Vol. 27, No. 4, pp. 765–76.

Stogdill, R.M. (1974), *Handbook of Leadership*, The Free Press.

Tannenbaum, R. and Schmidt, W.H. (1973). 'How to Choose a Leadership Pattern', *Harvard Business Review*, Vol. 51, May–June, pp. 162–80.

Taylor, F.W. (1911), *The Principles of Scientific Management*, Harper & Row.

Volenzi, E. and Dessler, G. (1978), 'Relationships of Leader Behaviour, Subordinate Role Ambiguity and Subordinate Job Satisfaction', *Academy of Management Journal*, Vol. 21, No. 4, pp. 671–8.

Vroom, V.H. and Yetton, P.W. (1973), *Leadership and Decision Making*, University of Pittsburgh Press.

Vroom, V.H. (1976), 'Leadership' in Dunnette, M.D. (ed), *Handbook of Organisational Psychology*, Rand McNally.

SECTION 8

A great deal has been written on the subjects of power and politics but from many different angles. Little·agreement seems to exist as to the definition, nature and basis of these topic areas or whether power and politics are integrally linked or conceptually separate. In this book, power and politics are treated as separate entities. Power is defined as the 'potential to do'. Politics is considered the 'ability to act and interact'. Not all writers and researchers would agree with such a distinction.

In order to gain a sensible picture of the literature on power, it is important to appreciate the origins of the concept of power, the various interpretations of power and the important links between power and culture. Despite the broad and scattered nature of the subject area, three texts (Pfeffer, 1978; Kakabadse and Parker, 1984; Cobb, 1984) provide a reasonably comprehensive analysis.

Emergence of power

Historically, power has been an important interest of community development theorists, such as Bohl (1957) and Wolfinger (1971), who concentrated on how to assist communities to improve their social facilities and standing. Consequently, power was seen in Weberian terms of coalition formation, strife, conflict and bargaining; namely 'A having the power over B to the extent that he can get B to do something that B would not otherwise do'. Although different interpretations of the term power have since been offered, a valuable text equating power with strife and bargaining is Bacharach and Lawler (1980). Two texts providing an in-depth examination of power in relation to community development are Domhoff (1980) and Libbert and Imershein (1977). From this tradition of the visible application of power to achieve desired outcomes emerged the concept of power levers, namely the different power strategies that can be applied in order to achieve certain ends. Texts to read are French and Raven (1959) and Raven (1965). In fact, it was French and Raven (1959) who identified five power levers, reward, coercive, legitimate, referent and expert power; Raven (1965) added information power to the list and Hersey Blanchard and Nortemeyer (1979) concluded that a seventh power lever exists, namely connection power.

Alternative views of power

The Cambridge academic, Steven Lukes (1974), challenged the community development interpretation of power as too simplistic and offered instead his three-dimensional view of power. Although the degree of sophistication increases from level 1 to level 3, Lukes considers the concept of power is only applicable at the individual level. Writers on power concentrating at the individual level tend to confuse the terms power and politics. The majority of texts in this area deal with the likely operational steps (means) towards more effective political behaviour. References to the various approaches to politics are offered in Section 9.

Other writers have attempted to measure power-oriented behaviour at the organisational subunit level. Hickson et al. (1971) postulates that power is the ability of the organisational subunit to determine its own strategies and activities. Hinings et al. (1974) and Benson (1961) use the Hickson approach for further exploration. These three groups of researchers offer a 'strategic contingencies' approach to power behaviour.

Other writers adopt a total organisational strategic view Mintzberg (1984) suggests that organisations pass through a number of power stages which in turn have strong implications for each entity's capacity to be responsive to societal or market needs. The more established an organisation becomes, the less it is likely to be proactive in its intra-organisational relationships. In contrast, Astley and Sachdera (1984) identify three sources of organisational power (hierarchical authority, resource control and network centrality) and consider structural power complex because the interactions between these three sources lead to tension and conflict.

As highlighted in the chapter, a number of writers equate various financial and policy strategic planning techniques with the concept of power. Wildavsky (1968) suggests that the budgeting process is really a form of power acquisition through the allocation of financial resources. Cyert and March (1964) consider that the budget represents the outcome of bargaining and leads towards organisational coalitions. Hofstede (1978) endorses both views, for he considers management control systems such as PPBS and MBO to be ineffective, since they are based on a cybernetic philosophy which is homeostatic in approach but are applied in organisational environments which are heterostatically oriented. Read also Dirsmith and Joblansky (1979), who explicitly identify zero-based budgeting (ZBB) as both a management technique and a power strategy to apply to poorly-understood problem areas, taking into account discrete decisions of which those involved in the situation may only be partially aware.

Certain researchers have studied decision-making patterns at the individual, subunit and organisational level and have presented their data as case studies. However, their conclusions emphasise power process in organisations rather than explicit decision-making behaviour. Hammer and Stern (1980) examined the role perceptions of workers and management in a furniture factory and concluded that the workforce preferred an internal equalisation of power. Hall's (1976) study of the fall of the *Saturday Evening Post* showed that the behaviour of groups in the magazine industry was as robust a predictor of any publishing organisation's future growth or demise as management's collective decision-making behaviour.

Power and organisation culture

Studies exploring the culture of organisations have developed independently of any work on power. However, Pettigrew (1979) and Mangham (1978) point out that a relationship between organisation culture and concepts or power does exist. Pettigrew (1979) indicates that any analysis of cultures could produce useful results in areas such as understanding the processes of legitimation and delegitimation in organisations, or desired leadership characteristics in certain situations or amongst entrepreneurs. Mangham's (1978) social dramas approach to the analysis of interventions in organisations leaves him to conclude that the power of an interventionist is dependent on his ability to diagnose the kinds of 'scripts' he sees his clients adopting and the scripts he encourages his clients to accept.

Other readings in the area of organisation culture place particular emphasis on how myths and accepted practices influence the formation of issues and patterns of interrelationships: Clark's (1972) examination of organisational sagas, Trice and Beyer (1984) in their analysis of multiple cultures or a more person-oriented analysis by Pasquale et al. (1978) of people who seem unable to 'fit' into certain organisations.

For more general reading, see Deal and Kennedy's (1982) and Schein's (1985) treatises on corporate cultures. An interesting collection of papers on organisational culture can be found in the September 1983 (Vol. 28) issue of *Administrative Science Quarterly*, devoted entirely to this topic.

Concluding comments

A number of writers (Cavanaugh 1984; Ryan 1984) have strongly argued that there is little agreement on the meaning of the word power. However, certain important themes need to be included in any discussion of power:

1 Power needs to be considered as a base from which to act.

2 The application of power involves the utilisation of resources.

3 Power has commonly been seen as a means of attaining particular goals, by the use of power levers.

4 Equally, power has been viewed as intrinsically linked to organisation culture. Hence, the manner of application of the power levers will be strongly influenced by the rise of values, myths and rituals and beliefs in the organisation. No analysis of power can take place without an analysis of organisational culture.

5 Power has been seen not just as a means of attaining goals, but also as a mechanism for identifying and highlighting perceived key issues.

These are the themes we have attempted to cover in the chapter.

References

Astley, W.G. and Sachdera, P.S. (1984) 'Structural Sources of Intra-organisational Power: A Theoretical Synthesis', *Academy of Management Review*, Vol. 9, No. 1, pp. 104–13.

Bacharach, S.B. and Lawler, E.J. (1980), *Power and Politics in Organisations*, Jossey Bass.

Benson, J.K. (1961), 'The Interorganisational Network as a Political

Economy', *Administrative Science Quarterly*, Vol. 6, pp. 229–49.

Burke, Warner W. (1976), 'Organisation Development in Transition', *Journal of Applied Behavioural Science*, Vol. 12, No. 1, pp. 22–43.

Cavanaugh, M.S. (1984), 'A Typology of Social Power' in Kakabadse, A.P. and Parker, C. (eds), *Power Politics and Organisations: A Behavioural Science View*, Wiley, pp. 3–20.

Clark, B.R. (1972), 'The Organisational Saga in Higher Education', *Administrative Science Quarterly*, Vol. 17, pp. 178–84.

Cobb, A.T. (1984), 'An Episodic Model of Power: Toward an Integration of Theory and Research', *Academy of Management Review*, Vol. 9, No. 3, pp. 482–93.

Cyert, R. and March, J. (1964), *A Behavioural Theory of the Firm*, Prentice Hall.

Dahl, R.A. (1957), 'The Concept of Power', *Behavioural Science*, Vol. 2, pp. 207–25.

Deal, T.E. and Kennedy, A.A. (1982), *Corporate Cultures: The Rites and Rituals of Corporate Life*, Addison-Wesley.

Dirsmith, H.W. and Joblansky, S.F. (1979), 'Zero-based budgeting as a management technique and political strategy', *Academy of Management Review*, Vol. 4, No. 4, pp. 555–65.

Domhoff, G.W. (ed) (1980), *Power Structure Research*, Sage.

French, J.R.P. Jr (1956), 'A Formal Theory of Social Power', *Psychological Review*, Vol. 63, pp. 181–94.

French, J.R.P. Jr and Raven, B. H. (1959), 'The Bases of Social Power' in Cartwright, D. (ed), *Studies of Social Power*, Ann Arbor MI: Institute of Social Research, The University of Michigan.

Hall, R.J. (1976), 'A System Pathology of an Organisation. The Rise and Fall of the old Saturday Evening Post', *Administrative Science Quarterly*, Vol. 21, No. 2, pp. 185–211.

Hammer, T.H. and Stern, R.N. (1980), 'Employee Ownership: Implications for the Organisation Distribution of Power', *Academy of Management Journal*, Vol. 23, No. 1, pp. 78–100.

Handy, C. (1976), *Understanding Organisations*, Penguin Education Series.

Harrison, R. (1972), 'How to Describe Your Organisation', *Harvard Business Review*, Sept/Oct.

Herman, S.M. (1974), 'Shadow of Organisation Development', Paper presented to the NTL Institute Conference on New Technology in OD, New Orleans, February.

Hersey, P., Blanchard, K.H. and Nortemeyer W.E. (1979), *Situational Leadership, Perception and the impact of power,*

Centre for Leadership Studies, Learning Resources Corporation, pp. 1–5.

Hickson, D.J., Hinings, C.R., Lee, C.A., Schneck, R.E. and Pennings, J.M. (1971), 'A Strategic Contingencies Theory of Intraorganisational Power', *Administrative Science Quarterly*, Vol. 16, No. 2, pp. 216–29.

Hinings, C.R., Hickson, D.J., Pennings, J.M. and Schneck R.E. (1974), 'Structural Conditions of Intraorganisational Power', *Administrative Science Quarterly*, Vol. 19, pp. 22–44.

Hofstede, G. (1978), 'The Poverty of Management Control Philosophy', *Academy of Management Review*, July, pp. 450–60.

Kakabadse, A.P. and Parker, C. (1984), 'Towards a Political Theory of Politics in Organisations' in Kakabadse, A.P. and Parker, C. (eds), *Power, Politics and Organisations: A Behavioural Science View*, Wiley.

Lawless, D.J. (1979), *Organisational Behaviour: The Psychology of Effective Management*. 2nd ed., Prentice-Hall.

Liebert, R.J. and Imershein, A.W. (eds) (1977), *Power, Paradigms and Community Research*, Sage Studies in International Sociology, Vol. 9, Sage Publications.

Lukes, S. (1974), *Power: A Radical View*, Macmillan.

Mangham, J.L. (1978), *Interactions and Interventions in Organisations*, Wiley.

Mintzberg, H. (1984), 'Power and Organisation Life Cycles', *Academy of Management Review*, Vol. 9, No. 2, pp. 207–24.

Pasquale, A.C., Sherman, N.K., Krinsky, L.W. and Yolles, S.F. (1978), *Misfits in Industry*, S P Medical and Scientific Books, Spectrum Publications.

Pettigrew, A.M. (1979), 'On Studying Organisational Cultures', *Administrative Science Quarterly*, Vol. 24, pp. 570–87.

Pfeffer, J. (1981), *Power in Organisations*, Pitman.

Raven, B.H. (1965), 'Social Influence and Power', in Steiner, I.D. and Fishbein, M. (eds), *Current Studies in Social Psychology*, Holt, Rinehart and Winston.

Ryan, M. (1984), 'Theories of Power' in Kakabadse, A.P. and Parker, C. (eds), *Power, Politics and Organisations: A Behavioural Science View*, Wiley, pp. 20–45.

Trice, H.M. and Beyer, J.M. (1984), 'Studying Organisational Cultures through Rites and Ceremonials', *Academy of Management Review*, Vol. 9, No. 4, pp. 653–9.

Vickers, Sir G. (1968), *Valve Systems and Social Processes*, Tavistock.

Weber, M. (1947), *The Theory of Social and Economic*

Organisation, Oxford University Press.

Wildavsky, A. (1968), 'Budgeting as a Political Process', in Sills, D.A. (ed), *The Interventionists' Encyclopedia of the Social Services*, Collier-MacMillan, pp. 192–9.

Wolfinger, R.E. (1971), 'Non-decisions and the Study of Local Politics', *American Political Science Review*, Vol. 65, pp. 1063–80.

SECTION 9

Like the concept of power, organisational politics has been defined and interpreted in numerous ways. The interpretation of organisational politics adopted for this book is that of the ability to act or interact in various situations. The ability to act implies a personal skill. However, the interpretation adopted is broader, encompassing concepts from social learning theory.

In order to appreciate why this view has been adopted, we divide the literature into three sections: the intents and means philosophy, dilemmas for management and organisation development, application of social learning theory. Read Kakabadse and Parker (1984a) for an overview of these three areas.

Intents and means philosophy

The bulk of the literature on organisational politics centres on the likely operational steps (means) towards more effective interpersonal behaviour in order for the individual to be able to achieve his objectives (intents). Hence, politics in organisations is largely viewed as individually-based behaviour. Pettigrew (1977) has probably been one of the more influential writers, identifying five strategies towards increasing the influence of internal consultants. Schein (1977) adds to Pettigrew's work by describing six strategies that change agents need to practise. Farrell and Petersen (1982) concentrate on a typology of political behaviour in organisations, but still at the individual level. In contrast, Fischer (1983) analyses politics at the organisational level by examining the external pressures that can be faced by any enterprise and the political strategies that the organisation can adopt to attempt to overcome its problems. Similarly, Mangham (1979) deals with politics at the organisational level but from the point of view of introducing major changes into organisations.

Dilemmas for management and organisational development

Kakabadse and Parker (1984a) strongly imply that in the fields of management and organisation development there has emerged an expressed philosophy of care, trust and affection for the individual. Although these values have dominated the field of organisation development, certain writers have questioned the practicability of such norms. Bennis (1969) recognised this development, stating that OD practitioners 'rely exclusively on two sources of influence, truth and love' (p 81). Such an approach is justified under conditions of collaboration. What of the other side of humanity – behaviours which Herman (1974) describes as anger, coercion, hate and aggression, which are as usual as love, peacefulness and compassion? There certainly has been a reluctance to develop conceptually what Warner Burke (1976) calls the 'darker side of humanity', lest it should taint and corrupt and give licence to practise the 'blacker arts of human behaviour'.

Until now, writers on OD have equated politics with behaviours which are considered unpleasant but nevertheless practical, pragmatic and necessary. Unpleasant as politics may seem to be, the need to find a new philosophical and conceptual base for OD and a disappointment with the operational results of OD interventions have stimulated a number of writers (Nord, 1974; Beer, 1976; Bowen, 1977) to explore the field of political behaviour.

Studies of political behaviour in OD circles have concentrated on examining both the intended outcomes of interventions and the necessary means of achieving those intents. Beer (1976), for example, emphasises an intents/means approach to interventions. Conceptually, however, the arguments have not progressed, as OD writers find themselves unable to develop beyond the good/evil view of political behaviour in dealings with human beings. Notions of power and politics have been defined as A intending to influence B, but in a way that B might not approve if he became sufficiently aware of A's intentions.

Application from social learning theory

Kakabadse and Parker (1984b) refute the assertion that politics is a series of behaviours that are negative or the only course that an individual can pursue because circumstances so dictate. They consider that individual behaviour is driven by cognitive maps. Fundamentally, the hypothesis offered is that human beings operate off cognitive schema: namely the way each individual receives, organises, plans, regulates and transmits information to other human beings. In other words, people learn to respond, manipulate and utilise their surrounding environment and thereby are capable of choice and self-regulation. Two social learning theorists, Bandura (1977) and Mischel (1977), suggest that people use symbolic processes to represent events and communicate with others. The famous sociologist Erving Goffman (1974) suggests that frames of individual reference are created through subjective interpretation of social interaction. Tolman (1924) considers that we structure our experience to form purposive maps which drive behaviour. Broadbent (1977 has suggested that subjective maps may be constructed on a hierarchical basis forming global and local schema. By global schema is meant the dominant values held by the individual, where the local schema represent the actions and functions associated with these values.

Drawing on such notions, Kakabadse and Parker (1984a, 1984b) view politics as an influence process which can be perceived as positive or negative depending on whether one's own purposive maps are being supported or threatened. A cognitive approach to the analysis of individual behaviour in organisations assumes that all behaviour in organisations is political. In most circumstances, most individuals find the behaviour of other persons or groups acceptable. Behaviour considered to be acceptable is behaviour that fits with the schema strategy or map of the individual. Problems arise when an individual or group rejects, misunderstands or responds with inappropriate behaviours to the actions or demands of another individual or group. In other words, the person concerned is unable to recognise or assimilate the demands and behaviours of the individual or group with whom he is interacting. Such negative consequences that may arise from individual or group interaction have largely been interpreted as 'political'.

Kakabadse and Parker (1984b) point out that no single logic or rationality exists which can adequately explain the range of behaviours adopted in an organisation. In fact, the way to view organisations and groups is through a multirational framework: different and often conflicting rationales exist in any organisation and each individual or group may change its rationale over time. Inevitably all behaviour in organisation, based on this logic, holds political connotations.

Concluding comments

Most texts on politics discuss, sometimes exclusively, the strategies and tactics for increasing an individual's interpersonal influence. Chapter 9 has pursued this path but more from the point of view of showing the reader the different ways of coping with unshared meaning. The two key texts (Kakabadse and Parker, 1984a, 1984b) emphasise the concept of multirationality, namely that different individuals and groups hold their own interpretations of situations. It is considered in these two texts that it is simply not easy to help people communicate and understand each other in situations where they have not only differences of views and values, but also different expectations, goals and personal objectives. Patterns of influence and interaction can be viewed and experienced as positive or negative, but it is imperative that each person has the means to negotiate outcomes that are to his satisfaction or at least tolerable.

References

Bandura, A. (1977), *Social Learning Theory*, Prentice-Hall.

Beer, M. (1976), 'On gaining influence and power for OD', *Journal of Applied Behavioural Science*, Vol. 6, pp. 44–51.

Bennis, W.G. (1969), 'Unresolved Problems Facing Organisation Development', *Business Quarterly*, Winter, pp. 80–4.

Bowen, D.D. (1977), 'Value Dilemmas in Organisation Development', *Journal of Applied Behavioural Science*, Vol. 13, No. 4, pp. 543–55.

Broadbent, D.E. (1977), 'Hidden Pre-Attentive Processes', *American Psychologist*, Vol. 32, pp. 109–17.

Burke, Warner W. (1976), 'Organisation Development in Transition', *Journal of Applied Behavioural Science*, Vol. 12, No. 1, pp. 22–43.

Farrell, D. and Petersen, J.C. (1982), 'Patterns of Political Behaviour in Organisations', *Academy of Management Review*, Vol. 7, No. 3, pp. 403–12.

Fischer, P.W. (1983), 'Strategies Toward Political Pressures: A Typology of Firm Responses', *Academy of Management Review*, Vol. 8, No. 1, pp. 71–8.

Goffman, E. (1974), *Frame Analysis: An Essay on the Organisation of Experience*, Penguin.

Herman, S.M. (1974), 'The Shadow of Organisation Development',

Paper presented to the NTL Institute Conference on New Technology in OD, New Orleans, February.

Kakabadse, A.P. (1983), *The Politics of Management,* Gower; Nichols Publishing Co., New York.

Kakabadse, A.P. and Parker, C. (1984a), 'Towards a Theory of Political Behaviour in Organisations', in Kakabadse, A.P. and Parker, C. (eds), *Power, Politics and Organisations: A Behavioural Science View*, Wiley.

Kakabadse, A.P. and Parker, C. (1984b), 'The Undiscovered Dimension of Management Education: Politics in Organisations' in Cox, C. and Beck, J. (eds) *Management Development Advances in Practice and Theory*, Wiley.

Mangham, I. (1979), *The Politics of Organisational Change*, Associated Business Press.

Mischel, W. (1977), 'Self-Control of the Self' in Mischel, T. (ed), *The Self: Psychological and Philosophical Issues*, Rowman and Littlefield, New Jersey.

Nord, W.R. (1974), 'The Failure of Current Applied Behavioural Science – A Marxian Perspective', *Journal of Applied Behavioural Science*, Vol. 10, No. 4, pp. 557–78.

Pettigrew, A.M. (1977), 'Strategy Formulation as a political process', *International Studies of Management and Organisation*, Vol. 7, pp. 78–87.

Schein, V.E. (1977), 'Individual power and political behaviour in organisations: An inadequately explored reality', *Academy of Management Review*, January, pp. 64–72.

Taylor, F.W. (1911), *The Principles of Scientific Management,* Harper & Row.

Tolman, E.C. (1924), *Behaviour and Psychological Man*, University of California Press.

The terms strategy and policy are difficult to define and have been used in the literature in a multiplicity of ways. Strategy and policy have been applied to organisations in terms of the mission and objectives pursued by organisations in the market place specifically, or society in general. Equally, the terms have been used to both analyse and describe the tensions, pressures and difficulties of the interface between internal organisation cultures and the external market, social and political environment. On this point, Stopford, Channon and Constable (1980) have published an excellent book of teaching cases, emphasising the internal/external tensions and difficult strategic choices faced by organisations.

Writers on strategy have adopted economic, historical, sociological and behavioural science angles. In fact, one world renowned business school academic, Professor Derek Pugh, at an Association of Teachers of Management Conference in 1976 questioned whether business policy/strategy was a subject at all.

In order to provide clarity, a loose distinction is offered between the broad-ranging analyses of nation states and trends in society, and the more specific view of strategy as applied to organisations.

Societal strategies

A popular approach to societal strategy is that championed by Alvin Toffler (1970; 1981) in such texts as *Future Shock* and *Third Wave*. Toffler, a futurist, projects the likely impact on society of new technological developments. Toffler's assumption that the new computers and attention paid to information technology is likely to disrupt certain primary institutions in society has been seriously challenged by Edwards (1985). Edwards (1985) considers that the growth of information technology is simply a passing phase which will be both encompassed and digested within the current structures of organisations.

Other interesting and also entertaining texts in the global societal strategy area are Naisbitt's (1984) *Megatrends* and Beckman's (1983) *Downwave*. A further valuable book is Hofstede's (1980) well-researched analysis of international differences of work-related values and how these differences influence the development of organisations in different nations.

Analyses of nation states are numerous and for most a traditional economic interpretation form the basis to the text. However, certain writers have recently departed from such a concentrated approach and have offered a far broader analysis encompassing economic and behavioural views. Kenny (1984a) attempts to show how government and enterprise are intertwined. He then specifically applies the concept to the Irish context in order to predict the problems and opportunities for the Irish Republic (Kenny, 1984b). Similar analyses have been published for both Europe and the USA. In particular, Benson (1982) examines business ethics in the USA and Young (1983) discusses the future potential and opportunities for the non-profit sector in the USA. Likewise, Norman (1984) examines the strategies and leadership styles of service businesses in Europe.

An interesting book is that by Castles, Murray, Potter and Pollit (1971), who attempt to bring together organisational strategic issues with societal strategic issues. Although a collection of papers worthy of attention, those contributions emphasising organisational strategy and decision-making processes would now be considered dated.

Strategy: an organisational perspective

A divide has emerged in the literature in the areas of business policy and organisational strategic decision-making processes. On the one hand, strategic processes are interpreted from a normative standpoint, whereby all-embracing models are offered so that the making and integration of strategic decisions in the wider organisational context is both feasible and desirable. The emphasis is on a scientific approach to contingency forecasting in order to draft comprehensive plans, designs and strategies. The early cybernetic interpretation of decision-making of Cyert and March (1963) or Scott (1967) arose from applying decision-making concepts with a strong economic perspective to the behavioural sciences. Equally, the normative approach has been applied in the clinical area (Inglefinger 1975, Lusted 1968), where the role of clinical judgement in diagnosing patients promotes the physician's scientific obligation to advance medical theory and practice. Meyer (1984) postulates that medical practitioners and health service administrators adopt the self-same model when involved in the purchase and evaluation of medical equipment and services. Hence, the normative school emphasises the strategic formulation process as highly rational and proactive, involving activities such as establishing goals, monitoring environments, assessing internal capabilities, searching for and evaluating alternative actions and, as a result, developing an all-embracing strategic plan to achieve identified goals. (Particular references in this line are Ansoff 1965, 1982; Grant and Kenny, 1982; Hoffer and Schendel, 1978; Thompson and Strickland, 1978; Perrow, 1970; Galbraith, 1977; Miles and Snow, 1978).

In complete contrast to normative thinking is the incrementalist approach (Frederickson and Mitchell 1984), where strategic decision-making is considered to be the result of countless loosely-linked planning decisions made over a period of time, but which at least adhere to a particular theme or trend. The trend may or may not be consciously recognised (Quinn, 1980; Miller 1982; De Vries and Toulouse, 1982). Protagonists of the normative school, such as Mintzberg (1973, 1978), Mintzberg and Walters (1982), Lindblom (1979) argue that incrementalist thinking is a far more accurate reflection of how organisations really make strategic decisions. For example, Wildavsky (1968) suggests that the budgeting process is an opportunity for individuals to negotiate the allocation of financial resources. In this way, Wildavsky (1968) sees strategy and policy as an arena of conflict over whose preferences are to prevail in the determination of policy. Hofstede (1978) endorses the view by indicating that management control systems such as PPBS and MBO are ineffective, as they are based on a cybernetic philosophy which is homeostatic in approach, as opposed to organisational environments which are heterostatic in approach.

Non-academics who write about strategic processes seem to fall more into the incrementalist school. The former chief executive of the UK motor corporation, British Leyland (BL), recounts his experiences there in a particularly interesting slim paperback (Edwardes, 1983). His descriptions of the feelings and attitudes of personnel in BL (including his own), the manner in which issues were formulated and decisions made, the opposition and frustrations he faced and the way he considered himself to be perceived, supports the loosely-linked nature of strategy formulation and implementation whereby negotiation and renegotiation of issues is the process which leads to particular outcomes.

Concluding comments

In the section, both normative and incrementalist philosophies are highlighted. Normative thinking helps to focus on all relevant issues and can relatively easily provide an overall strategic picture of an organisation. However, the sections in the chapter on strategic formulation, decision-making and strategy implementation have a strongly incrementalist flavour in that the manner of strategy application is emphasised. The ideas of Norman, Warren and Schnee (1981) are utilised, for they seem to encompass both philosophies neatly.

References

Ansoff, H.I. (1965), *Corporate Strategy*, McGraw-Hill.

Ansoff, H.I. (1982), 'Managing Discontinuous Strategies Change: The Learning Action Approach', in Ansoff, H.I., Bosman, A. and Storm, P.M. (eds), *Understanding and Managing Strategic Change*, North-Holland.

Beckman, R. (1983), *Downwave: Surviving the Second Great Depression*, Pan.

Benson, G.C.S. (1982), *Business Ethics in America*, Lexington.

Castles, F.G., Murray, D.J., Potter, D.C. and Pollitt, C.J. (eds) (1971), *Decisions, Organisations and Society*, Penguin.

Cyert, R. and March, J.G. (1963), *A Behavioural Theory of a Firm*, Prentice-Hall.

Edwardes, M. (1983), *Back from the Brink*, Pan.

Edwards, C. (1985), '*Managers and Information: Tomorrow's Opportunities and Problems*', Inaugural Professional Lecture, Cranfield Institute of Technology.

Fredrickson, J.W. and Mitchell, T.R. (1984), 'Strategic Decision Processes: Comprehensiveness and Performance in an Industry with an Unstable Environment', *Academy of Management Journal*, Vol. 27, No. 2, pp. 399–423.

Galbraith, J.R. (1977), *Organisational Design*, Addison-Wesley.

Grant, J.H. and King, W.R. (1979), 'Strategy Formulation: Analytical and Normative Models', in Schendel, D.E. and Hofer,

C.W. (eds), *Strategic Management*, Little, Brown & Co, pp. 104–22.

Hofer, C.W. and Schendel, D.E. (1978), *Strategy Formulation: Analytical Concepts*, West Publishing.

Hofstede, G. (1978), 'The Poverty of Management Control Philosophy', *Academy of Management Review*, July, pp. 450–60.

Hofstede, G. (1980), *Cultures Consequences: International Differences in Work-Related Values*, Sage.

Inglefinger, F.J. (1975), 'Decisions in Medicine', *New England Journal of Medicine*, Vol. 291, pp. 254–5.

Kenny, I. (1984a), 'Business, Politics and Society', in Kakabadse, A.P. and Mukhi, S., *The Future of Management Education*, Gower.

Kenny, I, (1984b), *Government and Enterprise in Ireland*, Gill & Macmillan.

Lindblom, C.E. (1979), 'Still Muddling. Not Yet Through', *Public Administration Review*, Vol. 39, pp. 517–26.

Lusted, L.B. (1968), *Introduction to Medical Decision-Making*, L.C. Thomas.

Meyer, A.D. (1984), 'Mingling Decision Making Metaphors', *Academy of Management Review*, Vol. 9, No. 1, pp. 6–17.

Miles, R.E. and Snow, E.E. (1978), *Organisational Strategy, Structure and Process*, McGraw-Hill.

Miller, D.J., De Vries, M.F.R.D. and Toulouse, J.M. (1982), 'Top Executive Locus of Control and its Relationship to Strategy-Making, Structure and Environment', *Academy of Management Journal*, Vol. 25, No. 2, pp. 237–53.

Mintzberg, H. (1973), 'Strategy-Making in three modes', *California Management Review*, Vol. 16, No. 2, pp. 44–53.

Mintzberg, H. (1978), 'Patterns of Strategy Formulation', *California Management Review*, Vol. 24, pp. 934–48.

Mintzberg, H. and Walters, J.A. (1982), 'Tracking Strategy in an Entrepreneurial Firm', *Academy of Management Journal*, Vol. 25, No. 3, pp. 465–99.

Naisbitt, J. (1984), *Megatrends: Ten New Directions Transforming Our Lives*, McDonald.

Newman, W.H. and Logan, J.P. (1981), *Strategy, Policy and Central Management*, 8th ed., South Western Publishing Company.

Newman, W.H., Warren, E.K. and Schnee, J.E. (1982), *The Process of Management: Strategy, Action, Results*, 5th ed., Prentice-Hall.

Norman, R. (1984), *Service Management: Strategy and Leadership in Service Business*, Wiley Interscience.

Perrow, C. (1970), *Organisational Analysis: A Sociological View*, Wordsworth.

Quinn, J.B. (1980), *Strategies for Change: Logical Incrementalism*, Richard Irwin.

Scott, W.G. (1967), 'Decision concepts', in Scott, W.G., *Organisation Theory*, Irwin, pp. 219–26.

Stopford, J.M., Channon, D.F. and Constable, J. (1980), *Cases in Strategic Management*, Wiley Interscience.

Thompson, A.A. and Strickland, A.J. (1978), *Strategy and Policy: Concepts and Cases*, Business Publications.

Toffler, A. (1970), *Future Shock*, Random Press.

Toffler, A. (1981), *Third Wave*, Bantam Press.

Wildavsky, A. (1968), '*Budgeting as a Political Process*' in Sills, D.L. (ed), *The Interventionists' Encyclopedia of the Social Sciences*, Collier-MacMillan, pp. 192–99.

Young, D.R. (1983), *If not for Profit, for what?*, Lexington Books.

SECTION 11

Organisation structures are well documented and extensively researched. No one particular text summarises this complex area. In fact, the literature is characterised by research papers and books offering, at times, conflicting and contradictory perspectives. The literature on organisation structures is classified here under four headings: structure theory; systems theory; solution-centred prescriptions and organisation design theory.

Structure theory

Until the early 1960's, organisational theorists had demonstrated unusual agreement about the nature of bureaucracy, agreement based on Weber's (1947) original formulation. Theorists such as Udy (1959), Barnard (1938), Berger (1956), Parsons (1956a; 1956b), in the absence of methodological development, concentrated on conceptual clarity. The debate centred on such issues as the nature of authority and leadership and the interface between bureaucratic structural forms and the external environment.

With the onset of the 1960's, thinking largely changed due to an upsurge in research activity based upon attempts to test empirically those categories laid down by Weber. Researchers recognised the valuable role that computers could play in terms of data analysis. In addition, certain statistical techniques such as factor analysis in particular, and multivariate analysis techniques in general, quickly became popular tools in the processes of hypothesis formation and testing. Research focused on the relationships between elements of structure such as organisation size, ownership, geographic location, technology of manufacture and the manner in which an organisation regulates its activities such as centralisation/decentralisation of decision-making, task allocation, exercise of authority and the co-ordination of functions.

In the UK, the Aston research group championed this area of research. The bulk of the work of the Aston group appears in two volumes (Pugh and Hickson 1976, 1977). Also of interest is Child's (1972) study of 62 organisations, whose conclusion was that Weber's unidimensional model is probably the most valuable description of bureaucratic structure in organisations. Hining and Foster (1973) confirmed this finding in their study of churches. Recently, and in keeping with the Aston tradition, a study of organisation structures has been examined within different national contexts (Mansfield and Zeffrone 1983).

Similar studies have been conducted in the USA. Key references are Hall (1962, 1963), Blau, Heydebrand and Stauffer (1966), Blau and Schoenherr (1971), Perrow (1970), Hage and Aiken (1967). Hall (1974) and Litterer (1969), although now somewhat dated, provide a comprehensive and detailed overview of this area of study.

More recent work in this area has concentrated on organisation structure and innovation (Aiken, Bacharrach and French, 1980), organisation structure and technology (Fry, 1982) and organisation structure and strategy (Herber, 1984). However, the popularity of the Weberian-based structuralist research has been superseded by systems thinking.

Systems theory

In contrast to the structural theorists, an equally powerful and concurrently emerging discipline in organisation theory is the systems perspective. A fundamental assumption in systems theory is that human behaviour in organisations does not occur in isolation. Unlike the structuralist theorists, who would relate, measure and interpret particular elements of structure with each other, systems theorists have attempted to interlink and understand the impact of all the different aspects of life in organisations. In other words, behaviour in organisations can be understood only in context. Human behaviour, therefore, is influenced by the design of the organisation and the way information and work flow through the organisation. Hence, it is important to understand the entire organisation as a complex system composed of interrelated subsystems.

The inspiration for systems thinking was taken from biology; any biological system is complex, composed of interrelated parts that cannot be viewed in isolation, each existing in its own environment, affecting and being affected by that environment (Bertalanffy, 1972). A particularly influential writer is Gouldner (1959), who attacked the rigidities of Weberian ideal organisational form as too rational, unnatural and restrictive. He offered instead the ideal of the open system, which he saw as the natural or whole system, which includes formal structures but further those aspects that can lead to neglect or distortion of goal-seeking behaviour. This has led to an open/closed systems dichotomy analysis of organisations and generated, in turn, a number of far-reaching and influential research studies. Burns and Stalker (1961) compared a rayon mill to an electronic plant. In the former, the technology and business environment were characterised by certainty and predictability. In these circumstances, the behaviour of members of the organisation was structured and based on set, but required, patterns of action. Any uncertainty could easily be dealt with by those at the top. The electronic plant represented the opposite, for the production process contained many uncertainties, the market was turbulent and people's behaviour could not be predicted, as numerous unforeseen problems occurred and had to be solved at different levels in the organisation. Burns and Stalker termed the structure required for the rayon mill *mechanistic*, and that for the electronic plant *organic*. The higher the degree of bureaucracy (ie defined role authority and behavioural boundaries), then the term mechanistic applied, the less the degree of bureaucracy, then the more organic the structure. It is important to appreciate that the concepts of mechanistic and organic, within a system's philosophy, are not ideal organisational types, but all-embracing organisational concepts (including structures, culture, business environment and people) that are extremes on a continuum which in turn reveal degrees of bureaucracy within an organisation.

Similarly, Lawrence and Lorsch (1969) used the two elements of technology and environment to identify the degree of mutual cooperation and corporate cohesion in the organisation. Lawrence and Lorsch indicated that separate sections of the organisation (departments, divisions, groups) develop their own environment or culture (see Chapter 8 for an explanation of culture). Hence, the more the environment of these departments differ in certainty and predictability, the greater the degree of *differentiation* (ie the greater the differences of structure, work patterns, attitudes coupled with a low need for mutual cooperation). Such differences may lead to conflicts and splits in the organisation. As the degree of differentiation increases, *integration* (ie the quality of co-operation and corporate identity) needs to be given greater attention. Whereas

Burns and Stalker (1961) utilised technology to explain degrees of bureaucracy, Lawrence and Lorsch (1969) used technology to show the different cultures in an organisation and the impact of these cultures on people's work performance.

Other key texts in this area include Katz and Kahn (1966), who further developed Gouldner's (1959) work and suggested nine common characteristics shared by all open systems. For detailed overview of systems thinking, read Blau and Scott (1963), Child (1977), Lorsch and Lawrence (1972) and Huse and Bowditch (1977).

Solution-centred prescriptions

In the UK the study of public administration is a well established discipline. Historically, public administration was conceptually linked to political philosophy (Sherif, 1976). However, with the onset of public sector reorganisations of national proportions in the 1960s and 1970s, namely the reorganisation of local government, health services and police organisations, the link between public sector administration and political philosophy was broken and extensive research began to specify ideal organisational forms (structures) for public sector organisations. One of the most active groups has been the research centre at Brunel University, BIOSS (Brunel Institute of Organisation and Social Studies). The greatest contribution made by the BIOSS group was in the health and social services field, where ideal organisation structures were recommended (see Kogan and Terry, 1971, Kogan et al., 1971, Rowbottom et al., 1974). These works were based on the original studies of Brown and Jaques (1965), and Jaques (1951) in the Glacier Metal Company, which were further developed by Newman and Rowbottom (1968) in terms of appropriate means for organisation analysis. Similar work conducted in police organisations is neatly epitomised in the work of Bunyard (1978).

Although practical and useful, such work has been criticised for its normative, inflexible nature which does not allow for variations of context or the flexibility required for contingency management (Kakabadse, 1982). Similar work in the private sector suffers the same criticisms (Frank, 1971). One notable exception is the work of Goldberg and Fruin (1976), which examines recording and review systems in the social services, in order to improve the quality of managerial decision making.

Organisation design

In addition to the threefold classification above, research and writings on organisation structure can be further subdivided into theoretical and practical. The bulk of the texts fall into the theoretical grouping (structural and systems theorists). Attempts to make the subject area more practically useful, such as the work of the Brunel group, have been criticised as inflexible and insensitive to local needs. Consequently, writers and researchers have tried to link the two groupings together under the term organisation design. Handy (1973) devotes one chapter to the topic and Kingdon's (1973) work on matrix structures can be classified under this heading. An in-depth and comprehensive discussion of organisation design is provided by Randolph and Dess (1984). From the business-man's/practitioner's point of view, two excellent texts which provide a bird's eye view of the organisation and equally discuss, in sufficient depth, key elements of organisation structure, are those by Drucker (1968, 1977). A most interesting book on organisation design is provided by Pfeffer (1978), but this is probably more attractive to academics.

Concluding comments

Chapter 11 was written from an organisation design angle, describing fundamental elements of the determinants of structure, alternative forms of structure, arguments for and against centralisation/decentralisation, and the impact of structure (or its constituent parts) on accountability, span of control and organisation culture. The emphasis of this comprehensive analysis of organisation design is on practice and implementation. The organisation can often benefit from the modifications of manage-ment practice and human behaviour that result from changing certain constituent parts of structure.

References

Aiken, M., Bacharach, S.B. and French, J.L. (1980), 'Organisa-tional Structure, Work Process and Proposal Making in Administrative Bureaucracies', *Academy of Management Jour-nal*, Vol. 23, No. 4, pp. 631–52.

Barnard, C.J. (1938), *The Function of the Executive*, Harvard University Press, Cambridge, Mass.

Berger, H. (1956), 'Bureaucracy East and West', *Administrative Science Quarterly*, Vol. 2, pp. 63–85.

Bertalanffy, L. (1972), 'The History and Status of General Systems Theory', *Academy of Management Journal*, Vol. 15, No. 4, pp. 411–27.

Blau, P.M., Heydebrand, W.V. and Stauffer, R.E. (1966), 'The Structure of Small Bureaucracies', *American Sociological Review*, Vol. 31, pp. 179–91.

Blau, P.M. and Schoenherr, R.A. (1971), *The Structure of Organisations*, Basic Books.

Blau, P.M. and Scott, W.R. (1963), *Formal Organisations: A Comparative Approach*, Routledge and Kegan Paul.

Brown, W. and Jacques, E. (1965), *The Glacier Project Papers*, Heinemann Educational Books.

Bunyard, R.S. (1978), *Police: Organisation and Command*, Police Study Series, Macdonald and Evans.

Burns, T. and Stalker, G.M. (1961) *The Management of Innovation*, Tavistock, London.

Child, J. (1972), 'Organisation, Structure and Strategies of Control: A Replication of the Aston Study', *Administrative Science Quarterly*, Vol. 18, pp. 329–48.

Child, J. (1977), *Organisation: A Guide to Problems and Practice*, Harper & Row.

Child, J. (1984), *Organisation: A Guide to Problems and Practice*, 2nd ed. Harper & Row.

Drucker, P. (1968), *The Practice of Management*, Pan Business Management.

Drucker, P. (1977), *Management*, Pan Business Management.

Frank, H.E. (ed) (1971), *Organisation Structuring*, McGraw-Hill.

Fry, L.W. (1982), 'Technology–Structure Research: Three Critical Issues', *Academy of Management Journal*, Vol. 25, No. 3, pp. 532–52.

Goldberg, E.M. and Fruin, D.J. (1976), 'Towards Accountability in Social Work: A Case Review System for Social Workers', *British Journal of Social Work*, Vol. 6, pp. 3–22.

Gouldner, A.W. (1959), 'Organisation Analysis', in Merton, R. K., Brown, L. and Cottrel, L.S. (eds), *Sociology Today*, Basic Books.

Hage, J. and Aiken, M. (1967), 'The Relationship of Centralisation To Other Structural Properties', *Administrative Science Quarterly*, Vol. 12, pp. 73–92.

Hall, R.H. (1962), 'Intra-organisational Structural Variation: Application of the Bureaucratic Model', *Administrative Science Quarterly*, Vol. 7, pp. 293–308.

Hall, R.H. (1963), 'The Concept of Bureaucracy: An Empirical Assessment', *American Journal of Sociology*, Vol. 69, pp. 32–40.

Hall, R.H. (1974), *Organisation: Structure and Process*, Prentice Hall International.

Handy, C. (1977), *Understanding Organisations*, Pan.

Handy, C. (1982), 'Where Management is Leading', *Management Today*, December.

Herbert, T.T. (1984), 'Strategy and Multi-national Organisation Structure: An Inter-organisational Relationship Perspective', *Academy of Management Review*, Vol. 9, No. 2, pp. 259–71.

Hinings, C.R. and Foster, B.D. (1973), 'The Organisation Structure of Churches: A Preliminary Model', *Sociology*, Vol. 7, pp. 93–106.

Huse, E.F. and Bowditch, J.L. (1977), *Behaviour in Organisations: A Systems Approach to Managing*. 2nd ed., Addison-Wesley.

Jaques, E. (1951), *The Changing Culture of a Factory*, Tavistock.

Kakabadse, A.P. (1982), *Culture of the Social Services*, Gower.

Kakabadse, A.P. (1983), *The Politics of Management*, Gower; Nichols Publishing Co., New York.

Kingdon, D.R. (1973), *Matrix Organisation: Managing Information Technologies*, Tavistock.

Kogan, M., Cang, S., Dixon, M. and Tolliday, M. (1971), *Working Relationships Within The British Hospital Service*, Bookstall Publications.

Kogan, M. and Terry, J. (1971), *The Organisation of a Social Services Department: A Blueprint*, Bookstall Publications.

Lawrence, P.R. and Lorsch, J.W. (1969), *Organisation and Environment: Managing Differentiation and Integration,* Irwin.

Litterer, J.A. (1969), *Organisation, Vol I*. 2nd ed. Wiley.

Lorsch, J.W. and Lawrence, P.R. (1972), *Organisation Planning: Cases and Concepts,* Irwin.

Mansfield, R. and Zeffrone, R. (1983), *Organisational Structures and National Contingencies*, Gower.

Mohr, L.B. (1971), 'Organisational Technology and Organisational Structure', *Administrative Science Quarterly*, Vol. 16, pp. 444–59.

Newman, A.D. and Rowbottom, R.W. (1968) *Organisation Analysis*, Heinemann Educational Books.

Parsons, T. (1956a), 'A Sociological Approach to the Theory of Organisations (Part I)', *Administrative Science Quarterly*, Vol. 1, No. 1, pp. 63–85.

Parsons, T. (1956b), 'A Sociological Approach to the Theory of

Organisations (Part II), *Administrative Science Quarterly*, Vol. 1, No. 3, pp. 225–39.

Perrow, C. (1970), *Organisational Analysis: A Sociological Review*, Tavistock.

Perrow, C. (1976), 'A Framework for the Comparative Analysis of Organisations', *American Sociological Review*, Vol. 32, pp. 194–208.

Pfeffer, J. (1978), *Organisational Design*, Organisational Behaviour Series, AHM Publishing Corporation, Arlington Heights.

Pugh, D.S. and Hickson, D.J. (eds) (1976), *Organisation Structure in its Context: The Aston Programme I,* Saxon House/Lexington Books.

Pugh, D.S. and Hickson, D.J. (eds) (1977), *Organisational Structure: Extensions and Reflections: The Aston Programme II.* Saxon House/Lexington Books.

Randolph, W.A. and Dess, G.G. (1984), 'A Congruence Perspective of Organisation Design: A Conceptual Model and Multivariate Research Approach', *Academy of Management Review*, Vol. 9, No. 1, pp. 114–27.

Revans, T.W. (1976), *Participation in What?* ACP International Publications.

Rowbottom, R.W., Hey, A.M. and Billis, D. (1974), *Social Service Departments: Developing Patterns of Work and Organisation*, Heinemann.

Schumacher, E.F.C. (1974), *Small is Beautiful*, Abacus.

Sherif, P. (1976), 'The Sociology of Public Bureaucracies', *Current Sociology*, Vol. 24, pp. 1–175.

Woodward, J. (1965), *Industrial Organisation*, Oxford University Press.

SECTION 12

Numerous writers have referred to the extent to which individuals in organisations identify with each other and with the organisation, but only a few have directly addressed the issue. Argyris's (1974) analysis of disharmony and discontent within a newspaper organisation is an important contribution in this field. Similarly, Jones and Lakin's (1978) fictionalised description of events and processes in a carpetmaking company makes excellent reading. In a similar fashion, Mars's (1984) analysis of workplace crime is fascinating. Kakabadse's (1982) quantitative analysis of the poor fit between the organisation structure and cultures of social work organisations provides a similar perspective but from a macro view.

From a non-data-based, more conceptual angle, Vickers (1983) emphasises that human systems form the basis to organisations and need to be treated as such. Lippitt's (1982) extensive treatise on organisational renewal offers a holistic, prescriptive and extremely valuable view on how to go about introducing changes and then attempt to integrate the various parts of the organisation. Garratt and Stopford (1980) directly address the issues of integration on an international level in their edited book *Breaking down Barriers*. Finally, Kimberly and Miles (1980) argue that organisations change dramatically over time, not in a haphazard way, but in a predictable pattern which they term the organisational life cycle. In this way, integration is seen as a phase in the life cycle rather than as an issue that needs thinking about and specifically acting on.

As can be seen, integration has been interpreted in a number of ways. In this chapter, the four areas of performance appraisal, team development, MBO and the role of the general manager have been taken to be integral elements of any attempt to introduce integration and cohesion into the organisation. Consequently, further references are provided in each of the topic areas.

Performance appraisal

Tyson and York's (1982) overview of personnel management is a
valuable and readable text. Performance appraisal is discussed in
detail and also linked with the other topic areas of personnel. Also
see Thomason (1976) for a further in-depth analysis of personnel
management. From a somewhat broader point of view, William's
(1983) collection of papers looks at how research in the personnel
area can be practically utilised in line management situations.
Further, performance appraisal can be seen as one part of
manpower planning. Two references on performance appraisal in
manpower planning are Bartholomew (1976) and Pettman (1984).

Team development

Cummings (1981) provides an interesting overview of the
group/team literature, where personal, group and organisational
values, group dynamics and group growth and development
processes are considered crucial to understanding group/team
behaviour. As stated in the chapter, the growth and social needs of
group members can only really be satisfied in participative, self-
regulating groups. Such groups function better if the values and
beliefs of the managers (Nightingale and Toulouse, 1977;
McGregor, 1960) and the values of the total organisation
(Kakabadse, 1982) support such interactions. In terms of group
dynamics, a number of factors could promote or upset positive
group dynamics, such as the effort required by individuals to
achieve positive interactions in the group (Hackman, 1976); the
influence of the group leader (Glisson, 1978); group compliance
(Janis, 1972); tasks (Blumberg, 1980, Comstock and Scott, 1977);
stable and unstable work environments (Duncan, 1973); and the
ability of groups to introduce change to their work environment
(Weick, 1979). In terms of group/team growth and development
processes, see Cummings (1978) and Hrebiniak (1974), who see the
group leader as the stimulus to generate a learning climate within
the group. Also read the orginal text by Bateson (1972) on learning,
on which is based the Argyris and Schon (1978) double loop
learning concept. Pay special attention to Boss and McConkie
(1981) for they attempt to define the limitations of team building.
Baker (1979), in contrast, provides a prescriptive step-by-step
approach to effective team development. Particularly successful at
identifying the approaches and stages of team development are
Margerison and McCann (1985), who give realistic and easy-to-

learn steps on how to lead a winning team. Finally, read Tuckman's (1964) original thesis on the team development wheel which formed the basis to this section.

Management by objectives (MBO)

Odiorne's (1979) text on MBO provides a comprehensive overview of MBO and is a book well worth perusing. For more specific analyses of MBO, see Pringle and Longenecker (1982), who examine the ethics of MBO, and Katz and Allen (1985), who investigate employee performance and locus of influence.

The general manager

For an overview of the general manager's role and the skills required for effective performance, pay particular attention to Hunt (1983), Kotter (1982) and Mintzberg (1973). Tricker (1978) confines himself to the role of the non-executive director, whilst Hoesu (1978), Dessler (1983), Margerison and Kakabadse (1984) and Myers and Myers (1982) concentrate on the skills required for effective executive performance.

Concluding comments

Integration has not been amply and directly discussed in the literature. Performance appraisal is traditionally viewed as an element of personnel management and hence as a subject would rarely appear in books on organisation behaviour. Similarly, MBO would not traditionally be seen as a part of organisation behaviour. If anything, it would be more associated with business policy, but even this would be tenuous as MBO has fallen out of favour. In practice, all organisations use MBO, but label the process with many different headings.

Team development often appears in the literature on groups or alternatively in individual papers prescribing how team processes could be improved.

The role, skills and behaviour of senior managers provide a relatively new area of exploration. Despite the lack of research, Kotter (1982) clearly indicates the essential linking role of the general manager in organisational performance. Despite their varied background, and from the writers' experience of management academics and consultants, these four areas are essential components in helping to integrate individuals, groups, teams, departments or even divisions with the values, characerics and styles of the organisation.

References

Argyris, C. (1974), *Behind the Front Page*, Jossey Bass.

Argyris, C. and Schon, D. (1978), *Organisational Learning*, Addison-Wesley.

Baker, H.K. (1979), 'The Hows and Whys of Team Building', *Personnel Journal*, Vol. 58, pp. 367-70.

Bartholomew, D.J. (ed) (1976), *Manpower Planning*, Penguin Modern Management Series.

Bateson, G. (1972), *Stepts to an Ecology of Mind*, Ballantine.

Blumberg, M. (1980), 'Job Switching in Autonomous Work Groups: an exploratory study in a Pennsylvania Coal Mine', *Academy of Management Journal*, Vol. 23, pp. 287-306.

Boss, R.W. and McConkie, H.L. (1981), 'The Destructive Impact of a Positive Team Building Intervention', *Group and Organisation Studies*, Vol. 6, pp. 45-56.

Comstock, D.E. and Scott, W.R. (1977), 'Technology and the Structure of Sub-units: distinguishing individual and work group effects', *Administrative Science Quarterly*, Vol. 22, pp. 625-34.

Cummings, T.G. (1978), 'Self-regulating Work Groups: a socio-technical synthesis', *Academy of Management Review*, Vol. 3, pp. 625-34.

Cummings, T.G. (1981), 'Designing Effective Work Groups' in Nystrom, P.C. and Starbuck, W.H. (eds), *Handbook of Organisational Design*, Vol. 2, Oxford University Press, pp. 250-71.

Dessler, G. (1983), *Improving Productivity at Work: Motivating Today's Employees*, Prentice-Hall.

Duncan, R.B. (1972), 'Characteristics of Organisational Environments and perceived environmental uncertainty', *Administrative Science Quarterly*, Vol. 17, pp. 313-27.

Garratt, R. and Stopford, J. (eds) (1980), *Breaking down Barriers*, Gower.

Glisson, C.A. (1978), 'Dependence of Technological Routinisation on Structural Variables in Human Service Organisations', *Administrative Science Quarterly*, Vol. 23, pp. 383-95.

Hackman, J.R. (1976), 'Group Influences on Individuals', in Dunnette, M.D. (ed), *Handbook of Individual and Organisational Psychology*, Rand McNally, pp. 1455-1525.

Hoesu, R. (1972), *Personal and Organisational Effectiveness*, McGraw-Hill.

Hrebriniak, L.G. (1974), 'Job Technology Supervision and work-group structure', *Administrative Science Quarterly*, Vol. 19, pp. 395–410.

Hunt, J.W. (1983), 'Developing Middle Managers in Shrinking Organisations', *Journal of Management Development*, Vol. 1, No. 2, pp. 10–22.

Janis, I.L. (1972), *Victims of Group Think*, Houghton-Mifflin.

Jones, R. and Lakin, C. (1978), *The Carpet Makers*, McGraw-Hill.

Kakabadse, A.P. (1982), *Culture of the Social Services*, Gower.

Katz, R. and Allen, T.J. (1985), 'Project Performance and the Locus of Influence in the R & D Matrix', *Academy of Management Journal*, Vol. 28, No. 1, pp. 678–87.

Kimberly, J.R., Miles, R.H. and Associates (1980), *The Organisational Life Cycle*, Jossey Bass.

Kotter, J.P. (1982), 'General Managers are not Generalists', *Organisational Dynamics*, Vol. 10, No. 4, Spring, pp. 5–19.

Lippitt, G.L. (1982), *Organisation Renewal: A Holistic Approach to Organisation Development*, 2nd ed., Prentice-Hall.

Margerison, C. and Kakabadse, A.P. (1984), *How American Chief Executives Succeed*, Monograph, American Management Association.

Margerison, C. and McCann, R. (1985), *How to Lead a Winning Team*, MCB University Press.

Mars, G. (1984), *Cheats at Work: An Anthropology of Workplace Crime*, Unwin Books.

McGregor, D. (1960), *The Human Side of Enterprise*, McGraw-Hill.

Mintzberg, M. (1973), *The Nature of Managerial Work*, Harper & Row.

Myers, M.T. and Myers, G.E. (1982), *Managing by Communication: An Organisational Approach*, McGraw-Hill.

Nightingale, D.V. and Toulouse, J.M. (1977), 'Toward a Multi-level congruence Theory of Organisation', *Administrative Science Quarterly*, Vol. 22, pp. 264–80.

Odiorne, G. (1979), *MBO II.*, Fearon Pitman.

Pettmann, B.O. (1984), *Manpower Planning Workbook*, 2nd ed. Gower.

Pringle, C.D. and Longenecker, J.G. (1982), 'The Ethics of MBO', *Academy of Management Review*, Vol. 7, No. 2, pp. 305–12.

Thomason, G. (1976), *A Textbook of Personnel Management*, IPM.

Tricker, R.I. (1978), *The Independent Director: A Study of the*

Non-Executive Director and of the Audit Committee, Tolley.

Tuckman, B.W. (1965), 'Developmental sequences in small groups', *Psychological Bulletin*, Vol. 63, No. 6, pp. 384–99.

Tyson, S. and York, A. (1982), *Personnel Management Made Simple*, Heinemann.

Vickers, Sir G. (1983), *Human Systems Are Different*, Harper & Row.

Weick, K.E. (1979), *The Social Psychology of Organising*, 2nd ed. Addison-Wesley.

Williams, A.P.O. (ed) (1983), *Using Personnel Research*, Gower.

Index

affection, need for 102-3
Albrecht, Karl
  communication theories 98
Alderfer, Clayton
  motivation theories 123-4, 149
  (summary)
assertiveness 109—11
assumptions 96-7
attitudes 315

behaviour, verbal 78
Behavioural School of Management 17
Belbin, R. Meredith
  and group research 174-7
"big bang" (City of London) 351
body language 97-8, 106-7
budgeting, and power 238-9
bureaucracy 9

career development and planning 45,
  55-7, 58-9
case studies
  corporate strategy 281-2, 285, 288,
    295-6, 300, 303-4, 306
  groups 152-3, 159-60, 163-5, 177-8
  induction 31-2, 35-6, 43-4, 50-1, 54
  integration 351-2, 356-7, 366-7,
    373-4, 377
  interpersonal communication 92, 96,
    100, 104, 108, 110-11, 113
  leadership 184- 5, 199-200, 204,
    206-7
  management 6-7, 14-15, 17-18, 22,
    26-7
  motivation 117-18, 132-3, 134-5,
    139-40, 145
  organisation structure 312-13, 321,
    325, 327-8, 339-41, 343-4, 345-6
  personality 61, 69-70, 73-4, 82-3,
    88-9, 100

politics in organisations 249-50,
  260-1, 262-3, 264-5, 267-8, 269-
  70, 272
power 211-12, 218-19, 221-2, 224-5,
  236-7, 240-1, 245
centralisation vs decentralisation 336-
  41, 349 (summary)
Centre for Creative Leadership 45, 71
communication 13-14, 16
  channels 98
  and motivation 146-7, 151
conflict 250, 252, 261, 299, 326, 360-1
  resolution 111-12
contingency studies 194-6, 208-9
  (summary)
control, need for 102
corporate strategy
  aims 305
  case study 281-2, 285, 288, 295-6,
    300, 303-4, 306
  and conflict 299
  economic influences on 286-7
  elements 288, 305-8
  and government 284-5
  influences on 283-8
  formulation 290-6, 308 (summary)
  implementation 296-301, 310
    (summary)
  terminology 289-90, 311
    (summary)
  types 301-4, 310-11 (summary)
Cranfield School of Management 40,
  67
  culture, organisational 225-37,
    344-6

decentralisation vs centralisation 336-
  41, 349 (summary)
decision making 21-2, 196-201, 209

Drucker, Peter
  management theories 196

ERG (Existence, Relatedness, Growth)
    theory 123-4, 149
expectancy theory 128-131, 149-50
    (summary)
  model 129
extroverts 70

family life and work 51-7, 59
Fayol, Henri
  management theories 10-11, 16
Freud, Sigmund
  personality theories 65-6
fringe benefits 144

Gantt, Henry 13
General and Industrial Administration
    (Fayol) 10
general manager, role 375-7, 378, 379
    (summary)
Gilbreth, Frank 13
groups
  behaviour 165-7, 168, 169, 172, 181-
    2 (summary)
  case study 152-3, 159-60, 163-5,
    177-8
  classification 154-6
  cohesiveness 172-4, 178, 182
  definition 154
  development 170-2, 182 (summary)
  dynamics 160-1, 181-2, 364
  effectiveness 178-9, 183 (summary)
  formal 154, 157-8, 180 (summary)
  functions 157-8
  heterogeneous 158, 181 (summary)
  homogeneous 158, 181 (summary)
  informal 155, 180 (summary)
  interaction 163-7
  and motivation 160-1
  primary 155-6, 180 (summary)
  process model 162
  roles 174-6, 182 (summary)
  secondary 156, 180-1 (summary)
  size 158
  s 154-5, 180-1 (summary)
  157, 181 (summary)

  81, 221
  les
  56-7

  ure theory 227-36

Henley Management Centre 174
Herzberg, Frederick
  motivation theory 125-6, 149
    (summary)
Homans, George
  on groups 161-7
Human Groups, The (Homans) 161
Human Relations School of
    Management 191-2

incentives
  and motivation 125, 149
induction
  case study 31-2, 35-6, 43-4, 50-1, 54
  effective 38-44
  problems 37-8, 58
influence, personal 250, 261-72
information
  and management 14, 20-1
  and power 222-3
information technology
  and organisation structure 319
INSEAD 51
integration, organisational
  case study 351-2, 356-7, 366-7, 373-
    4, 377
  methods 353
interpersonal activity 19-20, 93
interpersonal communication 93-6, 114
    (summary)
  case study 92, 96, 100, 104, 108, 110-
    11, 113
  skills 106-14, 115 (summary)
interpersonal needs 101-3, 115
    (summary)
interpersonal problems 105-6, 115
    (summary)
interviews, limitations 33-4
introverts 70

job enrichment 136-7, 142
Johari Window 83-6

Key person analysis
  and corporate strategy 291-2, 294
Kotter, John
  management theories 376-7

leadership
  beliefs about 188-9
  case study 184-5, 199-200, 204,
    206--7
  classification 208-9
  definition 186, 187

development 46-7
and expertise 220-1, 222
and organisations 205
and personality 189-90
situational 201-5
style 142-3, 185, 186, 188, 191, 205,
   207
theories 187, 188-205, 208-9
   (summary)
Lewin, Kurt
   on groups 365-6
life planning 55-7
listening skills 106-7, 108-9

management
   and communication 13-14
   case study 6-7, 14-15, 17-18, 22,
      26-7
   constraints 24-8
   effectiveness 28
   elements 10-11
   functions 10-12
   nature of 8-9, 15-16, 17, 29-30
      (summary)
   roles 17-23
   scientific 12-13, 150 (summary)
   theories 10-17
managerial grid, the 192-4
managerial mapping 89-90, 91,
   (summary)
Margerison, Charles
   managerial mapping 89
Maslow, Abraham
   motivation theories 121-2, 148-9
      (summary), 160-1
matrix management 333-5
Mayo, Elton
   management theories 16, 191
MBO (Management by Objectives) 378
   (summary)
   benefits 373, 375
   definitions 369-70
   principles 370-1
   uses 368-9
McGregor, Douglas
   Theory X and Theory Y 188-9
McLelland, David
   motivation theories 123, 149
      (summary)
Mintzberg, Henry
   management theories 18-23
   and corporate strategy 296

MIS (Management Information
   Systems) 14
   objectives of 325-8
money
   and motivation 126
motivation
   case study 117-18, 132-3, 134-5,
      139-40, 145
   and communication 146-7, 151
   definition 118
   determination of 131-2, 136-7
   and environment 133-4
   and groups 160-1
   improvement 140-8, 327
   model of 119
   and organisation structure 343
   theories 120-31, 148-51
      (summary)
Myers Briggs Type Indicator 67-9, 71,
   89, 90

networks 265-8

organisation
   and conflict 252-61
   culture of 225-37, 325, 344-6
   growth 320
   models 13-14
organisational strategy, see corporate
   strategy
organisational structure
   analysis 313-16, 347 (summary)
   case study 312-13, 321, 325, 327-8,
      339-41, 343-4, 345-6
   components 316-17, 328-41, 349
      (summary)
   divisional 332-3, 348
   flexibility 322-4
   functional 330-1, 348
   and information technology 319
   matrix 333-5, 348-9
   and motivation 343
   product-based 331-2, 348
   and technology 317-18
   roles 329
      types 330-5
   Oxford Management Centre 23

perceptions 90-1 (summary)
   difference 74-81, 90
   improvement 83-6
   and roles 86-8, 97

performance appraisal 378 (summary)
   and MBO 372
   methods 356, 357–8
   and motivation 141–2
   types 355
   use 353–4
personality 90 (summary)
   case study 61, 69–70, 73–4, 82–3, 88–
      9, 100
   definition 62–3
   development 64
   Freud's theories 65–6
   and leadership 189–90
   types 63
   and power 219–20
Peter Principle, The 81
politics
   in organisations 273–5 (summary)
   case study 249–50, 260–1, 262–3,
      264–5, 267–8, 269–70, 272
   and corporate strategy 297
potential, identification 45–6
power
   and budgeting 238–9
   case study 211–12, 218–19, 221–2,
      224–5, 236–7, 240–1, 245
   and change 241–6, 248
   characteristics 214
   and coercion 216, 246
   and contacts 224–5, 247
   definitions 213, 246
   and expertise 220–2, 247
   and groups 161
   and information 222–3, 247
   and legitimacy 216–19, 246
   levels 237–41
   and organisation culture 225–36, 247
   and personality 219–20, 246–7
   types 214–25, 246–7 (summary)
problems
   recognition 239–40
   solving 112–14
profit centres 46

Quality Circles 142

recruitment 33–5, 57 (summary)
results 45–6
roles 17–23, 71–3
   problems 86–8

Schein, Ed
   on careers development 48–50
   on recruitment 34–5, 36
Sheldon, William
   personality theories 63
socialisation 36–7, 38–44, 58
span of control 342, 349
stakeholders
   identification 262–3
   influencing of 264–5
   and organisation culture 343
stereotyping 53, 77–8, 80, 256
Stewart, Rosemary
   management theories 23

task forces 231–4
Tavistock Institute
   and organisation structure 318
Taylor, Frederick
   management theories 12–13, 254
   on work structure 133–4
teams
   building 364–5
   conflict 360–1
   formation 358–60
   growth 365–8, 378–9
   and organisation culture 231–4
   values 363–4
Theory X and Theory Y 188–9
thinking, models 75
time management 7, 21, 23
training 46, 47, 48–9, 142

values 259, 363–4
Vroom, Victor
   on expectancy theory 128–9
Vroom-Yetton decision tree model
      196–201, 209

Weber, Max
   on bureaucracy 9
   on power 237–8
Western Electric Company 16
women in management 52–4
Woodward, Joan
   on organisation structure 317
work and family life 51–7, 59
work structure, 133–4, 138, 143, 150–1
      (summary)